PUNISHMENT AND PROCESS IN INTERNATIONAL CRIMINAL TRIALS

INTERNATIONAL AND COMPARATIVE CRIMINAL JUSTICE SERIES

Series Editors:

Mark Findlay, *Institute of Criminology, University of Sydney*
Ralph Henham, *Centre for Legal Research, Nottingham Trent University*

This series explores the new and rapidly developing field of international and comparative criminal justice and engages with its most important emerging themes and debates. It focuses on three interrelated aspects of scholarship which go to the root of understanding the nature and significance of international criminal justice in the broader context of globalization and global governance. These include: the theoretical and methodological problems posed by the development of international and comparative criminal justice; comparative contextual analysis; the reciprocal relationship between comparative and international criminal justice and contributions which endeavor to build understandings of global justice on foundations of comparative contextual analysis.

Punishment and Process in International Criminal Trials

RALPH HENHAM

ASHGATE

Published by
Ashgate Publishing Limited
Gower House
Croft Road
Aldershot
Hants GU11 3HR
England

Ashgate Publishing Company
Suite 420
101 Cherry Street
Burlington, VT 05401-4405
USA

Ashgate website: http://www.ashgate.com

British Library Cataloguing in Publication Data
Henham, Ralph J., 1949-
Punishment and process in international criminal trials. - (International and comparative criminal justice series)
1. Criminal procedure (International law)
I. Title
345'.05

Library of Congress Cataloging-in-Publication Data
Henham, Ralph J., 1949-
Punishment and process in international criminal trials / by Ralph Henham.
p. cm. -- (International and comparative criminal justice)
Includes bibliographical references and index.
ISBN 0-7546-2437-4
1. Criminal procedure (International law) I. Title. II. Series.

KZ6310.H46 2005
345'.05--dc22

2004028062

ISBN 0 7546 2437 4

Typeset by IML Typographers, Birkenhead, Merseyside
and printed and bound in Great Britain by TJ International Ltd, Padstow, Cornwall

Contents

List of Figures

Acknowledgements

The material presented and discussed in this book arises from the author's work on the International and Comparative Criminal Trial Project, which was founded by the author and Professor Mark Findlay (University of Sydney) in 1999 and is based in the Centre for Legal Research at Nottingham Law School.

The purpose of this volume is to bring together several themes concerned with sentencing in international criminal trials that have been discussed in a number of articles and working papers produced by the author for the ICTP. A primary rationale for the collection is to emphasise the author's enduring concern with the ideology and legitimacy of international sentencing, and its broader significance for the philosophy and sociology of international criminal justice. In that sense, it is both a socio-legal and philosophical inquiry. However, it also has more pervasive theoretical and methodological implications for understanding socio-legal process comparatively (and internationally) due to the perspective of comparative contextual analysis which is adopted throughout the text. More particularly, it is argued that the theory, modelling and method suggested by this approach provides a tool for understanding the relationship between normative structures and human agency within the context of trial ideologies and cultures at the global and local level. As such, the analysis suggests a means for translating our aspirations for international penality into a reality which has moral legitimacy and delivers a form of collective justice that contributes to peace and reconciliation.

The author would like to thank Mark Findlay for his inspiration and perceptive criticism and also Roger Cotterrell for his encouragement and support. Thanks are also due to Nottingham Law School for its continued support of my work and the provision of a period of sabbatical leave. As always, I have benefited in innumerable ways from the constant support and encouragement of my wife Annemarie, to whom this book is dedicated.

I have drawn upon the following published materials in the preparation of this text, with substantial additions and revisions where appropriate:

'Some Issues for Sentencing in the International Criminal Court' (2003) *International and Comparative Law Quarterly* 52: 81–114

'The Philosophical Foundations of International Sentencing' (2003) *Journal of International Criminal Justice* 1/1: 64–85

'Conceptualising Access to Justice and Victims' Rights in International Sentencing' (2004) *Social & Legal Studies* 13/1: 21–55

Ralph Henham
Nottingham

Series Editors' Preface

This book is the first in a new series devoted to exploring the new and rapidly developing field of international and comparative criminal justice. The series aims to encourage authors from a wide variety of disciplines to engage with its most important emerging themes and debates, focusing on three interrelated aspects of scholarship which go to the root of understanding the nature and significance of international criminal justice in the broader context of globalisation and global governance.

Firstly, the series aims to address the theoretical and methodological problems posed by the development of international and comparative criminal justice. It therefore seeks to locate this new area of study within existing theoretical debates in criminology, legal philosophy, international relations, international law and the sociology of law. In addition, as editors, we wish to stimulate debate about the methodological issues raised in seeking to understand the relationship between human agency, structure and process within comparative and international justice contexts. The series will therefore include books dealing with such diverse topics as international criminal justice theory and comparative research methodology and policy.

The series also aims to promote scholarship that enhances our understanding of the operation of criminal justice processes and policy. In particular, it concentrates on developing comparative understandings of trial ideology, its transformation into normative structures, and the significance of trial process for trial participants and relevant communities of justice. In addition to comparative accounts of criminal justice processes, it includes discussions of comparative sentencing and penology and explores the interface between law and morality against the realities of cultural relativism.

Finally, the series reflects on the recursive relationship between comparative and international criminal justice and aims to build understandings of global justice on foundations of comparative contextual analysis. Significant areas include developments in the international legal order; contextual analyses of international criminal procedure and rights paradigms; victimology and international criminal justice; contemporary issues in alternative justice; and the role of the international criminal trial.

Mark Findlay

Ralph Henham

Introduction

The purpose of this book is to provide an integrated socio-legal analysis of the law and process of international sentencing. It considers the rationale and development of international sentencing structures and processes, the nature and scope of legal and procedural constraints on decision-making, access to justice and rights issues and, in addition, provides a detailed evaluation of the philosophical and theoretical difficulties raised by this rapidly developing area of international criminal justice.

The fact that the analysis claims to be both 'integrated' and 'socio-legal' requires some preliminary explanation. The basic premise which informs the work is that sentencing is *instrumental.* By this is implied a conceptualisation of sentencing that is purposeful, one which provides a context where the ideological and philosophical rationales that inform policy and structure are negotiated in ways that reflect meaningful connections between the institutions of punishment and citizens. As Tamanaha (1997, p.237) recognises, the exercise of judicial discretion has an autonomous quality which goes beyond rule-orientation and procedural concerns towards the attainment of social purposes; the direction and control of this cognitive framework being crucial to the consistent and principled development of sentencing practice. Such arguments invest the instrumentality of legal reasoning with a principled form of rationality which is oriented towards the social consequences of punishment. In the context of the nation state the instrumental rationality of judicial reasoning and what constitutes substantive justice are circumscribed by cultural parameters.

However, for sentencing in the international criminal trial institutions the connections between judicial attitudes and the instrumentality of discretionary behaviour are more difficult to draw and reconcile with the international dimensions of penality. For example, it may be argued that the ideological merits of international punishment are determined by the position taken on the legitimacy of western forms of liberal democracy to pursue their ambitions through war and the threat of military power. Alternatively, this argument may be countered by espousing the legitimacy of international punishment on the basis of the need for the international community to punish gross violations of international humanitarian law. Such arguments serve to highlight the fact that the ideological merits of international punishment and the motives for the establishment and operation of international punishment structures are conjectural and cannot be divorced from global politics. However, they also indicate the difficulties faced by sentencers in providing rationalisations for international punishment that transcend its symbolism and connect in some meaningful way with victims and communities.

It is also arguable that the problems faced by international institutions are *qualitatively* different from those faced by national trial institutions and, therefore, the development of international sentencing principles and normative procedures are essentially *sui generis* (Rubin, 2001). This view implies that since international institutions are dealing with distinctive international forms of criminality, domestic and regional jurisdictional practices, or inquisitorial and adversarial forms of trial (or their hybrids) have little (or no) relevance in determining the future development of international sentencing praxis.[1]

The position adopted in this book is very different in that it views the creation and development of international sentencing norms as essentially a recursive process grounded in social contexts which reflect diverse legal cultures and conventions. Pragmatically, this recognises that the forces that have informed the debates and substantive content of the foundation instruments and sentencing practices of the international institutions have been driven in equal measure by diverse ideologies, jurisdictional forms, process styles and rights paradigms as they have by multinational political imperatives (Dennis, 1997). However, the theoretical and methodological implications of this approach are profound, since it requires the integrated development of concepts, models and methods that are capable of delivering convincing comparative contextual accounts of process and ideology at different jurisdictional levels and describing their influence (if any) and impact on international sentencing praxis, and reciprocally, the impact on regional and domestic sentencing regimes of institutionalised global sentencing practice.

The remainder of this introductory chapter aims to clarify for the reader some of the theoretical concepts and methodological assumptions which underpin this endeavour and which are explicitly referred to throughout the substantive analysis that follows.

The Concept of Internationalisation

This book is essentially concerned with the description and analysis of international sentencing process and procedure in the United Nations International Criminal Tribunals for the Former Yugoslavia and Rwanda, and the more recently established International Criminal Court.[2] However, the notion of 'internationalisation' is deliberately invoked to suggest that international trial processes need to be understood in terms which are able to make sense of their origins. This injunction is more than just a plea for contextual analysis; it implies that to determine the content and parameters of international sentencing depends upon our ability to comprehend the origins and significance of structure and process. It also serves to draw a conceptual distinction between the creation and development of new, exclusive forms of international sentencing process and principles and those that signify accommodation and compromise between existing (or hybridised) domestic or regional jurisdictional forms upon which they are based. This imperative is also driven by a desire to appreciate the dichotomy between local jurisdictions with transplanted forms of process originating from other domestic jurisdictions (hybridised), and the internationalisation of process in domestic jurisdictions achieved through the transplantation of international forms of process (internationalised).

---

[1] It nevertheless remains consistent with the notion that the international tribunals are distinguished from national systems through their humanitarian mission (Cassese 1999).

[2] Hereinafter referred to as the ICTY, ICTR and ICC respectively.

The phenomenon of internationalisation in sentencing is an enigma. Internationalisation suggests movement or transition, in the sense of some form of development or evolutionary process towards harmonisation and uniformity in sentencing process across and beyond specific jurisdictional contexts. Like globalisation, it is a notion which conveys a sense of inevitability and relentlessness. It also implies that there are beneficial consequences to be derived for sentencing from the merging of trial traditions, or their hybridisation. However, such an assertion cannot be made by simply extrapolating from descriptions derived from the juxtaposition and comparison of process styles from different legal cultures (Nelken, 2000). Our understanding of internationalisation in sentencing is shaped by our capacity to deconstruct the relationship between domestic, regional and international sentencing contexts.

As Figure I.1 suggests, the cultural transmission of process styles is reciprocal, and has both horizontal and vertical effects. Hence, the essence of internationalisation is concerned with the extent to which we are able to provide meaningful descriptions of sentencing process at different jurisdictional levels and to draw conclusions about the emergence of common themes, process styles or procedures which are truly based on shared experience (Findlay and Henham, 2005).

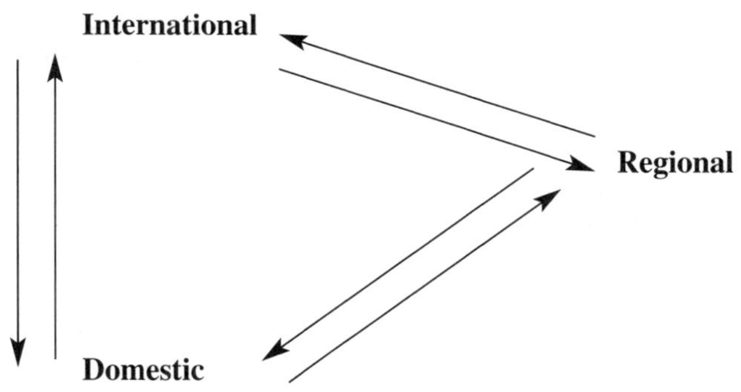

Figure I.1 Cultural transmission of process styles

In adopting this perspective this book seeks to address several complex issues raised by the phenomenon of internationalisation in sentencing. The most fundamental of these is whether meaningful comparative generalisations can be made regarding the extent (or not) of any merging in trial traditions, as reflected in the foundation instruments and sentencing practices of international institutions. As suggested, this depends on our ability to generalise about areas of synthesis and difference (Findlay, 2001).

The notion of internationalisation also provides an important perspective from which to explore the extent to which international sentencing practice conforms with particular rights paradigms that might be taken as measures of international criminal justice, and to test the adequacy of such paradigms. Such normative evaluation leads to a consideration of the relationship between law and morality and its reflection in sentence decision-making at the international level. More particularly, it questions whether international sentencing should be regarded as in some way transformative, in the sense that it forms part of the institutional machinery which enables the moral sentiments of the international community with respect to serious breaches of international humanitarian law to find practical expression, or, alternatively, whether the legitimacy of international sentencing ultimately depends on its ability to link retributive and communitarian aspirations for punishment. These interrelated issues of principle and practice force us to (re-)examine the philosophical rationales for international criminal trials and their effect on shaping process. More broadly, they also invite a reconsideration of the nature of penality in the late postmodern era and its meaning for international criminal justice.

The Concept of Integration

The approach adopted in this book presupposes the desirability of integrated sentencing. However, the meaning of this concept is dependent upon perspective.[3] Firstly, the notion of integrated decision-making as it relates to international sentencing recognises that the sentencing decision should be conceived as an amalgam of relevant process decisions, rather than simply representing the processual climax of those decisions. It also acknowledges the problematic nature of focusing on the relevance of sentencing within the 'trial' as the context for analysis, particularly the relativity of meaning and significance for the concept of 'trial' in different jurisdictional contexts.

Secondly, a distinction is drawn between the conception of integration as representing a distillation of relevant decisions, and the notion of integration promoted through the fusion of process; the latter recognising that the meaning accorded to 'sentencing' within the criminal process not only depends on cultural context, but is also distinguished by the significance it is accorded within different regimes of criminal process and procedure.

Thirdly, the notion of integration encompasses the adequate representation of both lay and professional interests in trial decision-making, and is concerned with evaluating different modalities of discretionary behaviour and intervention regarding the perception, evaluation and use of information for sentencing purposes. These are ultimately reflected in the connections that are made between penal justifications, policy and decision-making.

Finally, this conceptualisation of sentencing also moves beyond the notion of decision sites and their relative significance as process variables and focuses on *context*; more specifically, the cultural contexts in which significant trial relationships are created and merge to determine the exercise of discretionary power at significant decision sites for sentencing in the trial process. In this sense, the analysis seeks to determine how sentencing serves to integrate the requirements and aspirations of disparate cultural contexts.

---

[3] Integration in the present context is distinguished from the integration of theory and method in socio-legal analysis referred to earlier.

Theoretical Dimensions

The notion of internationalisation presupposes the existence of discernable contexts of rationality and purpose, and social processes which facilitate the achievement of principled objectives through international forms of punishment. It also countenances the possibility that penality[4] is a fluid conceptualisation whose elements are readily transformed and capable of transgressing jurisdictional boundaries, whether laterally (as between nation states or regional entities), or vertically (as between local and global contexts). Internationalisation implies some synergy of ideology, structure and normative practice in sentencing reflective of local and regional contexts. However, our understanding of the complexities and significance of sentencing as a social process in transition is inevitably conditioned and constrained by our ability to explain it as a phenomenon in any context. Such epistemological and methodological difficulties are compounded by the comparative dimensions of the analytical endeavour and must be adequately addressed from the outset.

As a decision-site implicated in publicly resolving the consequences of 'criminality' or 'criminalised' behaviour,[5] the processual activity which is sentencing suggests a convergence of certain moral, legal and sociological imperatives. The identification, description and explanation of each constituent of process is, therefore, epistemologically conjectural terrain, reflecting broad and fundamental disagreements in legal and social theory (Cotterrell, 1998a; Nelken, 1998; Banakar, 2000). This book does not engage directly in this debate, but makes explicit a commitment to the need for legal contexts to be interpreted sociologically (Cotterrell, 1998a). Understanding sentencing is essentially an exercise in legal sociology; one which seeks to ask questions about the nature of law in a social context, rather than the nature of a social process which involves law (Henham, 2001, p.257). The argument between the relative contributions of legal sociology and mainstream sociology is well summarised by Cotterrell (1998a, p.175) in his suggestion that 'as sociology interprets law, law is reduced to sociological terms'. However, the crucial question is the extent to which sociological approaches are capable of delivering understanding and explain the motivations and meanings of legal phenomena such as sentence decision-making. As an alternative to legal positivism, a sociological approach to deconstructing legal contexts should at least provide us, as Banakar (2000, p.284) puts it, 'with systematic empirical knowledge of the limits of institutional action'.

Nevertheless, the position adopted here goes further in insisting that there are two key issues to be considered. The first concerns the relationship between values,

---

[4] 'Penality' is used here to describe the dimensions of punishment as a social phenomenon which, for Garland, entails a recognition that '... penality communicates meaning not just about crime and punishment but also about power, authority, legitimacy, normality, morality, personhood, social relations, and a host of tangential matters' (Garland 1990, p.252). This clearly includes the ideological, normative and empirical dimensions pertaining to punishment.

[5] The observations of labelling theorists such as Becker (1973) are particularly apposite in analysing the social forces that determine the limits of criminality and deviance. It is significant, for example, that mass atrocity may not be conceived as deviance within specific social contexts (Drumbl 2003). Furthermore, these parameters may be culturally influenced by rationalisations similar to the 'techniques of neutralisation' described by Matza (1969). Sentencing is, of course, implicated in the symbolism of labelling and the public affirmation of definitions of deviance through the exercise of hegemonic power.

norms and process. In particular, it is argued that the relationship between legal reasoning and punishment in sentencing needs to be explained in terms which are capable of accounting for the transformation of sentencing law's narrative principles into morally significant reasons for action. In other words, an examination of the law and process of sentencing at any level must explain how (and in what sense) law is transformed into normative guides to conduct for relevant audiences (Henham 2001, p.267). As suggested, this does not require law's reality to be subsumed or distorted by sociological interpretations, but rather an acknowledgement that sociological insights are capable of providing conceptual settings which facilitate the deconstruction of different legal discourses (and systems) (Nelken, 1998).

The second issue is concerned with the theory and method of comparative contextual analysis. From the outset it is necessary to re-emphasise that understanding the internationalisation of sentencing is essentially a problem of comparative method for socio-legal analysis. This is implicit in the proposition that the social reality or practice of sentencing is an activity which both reflects and creates *context*. As elaborated in Chapter 7, existing models of criminal process provide inadequate paradigms through which to explain the relevant dimensions of trial praxis at the comparative level. In particular, sentence modelling has largely reflected the narrow positivist preoccupation in criminology with identifying and measuring presumed 'explanatory' variables in an effort to understand the reasons for *inconsistent* sentencing. A more appropriate context in which to conceptualise sentencing is suggested by Skolnick (1966). In his opinion, a study of law in action (such as discretionary decision-making in the sentencing process) is in essence concerned to deconstruct the meanings attributed to action by social actors through studying the interrelationship and transformation of legal principles and rules within legal institutions. An important recognition in Skolnick's analysis is that revealing contexts of meaning is contingent on multifaceted sociological interpretation. This analysis is consistent with the approach to sentence modelling developed later in this book.

This book also adopts the view that the conceptual framework implicit in Giddens's (1979, 1984) theory of structuration can be refined to provide a macro-theoretical conceptualisation which is capable of distinguishing and accommodating the contextual analysis of sentencing process at three significant levels of understanding; namely the legal, organisational and interactive components of sentence decision-making.[6] More particularly, it is argued that such levels signify interconnected aspects of the same social practice, offering three levels of understanding depending on context. They are essential preconditions to understanding the comparative analysis of social interaction in international sentencing (Figure I.2). Hence, a key theoretical assumption underlying the following analysis is that structuration theory provides an important conceptual tool which facilitates the identification of elements and processes concerned in the recursive nature of the application of legal rules and resources in sentencing, both global and local (Layder, 1994).

---

[6] It is not proposed to elaborate the arguments supporting this view in this book. For detailed exposition of the theoretical, modelling and methodological foundations of comparative contextual analysis the reader is referred to Findlay and Henham (2005); Henham and Findlay (2001; 2002). See also Chapter 7 for further consideration of these issues in the context of international sentencing.

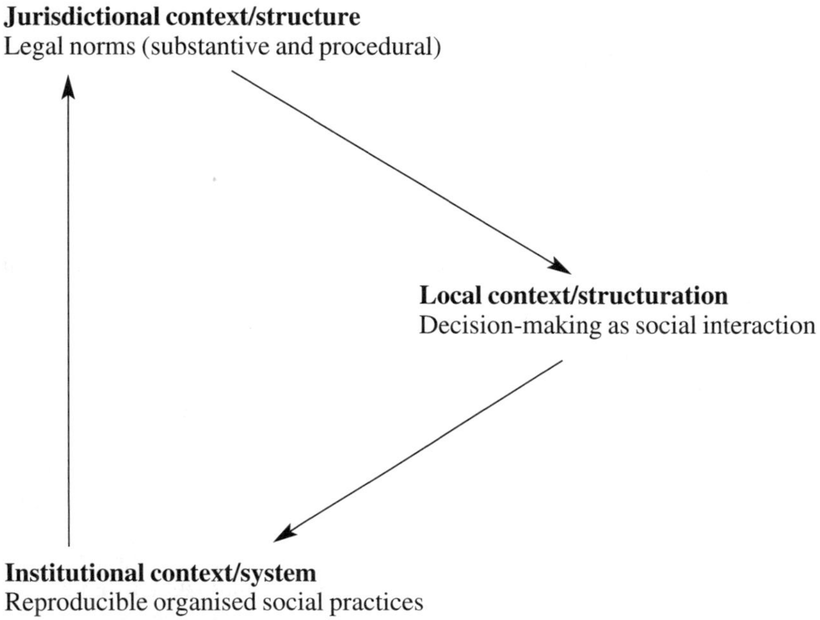

Figure I.2 Conceptualising sentence decision-making as a process of structuration[7]

Finally, it is widely acknowledged that the contextual appreciation of law and legal processes within different legal cultures and across legal jurisdictional boundaries is problematic (Nelken, 1997), and that, as Hodgson puts it (2000, p.141), may create only 'an illusion of understanding'. The objectivity of process exists to the extent that we are able to identify the criteria whereby relevant participants recognise external reality, i.e. the reality of objects, events or states. The connections between subjective experience and objectivity therefore exist in so far as there are common definitions of process as objective reality. As Bell suggests:

7 This sentencing model is a micro-representation of structuration adapted to show the predominant influences on sentence decision-making within the framework for action suggested by structuration theory. Essentially, it is a conceptualisation which is designed to elucidate the various dimensions of sentence decision-making. Hence, processes of decision-making are conceptualised as a series of frames of action with each frame of action contributing to mould the sentencing process. The social reality and significance of the sentencing process is therefore dependent on the constituents of previous frames of action because structuration recursively contructs contextualised social action. Thus, context is three-dimensional and *dynamic* across time and space, whilst the relationship between structure and agency depends for its relative existence upon context from which it is never separate or autonomous. As such, the relativity of each frame of action is established through our ability to consider interaction within the context of the frame against past and present action outcomes. In summary, this approach envisages various dimensions of sentence decision-making and sees their contextualisation and comparison in terms of a series of frames which comprise a moving picture – contextualised social action.

> ... categorisation depends on what the various legal actors think is happening in a legal situation ... Although the participant has a personal perspective on legal events, culture is a collective phenomenon where groups use the same language and have a common identity despite other differences ... assignment of meaning to natural facts depends on collective intentionality ... the community acting creates the institutional reality, which individuals can then use to explain events. But it is clear that this institutional system and practice precedes them (2001, Ch. 1).

However, in our interpretation of legal culture we must, as Hodgson (2000) also observes,[8] be mindful of the fact that legal language exists within the *context* of legal culture, and that mere categorisation and comparison does not equate with objectivity (Casanovas, 1999). In this sense the challenge for comparative contextual analysis is to provide authentic descriptions and explanations of the commonality of shared experience across jurisdictional boundaries.

In addition to the different levels of meaning and understanding attributed to action and process by researchers, comparative scholars such as Twining (1999) have also highlighted the problems caused by the absence of any definite and uniform legal vocabulary. The rules which operate within any legal context have deliberate narrative structure and form, and, as Bennett and Feldman (1981) suggest, both actors and interpreters have an important margin of control over the definition of what constitutes the reality of legal process. For interpreters of international sentencing praxis,[9] therefore, a fundamental prerequisite is the ability to infer that interpretative methodologies are addressing culturally meaningful questions.

Structure of the Book

This book contends that understanding must proceed at the levels of inference and meaning to produce accounts of how rules, procedures and processes are conceptualised and understood by trial participants in the daily interaction of sentencing. As Rogers and Erez (1999) suggest, the social reality of sentencing for trial participants is revealed by exploring the 'objectivity' or common experience of process whilst also deconstructing its 'subjectivity'. These theoretical and methodological imperatives are critical for understanding international forms of process where comparable definitions of what participants in the sentencing process understand by a particular event and its significance must be established (Ewald, 1998). Furthermore, it only through developing concepts and methodologies for comparative contextual analysis that progress can be made towards providing meaningful evaluations of international sentencing praxis.

The chapters which follow refer to and develop the concepts and implicit assumptions upon which this analysis is based in terms of their relevance for understanding particular aspects of international penality, as expressed or represented in the sentencing practices of the *ad hoc* criminal tribunals and the newly

---

8 For Crawford (2000, p.225) this means developing 'ways of understanding *contrasts* and *differences* without slipping into cultural relativism'.

9 This expression is holistic in that it refers to everything that is to do with the conception of international sentencing in terms of its ideology and institutional practice.

created ICC. Within this framework the analysis and evaluation of international penality is developed critically, from a perspective which is sensitive to the relativity of justice as reflected in international criminal trials. Throughout the analysis questions are asked about the moral significance and legitimacy of international punishment and process for individuals, groups and states implicated in social conflict and war, and how international penality can best serve the interests of peace and reconciliation.

Chapter 1 analyses the nature and extent of internationalisation in sentencing. It focuses particularly on those factors influencing the sentencing structures of the ICTY, ICTR and the ICC. It is argued that understanding discretionary sentence decision-making in international criminal trials is pivotal for developing meaningful interpretations of international criminal justice. It is suggested that the absence of penological justifications in the foundation instruments of the *ad hoc* tribunals and the ICC weakens their claims to provide a rational foundation for the exercise of any universally accepted principles of criminal justice. The chapter also evaluates internationalised sentencing structures (such as East Timor and Kosovo) and alternative processes (such as Truth and Reconciliation Commissions, or TRCs) in the context of providing moral and legitimate resolutions for breach of international humanitarian law.

In Chapter 2 the procedural rules and trial practice of international criminal process are analysed in so far as they relate to sentencing. Consequently, the analysis focuses on evidential stages relevant to sentence and the nature and quality of the evidence permitted. It focuses particularly on the roles of the judge, prosecution and defence in relation to the presentation and assessment of such evidence, and the significance of victim evidence for sentencing. The analysis also questions the heuristic value of conventional criminal process models in the comparative contextual analysis of international sentencing. It suggests that process models should not only be capable of accommodating propositions associated with competing goals, but also their normative implications, and the rationales which should determine the balance to be accorded to each.

Chapter 3 describes the context in which the process of sentencing takes place in international criminal trials, concentrating on the nature and significance of sentence decision-making and delivery, particularly the interplay between legal form and discretion, and issues of transparency and integration in international sentencing. The analytical focus for this chapter is the social reality of decision-making in international criminal trials and the deconstruction of sentence decision-making; issues whose understanding is crucial before we can begin to address questions of rationality and purpose for international penality.

Chapter 4 analyses the structural constraints that threaten notions of fair trial within international sentencing processes, particularly procedural mechanisms for sentence reduction, by considering the nature and form of plea bargaining in international criminal tribunals and the discretionary power of professional trial participants. The implications are assessed in terms of victims and process transparency, in addition to the paradigms of proportionality and desert, and contrasts between adversarial/inquisitorial process styles. The argument seeks to demonstrate that international procedural justice cannot be satisfactorily evaluated on the sole basis of the extent to which procedures conform to 'objectively' defined characteristics, since ideology and power are invariably crucial to the development of procedural norms and the policies which inform them. It is suggested that, for generalised notions of justice to be developed which transcend process constraints and are tolerant of representative participation and communitarian objectives, a wider role for the victim in the penality of international justice must be elaborated.

The relevance of conventional notions and justifications for punishment as they relate to institutionalised forms of international sentencing are addressed in detail in Chapter 5. After analysing the philosophical justifications for international punishment, reasons are suggested for challenging the legitimacy and relevance of current justifications for international sentencing. It is argued that the morality and symbolism of sentencing in international criminal trials should provide a means for connecting the citizens of communities affected by conflict and victims to the values and norms of international humanitarian law. The chapter explores the degree to which particular philosophical justifications might validly be utilised to promote competing moral claims for punishment. Arguments are put forward for the adoption of philosophical paradigms for international sentencing which appear more reflective of communitarian concerns.

Chapter 6 focuses on issues relating to the conceptualisation of access to justice and rights in international sentencing. It discusses why it is necessary to understand how the dynamics of power exercised within the context of international penal structures actually determine the relationship between the normative and factual dimensions of rights law and what this reality actually signifies in a comparative context. It is argued that due process principles are meaningless unless they are truly effective in enabling victims and citizens of victim communities to assert rights which have some relevance to the institutions of international penality.

In Chapter 7 the theoretical and methodological issues facing the comparative contextual analysis of international punishment and process are addressed, especially the potential for developing alternative theoretical paradigms for international sentencing and assessing their validity. The chapter explores the potential for utilising contextual modelling as a methodology for reconstructing judicial discretionary sentence decision-making and engaging restorative justice as a significant rationale for international criminal justice.

The concluding chapter suggests how the debates over punishment and penal philosophy, consistency and discretion, crime control and due process and access to justice in international sentencing may be resolved. The chapter argues strongly that the ideological purposes of the international criminal trial need to be carefully redefined to reflect competing purposes for punishment, and penal measures focused on those areas where the most productive outcomes for all parties can be forged. I argue that international penality should be reconceptualised and reconstructed to facilitate the implementation of dynamic, creative and innovative solutions and strategies for peace and reconciliation, rather than symbolic outcomes for international criminal trials.

This book is therefore timely and significant in addressing important issues and questions regarding the nature and justifications for punishment in international criminal trials. However, it is not simply an atheoretical inquiry about the technicalities of sentencing practice. It is much broader in scope and puts the issues about trial outcomes in wider perspective. In essence, it is a book about victims, trial process, procedure and fair trial, the philosophy of punishment and problems of legal comparisons. The book is a socio-legal and philosophical inquiry that engages with the themes and influences that shape discretionary decision-making in international criminal trials. It seeks to comprehend the punishment of international crimes through the comparative contextual analysis of trial processes so that it becomes possible to understand how and why particular sentencing outcomes are produced.

Chapter 1

Internationalisation and Sentencing

This chapter analyses the nature, extent and implications of internationalisation for sentencing, and identifies the main themes of internationalisation that are explored in later chapters. More specifically, it aims to evaluate the theoretical arguments and empirical evidence that argue for the internationalisation of sentencing practice within the wider context of the globalisation of criminal justice. It focuses particularly on the factors that have influenced the sentencing structures of the ICTY[1] and ICTR,[2] in addition to the newly created ICC.[3] The chapter also evaluates internationalised sentencing structures (such as those established in East Timor and Kosovo) and alternative processes (such as Truth and Reconciliation Commissions).

Introduction

The relative instability of the new international world order and the growth of global terrorism have focused attention on critical deficiencies in the purpose, coherence and operation of the international mechanisms developed for dealing with the punishment of gross breaches of international humanitarian law (Beresford, 2002; Henham, 2003a). Furthermore, these sharp ideological and political divisions have more recently been reflected in the sustained opposition of the US to the ICC and attempts to undermine its credibility (Evered, 1994; McGoldrick, 1999, p.644; Ball, 2004).

Such concerns force us to re-examine questions which relate to the penality of the international trial process (such as its philosophical justifications), the construction of criminality and the impact of globalised systems of punishment on regional and

---

[1] The ICTY was established by United Nations Security Council Resolution 827 of 25 May 1993, UN Doc.S/RES/827.

[2] The ICTR was established by United Nations Security Council Resolution 955 of 8 November 1994, UN Doc. S/RES/955.

[3] The Rome Statute establishing the ICC came into force on 1st July 2002. There is a paucity of substantive analyses which evaluate the implications for international criminal justice theory and policy of sentencing in the ICC. For a general overview, see Schabas (2001a; 2004, Ch. 7). Note that the jurisdiction of the ICC is limited to 'the most serious crimes of international concern'; 'the most serious crimes of concern to the international community as a whole' (Preamble, Articles 1 and 5.1 of the ICC Statute); it does not extend (*inter alia*) to terrorism. The main reason for its exclusion has been the fear of politicisation of the ICC, such that no generally acceptable definition of 'terrorism' has been forthcoming, although general agreement exists regarding the legality of prosecuting states which aid or sponsor state terrorism; see further, Kittichaisaree (2001, p.227). However, informed opinion suggests that crimes on the scale of those perpetrated on 9/11 amount to the commission of 'crimes against humanity' within the meaning of Article 7 of the ICC Statute; Dennis (2001) and see generally Kittichaisaree (2001, Ch. 5).

domestic criminal justice process and policy.[4] Consideration of these pressures is also provoked by the fact that it is in the context of international courts, judges and trials that the guarantees provided by the separation of powers for democracy appear at their weakest.[5] These are reflected in the problems of asserting the independence of the international judiciary experienced in the war crimes tribunals,[6] and the paradox of the international rights paradigm of fair trial which is proclaimed against the universal (i.e. inclusive) mandate claimed for institutional and procedural penality.

Thus, cogent arguments exist for regarding the international trial process as symbolic of hegemonic power, authority and control. It may not be an exaggeration to suggest that the *locus* of the international trial may, in future, provide the forum for global acts of retribution and vengeance on an unprecedented scale, with international punishment a distortion of the role of penality for ends which have previously not been recognised (such as political domination and waging war).[7] Therefore, although the trial's existence at the global level may argue for the unity and generalisation of justice, it may also provide the interactive context for the disempowerment and marginalisation of social, political and economic minorities.[8]

The analysis which follows provides an overview of the position of international sentencing from the following perspectives:

- *Penality* – it is argued that there is substantive irrationality and an absence of penological justifications for international sentencing praxis. In this sense the intention is to expose the underdeveloped and conflicting penal justifications and the irrationality of praxis in an international setting, rather than the conventional contradictions that lie behind sentencing principles.[9]
- *Trial process* – this concerns the contexts of sentence determination and delivery. The emphasis here is on the pivotal role of discretion and the relationships between trial participants that influence the sentencing outcome.[10]

---

[4] The latter may be expected both to reflect and influence the transformation or fragmentation of internationalised trial process.

[5] The future development of measures of democratic accountability for international criminal trial mechanisms raises difficulties at several levels: firstly, whether the emergence of a 'culture of accountability' will, in reality, simply reflect the a process of 'Westernisation', whose parameters and dynamics are unknown; Secondly, whether international criminal trials and process norms are capable of accounting for the different historical, social and cultural contexts in which the norms are applied; and, thirdly, the extent to which local process is likely to be undermined by the universality of international criminal process norms (Cockayne 2001). For an exploration of possible normative frameworks of accountability, see Bassiouni (1996).

[6] In the sentencing context this was exacerbated by the absence of any coherent sentencing guidance following Nuremberg,Tokyo and the other post-World War II tribunals which preceded the ICTY and ICTR, or the provision of any separate context for sentence decision-making.

[7] Arguably, these effects may in turn infiltrate the principles and expectations for sentencing at the local or regional levels.

[8] As Mathiesen (1990) suggests, imprisonment within advanced capitalist societies may serve expurgatory, symbolic and diversionary functions.

[9] These issues are explored further in Chapter 7.

[10] These issues are considered in Chapter 3; Chapter 2 examines procedural form and Chapter 4 procedural constraints.

- *Access to justice and fair trial* – this examines the relationship between state interests and offenders' and victims' rights from the perspective of humanitarian law.[11] Although given a much sharper focus by the well-developed and prevailing rights paradigms for international justice, the designation and substantive form of rights within the international criminal trial process remain conjectural.[12]
- *Internationalisation* – as discussed in the Introduction, this is particularly concerned with the reciprocal effects of institutionalised global sentencing practice on domestic and regional sentencing regimes, and raises questions regarding the extent to which comparable evaluations of sentencing practice across cultures and contexts can be provided.

Additionally, the discussion is couched in the wider context of some important questions concerning the relevance and future direction of criminal justice theory and its ability to anticipate or conceptualise internationalised sentencing praxis. More specifically, it develops some earlier arguments which suggest that internationalised procedural fairness paradigms are inadequately theorised, particularly as they relate to the role and outcome of sentencing (Henham, 2000b, 2001). The practical implications of this theoretical lacuna, and its implicit distortion of conventional models, are pertinent in that rights law can be seen as instrumental in sustaining the boundaries of permissible international and national state action against citizens. It is, therefore, important for any analysis to consider the extent to which the sentencing functions of international institutions are (and may be) infected by state and regional interests, and how this tendency might be resisted both normatively and practically.

It may be argued that the functional significance of international legal codes is considerable, if we are to accept the Durkheimian notion that the function of punishment (as expressed in sentencing law and practice) is to reflect and reaffirm society's (or, in this case, the international community's) moral opprobrium. Despite the known weaknesses of Durkheim's position (Garland, 1990), and, in particular, his failure to theorise notions of hegemony and inequality in social position, Cotterrell (1999, p.199) has argued that the strength of Durkheim's approach lies in his exhortation that law must be viewed in terms of its actual or potential moral worth.[13] Indeed, Cotterrell (1999, p.205) suggests that, far from ignoring questions about power and social control, Durkheim equates power with legitimate authority, a legitimation derived from an expressed moral consensus in society. It is, therefore, important to recognise that the normative significance of internationalised legal rules and processes as representing a form of moral legitimacy is derived through the recursive exercise of judicial and state power in international institutions.

The pivotal nature of discretionary judicial power in international sentencing is re-enforced by the absence of mechanisms for realising the aspirations for punishment expressed in the foundation instruments of international institutions. Hence, there is no institutionalisation of policy through which the linkage between purposes of

---

[11] More particularly, the European Court of Human Rights (ECHR) and the International Covenant on Civil and Political Rights (ICCPR); see Findlay (2001) for discussion of how the former might provide a context for internationalised procedural synthesis through expansion of the notion of fair trial.

[12] Further development of these arguments is provided in Chapter 6.

[13] For further exploration of this theme in the context of sentencing, see Henham (2001).

punishment and the means of their achievement are prescribed and developed. As Carcano (2002, p.591) suggests in the case of the ICTY and ICTR, it is for the judges to establish the appropriate parameters of the relationship between the purposes of punishment and the gravity of international crimes.[14]

Hence, discretionary sentence decision-making in the international institutions represents judicial signification and justification of legal rules as morally appropriate, since sentencers effectively operationalise policy-justified principles of punishment by transforming law into appropriate sanctions through the international penal process.[15] This leads us to consider the boundaries of judicial discretion and the extent to which conventional sentencing discretion is fettered in the international context. It also provides an opportunity to examine the implications for realising (or frustrating) a credible and convincing theory of international sentencing and punishment which recognises the political and ideological interests at work on the court and its judges (and the reasons for their existence).

The significance of this debate is not, therefore, just at the level of substantive law, legal sociology or the sociological analysis of judicial decision-making. Discussion of the principles of punishment and any associated theory of sentencing must proceed at the levels of politics, ideology, symbolism, compromise and accommodation. My argument is that the contextual analysis of international sentencing and the development and implementation of future policy demand a multilevelled description and evaluation of *process*.[16] For this, as Findlay (1999, p.vii) suggests, we must acknowledge, nurture and extend (but not ignore) our appreciation of theoretical insights which facilitate understandings of key procedural components within the international criminal justice process and their significance, at both the local and global level.

The following discussion addresses these questions by directing them at the ICC and drawing upon the practice and evaluation of ICTY and ICTR sentencing practices.

Purposes and Principles of Punishment

The Rome Statute of the International Criminal Court is virtually silent regarding the purposes and principles which should inform the sentencing of offenders convicted before the ICC. As Schabas (2001a, p.138) implies, this is largely due to the absence of any substantive debate on the subject at the Rome Conference in 1998. The discussions were instead dominated by the debate about capital punishment, and,

---

[14] Carcano (2002, p.591) takes the view that the use of the words 'halted' and 'redressed' in the United Nations Resolutions establishing the ICTY and ICTR (*supra*, notes 1 and 2), invariably suggest general deterrent and retributive purposes for punishment. However, as Schabas (1997, p.21) suggests, what constitutes redress may be separated from retribution, since these are relative concepts for victims and victim communities.

[15] Garland's (1990) insistence on the nature of punishment as process is also relevant here. The international criminal trial and its verdict is a ceremony and the sentence is a balance to justice and justification of a just cause delivered by the judge as controller of the ceremony.

[16] This process being international sentencing and its place in the imposition of punishment at the core of international criminal justice.

whilst the ultimate decision to exclude the death penalty from the sentences available to the ICC can no doubt be justly hailed as a humanitarian victory, the failure to establish which objectives and principles should characterise the penality[17] of the ICC constitutes a significant omission.[18]

It may be argued that the forum of the ICC should exist as public ceremony to give substance and form to previously articulated penal purposes. Instead, these purposes remain largely implicit; and remain to be discerned from statements previously made at the Nuremberg and Tokyo war crimes tribunals which suggest that retribution[19] should be the main objective of such prosecutions (Wexler, 1996; Schabas, 1997). As a moral position the desire for retribution is justified by a need to reassert the fundamental virtues of humanity as represented by the international community and democratic principles of justice.[20] This was clarified by the Appeals Chamber of the ICTY in *Aleksovski*:[21]

> This [retribution] is not to be understood as fulfilling a desire for revenge but as duly expressing the outrage of the international community at these crimes ... Accordingly, a sentence of the International Tribunal should make plain the condemnation of the international community of the behaviour in question and show that the international community was not ready to tolerate serious violations of international humanitarian law and human rights.

---

[17] 'Penality' is here used in the sense proposed by Garland (1990, p.17) to refer to 'the networks of laws, processes, discourses, representations and institutions which make up the penal realm'. As an aspect of penality, the rationale(s) for sentencing are particularly significant in the present context. Because it occurs outside national contexts, international trial process alters or distorts the central objectives of the sentencing process, which may arguably include retribution or deterrence, pedagogical performance, national reconciliation, or exculpation; see further Alvarez (1998); Howland and Calathes (1998). Howland and Calathes (1998, p.154), for example, make a strong case for developing the ICTR's objectives through a combination of human rights and restorative perspectives, noting significantly: 'The ICTR cannot adopt traditional and Western criminal justice punishment objectives such as deterrence, retribution, or incapacitation when these objectives so clearly cannot be achieved in the context of mass human rights violations ... As currently conceived and understood the ICTR's objectives provide little guidance.' These arguments are developed further by Drumbl (2000) and Parmentier (2003).

For an excellent discussion of life imprisonment as an aspect of the penality of international law, see van Zyl Smit (1999). In this context it is significant that the death penalty was excluded in the case of the ICTR despite the fact that the Rwandese government wished to retain it for persons convicted of crimes of similar magnitude

[18] See further Hall (1998). Similarly, both the Statutes of the ICTY and the ICTR fail to allude to the objectives of sentencing, or the principles of punishment to be adopted by judges in sentencing; see Schabas (1997); Grosselfinger (1998). Only the ICTR mandate includes a reference to the need to contribute to 'national reconciliation' in its Preamble.

[19] Here 'retribution' is used in the wider sense of requiring that offenders should be made to atone for their crimes by suffering. Support for the view that the context of the *ad hoc* tribunals is vindication and western exculpation derives from their primacy over national jurisdictions, subordination of the tribunals' jurisdictions through case selection and other Security Council pressure; see Bassiouni and Manakas (1996, pp.228–231). On the limited resources provided to the tribunals, see Forsythe (1994).

[20] The associated desire for revenge or vengeance being regarded as a negation of such principles; see *Prosecutor v Delalic et al.* (Case No. IT-96-21-T), Judgement, 16 November 1998, para.1231 (the '*Celebici*' case).

[21] *Prosecutor v Aleksovski* (Case No. IT-95-14/1-A), Judgement, 20 March 2000, para. 185.

Nevertheless, the morality of retribution itself is questioned without the concomitant requirements of consistency and a rationale which determines how the severity of sentence should relate to the harm sustained by the offending behaviour. In this, it may be argued that the absence of any meaningful discussion of penal purpose in the establishment or foundation documents of the ICC undermines its legitimacy as a mechanism which can deliver democratic principles of justice.[22] This would seem, therefore, to render meaningless assertions, such as those expressed in the following extract from the ICTY's judgement in *Furundzija*:[23]

> It is the *infallibility* of punishment, rather than the severity of the sanction, which is the tool for retribution, stigmatisation and deterrence. This is particularly the case for the International Tribunal; penalties are made more onerous by its international stature, moral authority and impact upon world public opinion, and this punitive effect must be borne in mind when assessing the suitable length of sentence [emphasis added].

Such obfuscation of purpose is compounded by the rhetoric of moral justification expressed by the tribunal, and the implication that the ICTY (or any other such international forum) might be in a position to turn these sentiments into a fully articulated penality of proportionate retribution. Furthermore, the relativity of concepts such as justice and penality is ignored, it being assumed that these are synonymous for both the ICTY and international trial justice. This threatens the implicit presumption that international justice and penality could be regarded in any conventional sense as democratic and, thus, the legitimate manifestation of a global moral consensus.

The insights of liberal thinkers of the Enlightenment period such as Beccaria (1764) are surely significant in this context. Faced with the unimaginable horrors of the *ancien régime* the liberal theory of criminal law espoused a doctrine which (although ignoring power and social inequality) emphasised individual rights and principles of equality before the law to provide essential safeguards against the tyranny of social and political inequality. Significantly, the individual's relationship with the state was redefined so that the administration of justice was seen to embody and reflect principles of clarity and certainty which saw the moral justification for the criminal law as emanating from the needs of a particular society.[24] In other words, specific guarantees in addition to (and supporting) declarations of intent or moral purpose were required in order to legitimate penality. I would argue that these postulates are equally pertinent in the contemporary contexts of international criminal law and, although reflected in certain principles of international humanitarian law, require to be mirrored and fully articulated in the statutes and procedural rules of the ICC (and similar international fora). As Kittichaisaree (2001) suggests, international criminal law has evolved in order to reflect the moral judgements of the community of nations which, in the case of the Nuremberg and

---

[22] The expression 'democratic' is used deliberately to imply the need for principles which sustain and protect individual liberty against the incursions of state or inter-state power.

[23] *Prosecutor v Furundzija* (Case No. IT-95-17/1-T), Judgement, 10 December 1998, para. 290.

[24] For comprehensive analysis, see Radzinowicz (1966, Ch. 1). As van Zyl Smit (1999, p.27) points out, Beccaria argued that sentence severity should be predetermined, proportionate to the crime and sufficient to meet the minimum requirements of deterrence.

Tokyo tribunals, consisted largely of the enforcement of victor's justice reflecting principles of communal vengeance rather than deterrence. It is this connection between retribution and international justice which has motivated and legitimated current mechanisms for international criminal trial.

As I have contended, the absence of penological justifications in the foundation documentation and Statute of the ICC weakens its claims to provide a rational foundation for the exercise of democratic principles of criminal justice. Yet this deficiency is further compounded by confusion relating to the possible ambit and meaning accorded to penal justifications in the proceedings and practice of the *ad hoc* Tribunals and, therefore, liable to be reflected in the position of the ICC in relation to such matters. A clear example concerns the role of deterrence, which has frequently been cited as a penal justification by both the ICTY and the ICTR. For instance, as Morris and Scharf (1995) point out, one of the five enumerated goals of the ICTY was explicitly to deter future violations of international criminal law. Indeed, in *Erdemovic*,[25] the Trial Chamber of the ICTY discussed (*inter alia* at para. 58) the objective of deterrence in the context of the United Nations Security Council's overriding concern to maintain peace and security in the former Yugoslavia. In so doing, it drew clear distinctions between 'general prevention (or deterrence), reprobation, retribution (or 'just deserts'), as well as collective reconciliation', suggesting that these purposes would provide guidance in determining the appropriate punishment for a crime against humanity. Yet no attempt was made to define these purposes, or explore their meaning in the trial context. Still less was there any suggestion of exactly how purposes might be linked to guidance in determining punishment.

Further instances of such inconsistency revealing an absence of applied principles are common. For example, in *Rutaganda*[26] the ICTR stated that there was a clear dichotomy between retribution and deterrence, suggesting that the former objective should be subsumed to the overwhelming need to 'dissuade for good, others who may be tempted in the future to perpetrate such atrocities by showing them that the international community shall not tolerate the serious violations of international humanitarian law and human rights'. But how might deterrence achieve its end; indeed, what evidence exists to suggest that deterrence has any impact whatsoever as a consideration in the motivation of such offences?[27] Similarly, in *Tadic*[28] the ICTY gave equal emphasis to retribution and deterrence, but went on to suggest (para. 61) that incapacitation of the dangerous and rehabilitation were also desirable objectives, implying that the latter promoted the 'modern philosophy of penology that the punishment should fit the offender and not merely the crime'. Again, no consideration was given to balancing or defining these objectives[29] in the context of the demands for collective retribution personified by state interests and the adopted common law tradition which favours the individualisation of sentences.

---

[25] *Prosecutor v Erdemovic* (Case No. IT-96-22-T), Sentencing Judgement, 29 November 1996.

[26] *Prosecutor v Rutaganda* (Case No. ICTR- 96-3), Judgement and Sentence, 2 February 1999.

[27] Surely, the advent of suicide terrorism is manifest proof of the irrelevance of deterrence in the present context.

[28] *Prosecutor v Tadic* (Case No. IT-94-1-S), Sentencing Judgement, 14 July 1997.

[29] Von Hirsch (1993, p.13), for example, suggests that the preventative function of a sanction should be tied to the normative reasons for penal censure.

More recent attempts by the ICTY to clarify the relationship between deterrence and other general justifying aims for international punishment have done little to resolve these difficulties. The Trial Chamber in *Todorovic*[30] concluded that retribution and deterrence provided 'the main principles in sentencing for international crimes' that formed 'the backdrop against which an individual accused's sentence must be determined'. It then went on to consider the meaning and implications of the principle of retribution for sentence determination, but failed to do so in the case of deterrence, merely accepting instead the approach of the ICTY Appeals Chamber in *Aleksovski*[31] that deterrence should be a legitimate consideration in sentencing for international crimes. In *Krnojelac*[32] the Trial Chamber simply acknowledged retribution and deterrence as the main sentencing factors and confirmed that general deterrence was not to be accorded undue prominence in the determination of sentence, again without providing any rational explanation for its conclusions.

In addition, the failure of the international tribunals either to satisfactorily define or draw a considered distinction between retribution and deterrence has concealed a fundamental misconception. This concerns the tendency to regard the overriding deterrent purpose of international punishment as somehow distinct from that of reprobation or denunciation,[33] since the latter may be considered to be an implicit purpose of deterrence (Walker, 1969, p.36). However, it is reasonable to suggest that the relative purpose(s) of denunciation ought to be deconstructed before any such assumptions regarding its rationale and direction are made. If denunciation exists in order to demonstrate abhorrence or disapproval it must seek to do so through punishment – the public manifestation of a view that regards the activity in question as incompatible with civilised human conduct. Consequently, it must be declared through the punishment process and the way in which it is to be delivered made explicit in an expression of purpose, be it retribution[34] or deterrence. However, denunciation may be regarded as equally appropriate for other cogent reasons; for example, to re-enforce the collective conscience of a society or social group in the Durkheimian sense, or where it is considered as essentially justified for its own sake – as exemplified by nineteenth century penality. Nonetheless, it is apparent that the overriding sentiment of punishment in the international arena consists of revenge and retribution tempered by poorly articulated allusions to deterrence (and occasionally rehabilitation and reconciliation). As Schabas suggests:

> What is desired is a judgment, a declaration by society, and the identification and stigmatisation of the perpetrator (1997, p.21).

Yet, as acknowledged by the ICTY in *Celebici*,[35] retribution and international justice may be irreconcilable aims.

---

30 *Prosecutor v Todorovic* (Case No. IT-95-9/1-S), Sentencing Judgement, 31 July 2001, paras 28, 29.

31 *Aleksovski*, *supra*, note 21.

32 *Prosecutor v Krnojelac* (Case No. IT-97-25-T), 15 March 2002, para. 508.

33 *Erdemovic*, *supra*, note 25, para. 58.

34 As Walker (1991, p.31) points out, retributivism implies the actual infliction of punishment, whilst denunciation merely requires a belief in its infliction.

35 *Delalic et al.*, *supra*, note 20 .

If retribution and denunciation direct the so-called search for 'truth' as the dominant forces which drive the international trial process, then it is unsurprising that the trial as symbolism predominates in trial interaction.[36] Where sentences fall short of retributive expectations they may be rationalised in terms of rehabilitation and reconciliation.[37] But such penal objectives are treated as subsidiary rationales, whilst the international tribunals continue to function on the basis that retributive punishment exercised in a manner consistent with a fundamentally just moral purpose leads inexorably to reconciliation. However, the evidence for such linkage, and the extent to which rehabilitation and reconciliation are regarded as relevant imperatives for international penal praxis, may be questioned.

Rehabilitation has not been considered significant in so far as the *ad hoc* tribunals have failed to articulate the need for retributive punishment to comply with human rights norms.[38] Neither is it mentioned in the ICC Statute.[39] Indeed, the theoretical discussion in the *Erdemovic* judgement plainly regarded rehabilitation as a subsidiary consideration to retribution, deterrence and stigmatisation as pre-eminent factors. Although there is scope for the individual rehabilitation of offenders to be accommodated within the ambit of sentence individualisation permitted under Article 78(1) by implication, there is no attempt made to define the possible meaning of rehabilitation in the wider context of international trials, or explain the nature of the values and attitudes which underpin it.

As Garland (1990, p.186) convincingly argues, in the postmodern era the rehabilitative ethos has become closely associated with the power-knowledge network of social control. Thus, the rationalisation of penality in the late twentieth century became characterised by the technical displacement of moral judgements as determinants of rehabilitative ideology and the substitution of administrative and political imperatives. As such the notion of rehabilitation has, in common with other conceptions of penality, drifted from the communitarian ideals of social justice and moral education to become symbolic of state interests. It has instead formed part of the panoply of institutional practice which needs to connect with its intended audience. Symbolism and rhetoric are paramount in this endeavour, and, crucially, 'the envisaged audience and its characteristics may be crucial in shaping the general form which the signifying practice will adopt' (Garland, 1990, p.260).

In the context of ICC sentencing the envisaged audience is global, yet the moral values which will be significant in the shaping of its penality are those considered and adopted in the principles for normative practice contained in its foundation instruments. However, as with the *ad hoc* tribunals, such normative principles exist as rules and procedures borne of political compromise and accommodation, and,

---

[36] This may cause us to question whether the search for truth and the imposition of punishment as competing objectives are consistent with a more civil professional judicial role.

[37] *Prosecutor v Kambanda* (Case No. ICTR-97-23-S), Judgement and Sentence, 4 September 1998, para. 50. Such rationalisations may not be endorsed at the local level.

[38] Although, as Schabas (1997, p.22) points out, rehabilitation is generally recognised as an essential component of international humanitarian law.

[39] Article 76 simply refers to the 'appropriateness' of any sentence, whilst Article 78(1) (determination of sentence) permits the individualisation of sentences. However, Article 75(1) deals specifically with the need for the court to establish principles relating (*inter alia*) to rehabilitation for victims in the context of reparations.

additionally for the ICTY and ICTR, the relative recognition and reflection of local processes which are (in any event) merely indicative of the sentence which should be adopted in any particular case. Hence, the future challenge for the ICC lies in the extent to which it succeeds in developing its penality by adopting principles and approaches designed to reconcile the local with the global at the moral and normative level, or whether it is destined to function merely as a symbolic component of globalisation that exists to provide a language and mechanism for asserting hierarchies of international power. As with the *ad hoc* tribunals, this will depend on the ability of the ICC to extend beyond performance and legitimise its sentencing practice in terms designed to engage successfully with local mechanisms of accountability and the institutions of punishment.[40]

There also exists cogent evidence to suggest that international agreement on matters of sentencing rationales and principles is problematic.[41] Consequently, not only may global and local contexts suggest contrary values which lead to conflict (Bauman, 2000), paradox and disharmony are disguised, submerged and ignored in the overwhelming nature of the rhetoric of retribution and vengeance. Thus, assertions, such as that in *Celebici*,[42] that 'retributive punishment by itself does not bring justice', conceal the institutional failure to confront contradiction and relativity in the context of developing an international penal rationale for the ICC. It fails to reach beyond the personification of the ICC as the global arbiter of guilt and punishment acting in accordance with fundamental principles of morality.

Such a scenario not only conceals and obfuscates the possible rationales of rehabilitation and its relationship with other sentencing rationales, it also fails to consider the possibly constructive import of restorative justice principles prevalent in domestic justice paradigms and how these may be linked to mechanisms which could provide the path to reconciliation. We can postulate significant elements of restorative justice to include the following:[43]

- humanitarian treatment of offenders
- elements of compensation, restitution, reparation (possibly reintegration)
- diversionary and mediatory processes
- victim participation.

These factors (with the exception of diversion and mediation) are already characterised in the ICC Statute and the Rules of Procedure and Evidence, Section III. Nevertheless, despite vague assertions that legal accountability contributes to rehabilitation of the victim's dignity and the reconciliation of opposing factions (Wexler, 1996, p.711), the documentation remains notably silent on a singularly vital

---

[40] It is arguable that the ICC, perhaps even more than the *ad hoc* tribunals, is a politically/diplomatically engineered institution meant to function as a kind of global conscience in order to provide diplomats and politicians with a reference point when things go wrong.

[41] An example is provided by the failure of the Council of Europe's recommendation on consistency in sentencing to suggest any specific sentencing rationale; see Council of Europe (1993).

[42] *Delalic et al.*, *supra*, note 20, para. 1231.

[43] The nature of the restorative justice paradigm is notoriously elusive; see Zedner (1994); Dignan and Cavadino (1996). For analysis of restoration and retribution in the context of international criminal justice, see Roberts (2003).

issue; namely, how might the formal legal rules and procedures of the ICC actually provide a guide towards the achievement of a communitarian philosophy of punishment through the discretionary decision-making process of international sentencing?

If the notion that law exists as an integrative mechanism is accepted (Cotterrell 1992, p.71), this must imply an acknowledgment that legal norms reflect notions of justice compatible and supportive of ideology at several levels.[44] However, it also implies a Durkheimian imperative which suggests a need to provide interpretations and adopt practices that might allow us to make the link between the recognition of law as a representation of morality and the existence of forms of expressed morality in civil society which exist in notions of communitarianism. Thus, the moral legitimacy of the international penal regime is constituted through its capacity to reflect socially meaningful (i.e. pluralistic) conceptions of morally unacceptable behaviour. This in turn requires an acknowledgement that it is the international sentencing *process* itself which provides the transformative mechanism and supplies linkage between moral purpose, legal norms and social behaviour. It follows, therefore, that these purposes (if they are to include reconciliation, or provide linkage between rehabilitation and reconciliation) must be articulated. They cannot simply remain pragmatic contexts.[45]

It was acknowledged in *Erdemovic*[46] that, whilst the ICTY has a clear mandate to investigate, prosecute and punish violations of international humanitarian law, the exercise of its judicial functions must contribute to the resolution of wider issues such as accountability, reconciliation and the establishment of the 'truth'. As the Trial Chamber put it:

> Discovering the truth is the cornerstone of the rule of law and a fundamental step on the way to reconciliation: for it is the truth that cleanses the ethnic and religious hatreds and begins the healing process ... On the other hand, the International Tribunal is a vehicle through which the international community expresses its outrage at the atrocities committed...

Such observations clearly illustrate and re-enforce what will become an urgent need for the ICC to balance retributive and reconciliatory demands through the

---

44 Namely, global or regional, but also as suggestive of a morality of sanctioned punishment.

45 It may be that South Africa's Truth and Reconciliation Commission (which did not possess prosecutorial power) provides a more convincing mechanism than legal accountability to promote the re-establishment of coexistence; for discussion, see Cohen (1995); Osiel (1995); van der Vyver (2004).

46 *Erdemovic*, *supra*, note 25, para. 21. Similar sentiments were expressed by the ICTR in *Kambanda*, *supra*, note 37, paras 26 and 28. However, different members of the international community interpret the ICTR's objectives in very different ways. Many focus on the goal of prosecution and punishment, while others recognise a greater role for the ICTR in national reconciliation; see Howland and Calathes (1998). Cockayne suggests that the major role of the ICTR is one of performance, not scrutiny. This is highlighted by the ICTR's failure to place great emphasis on its statutory 'reconciliation' mandate, particularly by failing to engage directly with the Rwandese people. Even in *Kambanda*, where the former prime minister pleaded guilty to genocide, little effort was made to capitalise on the confessions and admissions of guilt in the process of reconciliation at a local level. Similar comments apply to the ICTY. As Cockayne points out, such isolation undermines the educative and reconciliatory purposes of the trial process, and its legitimacy; see Cockayne (2001).

development of appropriate sentencing norms based on articulated purposes. Precedent and judicial authority cannot reconcile such fundamental contradictions in the ICC's rationale. Failure to address this issue risks producing a tribunal founded on principles of revenge, prejudice, discrimination and oppression.

Aspects of Sentencing Process

One of the fundamental aims of retributivism in the context of ICC sentencing practice will be to ensure that in future there exists no justification for severe violations of human rights (Nemitz and Wirth, 1999). However, respect for human rights also provides the context for establishing the parameters for the operation of retributive principles in international sentencing. As Schabas notes:

> Accompanying the new focus of human rights law upon the battle against impunity, the significance of retribution as an objective in sentencing is heard with disconcerting frequency ... surely a human rights approach must aim at combating these tendencies in society, which run counter to the rule of law and the protection of individual rights (1997, p.21).

Consequently, human rights considerations should not only determine the legitimate boundaries for retributive justifications,[47] but also their implementation. More particularly, if it is argued that this objective can only be achieved through the development of a just and consistent sentencing practice, then it is necessary to confront several paradoxes. Essentially, these relate to problems concerned with balancing elements of proportionality and culpability. The limited form of retributivism characterised in the approach adopted by the *ad hoc* tribunals requires adherence to two fundamental principles:

- that consistency demands similar crimes be dealt with by similar punishments
- that the severity of any sentence should be related to the amount of harm caused by the offending behaviour.

These principles are, nevertheless, problematic in that they do not readily accommodate notions relating to the individualisation of sentences. This is well-illustrated by the ICTY's judgment in *Todorovic*,[48] where the Trial Chamber stated:

> The principle of retribution, if it is to be applied at all in the context of sentencing, must be understood as reflecting a fair and balanced approach to the exaction of punishment for wrongdoing. This means that the penalty imposed must be proportionate to the wrongdoing; in other words, that the punishment be made to fit the crime.

[47] Nevertheless, as Schabas (1997, p.21) contends, for victims and the wider public, the actual consequences of conviction may be far less important than its symbolic significance.

[48] *Prosecutor v Todorovic* (Case No. IT-95-99/1-S) Sentencing Judgement, 31 July 2001, paras. 28–30.

This difficulty is compounded by the fact that Article 78(1) of the ICC Statute emphasises the importance of offence gravity and sentence individualisation by implication,[49] but fails to indicate what factors should determine the relative weight to be accorded to these principles.[50] Similarly, Rule 145(1)(a) of the Rules of Procedure and Evidence acknowledges the culpability of the offender as relevant only in so far as it relates to issues regarding the totality of sentence.[51]

As von Hirsch (1976, Ch. 8) has explained, commensurate desert systems (as personified by the international tribunals) need to recognise that sentencing policy must consider the extent to which deserved punishment is applied in individual cases. It is, however, an unresolved weakness in deserts theory that the approach is unable to distinguish convincingly between different degrees of responsibility, or quantify harm (Ashworth, 1983, pp.173–181; Ashworth, 1989a, p.346). It is, therefore, difficult to establish a relationship between the relative seriousness of behaviour (cardinal proportionality) and the relative severity of sentence (ordinal proportionality), as it is to define those moral values which should inform the setting of penalty levels.[52]

Modern social contract theorists such as Murphy (1979) have taken account of political obligation and sought to justify retributive punishment on the basis of the State seeking to achieve equilibrium between State interests and individual rights by maintaining the balance of advantage in favour of law-abiding citizens. However, in the international context, this notion implies the need to address the basis upon which such a moral imperative might be translated into a moral obligation on the part of the international community. This does not take effect in either the Statute or the Rules of Procedure and Evidence for the ICC. Consequently, the notion of individualisation is

---

[49] It states 'In determining the sentence, the Court shall, in accordance with the Rules of Procedure and Evidence, take into account such factors, as the gravity of the crime *and the individual circumstances* of the convicted person' [emphasis added].

[50] The concept of individualisation is problematic. For example, it may suggest a choice for sentencers to follow sentencing principles based on consequentialist justifications designed to operate independently from retributive considerations, or in conjunction with them. In the latter case, the choice of a retributive sentence may be forced on the sentencer due to the unsuitability of available individualised measures, or the inherent seriousness of the offence may preclude individualisation. As Thomas (1979, Ch. 1) describes, such was the distinction drawn between tariff and individualised sentencing drawn in England and Wales before the Criminal Justice Act (1991). According to this approach the primary decision was determined by the nature of the offence and the social importance of marking its gravity, which could outweigh the perceived benefits of an individualised sentence for the offender. Alternatively, in appropriate circumstances (such as 'treatable' psychiatric illness), it was possible for individualisation to replace retributive considerations completely. Such fundamental distinctions do not seem to have been considered in formulating the approach of the ICC to individualisation, although the relevant foundation provisions suggest a balancing of offence, offender and victim-related factors.

[51] There is a notable absence of any framework which might assist sentencers in developing a considered (and consistent) approach to sentence decision-making. These issues are explored further in Chapters 2 and 3.

[52] See von Hirsch (1986, p.87). Notwithstanding, as Gardner (1998, p.39) points out, both cardinal and ordinal principles of proportionality need to be applied with the State's duty of humanity in mind, since this forbids cruel and brutalizing punishments even when these would be proportionate. For a consideration of proportionality in the context of life imprisonment, see van Zyl Smit (1999, pp.35–40).

considered against a background where the primary consideration is overwhelmingly retributive rather than consequentialist.[53]

If it is accepted that the predominant rationale for individualisation should be consequentialist[54] in the context of international sentencing, then it becomes necessary to conceptualise and implement rational principles which sustain the linkage between retributivism and constructive communitarian process. Furthermore, it may be argued that such linkage of retributive and reconciliatory purposes at both the individual and inter-state levels may best be achieved through emphasising the educative or communicative aspects of retributive punishment itself (Duff and Garland, 1994). Such a consequentialist notion of communicative punishment should, therefore, extend beyond Duff's repentance/penitence paradigm to accommodate the concept of punishment as moral education designed to re-legitimate (pre-supposed) shared beliefs and aspirations. Thus, sentencing purposes for the ICC which combine an enlightened approach to retributive sentencing with clearly articulated consequentialist aspirations would constitute a significant step towards implementing communitarian notions of (re)constructive international criminal justice.[55]

The issue of consistency in sentencing practice is also likely to become a significant one for the ICC as the throughput of cases increases. The possibility of unjust and disproportionate sentences is addressed only in Part 8 (Appeal and revision) of the ICC Statute where Article 81(2)(a) provides:

> A sentence may be appealed, in accordance with the Rules of Procedure and Evidence, by the Prosecutor[56] or the convicted person on the ground of disproportion between the crime and the sentence.

However, the demonstration of disproportionality between offence and sentence will be problematic[57] since the Statute does not create a hierarchy of offence categories which might be developed into meaningful sentencing principles by the courts.[58] In

---

53 This was confirmed in both the *Celebici* case; *Prosecutor v Delalic et al* (Case No. IT-96-21), Appeals Judgement, 20 February 2001, para. 731, and *Prosecutor v Kupreskic* (Case No. IT-95-16-T), Judgement, 14 January 2000, para. 852.

54 To accept the reverse merely forces an accommodation with the notion of retributive punishment.

55 The concept of communitarianism is used here to invoke the notion that international sentencing norms must serve a reintegrative function at both the global and local levels. It is significant, therefore, that attention should focus on the rationalisation or modification of *process*.

56 An unfettered prosecution right of appeal in such circumstances is not widely available. In England and Wales, for example, prosecution appeals are limited to unduly lenient sentence determinations under the provisions of S36 of the Criminal Justice Act (1988). The test of what constitutes 'undue leniency' is strictly legalistic; for criticism, see Henham (1994).

57 The Appeals Chamber in *Celebici*, *supra*, note 53, cautioned, '... While [it] does not disagree with a contention that it is to be expected that two accused convicted of similar crimes in similar circumstances should not in practice receive very different sentences, often the differences are more significant than the similarities, and the mitigating and aggravating factors dictate different results. They are therefore not reliable as the *sole* basis for sentencing an individual' (paras 717, 719).

58 More particularly, by facilitating the ascription of weights to significant factors. Restrictions on the use of penalties beyond imprisonment and lack of clarity regarding the appropriate use of alternatives merely exacerbates this problem. For an exploration of the issues in the context of sentencing, see Carcano (2002).

addition, the only individual circumstances[59] specifically referred to as relevant to the Court on a review concerning reduction of sentence relate to willingness to cooperate with the prosecutor, assistance in locating assets and the enforcement of the Court's judgements and orders in other cases; Article 110(4)(a) and (b).

Failure to deal adequately with consistency and the disproportionality issue raises fundamental questions regarding the capacity of the ICC to deliver a sentencing praxis which corresponds with contemporary due process paradigms promoting access to justice and fair trial, such as the European Convention on Human Rights. Since, as Findlay (2001, p.49) points out, both substantive and procedural rights have featured prominently in the foundation instruments of the international tribunals, their interpretation against the norms and principles developed by (*inter alia*) the European Human Rights Convention is expected to provide a further context for synthesis.[60]

In the context of dangerousness legislation in England and Wales, for example, we find that challenges are possible under Convention Articles with regard to fundamental concepts, such as the meaning and acceptability of 'preventative detention'; how decisions as to 'commensurability' are reached; what is meant by 'punitive' and 'inhuman and degrading' treatment; when sentencing is 'discriminatory', and what the extent of victims' rights should be in the sentencing process. The potential for state sentencing norms to conflict with normative imperatives demanded by transnational rights agendas such as the European Convention is well-illustrated by the Commission's decision in *Mansell v United Kingdom.*[61] The general point at issue was whether a particular form of extended sentence designed for dangerous violent and sexual offenders[62] should be regarded as wholly punitive, or as containing a preventative element. If punitive, there exists an obligation for English courts not to pass disproportionate sentences which could be regarded as inhuman punishment under Article 3 of the Convention, whereas no proportionality requirement applies to the preventative element in a sentence, although that element must satisfy Article 5(4) which allows for sentence review. The Commission reached the bizarre decision that the sentence was essentially retributive and deterrent in character and therefore the controls and safeguards required by Article 5(4) were inappropriate, these having been incorporated in the original conviction and sentence. Ironically, it is difficult to imagine a clearer case of a sentence originally imposed for preventative purposes on the basis of the defendant's dangerousness and likely recidivism.

It may be argued, therefore, that in failing to provide the potential for the development of a coherent sentencing jurisprudence from a hierarchical categorisation of offences, the ICC may produce similar normative interpretations of key concepts (such as proportionality) which do not accord with the distinct moral and normative meanings attributed to them by state or regional jurisdictions.

---

59 These may be raised either during the trial, at a pre-sentence hearing, or during the appeal process.

60 And (possibily) disharmony. For an analysis of the difficulties for sentencing theory and process produced by the globalisation of rights norms, see Henham (2000b).

61 (1997) EHRR 66. The English Court of Appeal decision is reported at (1994) 15 Cr.App.R.(S) 771.

62 Namely, S2(2)(b) of the Criminal Justice Act 1991. This provision was repealed by a new regime for dealing with dangerous offenders introduced by Chapter 5 of the Criminal Justice Act (2003). Nevertheless, the point made herein is still valid.

Furthermore, the problem may be compounded if sentencing praxis is developed against particular notions of fair trial, such as those demanded by paradigms like the European Convention on Human Rights.

The potential for the systemic dysfunction of sentencing practice in the ICC is significantly enhanced by the absence of mechanisms designed to secure consistency. Inevitably, this will invite comparison, adoption or expansion of existing paradigms drawn from either state or inter-state jurisdictions. Although the conundrum of achieving consistency in sentencing practice has exercised the minds of sentencing scholars and practitioners in common law jurisdictions for many years (Ashworth 2000a, Ch. 13), it has mainly been addressed in contexts combining common law and civil law traditions during the deliberations of EC institutions. For example, in a report presented to the Council of Europe's eighth Criminological Colloquium in 1987 on disparities in sentencing (Council of Europe, 1989), Ashworth specifically considered the difficulty of providing credible mechanisms to reduce disparity in mixed sentencing systems. In particular, it was acknowledged that systems, such as those of France or Portugal, consider that the philosophy of individualisation should be the guiding principle in each case, whilst most other member states have 'mixed' systems in the sense that, although proportionality is the primary aim, there are spheres of sentencing where other aims (such as individual and general prevention, incapacitation and rehabilitation) predominate. In order to combat the problem of 'subjective disparity'[63] it is necessary to establish the ideal sentencing pattern for a given jurisdiction. This could be achieved by first deciding upon the aim of sentencing, or the order of priority among competing aims. As Ashworth put it:

> Without a clear declaration of priority or a statement of the categories of offence or offender to which each aim is to apply, the crucial piece of guidance is missing and the system constitutes a veritable invitation to subjective disparity (1989b, p.107).[64]

Accordingly, the Council of Europe's (1993, p.7) recommendations on consistency in sentencing fully endorsed this approach, suggesting:

> 3. a. Wherever it is appropriate to the constitutions and traditions of the legal system, some further techniques for enhancing consistency in sentencing may be considered.
>   b. Two such techniques which have been used in practice are 'sentencing orientations' and 'starting points'.
>   c. Sentencing orientations indicate ranges of sentence for different variations of an offence, according to the presence or absence of various aggravating or mitigating factors, but leave courts with the discretion to depart from the orientations.

---

63 It was acknowledged that the concept of 'subjective disparity' can have no constant point of reference, since its essence lies in deviations from the 'ideal sentencing pattern' in a given jurisdiction; Council of Europe (1989, p.101).

64 Ashworth goes on to dismiss as inadequate provisions which purport to address the problem of subjective disparity by:

(1) providing authoritative lists of aggravating and mitigating factors, or

(2) maintaining proportionality as the guiding principle giving way to individualisation in various types of cases, or

(3) relying on appeal systems to remedy subjective disparities.

d. Starting points indicate a basic sentence for different variations of an offence, from which the court may move upwards or downwards so as to reflect aggravating and mitigating circumstances.[65]

Whilst firmly supporting clarification of the rationales for sentencing as an essential prerequisite for consistency, the Council of Europe (1993, p.21) in its recommendations failed to suggest what primary rationale(s) might be appropriate for member states, leaving the matter to be determined instead by reference to the constitutional principles and legal traditions of each country. It did emphasise, however, that, whatever sentencing rationales were declared, 'disproportionality between the seriousness of the offence and the sentence should be avoided' (Council of Europe, 1993, p.6).[66]

It is apparent that neither the ICC Statute nor the Rules of Procedure and Evidence provide for any similar techniques for securing consistency. In fact, the ICC Statute positively encourages the conception of unfettered discretion in Article 76(1)[67] without considering any stated primary rationale(s) or purposes in sentencing. A similar situation pertains in the case of the *ad hoc* tribunals, where, as discussed, practice has re-enforced an overriding consideration to have regard to the gravity of the offence[68] without any principled linkage to rationales such as retribution and deterrence. Although it might be possible for either the ICC or the Assembly of State Parties to develop techniques for securing consistency such as those described by the Council of Europe, a fundamental obstacle concerns the boundaries of the concept of gravity itself within the wider context of international sentencing norms.

A significant paradox and circularity results from an inability or unwillingness to rank crimes falling within the ambit of international courts and tribunals in terms of their respective gravity for the purposes of sentencing.[69] The consequences are exemplified by Article 77(1) of the ICC Statute which indicates imprisonment as the preferred sanction for any crime referred to under Article 5,[70] with fines and

---

65 Recommendation 4.b. suggests that 'Wherever it is appropriate to the constitution or the traditions of the legal system, one or more of the following means, among others, of implementing such orientations or starting points may be adopted:

(i) legislation
(ii) guideline judgments by superior courts
(iii) an independent commission
(iv) ministry circular
(v) guidelines for the prosecution.'

66 The issue of what might constitute an appropriate mechanism to promote consistency in the future sentencing practices of the *ad hoc* tribunals is considered by Beresford (2002). Regrettably, Beresford fails adequately to distinguish between the self-regulation of judicial discretion, legislative orientation of sentencing policy, and the numerous variations in guideline sentencing systems.

67 This merely states: 'In the event of a conviction, the Trial Chamber shall consider the appropriate sentence to be imposed and shall take into account the evidence presented and submissions made during the trial that are relevant to the sentence.'

68 *Aleksovski*, *supra*, note 21, para. 182.

69 For further comment on the problems of ranking international crimes experienced by the *ad hoc* tribunals, see generally Kittichaisaree (2001, p.317); Bohlander (2000); Carcano (2002).

70 Article 5 specifies genocide, crimes against humanity, war crimes and the crime of aggression to be within the jurisdiction of the ICC.

forfeiture regarded as additional under subsection (2).[71] Such difficulties of approach are undoubtedly attributable to the magnitude of international criminality in its various forms, but, allied to unfettered judicial discretion, it reduces considerably the potential for rationality.[72] The difficulty is clearly illustrated in remarks made by the Trial Chamber of the ICTR in *Kambanda*:[73]

> There is no argument that, precisely on account of their extreme gravity, crimes against humanity and genocide must be punished appropriately ... the Chamber will prefer to lean more on its *unfettered discretion* each time that it has to pass sentence on persons found guilty of crimes falling within its jurisdiction ... [emphasis added].

In consequence, the question of disproportionality as regards sentence severity is worked out at the level of sentence individualisation. No attempt is made in the foundation instruments of the international institutions to relate offence seriousness to sentence severity, nor to suggest mechanisms which might provide some linkage between the principles of cardinal and ordinal proportionality.

Again, this may be illustrated by exploring the context of recent remarks of the Trial Chamber in the *Celebici* case.[74] In considering a claim by the appellant Delic, that the sentence imposed by the Trial Chamber had been excessive and disproportionate to the severity of the crimes committed by him (even allowing for mitigation), the Trial Chamber confirmed the importance of the principle applied earlier in the original Trial Chamber's judgment,[75] that 'gravity is determined *in personam* and is not one of universal effect'. Hence, the standard measure of proportionality to be applied to sentences is that which exists between the gravity of the crime and the individual culpability of the offender. In order to facilitate the construction of mechanisms to regulate the consistency of sentencing in the international tribunals (including the ICC) it is necessary to suggest ways of describing how offence gravity at the level of international crimes can be rationalised for sentencing purposes. Such a mechanism needs to reach out beyond the substantive procedural concerns of *process* (Lacey, 1987, p.229) by ensuring some

---

[71] It is worth noting that this approach is completely at odds with the primacy accorded to imprisonment in most western jurisdictions, or by the Council of Europe (1993, p.8) recommendation 5.a.

[72] This is magnified by the failure of the ICC Statute to suggest any mechanisms for providing guidance on the relative significance of aggravating or mitigating factors; see Rule 145(2) of the Rules of Procedure and Evidence.

[73] *Kambanda, supra*, note 37, paras 17, 25; the latter cited in *Prosecutor v Serushago* (Case No. ICTR 98-39-S), Sentence, 5 February 1999, para 18.

[74] On 11 April 2001 the President of the ICTY remitted the case to the Trial Chamber for review of the sentences passed on Delic, Mucic and Landzo. These sentences were passed after their conviction by Trial Chamber II at the conclusion of a trial on 16 November 1998. The Appeals Chamber allowed appeals against conviction and sentence on some of the counts in its judgement delivered on 20 February 2001, and remitted the question of what adjustment, if any, should be made to the original sentences to a Trial Chamber to be nominated by the President. The judgement of that Trial Chamber was delivered on 9 October 2001; *Prosecutor v Mucic et al.* (Case No. IT-96-21), Sentencing Judgement, 9 October 2001, para. 30.

[75] *Delalic et al., supra*, note 20, para. 1226. For discussion of the relevance of subjective seriousness to sentencing and its relationship to objective seriousness in the context of the *ad hoc* tribunals, see Kittichaiseree (2001, p.318).

conceptual and practical linkage between the substantive features and definitions of international crimes and their relative reality (as perceived constructs) for the purpose of individual sentencing. In other words, adopting the terminology of the *Celebici* Trial Chamber,[76] there should be some accommodation between the notions of criminal conduct and criminality.[77]

In this sense, I concur with Gardner (1998, p.41), that it is necessary to 'grasp not only the crime's legal definition but equally of what counts as the *substance* or the *gist* or the *point* of the crime as legally defined'. One still needs a 'moral map' of the crime for the purposes of assessing the proportionate *prima facie* sentence.[78] Gardner (1998, p.48) nevertheless acknowledges the limitations of the proportionality principle in providing a just methodology for scaling criminal sentences (such as the fact that the axes of gravity of crimes and sentences do not reflect each other). Instead, the sentencing stage should promote rational variation between cases rather than suppress them as does the trial stage. Notwithstanding, the moral sentiments engendered by the egregious nature of international crimes such as genocide are necessarily reflected in the construction of globalised notions of criminality. Such sentiments, whatever their justification, are further transformed through process into sentencing judgments (MacCormick and Garland, 1998, p.26).

Finally, it is significant that unresolved issues relating to rationale and consistency in sentencing are likely to be exacerbated by the fact that the operation of the ICC Statute is predicated on the principle of 'complementarity', through which the ICC's jurisdiction is regulated by strict conditions of admissibility (Schabas, 2001a, pp.66–70), which, if unfulfilled, leave national systems free to investigate and prosecute offences over which the ICC would otherwise have jurisdiction.[79] Since, as McGoldrick (1999, p.631) suggests, the structural relationship between the ICC and national courts is best conceived at a horizontal level, the potential for further obfuscation of the purposes and normative principles which will in future govern the

---

76 *Supra*, note 74, paras 32 and 33.

77 Interestingly, Grosselfinger (1998, p.14) suggests that indirect categorisation of sentences in terms of their severity will be possible through the security classifications adopted in States designated by the ICC to enforce sanctions under Article 103. In *Prosecutor v Blaskic* (Case No. IT-95-14-T), Judgement, 3 March 2000, the Trial Chamber proposed a mixed objective/subjective method for assessing crime seriousness whereby legal characterisation of the crime would be determined by its intrinsic seriousness, with subjective considerations relating to the individual circumstances of the case being reserved for sentencing. Sentence levels would depend on a determination of the appropriate balance between objective and subjective seriousness factors, although the weight to be accorded to the latter would not (except in exceptional circumstances) be permitted to override the former (see Carcano (2002) for arguments supporting this approach). However, the later Appeal Chamber decision in *Furundzija* (*Prosecutor v Furundzija* (Case No. IT-95-17/1-A), Appeals Judgement, 21 July 2000) did not refer to *Blaskic*, preferring instead an approach which retained greater flexibility for individual decision-makers to determine the appropriate relationship between individual factors and the relative gravity of crimes against humanity and war crimes for sentencing purposes.

78 Emphasis in the original. For arguments supporting the view that proportionality should form a key component in shaping the structure of the criminal law, see Ashworth (1999, pp.18–22).

79 Issues of admissibility are governed by Article 17 of the ICC Statute. The International Criminal Court Act 2001 gave effect to the ICC Statute in the UK. A collateral purpose of the Act, as Dennis (2001) suggests, was to enable the UK government to ratify the Rome Statute at an early stage and exercise some influence over the future development of the ICC.

sentencing of those convicted of 'the most serious crimes of international concern' will be even greater than currently exists with the *ad hoc* tribunals.[80]

Victims' Rights and State Interests

The importance of due process and its relationship to notions of fair trial and procedural justice in the future development of ICC sentencing praxis can be highlighted by focusing on the positions of victims' rights and access to justice.[81] Tochilovsky (1998, p.59) makes the point that the procedural rights enjoyed by victims in trials conducted by the *ad hoc* tribunals approximate those available in many civil law jurisdictions,[82] and are consistent with the general obligation of international judges to call whatever evidence is necessary in order to establish the 'truth'. Notwithstanding such attempts to remedy the deficiencies of adversarial process, are we really justified in suggesting, as does Schabas (2004, p.172), that this somehow reflects a wider 'important trend in criminal justice towards what is called "restorative justice"'? I contend that this is certainly not the case, for two reasons:

1. The suggestion is based on vague notions regarding the significance of restorative justice in the international context.[83]
2. There is no apparent rationality in defining the purposes of international sentencing. As already explained, consequentialist justifications currently sit uneasily within the context of a predominantly retributive rationale.

If it is accepted (as argued earlier) that sentencing in the international tribunals must include retributive considerations, but go beyond them to include mechanisms supportive of reconciliation, then notions of restorative justice should be developed to facilitate the achievement of this objective through sentencing praxis.[84] These mechanisms should be predicated on principles which are concerned to re-establish recognised conduct norms and the rights and obligations existing between citizens, and citizens and the state in victim communities. However, such mechanisms must be transformative at both the local and global level, a process which has often failed in the *ad hoc* tribunals.[85]

---

[80] This is due to the fact that both the ICTY (Article 9) and ICTR (Article 8) assert the primacy of their respective tribunals over national jurisdictions.

[81] This is explored in detail in Chapter 6.

[82] For example, the right to present evidence and put questions to the accused, witnesses and expert witnesses.

[83] This is not surprising given the difficulties encountered in conceptualising notions of victim participation evidenced in common law jurisdictions; see, for example, Dignan and Cavadino (1996); Edwards (2001); Johnstone (2002).

[84] The route to reconciliation through amnesty offered by mechanisms such as the South African Truth and Reconciliation Commission was rejected by the *ad hoc* tribunals as incompatible with the primary purpose of prosecution and the willingness of a state to bring the perpetrators of atrocities to justice. For arguments supporting a holistic approach; see Moghalu (2001).

[85] The difficulties encountered by the United Nations in establishing domestic criminal courts in Cambodia, Kosovo and Sierra Leone exemplify the problems of enforcing universal jurisdiction over international crimes; see further Bohlander (2001).

Moreover, conceptions of restorative justice, whilst being more suggestive of non-adversarial procedures, are not necessarily at variance with deserts-based retributive sentencing (Dignan and Cavadino, 1996). Furthermore, as Zedner (1994, p.248) suggests, both reparation and retribution are predicated upon notions of individual autonomy,[86] although ignoring the impact of structural inequality, power and social control variables. An additional difficulty lies in the fact that, whilst retribution equates proportionality with an objective assessment of offender culpability (and harm), reparative justice is proportionate to victim harm. Zedner goes on to suggest that:

> ... if reparative justice is to be more than a criminal analogue to civil damages, then it should go beyond the offence itself to enquire about its wider social costs and the means to making them good (1994, p.249).

Although cautioning that this process invites social intervention going beyond the normal boundaries of conventional crime prevention, it is precisely the need to address significant structural and ideological concerns that characterises those crimes of the magnitude with which we are concerned. Thus, notions of criminality as reflective of destruction, disintegration, conflict and breakdown go beyond traditional models which equate crime with social injustice. Instead, they lead directly to imperatives for reconstruction and reparation compatible with restorative justice principles aimed at increasing understanding, empowering victims and citizens and increasing their potential for participation and the resolution of conflict.[87] Certainly, in the arena of conventional crime, restorative justice principles are seen as potentially capable of re-empowering citizens and a force for social cohesion (Garland, 2001).

Whatever the potential for restorative justice, its value and relevance in the present context is its capacity to challenge conventional notions of the relationship between retributivism and other conceptualisations of penality in international sentencing. This includes a recognition that restorative objectives are *necessary* for the resolution of social conflict, and that notions of reparation and reconciliation should direct sentencing rather than be accommodated by retributive practices which are inconsistent and so lacking in any coherent philosophical basis as to threaten their legitimacy.

Internationalised Sentencing Structures and Alternative Processes [88]

Finally, this section reflects upon the implications for the internationalisation of sentencing of internationalised criminal courts and tribunals (such as Cambodia, East

[86] These issues are explored further in Braithwaite (2002).

[87] Some writers, such as Bush and Fogler (1994, pp.84–85) would argue that practices like mediation have the potential to transform conflict through empowerment and recognition by citizens of the need to acknowledge and be responsive to the needs of others.

[88] It should be noted that I do not deal with sentencing issues which relate to states exercising universal jurisdiction over international crimes (see further Ratner, 2003, van der Vyver, 2004b); domestic courts (as

Timor, Kosovo and Sierra Leone) and alternative processes (such as the Truth and Reconciliation Commissions). The purpose is not to provide the reader with a detailed analysis of the structure and operation of these institutions but to concentrate on identifying the underlying rationales for decision-making in terms of their relationship to truth and reconciliation. An attempt is also made to locate these arguments within the terms of the debate surrounding the justifications and significance of international punishment.

Internationalised Sentencing Structures

Superficially, the reasons for the establishment of internationalised structures and alternative processes differ fundamentally, since the former seek to establish some form of alternative criminal trial process whilst the latter (by definition) are aimed at finding alternative means of satisfying the particular requirements for truth and justice. International sentencing structures have generally been created in circumstances where the available criminal trial process in the country concerned is virtually non-existent (as in East Timor),[89] or inadequate, coupled with an

---

in Bosnia) established to hear cases transferred from international tribunals (see Bohlander, 2003); or special domestic courts (as in Iraq) established essentially to hear cases which involve alleged breaches of international criminal law.

In relation to the latter, it should be noted that the jurisdiction of the Iraqi Special Tribunal (IST) is limited to Iraqi nationals or residents accused of crimes listed in Articles 11 to 14 of the Statute of the Iraqi Special Tribunal (i.e. genocide (Article 11), crimes against humanity (Article 12), war crimes (Article 13), violations of certain Iraqi laws (Article 14)) committed between 17 July 1968 and 1 May 2003 in Iraq or elsewhere, including Iraq's wars against Iran and Kuwait. It is significant that, whilst Iraqi law applies to alleged breaches of Articles 11 to 14, Trial Chambers and the Appellate Chamber may resort to relevant decisions of international courts or tribunals as persuasive authority for their decisions (Article 17 b). Sentencing measures will no doubt be hard to balance, given the fact that capital punishment has been readopted in Iraq. Ironically, The Coalition Provisional Authority removed the death penalty in 2003 among some other cruelties in the Iraqi Penal Code. Article 24 of the Statute provides that, where no counterpart penalty exists under Iraqi law for crimes under Articles 11 to 13, the Trial Chamber should determine the penalty by taking into account such factors as the gravity of the crime, the individual circumstances of the offender and *relevant international precedents*. Finally, Article 29 stipulates that the IST has primacy over all other Iraqi courts with respect to the crimes stipulated in Articles 11 to 13 of the Statute.

[89] The re-building of East Timor's judicial system was established by the UN Transitional Administration for East Timor (UNTAET) under UNTEAT Regulation no. 2000/1 which created a system of District Courts and a Court of Appeal. Jurisdiction over the serious crimes of genocide, war crimes, crimes against humanity, murder, sexual offences and torture were reserved to the Dili District Court, and a Serious Crimes Panel was created within this court under Regulation no. 2000/15 to hear cases within the serious crimes jurisdiction. The Serious Crimes Panels apply the law of East Timor as promulgated by UNTAET. It has laid down substantive criminal norms which in part defer to the Indonesian Criminal Code (in respect of murder and sexual offences) and in part replicate the ICC Statute (on genocide, war crimes and crimes against humanity). Regulation no. 2000/15 also lays down a set of principles of international criminal law based on the ICC Statute, and the ICC Rules of Procedure and Evidence are incorporated as the applicable rules of procedure; see further Linton (2001a, 2001b); Strohmeyer (2001); Katzenstein (2003); Sriram (2004).

unwillingness to create a fully international tribunal. In Sierra Leone[90] and Kosovo,[91] some practical advantage may be claimed through the internationalisation of the criminal jurisdiction since it ensures that charges arising from internal conflicts are dealt with 'impartially'. However, in other cases, such as Cambodia,[92] it is less clear how internationalisation has contributed to any 'improvement' in the trial process, and, indeed, intervention may instead be seen more in terms of lending international political support to the trial process (Cockayne, 2002).

In legal terms, each jurisdiction is challenged with developing a body of substantive and procedural law which combines local and international sources. In Kosovo and East Timor, international norms have clear normative priority over local rules, especially on procedural issues. In the Special Court for Sierra Leone, however, international rules (the ICTR Rules) may be amended by the judges 'guided' by local rules.[93] In Cambodia, domestic criminal procedure (civil law style) applies subject to any amendment authorised by the UN to force compliance with international norms. There is no clear systematic hierarchy of international and domestic procedural rules. The process of internationalisation appears to be *ad hoc* and left to the discretion of inexperienced and under-resourced judges.

More recently, commentators have pointed to a number of particular difficulties with internationalised fora which have significant implications for their relationship with alternative processes. For example, in relation to Cambodia, Pangalangan (2002) suggests that, rather than providing a model of criminal justice and procedure, the insertion of internationalised chambers into national systems could 'immunise' the rest of the judicial system against amendment in correspondence with international norms. In effect, the creation of an enclave of international standard

---

[90] The Special Court for Sierra Leone is independent of both local judicial institutions and the UN Mission in Sierra Leone (UNAMSIL). It is a *sui generis* mechanism established by treaty between the UN and Sierra Leone (completed on 15 January 2002). The Statute of the Court provides for a mixed jurisdiction, including both international crimes (war crimes, crimes against humanity) and crimes taken from Sierra Leonean law (including abduction of girls and destruction of property). The Statute further provides for the Court's rules of procedure to be the Rules of Procedure and Evidence of the ICTR (as amended by the Special Court judges guided by the Sierra Leone Criminal Procedure Act 1968); see further Linton (2001a).

[91] The Kosovo Courts were created by virtue of UN Security Council Resolution 1244 which provided the UN Interim Administration Mission in Kosovo (UNMIK) with the tasks of (*inter alia*), 'performing basic civilian administrative functions', 'maintaining civil law and order', and 'protecting and promoting human rights'. Accordingly, an 'Emergency Judicial System (EJS)' was created (now overseen by an Advisory Judicial Commission established under UNMIK Regulation 1999/7), and international judges and prosecutors were inserted into the EJS in February 2000 (expanded into a Kosovo-wide Programme of International Judicial Support in May 2000); see further Bohlander (2001, 2002, 2003); Strohmeyer (2001).

[92] The Extraordinary Chambers of the Courts of Cambodia were established by King Sihanouk on 10 August 2001 in the *Law on the Establishment of Extraordinary Chambers in the Courts of Cambodia for the Prosecution of Crimes Committed during the Period of Democratic Kampuchea.* The level of control exercised by Cambodia is greater than other internationalised systems, since all appointments are made by the Cambodian Supreme Council of the Magistracy, power being exercised in accordance with existing procedural law. Where gaps exist guidance may be sought in procedural rules established at the international level (Article 20); see further Linton (2001a).

[93] Sierra Leone Criminal Procedure Act 1968.

justice might remove the pressures on the rest of the system to reform. It also threatens to erode rather than enforce domestic stability, by creating a two-tier system; international standard justice for the leaders of atrocities, and domestic standard justice for their underlings.

Similarly, commenting on East Timor, Othman (2002) points to a number of normative questions regarding to the hierarchy between crimes, and practical issues relating to the concurrent operation of two procedural systems in trials where the accused is charged with both 'international' and domestic crimes. Furthermore, the international authority of (as yet) untested international ICC norms might be undermined because of inadequate resources being provided to the processes which were intended to give them substance.[94]

As with international structures, the procedures for establishing internationalised forms in themselves raise a number of important legal and policy questions regarding their legitimacy, as summarised by Nollkaemper (2002):

1. Whilst three procedures for establishing such tribunals can be identified,[95] the central question is political; namely, who has the means to organise and sustain the court?
2. What (or whose) normative order underpins the process of criminalisation manifested in the trial? What is the context from which the criminal norms issue, and against which the conduct of the individuals concerned is to be measured? As for international sentencing, this issue is fundamental for the rationalisation of punishment.
3. In Sierra Leone, does the fact that the UN dealt solely with government forces threaten to taint the perceived impartiality of the trial process, and therefore undermine the deterrent objectives of the trial as symbolic of a process of criminalisation? Does it instead suggest that trial and sentencing in internationalised tribunals is less focused on deterrence than retribution by the international community and its chosen local partners?
4. The question of direct effect of international law within national legal orders has a direct bearing on criminal trial processes, since it influences the manner in which international and domestic processes are reconciled.[96] For example, in certain constitutional orders, international norms may have effect only to the extent that they do not derogate from fundamental principles guaranteed by the national constitution. In such cases, national procedural norms take primacy, with international norms playing only an influencing role. Under the trusteeship approach, however, international law predominates so that local norms play a minor influencing role.

---

[94] In relation to Sierra Leone, underfunding raises serious questions about international standards of judicial independence (Schabas, 2002).

[95] These are:

(1) unilateral establishment by the UN

(2) establishment after negotiation between the UN and a State

(3) establishment after inter-state negotiations.

[96] As Nollkaemper (2002) points out, in both the Kosovo and East Timor cases, the situation can be construed in two alternate (but equally novel) ways. Firstly, international norms may take their direct effect through a combination of the coercive power of the UN Security Council under Chapter VII and

All four points question the nature and significance of the relationship between international and national structures in an internationalised context. The most important aspect of this relationship for sentencing concerns the interaction between international and national normativity and its manifestation in hybrid trial processes.[97] As Romano (2002) suggests, the key factor here is how individual judicial discretion modulates this effect to conduct the process of criminalisation.[98] However, as I have argued here and elsewhere (Henham, 2003a, 2003b), the crucial issue remains one of understanding what this process of criminalisation actually signifies for victims and victim communities. In other words, whilst the international (and internationalised) judiciary may be the mediators of some form of penality,[99] the implications of this cannot be worked through without a consideration, on the one hand, of what the constituent elements of that penality mean and signify in ideological and political terms, and, on the other, the extent to which the exercise of judicial discretion in sentence decision-making is transformative of the morality and normative framework such penality represents. As discussed, this conceptualisation requires us to make certain assumptions regarding the nature of law and the process of legal reasoning in sociological terms. However, it also forces us to address the *legitimacy* of the penality which relates to international (internationalised) institutions because it seeks to make connections between the ideology of punishment and its moral legitimacy. The latter is considered at the level of the moral values that underpin the normative principles embodied in the institutional frameworks of international

---

consent of the sovereign within whose territory that direct effect occurs (originally, Indonesia and Serbia, respectively). Secondly, the prior sovereignty might be said to be ceded to a UN trusteeship system, which would remove the requirement of constitutional incorporation usually needed to see international norms take effect within national legal orders.

More generally, Schabas (2002) suggests that a common feature existing between the four internationalised tribunals is the process of encroachment by the international community upon national processes with a view to ensuring the prosecution of human rights abuses. This observation suggests how the internationalisation of criminal trial process is a constitutional process, a re-ordering of global governance, in which the international community is arrogating to itself the right to use penal repression to defend its own norms. As Cockayne (2002) observes, this process involves a fundamental redefinition of sovereignty and a basic reallocation of power over the use of violence as a repressive tool.

[97] See Henham (2000b) for a discussion of this phenomenon in the context of the ECHR. Condorelli (2002) makes the important point that the hybridisation of criminal processes also reflects a wider trend towards the internationalisation of domestic judicial functions even in purely national contexts involving not just formal institutional processes but also the growth of comparative judicial methodology by judicial actors.

[98] Romano (2002) suggests that 'local' judges will exercise a kind of 'local' discretion, embedded in local norms, and 'international' judges a generalised or abstracted 'international' discretion, freed from any particular perspective that would threaten its impartiality. Notwithstanding the fact that such an analysis appears to ignore the possibility that so-called 'international' discretion is partial rather than generalised and unfocused, the alternative scenario envisaging the fusion of two normative orders to constitute a uniform unilateral criminalisation of the conduct in question seems a remote possibility. More likely, where mixed benches are involved, is the effect that there may be multiple (rather than one) trial process occurring in each trial in these hybrid tribunals.

[99] This proposition is consistent with the findings of other work; see Findlay and Henham (2005); Henham and Mannozzi (2003).

(internationalised) criminal processes and the connections that can (and should) be made between these and the penality of post-conflict societies. Consequently, a major theme of this book is directed towards understanding the linkage between the conditions of moral and legal pluralism and their implications for international punishment.

As Condorelli (2002) intimates, whilst the advent of the ICC might supercede the need for internationalised tribunals, the important lesson to be drawn from them relates to the need for justice to be made local. Certainly, the necessity for the *ad hoc* international criminal tribunals and the ICC to engage international punishment norms with those of the communities where they are to be enforced has been strongly argued (Alvarez, 1999; Drumbl, 2000; Henham, 2003b). However, it must be emphasised that the nature and significance of this transformative enterprise differs as between international and internationalised punishment models. This point is made clear by Linton in describing the significance of the Serious Crimes Panels in East Timor:

> Beyond the obvious prosecution of atrocities, it is unclear what the aim of the Serious Crimes experiment is meant to be. Is it an end in itself, in other words, with no greater purpose beyond retributive justice in the individual case? Or is the purpose to contribute towards reconciliation in a nation struggling to come to terms with a violent history, with the courts used as a means for checking impunity, establishing the rule of law and determining the wider truth of what occurred? (2001a, p.217).

More particularly, it needs to be established whether, as Linton (2001a, p.243) suggests, the purpose of the enterprise is for justice to be seen as an end in itself, or whether it is part of a nation's strategy for moving forwards towards peace and reconciliation.[100]

Allied to this is the relationship between internationalised forms and other domestic processes of accountability such as truth and reconciliation commissions. Although such processes have been initiated in Sierra Leone, East Timor and Serbia to sit alongside existing institutions, the distinctions between TRCs and criminal trial processes are largely unclear, as are understandings of how each operates and interacts.

Alternative Structures

Part of the conceptual difficulty in reconciling the purposes of internationalised structures with those of alternative mechanisms[101] is the fact that it is impossible to draw meaningful generalisations about their relationship since each structure is unique. For example, the South African Truth and Reconciliation Commission remains the only commission which has had the power to grant amnesty to individual

---

[100] In the case of Sierra Leone she suggested the need for a clear policy of transitional justice to ensure that the existing work of the Serious Crimes Panels was not compromised in any way. Failure to do so would threaten notions of fair trial, including trial by media, prejudice to the presumption of innocence, the tainting of evidence and the risk of inconsistent testimony; Linton (2001a, p.223).

[101] See generally, Roht-Arriaza (1995); Osiel (1997); Minow (1998); Hayner (2001).

perpetrators and was notable for its public sessions.[102] Other commissions are more victim-orientated and likely to deal with crimes specific to vulnerable or minority groups such as women and children. The East Timor Commission for Reception, Truth and Reconciliation, for example, is particularly concerned with the return and reconciliation of low-level offenders by their communities, where perpetrators and victims are generally well-known to one another.

Hayner (2001) suggests that, far from being a poor second choice to 'real' (i.e. trial) justice, Truth Commissions should be seen as complementary processes that can actually strengthen justice.[103] Similarly, Moghalu (2001) also argues that a holistic approach to the resolution of conflict is needed, and that Truth Commissions and prosecutions should not be regarded as mutually exclusive alternatives. However, it is necessary to recognise the political realities (Allen, 1999), such as the fact that TRCs are often chosen to avoid criminal prosecution, or may not even be considered an option as, for example, in the case of genocide where there appears to be a consensus in the international community that it should be prosecuted.

Nevertheless, the key to understanding the nature and significance of the alternative conceptions of justice apparently administered by TRCs and Courts (whether international or internationalised) is to examine the bases upon which such competing versions of 'truth' claim moral legitimacy. Moghalu (2001) intimates that the TRC process propagates a *false* differentiation between 'truth' and 'justice'; but, what does this assertion actually mean? If we equate the notion of justice with resolution, then it may be argued that trials are more likely to provide the kind of lasting resolution which victims seek; that to try individuals assists in demystifying collective responsibility; and that they provide closure – they establish a form of binding historical 'truth' (a political space freed from the past) with legal consequences. Alternatively, if we consider the nature of trial justice in qualitative terms, then, as discussed elsewhere in this book, there are several ways in which the moral integrity of international sentencing may be impugned. It may, therefore, be questioned whether the supposed advantages claimed for trial justice as establishing truth through closure are sustainable, since its morally relative nature is undeniable.

The very same arguments apply in the case of TRCs where the relative differentiation between notions of 'truth' and justice is equally difficult to reconcile with their supposed strengths; namely, that they empower and engage victims and victim communities by placing them at the heart of the process. Whilst this may (or may not) be true, again the emphasis is on the fact that moral legitimacy is equated with the nature and function of the process rather than what it *actually* signifies. As I have argued, in order for legitimacy to be considered in such terms requires us to establish some conceptual linkage between the moral justifications for the process and how these are transformed in processual terms to connect with notions of moral legitimacy in victim communities. In the context of sentencing, this position forces us

---

[102] As Wilson notes: 'The theatricalisation of power gives us one clue as to why democratising governments set up truth commissions rather than relying upon an existing legal system: truth commissions are transient politico-religious-legal institutions which have much more legitimising potential than dry, rule-bound and technically obsessed courts of law' (2001, p.20).

[103] In Argentina, for example, the Prosecutor's pursuit of generals of the junta relied heavily on information gathered by the Truth Commission.

to examine the rationalisations for process, what they represent as moral values, and how they are embodied in legal norms and transformed into relevant normative imperatives.

An illustration of this argument is provided by Wilson (2001) in his contextual analysis of the South African Truth and Reconciliation Commission and the alternative conceptualisations of justice that existed in numerous townships during the time of its operation. A pervading theme in his analysis is the failure of the TRC process to achieve moral legitimacy within certain townships because it could not engage in any meaningful way with their punitive conception of justice. Wilson (2001, p.160) suggests that this phenomenon was facilitated because human rights were reconceptualised as restorative justice and forgiveness in the TRC process, this being coupled with the attribution of revenge and retribution as morally unacceptable. Wilson concludes:

> The most damaging outcome of truth commissions is as a result of their equating of human rights with reconciliation and amnesty. This delegitimizes them enormously in relation to popular understandings of justice and can lead to greater criminal activity in society ... Human rights talk has become the language of pragmatic political compromise rather than the language of principle and accountability (2001, p.228).

In addition to his attack on human rights as a 'product of modernist rationalisation', Wilson (2001, p.225) concludes that 'truth' and moral legitimacy is to be found in 'striking the right balance between legal-forensic investigations and historical approaches to truth'. Whilst acknowledging the contentious nature of community justice, he argues, on the basis of a detailed study of localised forms of tribal justice,[104] that a retributive understanding of human rights is necessary to provide a meaningful basis for legitimising legal institutions.

Notwithstanding that Wilson's specific conclusions cannot be generalised beyond their socio-historical and political context, they argue persuasively the need for notions of accountability and justice to be grounded in terms which resonate with the moral legitimacy attached to notions of penality in victim communities. Thus, it is crucial that different approaches to the meaning and signifying nature of penality should be reflective of generally understood contextualised meanings of crime and punishment (Garland, 1990). This suggests that, particularly where Truth Commissions operate in tandem with internationalised courts, the rationality for such mechanisms should be informed by a relational approach to the conceptualisation of justice. This implies that, instead of rationales for internationalised or alternative processes being imposed or presumed, such rationales should be community-based so that localised notions of moral legitimacy are mirrored in national and international structures.

---

[104] More particularly, he analysed the penality of the local court (or *imbizo*) existing in the small township of Boipatong, observing its retributive approach to the pursuit of 'truth' and the conceptualisation of justice. For example, Wilson concludes that: 'In contrast to anonymous encounters between strangers at human rights commissions, *imbizo* members hold that cross-examination from members of the same community always finds out the guilty, and achieves justice through vengeful punishment, rather than "reconciliation" and amnesty' (2001, p.207).

Conclusion

At the level of symbolism, the expressive function of punishment in the ICC's Trial Chamber will be of major significance in reasserting the primacy of the prevailing international moral order (Amann, 2002).[105] It represents the re-enforcement of moral legitimacy and legal ideology in the hegemonic struggle among social groups (or societies) intent upon asserting their own version of morally acceptable rules. Yet within such a context it becomes problematic to envisage international sentencing as a coherent and credible unilateral force which is capable of creating and facilitating opportunities for transforming moral principles that combine retributive and restorative aspirations into practice. Consequently, it is crucial to view the achievement of these objectives within the context of universally accepted rights paradigms which satisfy the functional requirement of legitimating the boundaries of international action against citizens and states. As Cotterrell (1997, p.91) implies, this requires a pluralistic vision of law which reaches beyond parochial state interests to reflect communitarian concerns at the international level. Accordingly, such communitarian aspirations, whether at the global or local level, must reflect adequately individual demands for guaranteed freedoms against power exercised arbitrarily in the name of the international community. In this respect, this chapter has highlighted significant imperatives for the future development of principled sentencing in the ICC which should sustain these aspirations. More specifically, these consist of the need for:

- a statement of principles or purposes for sentencing
- mechanisms to provide guidance and ensure consistency through the development of a principled sentencing jurisprudence
- additional safeguards against bureaucratic and managerial agendas which compromise due process
- the development of due process norms which adequately address victims' concerns
- the de-politicisation of the international criminal trial process[106]
- a re-engagement beyond retributive concerns to address more adequately communitarian notions which resonate with rehabilitation, reconciliation and restorative justice.

These prescriptions also reflect on the need to reconcile 'an acute sensitivity to the peculiarities of the local' with 'the universalising imperative' in the contextual analysis

---

[105] This is not meant to imply support for any particular moral position. In the late postmodern world moral legitimacy is ambivalent and conjectural. For example, as Caplan (2001) rather cynically commented on the Bill providing for UK ratification of the ICC: 'Perhaps the Prime Minister should authorise the Foreign Office Minister, Baroness Scotland of Asthal, to table an amendment to the ICC Bill saying that it does not apply when NATO has the moral right to intervene. If so, who will decide when it is acceptable morally to invade or bomb a country in the name of international justice?' Similar arguments no doubt apply regarding the continued reluctance of some countries (notably the US) to ratify the ICC Statute, and the willingness of those who have to restrict its effectiveness in times of impending conflict.

[106] This does not imply that political realities should be ignored in formulating credible objectives for international sentencing.

of international justice, or, in other words, provide a more general consideration of the means whereby localised criminal trial procedures may be recognised as instrumental (or reflective) in the transformation and internationalisation of criminal procedure in the sentencing context (Findlay, 1999).

Hence, it is important to recognise that we have, in this chapter, been concerned with deconstructing the contexts of international sentencing at several levels, both horizontal and vertical. For instance, our evaluation of fair trial paradigms against the practices of international sentencing must recognise the relativity of particular notions of justice. As Findlay (2001, p.50) correctly suggests, access to justice as measured by adherence to principles of fair trial can only be understood by research which considers the dynamic of practice and process through a detailed examination of the developing contexts of discretionary decision-making within particular sites of the international trial, such as sentencing. The prospects and reality of synthesis in institutional and procedural form is, therefore, dependant on a careful observation of these processes and their effects at both the international and local level. At the international level, however, symbolism and judicial dominance will be important determinants of the discretionary decision-making aspects of sentencing procedure in the ICC. Nevertheless, the forces of greatest significance are likely to remain those ideological and political dynamics which forged the ICC's Statute and Rules. These are liable to re-enforce and sustain such philosophical compromises and pragmatic contexts as have been revealed by the sentencing practices of the *ad hoc* tribunals.

For criminal justice theory, there is the further recognition that its role in the international sphere is to provide the appropriate epistemological contexts for developing penal strategies (Henham, 1999b, p.178). These may reflect communitarian desires for justice in the sentencing process. For example, Cotterrell (1995, p.316) argues that, whilst justice must be predicated on order, the balance and interplay between them should 'determine the level of legitimacy accorded to legal doctrine and the agencies involved in its institutionalisation'. Hence, although not prescriptive of the social values to be ascribed to order and justice, Cotterrell's position is tolerant of a communitarian vision of rights which is predisposed to recognise diversity and pluralism in the world order.

Recognising the need to reflect upon the diversity and instrumental desires of public opinion at the level of the international criminal trial and sentencing forces criminal justice theory to develop strategies for understanding the moral contexts of international law's implementation at both the international and domestic level. This acknowledges that our appreciation of such social experience, including the development of penality,[107] is contingent upon our knowledge of how international legal norms are transformed and understood as conduct norms and values at these levels through sentencing practice. I would argue that coherent policy and the future development of sentencing purposes and principles for the ICC depend on conceptualising in this manner.[108]

---

[107] This includes the ambit of rights norms within criminal procedure.

[108] In this endeavour autopoietic theory may assist us to conceptualise and contextualise discourses which present competing interpretations of the legal and social meaning of forms of justice; see further King (1993); Nobles and Schiff (1995).

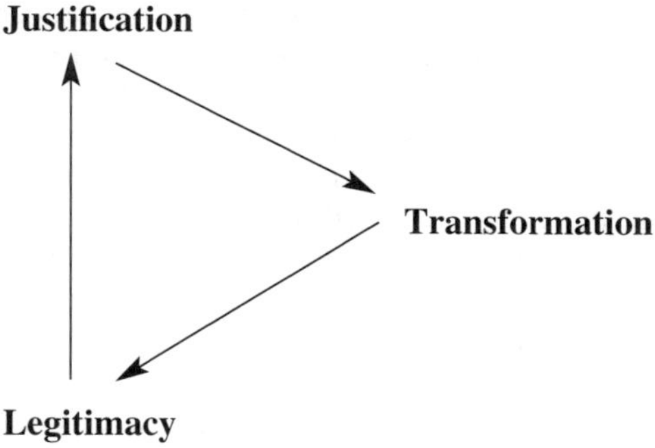

Figure 1.1 Conceptualising the relationship between legitimacy and justification

Thus, portrayed diagrammatically (as in Figure 1.1), the relationship between the justifications for international punishment and the moral legitimacy attached to them can be conceptualised as constituted recursively through process. Consequently, relationality as between the moral justification for punishment and the moral legitimacy accorded to it is determined by the extent to which the process of transformation (through discretionary decision-making) engages with localised (relevant and meaningful) conceptions of legitimacy.

At the micro-level, understanding the significance of discretionary decision-making in sentencing at the international level suggests a need to reconsider how sentencing decisions can be conceptualised, described and analysed (Henham, 2001). This raises crucial issues relating to the merging (or otherwise) of adversarial and inquisitorial styles in the international criminal trial as evidenced in the process of judicial decision-making. For instance, as Tata (1997) suggests, sentencing decisions should be analysed at the discrete level from the standpoint of the description and explanation of sentencers' accounts of 'similarity' and the construction of 'whole offence stories'. However, intuitive accounts must also be balanced against accounts of how the formal exercise of discretion becomes patterned, normalised and typified as an exercise in contextual analysis.[109] Descriptions at the level of legal formalism are patently inadequate as a methodology which might contribute to our understanding of the comparative analysis of trial process (Roberts, 2002).

I have suggested that the sentencing practices of the *ad hoc* tribunals have done little to promote principles which argue for the unity or generalisation of justice, and have failed to appreciate fully the fact that our interpretation of justice is dependent on social context. In addition, the contextual stage must be considered as multi-layered and responsive to the demands of justice as perceived at both the international and domestic state levels. Therefore, whilst appearing to have reconciled and

[109] The analysis of trial transcript material is one element in this process. Neither this, nor the adoption of other methodologies for deconstructing sentence decision-making, can be adopted in a theoretical vacuum; see Henham and Findlay (2001).

synthesised some aspects of adversarial and inquisitorial procedural approaches in their respective Statutes and Rules, these practices are currently more reflective of judicial pragmatism and style than a concerted attempt to forge an influential procedural hybrid sentencing process which might serve as a paradigm for future international sentencing. Nevertheless, whereas focusing our attention on style also directs us to examine judicial practice (Pakes, 2001, 2004), this does not address context, nor resolve the manifest inconsistencies and paradoxes that have produced and sustained the present arrangements. Such relative insularity and irrelevance contributes to weaken any claim for international sentencing to exercise democratic principles of justice.

Rather than perpetuating sterile arguments over the relative seriousness of heinous crimes, it has been argued that[110] the prospects for a more integrated sentencing regime for the ICC would be much enhanced by relating those considerations to a principled reassessment of its penality. Such a move would ultimately invest the crucial process of sentencing by the ICC with greater credibility and legitimacy at both the international and local level, and help dissipate its otherwise likely place in history as the twenty-first century forum for international public retribution.

[110] Limitations on the use of penalties beyond imprisonment militate against restorative development. Removal would also facilitate a more constructive debate concerning the sentencing potential for rehabilitation and reconciliation as realistic primary sentencing objectives.

Chapter 2

Procedural Rules and Trial Practice

The rationale for this and the following chapter is interconnected. In essence, the purpose of these chapters is to develop an appropriate conceptual framework against which those procedural rules of the *ad hoc* tribunals and the ICC that concern sentencing can be interpreted and evaluated. The following chapter utilises the same approach, but extends the analysis to consider the wider social context within which these rules and procedures operate and the implications for internationalisation in sentencing.

This chapter begins by outlining a framework for analysis which seeks to build upon existing paradigms for modelling the operation of criminal justice processes and thereby provide a conceptual tool for process evaluation. The analysis itself concentrates on describing the mechanics of international sentencing within this paradigm, focusing especially on those stages in the trial process which deal with evidence relevant to sentencing; the nature and quality of the evidence permitted; the roles of the judge, prosecution and defence in relation to the presentation and assessment of such evidence; and the significance of victim evidence for sentencing.

Introduction

Before embarking on the analytical exercise it is necessary to explain what is meant by modelling in this context, and why it is regarded as fundamental to the understanding of international sentencing. Dealing with these questions in reverse order, the functional value of assessing procedural rules and practice in terms of a paradigmatic approach is twofold. Firstly, it can provide a heuristic device, a theoretically grounded construct that allows us to link what is discovered to existing knowledge about sentencing. Secondly, it permits systematic evaluation regarding the operation of existing models of sentencing and their ideological context, thereby allowing us to test certain assumptions about preferred criminal justice processes based on such models (such as those reflecting adversarial or inquisitorial trial styles).

The first question is more difficult to answer since conventional criminal justice models may be characterised as either theoretical or ideological in purpose. In a theoretical sense, the function of a model is seen in conventional sociological terms; to facilitate the emergence of new 'knowledge' by providing a conceptual framework which has the heuristic capability to promote methodologies designed to test the postulates of a particular theoretical position (Rudner, 1966; Ryan, 1970). It therefore facilitates theoretical verification and development.

Alternatively, it is possible to characterise certain types of modelling as atheoretical in the sense of being, *in essence*, either normative or ideological in nature. Criminal justice modelling may be described as normative where its primary objective is to provide a principled basis for the reform of criminal justice (see Ashworth, 1994, 1998). Ashworth's rights-based approach is concerned chiefly with the identification of principles of substantive and procedural fairness in the criminal justice context and, as a statement of normative principles, does not address significant wider theoretical and analytical issues. More particularly, it fails to conceptualise power by neglecting the contexts in which rights and principles may or may not operate, including its wider symbolic dimensions in terms of domination, exploitation and oppression. [1]

Ideological modelling is frequently described as template analysis, or what Nelken (1997) refers to as 'comparison by juxtaposition'. In this, historically the traditional approach of comparativists, the atheoretical model is constructed of postulates which exemplify the empirical practice pertaining in one particular jurisdiction, usually a western industrialised democracy such as the US or the UK, i.e. a model based on adversarial practice. The crucial point is that the resulting model is treated as valid and authoritative; it is used as a measure against which to evaluate other jurisdictional approaches and, arguably, merely disguises, or exemplifies, a more sinister trend towards ideological imperialism to be achieved through intellectual and administrative infiltration of key cultural processes (Zedner, 1995). The so-called template approach to modelling is fundamentally flawed since it is patently invalid and speculative to base conclusions on an attempt to measure the principles of an adversarial system against those of an inquisitorial model (or vice versa) without a consideration of context, both within and across cultures (Leigh, 1977; Findlay, 1999; Henham and Findlay, 2001). As Vogler (2000) points out, the template approach simply produces accounts of process in different jurisdictions which have been distorted by the dominant perspective, since although the tasks to be achieved by criminal procedure are basically the same, 'the ways in which such tasks are accomplished are so various and so functionally different as to defy universal categorisation'.

Notwithstanding, the continuing trend towards the hybridisation of criminal justice systems worldwide suggests that the modelling of processes such as sentencing should contain propositions based on adversarial and inquisitorial principles, and extend beyond mere description through the inclusion of normative and ideological assumptions. In other words, although we should acknowledge that the modelling of international (and internationalised) criminal justice processes should have heuristic aims, these should be formulated in recognition of the ideological and ethical consequences of existing practices. Frase (1998) makes some important observations in this context. In particular, he points out that many existing practices (such as plea bargaining) simply cannot be explained in terms of the dichotomous characterisations included in conventional models, and, significantly, that traditional theoretical models tend to obscure the common practical problems that have resulted in the increasing hybridisation of criminal justice processes around the world (Frase, 1998, p.115).

Hence, the challenge for comparative and international process modelling is for the development of theory to be informed by empirical reality; that theoretical

[1] As Findlay (2001) suggests, the social and political context in which rights are examined can only be discovered through the adoption of models that identify (or facilitate the identification of) competing interests.

models should not simply reflect the features of some idealised form of process (such as Packer's (1968) due process/crime control paradigm), or rigid dichotomy (such as between adversarial/inquisitorial or common law/civil/law styles). As Figure 2.1 suggests, an ideal-type model of due process (such as Packer's) is not normatively prescriptive. It can be used to judge whether process measures up to a taxonomy of idealised due process characteristics. That is the extent of its heuristic capability. The implication of any such evaluation may be normative prescription (such as increased rights for victims), but the taxonomy ignores social context.

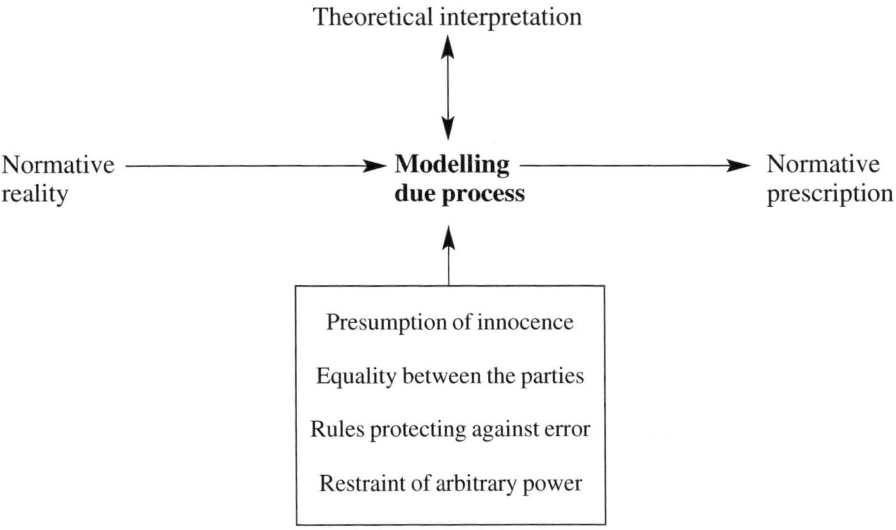

Figure 2.1 Ideal-type due process modelling

For models like Packer's the normative reality may be in terms of adversarial, hybridised or inquisitorial process norms. The reality of the relationship between these modalities and international norms is portrayed in the Introduction (Figure I.1). However, the taxonomy is value-free, and so context-free. It assumes we can recognise the existence of states of affairs in the operations of any process style that can be objectively characterised in terms of the taxonomy. However, the significance of any process style in terms of fact/value depends on context. The interpretation of the empirical reality depends on theoretical predisposition which in turn influences policy (normative prescription).

Process models should not only be capable of accommodating propositions associated with (possibly) competing goals, but also their normative implications, and the rationale(s) which should determine the balance to be accorded to each. In terms of the pure description and interpretation demanded of doctrinal analysis or legal positivism, the ambit of the empirical endeavour does not extent beyond 'law in books'. Thus, the analysis of legal narrative is essentially teleological and utilises conventional interpretative techniques. This exercise, although limited in scope, is a necessary prerequisite to the description and evaluation of legal criteria (or propositions based upon them) that may be included within any paradigm of the international sentencing process. In short, such narrow process models facilitate the assessment of one dimension in the model – legal doctrine, and speculation at that level.

The evaluation of legal process in its socio-political and historical context demands the adoption of methodological techniques that follow on from the deconstruction of specific contexts for comparison, and the development of a comparative contextual model to facilitate this task (Henham and Findlay, 2002).[2] For international sentencing, the empirical context for normative speculation may be provided (*inter alia*) through the broader interpretation of trial narrative, expert commentary and non-participant observation of the sentencing activities in international criminal trials.[3] Chapter 3 develops the conceptual basis for modelling international sentencing process informed by the analysis of legal norms that now follows.

Figure 2.2 summarises the argument as so far developed, which gives rise to the following broad distinctions between the various approaches to modelling criminal justice processes.

Ideal-type modelling – Propositions that assume we can recognise the existence of states of affairs in the operations of any process style that can be objectively characterised in terms of the model's taxonomy
Normative modelling – Propositions that identify desired principles of substantive and procedural fairness for criminal justice process
Descriptive modelling – Propositions that merely describe; produces template analysis or 'analysis by juxtaposition'; 'ideological imperialism'
Contextual modelling – Propositions that purport to describe the meaning of process as fact/value through the deconstruction of context

Figure 2.2 Modelling criminal justice process

To construct a model of international sentencing having heuristic value depends initially therefore on the identification and description of legal norms. Since any understanding, assessment and evaluation of such norms in doctrinal terms is context-specific, dependant on legal culture (Bell, 2001), the significance of legal norms for international sentencing practice cannot simply be extrapolated from whether or not they represent aspects of adversarial or inquisitorial justice included as propositions in a model. As Spencer points out:

---

2 This is developed in Chapter 7.

3 Trial narrative and expert commentary are the only empirical sources used in this study.

> ... the ingredients of the terms 'inquisitorial' and 'accusatorial' mean so many different things to different people, and confusion consequently abounds as to what the essence of the distinction between them is (2002, p.20).

It follows that the modelling of these process styles and their significance for understanding the rules and practices of international criminal sentencing must be contextual.

Figure 2.3 suggests some broad[4] distinctions characterising adversarial/ inquisitorial process styles that have potentially important repercussions for international sentencing.

The role of the prosecution and the defence
The status of written evidence
The significance of the guilty plea[5]
The role of the judge in questioning witnesses and the admissibility of evidence
The distinction between verdict and sentence
The presence or absence of a separate sentencing phase
The extent of discretionary power in determining sentence
The status of the victim

Figure 2.3 Distinguishing adversarial/inquisitorial process styles

The following chapter develops the heuristic capability of this taxonomy through the systematic evaluation of international sentencing practice in its wider ideological, ethical and social context. This provides a firm basis from which to test certain assumptions about the possible future development and direction of international sentencing process styles and their implications for international penality.

---

[4] Spencer (2002, pp.27-37) suggests the following areas of major difference between continental and English criminal procedure today:

(1) guilty pleas
(2) a different notion of appeals
(3) the status of the public prosecutor
(4) the status and organisation of the police
(5) the status, recruitment and training of judges
(6) speed of proceedings – use of pre-trial detention
(7) legal status of the victim.

[5] This issue is dealt with in Chapter 4.

Sentencing Rules and Procedure

The purpose of this section is to provide the reader with an overview of the relevant legal context for sentencing in the *ad hoc* tribunals and the ICC. This is followed by a more detailed consideration of evidential matters relevant to sentencing in terms of the issues emphasised in Figure 2.3.

ICTY and ICTR [6]

In relation to the appropriate penalties, Article 24 of the ICTY Statute[7] provides:

1. The penalty imposed by the Trial Chamber shall be limited to imprisonment. In determining the terms of imprisonment, the Trial Chamber shall have recourse to the general practice regarding prison sentences in the courts of the Former Yugoslavia.
2. In imposing the sentences, the Trial Chamber should take account of such factors as the gravity of the offence and the individual circumstances of the convicted person.
3. In addition to imprisonment, the Trial Chamber may order the return of any property and proceeds acquired by criminal conduct, including by means of duress, to their rightful owners.[8]

Appellate proceedings are provided for by Article 25 on the basis of either an error of law invalidating the decision, or an error of fact having resulted in a miscarriage of justice; the Appeals Chamber having the power to either affirm, reverse or revise the Trial Chamber's decisions. Significantly, possible grounds include appeals against sentence, with action being commenced by the individual concerned or the Prosecutor. The latter represents an important strengthening of the prosecution's powers when compared to the position under the Nuremberg Charter and in most jurisdictions (whether adversarial or inquisitorial).[9] This avenue was successfully exploited by the prosecution in *Aleksovski*[10] on the basis that the sentence imposed was 'manifestly disproportionate' to the crimes committed by the accused.

In addition to setting the maximum term upon conviction to life imprisonment,[11] Rule 101 of the ICTY Rules of Procedure and Evidence[12] goes on to provide:

---

[6] For recent detailed evaluation of the sentencing practices of the *ad hoc* tribunals, see Beresford (2002). Although valuable, Schabas's (1997) analysis does not extend beyond the first sentencing judgement of the Trial Chamber in *Erdemovic*; see *Prosecutor v Erdemovic* (Case No. IT-96-22), Sentencing Judgement, 29 November 1996.

[7] Article 23 of the ICTR Statute is similar, except that the word 'Rwanda' replaces 'Former Yugoslavia' at the end of paragraph 1.

[8] Issues concerning the restitution of property are dealt with by Rule 105 of the ICTY Rules of Procedure and Evidence.

[9] In England and Wales, for example, the Attorney-General may refer a case to the Court of Appeal on the ground that the sentence was 'unduly lenient'; S36 Criminal Justice Act (1988). A prosecution right of appeal in relation to judge-ordered acquittals was introduced by Part 9 of the Criminal Justice Act (2003).

[10] *Prosecutor v Aleksovski* (Case No. IT-95-14/1), Appeals Chamber, Judgement, 24 March 2000.

[11] See further Schabas (1997).

[12] Again these provisions are mirrored by those of the ICTR.

(B) In determining the sentence, the Trial Chamber shall take into account the factors mentioned in Article 24, paragraph 2, of the Statute, as well as such factors as are:
   (i) aggravating circumstances;
   (ii) any mitigating circumstances including the substantial cooperation with the Prosecutor by the convicted person before or after conviction;
   (iii) the general practice regarding prison sentences in the courts of the Former Yugoslavia;[13]
   (iv) the extent to which any penalty imposed by a court of any State on the convicted person for the same act has already been served, as referred to in Article 10, paragraph 3, of the Statute.

(C) Credit shall be given to the convicted person for the period, if any, during which the convicted person was detained in custody pending surrender to the Tribunal or pending trial or appeal.

Both the ICTY and the ICTR have adopted an individualised approach to sentencing within these broad parameters since, as observed in Chapter 1, judges have a largely unfettered discretion to develop sentencing jurisprudence under the terms of their respective foundation instruments. Sentences are largely determined by the gravity of the offence[14] and the degree of responsibility of the accused, together with the impact of relevant aggravating circumstances. Although sentencers have access to a broad range of information to assist them in achieving their objectives,[15] the weight to be accorded to the evidence remains dependant on the judicial discretion exercised according to the circumstances of each individual case.

In his recent detailed analysis of the sentencing practices of the ICTY and ICTR, Beresford (2002) identified the following main aggravating factors as commonly taken into account: the scope of the crime; number and suffering of the victims; form of participation; motive; and superior responsibility. Mitigating circumstances included the following: the plea of guilty; personal circumstances (emotional condition of the accused, background of the accused, effect of sentence on others where unusual hardship likely to result, conduct of the accused since the commission of the offence); good character; superior orders; level of participation in the crimes; and disorder ensuing from an armed conflict. However, Zappala (2003, p.201) suggests that Rule 101 of the Rules of Procedure and Evidence of the ICTY and ICTR consists of so vague a reference to aggravating circumstances as to be contrary to the principle of legality. This prompts him to advocate the deletion of such requirements[16] and the substitution of a definitive list of aggravating circumstances to be taken into account at the sentencing stage. Zappala relates the issue of delimiting aggravating circumstances to the question of the unrestricted use of judicial discretionary power in establishing a hierarchy of crimes in international criminal law. In this sense, a distinction is drawn between the circumstances that might aggravate an offence in any individual case, and the effect of that decision on the relative perception of crime seriousness.

---

13 See further Schabas (1997, p.5) on this issue.

14 See further Frulli (2001); Carcano (2002).

15 For example, Rule 85(A)(vi) of the ICTY Rules provides that the parties may produce 'any relevant information that may assist the Trial Chamber in determining an appropriate sentence if the accused is found guilty on one or more of the charges in the indictment'.

16 Rule 145, paragraph 2(b)(vi) of the ICC Rules of Procedure and Evidence replicates this provision.

The argument is an important one because it seeks to delineate the appropriate connections which can be made between those factors that determine the relative severity of different offences under international criminal law and their relevance to sentencing decisions made in individual cases. As Bohlander (2000, p.246) suggests in his extensive commentary on *Tadic*,[17] a consideration of sentencing factors beyond the realms of the facts of the particular case come into play where the same conduct can be charged differently. Bohlander uses the distinction between the offence of murder as a war crime and a crime against humanity to illustrate his point. In the latter case the *mens rea* requirement is higher since the criminal act must be committed in the knowledge that it is part of a widespread campaign of murder. This would be reflected in the more lenient sentence for a person convicted of murder as a war crime, since that individual would not have had such knowledge. However, the distinction is important in terms of the source of the sentencing factors taken into account. In effect, because knowledge of the widespread character of the murder campaign forms part of the offence description for murder as a crime against humanity, Bohlander suggests that this becomes a general sentencing factor for murder as a war crime; one that acts to aggravate the offence charged and elevate it to a higher plane of seriousness for the purpose of determining sentence. He concludes:

> And in this way, when it comes to sentencing, especially without a sentencing scale, one may of course take all the typified elements of one type of offence and use them as general sentencing factors for others requiring some element of the former, thereby equalising the abstract distinction of criminal repugnance.

I would argue that this argument reflects the conceptual confusion in the foundation instruments of the *ad hoc* tribunals caused by the failure to clarify the relationship between substantive offence elements and sentencing principles. The conventional common law approach for dealing with the conceptual problems of culpability and harm has followed the notion that the substantive law exists to fix the minimum conditions for liability whilst sentencing principles should determine the degree to which any offender can be held responsible for the consequences that follow from his actions. The moral distinctions between offences are drawn through the framing of substantive offences with specific factors bearing on an individual's responsibility for harm and culpability being reserved for sentencing purposes. In *Aleksovski*[18] the ICTY endorsed the view that the gravity of an offence should be determined through the application of the abstract offence provision to the concrete circumstances of the case and the accused in such a way as to reflect his own personal circumstances (in so far as these may be taken into account), and his culpability in relation to the events as charged and for which he has been convicted. The extension of this approach to include the consideration of offence gravity in relation to other offences (cf. Bohlander, 2000) introduces an assessment relevant for sentencing which depends on some objective ranking of the constituent elements of each offence (offence seriousness), or what Carcano (2002, p.590) describes as assessment *in abstracto*.[19] The obfuscation results from a failure to differentiate the consequences of assessing

---

[17] *Prosecutor v Tadic* (Case No. IT-94-1), Judgement in Sentencing Appeals, 26 January 2000.

[18] *Supra*, note 10, para. 182.

[19] Although favouring the ranking of international crimes, Carcano (2002, p.594) appears to recognise the limitations of such comparisons for the purposes of sentencing in individual cases.

offence seriousness for the purposes of determining the substantive issue of criminal liability from that of determining sentence; a divergence that has been exacerbated by the different approaches of the ICTY and the ICTR (Carcano, 2002).

Despite the fact that the notion of the individualisation of sentences is apparently enshrined in Article 24(1) of the ICTY Statute (Article 23(1) ICTR Statute), through the reference to 'individual circumstances', the exact parameters of this concept are not elaborated. As a result confusion also persists in the sentencing decisions of the *ad hoc* tribunals regarding the interpretation of 'individualisation' as a sentencing concept. Zappala (2003, p.204), in particular, seems to elevate 'individualisation' for crimes under international law to the level of a due process right on the basis that it is instrumental in defining the limits of individual criminal responsibility for acts committed during the course of armed conflicts, although falling short of recognising an allied right to rehabilitation on the part of the convicted person. In any event, the precise ambit of the 'individualisation' concept and its relationship to rehabilitation as a possible sentencing objective for the *ad hoc* tribunals remains conjectural. It is difficult to see how individualisation as a philosophical approach to the resolution of the conflicting demands of sentencing can be conceptualised as an enforceable legal right in international sentence decision-making. This would only be possible should the rationale(s) for sentencing international crimes accommodate such an approach. As things stand, the predominant ideological framework of retributivism and deterrence for international sentencing suggests a particularly narrow interpretation of individualisation; certainly not one that engages constructively with the wider social context of sentencing outcomes.

An earlier study by Schabas (1997) also considers the general applicability of the provisions of the Universal Declaration of Human Rights (1948) and the International Covenant on Civil and Political Rights (1976), and especially Articles 7, 10 and 15 in relation to the latter.[20] Schabas suggests that Article 7 'encompasses the notion of proportionality in criminal punishment', whilst Articles 7 and 10 effectively insist on the importance of rehabilitation. Again, the normative significance of these aspirations is ignored, as is the possibility of their realisation within the existing philosophical context of international penality.

ICC[21]

Article 76(1) of the ICC Statute provides:

> In the event of a conviction, the Trial Chamber shall consider the appropriate sentence to be imposed and shall take into account the evidence presented and submissions made during the trial that are relevant to the sentence.

---

[20] Article 7 provides: 'No one shall be subjected to torture or to cruel, inhuman or degrading treatment or punishment. In particular, no one shall be subjected without his free consent to medical or scientific experimentation'.

Article 10 provides: '1. All persons deprived of their liberty shall be treated with humanity and with respect for the inherent dignity of the human person ... 3. The penitentiary system shall comprise treatment of prisoners the essential aim of which shall be their reformation and social rehabilitation ...'

Article 15 prohibits retroactivity in respect of crimes and punishments (*nullum crimen nulla poena sine lege*).

[21] For further analysis, see Henham (2003a); Schabas (2004).

Patently, this provision neither provides nor refers to any rationale or statement of purposes for sentencing. Neither does it indicate (even in outline form) the nature and form that any sentencing guidance might take. Instead, it does little to improve on the unfettered discretion that is accorded to judges sentencing in the Trial Chambers of the ICTY and ICTR.[22]

The framework for the fixing of penalties in the ICC is provided by Article 77 of the ICC Statute as follows:

> 1. Subject to Article 110, the Court may impose one of the following penalties on a person convicted of a crime referred to in Article 5 of this Statute:
>   (a) Imprisonment for a specified number of years, which may not exceed a maximum of 30 years; or
>   (b) A term of life imprisonment when justified by the extreme gravity of the crime and the individual circumstances of the convicted person.
> 2. In addition to imprisonment, the Court may order:
>   (a) A fine under the criteria provided for in the Rules of Procedure and Evidence;
>   (b) A forfeiture of proceeds, property and assets derived directly or indirectly from that crime, without prejudice to the rights of bona fide third parties.

Specific grounds for appeal against sentence are (unlike the ICTY and ICTR Statutes) specifically referred to in Article 81(2)(a) of the ICC Statute which provides that a sentence may be appealed (in accordance with the Rules of Procedure and Evidence) by the Prosecutor or the convicted person on the ground of disproportion between the crime and sentence. This, in effect, codifies existing ICTY and ICTR practice. More broadly, an appeal against sentence may come within the general provisions of Article 81(1) which provides that the Prosecutor, the convicted person, or (even) the Prosecutor on behalf of the convicted person, may make an appeal on the grounds of procedural error or error of fact or law. It is significant that Article 81(2)(b) adds a further broad ground available to the convicted person only (or the Prosecutor on that person's behalf), namely, any other ground that affects the fairness or reliability of the proceedings or the decision.

Furthermore, according to Article 83(2) of the ICC Statute, where the Appeals Chamber finds that the original proceedings were 'unfair in a way that affected the reliability of the decision or sentence, or that the decision or sentence … was materially affected by error of fact or law or procedural error', it has the power to reverse or amend the decision or sentence, or order a new trial before a different Trial Chamber. It is worthy of note that a decision or sentence appealed only by the convicted person (or the Prosecutor on that person's behalf) cannot be amended to their detriment. Where a sentence is found on appeal to be disproportionate to the crime it may be varied as provided for in Part 7 (Articles 77–79) of the ICC Statute.

Although, as Zappala (2003, p.173) observes, the broader approach adopted in drafting the ICC appeals provisions than those of the ICTY and ICTR probably reflects a move towards a civil law approach to appeal proceedings, it is difficult to

---

[22] The consequences of this are discussed in Chapter 1.

envisage how the Appeals Chamber will use its powers to develop a coherent sentencing jurisprudence which is informed by a rational statement of aims.[23] The restriction of separate and dissenting opinions to points of law[24] is not encouraging in

---

[23] The general approach of the ICTY is to be found in the *Celebici* Appeals Judgement of 20 February 2001; see *Prosecutor v Delalic et al.* (Case No. IT-96-21) Appeals Chamber, Judgement, 20 February 2001, paras. 710–724. The following contains the most significant passages: 'The Prosecution submits that the Appeals Chamber should determine "basic sentencing principles which should be applied by the Trial Chambers". The Appeals Chamber notes that the Prosecution made similar submissions in the case of *Furundzija* before the Appeals Chamber, arguing that such principles would assist in order to achieve consistency and even-handedness in sentencing before the Trial Chamber. The Appeals Chamber in that case decided that, since only certain matters relating to sentencing were at issue, it was inappropriate to set down a definitive list of sentencing guidelines for future reference.

The benefits of such a definitive list are in any event questionable. Both the Statute (Article 24) and the Rules (Rule 101) contain general guidelines for a Trial Chamber to take into account in sentencing. Other than these general principles, no detailed guidelines setting out, for example, what particular factors may be taken into account in mitigation or aggravation of sentence are provided in either the Statute or the Rules.

Trial Chambers exercise a considerable amount of discretion (although it is not unlimited) in determining an appropriate sentence. This is largely because of the over-riding obligation to individualise a penalty to fit the individual circumstances of the accused and the gravity of the crime. To achieve this goal, Trial Chambers are obliged to consider both aggravating and mitigating circumstances relating to an individual accused. The many circumstances taken into account by the Trial Chambers to date are evident if one considers the sentencing judgements which have been rendered. As a result, the sentences imposed have varied, from the imposition of the maximum sentence of imprisonment for the remainder of life, to imprisonment for varying fixed terms (the lowest after appeal being five years). Although certain of these cases are now under appeal, the underlying principle is that the sentence imposed largely depended on the individual facts of the case and the individual circumstances of the convicted person.

The Appeals Chamber accordingly concludes that it is inappropriate for it to attempt to list exhaustively the factors that it finds should be taken into account by a Trial Chamber in determining sentence. The sentencing provisions in the Statute and the Rules provide Trial Chambers with the discretion to take into account the circumstances of each crime in assessing the sentence to be given. A previous decision on sentence may indeed provide guidance if it relates to the same offence and was committed in substantially similar circumstances; otherwise a Trial Chamber is limited only by the provisions of the Statute and the Rules. Therefore, while the Appeals Chamber does not discount the assistance that may be drawn from previous decisions rendered, it also concludes that this may be limited. On the other hand, it reiterates that, in determination of sentence, "due regard must be given to the relevant provisions in the Statute and the Rules which govern sentencing, as well as the relevant jurisprudence of this Tribunal and the ICTR, and of course to the circumstances of each case".

The test to be applied in relation to the issue as to whether a sentence should be revised is that most recently confirmed in the *Furundzija* Appeal Judgement. Accordingly, as a general rule, the Appeals Chamber will not substitute its sentence for that of a Trial Chamber unless "it believes that the Trial Chamber has committed an error in exercising its discretion, or has failed to follow applicable law". The Appeals Chamber will only intervene if it finds that the error was "discernible". As long as a Trial Chamber does not venture outside its "discretionary framework" in imposing sentence, the Appeals Chamber will not intervene.'

[24] The views of the minority must be recorded where there is no unanimity (Article 83(4)).

this respect.[25] Further, since appeals by the Prosecutor are likely to focus on the question of undue leniency in sentences determined by the Trial Chamber, it is interesting to speculate whether the Appeals Chamber will use such appeals to affirm the parameters for sentencing practice. One problem eventually likely to be faced by the Appeals Chamber if it wished to develop some coherence in sentencing practice will be the basis upon which the issue of undue leniency is to be determined; a decision that will reflect on whether the broad discretionary power of ICC judges can be harnessed to engage in any relational sense with particular aims or purposes for sentencing. The reason for this stems from the fact that there are several possible approaches. The conventional view would be for the Appeals Chamber to apply an objective test, determining the basis upon which a sentence might be considered as unduly lenient according to whether the Trial Chamber had committed an error of principle. In essence, this is a finding suggesting that a decision was reached which no judge could reasonably consider appropriate in the circumstances, having applied his mind to all the relevant factors and considered the possible range of sentences.[26] The relationship between such an objective approach and public perception is that it appears to represent a reaffirmation of the traditional social contract theory approach; namely, that the penal aspirations and desires of (in this case) the 'global community' are satisfied if the institutions of international punishment are deployed to safeguard the integrity of its legal norms and their interpretation through everyday procedural process.

However, as discussed, such connections are at present tenuous and under-developed. It is also an approach that is essentially negative for the future extension of sentencing guidance for the ICC since it accepts the principle that the desire for justice is capable of being fulfilled through the application of existing sentencing norms and practice, and it restricts the development of sentencing guidance through being backward-looking – concerned with legal form rather than being innovative and responsive to contemporary penal concerns. This is particularly unfortunate

---

[25] In *Erdemovic* Judge McDonald and Judge Vorah took the view that the tribunal was entitled to move beyond the purview of the ICTY Statute or Rules of Procedure and Evidence (unless there was any indication to the contrary) where it felt it necessary to ensure the proper administration of justice; *Prosecutor v Erdemovic* (Case No. IT-96-22), Appeals Chamber, Joint Separate Opinion of Judge McDonald and Judge Vorah, 7 October 1997, paras 3–5: '… the first step in the proper construction of the Statute and the Rules must always involve an examination of the provisions of the Statute and the Rules themselves. The terms used in these instruments must be construed according to their plain and ordinary meaning. … We would add that regard may also be had to the preparatory work relating to the formulation of the Statute and the Rules for the purpose of statutory interpretation. … The second step in the proper interpretation of the Statute and the Rules involves a consideration of international law authorities which may offer further elucidation of the meaning of terms employed in the Statute and the Rules. We would, however, state the caveat that no credence may be given to such international authorities if they are inconsistent with the spirit, object and purpose of the Statute and the Rules as discerned from the plain meaning of the terms used therein. In the event that international authority is entirely lacking or is insufficient, recourse may then be had to national law to assist in the interpretation of terms and concepts used in the Statute and the Rules. We would stress again that no credence may be given to such national law authorities if they do not comport with the spirit, object and purpose of the Statute and the Rules.'

[26] Such a test reflects the approach adopted by the English Court of Appeal in determining undue leniency on a reference by the Attorney-General under S36 of the Criminal Justice Act 1988 (as amended).

because there is opportunity for a full consideration of the arguments and principles from both the Prosecution and the Defence in the Appeal proceedings. A more constructive way forward would be for the Appeal Chamber to elaborate a dichotomous approach to the question of developing principles for deciding undue leniency. In particular, whilst retaining an objective test,[27] such an approach could be based primarily on expounding a body of sentencing principles built principally upon considerations which engaged with public perceptions of justice with due regard to sentencing convention.

This debate also raises some significant issues relating to the status of the sentencing principles produced by the international criminal institutions. The Appeal provisions of the ICC (more so than the *ad hoc* tribunals) acknowledge the possibility of appeals against sentence involving errors of fact or law, in addition to procedural errors. Commentators[28] acknowledge that the establishment of some form of sentencing guidance would help to ensure the independence of the judicial process and provide the appropriate discretionary framework for the future development of sentencing jurisprudence in both the *ad hoc* tribunals and the ICC.[29] Whilst acknowledging their local limitations, Beresford (2002, p. 85) advocates the formulation of guideline judgements similar to those utilised by the English Court of Appeal for the *ad hoc* tribunals.

Ignoring for now the ideological and structural issues involved in pursuing such a course, I would argue that some clarification of the legal status of such guidelines and principles is first necessary, particularly for the purposes of appeal. In the English context, for example, the development of sentencing principles by the Court of Appeal provides a mechanism for shaping sentencing policy in inferior courts and providing a degree of internal consistency. However, within the sentencing system, the decisions of the Court of Appeal have never been clearly ascribed the status of rules of substantive law. Although there have been occasions when they have been treated as rules of substantive law for the purposes of the precedent system and where the interests of justice so required, the Court has been unwilling to certify a sentencing principle as giving rise to a question of law of general public importance for the purposes of appeal to a higher authority (the House of Lords). Thomas (1979), a leading authority on English sentencing, suggests that this amounts to a recognition on the part of the Appeal Court that decisions on the exercise of sentencing discretion do not create rules of law *stricto sensu*, but that they should be treated as such for the purposes of the precedent system, in that they are intended to be binding on inferior courts.

This analysis raises some interesting questions in the context of international sentencing should it be considered appropriate that principles and guidelines be developed for the international institutions along the lines of the English paradigm. Firstly, whilst the exact status of such mechanisms has not been clarified in the foundation instruments of either the *ad hoc* tribunals or the ICC, Article 21(2) of the ICC Statute does at least suggest that the ICC may, although is not obliged to, follow its own previous decisions, and, as such, is likely to follow ICTY and ICTR practice

---

27 Clearly, a subjective approach would simply re-enforce the *status quo*.

28 See Beresford (2002); Henham (2003a).

29 See the attempt by Pickard (1997) to design such guidelines for the ICC.

in this area. The leading ICTY authority on the precedent issue is the Appeals Chamber's decision in *Aleksovski*[30] where the general rationale and practice of precedent was approved largely adopting a common law approach. In *Furundzija*,[31] for example, the ICTY Trial Chamber followed previous decisions of the ICTY relating to the imposition of sentence where there are multiple convictions. Notwithstanding, despite the copious citing of previous authority for the purposes of determining the appropriate sentencing principle to be deduced and applied, the *ad hoc* tribunals have yet to confront the issue of whether or not it is a *legal* principle that is being followed. If sentencing principles are to be treated as equivalent to legal principles then it falls upon the Appeals Chamber to make definitive rulings regarding the legal status of those principles, in addition to decisions relating to the facts.[32] However, if they are regarded merely as authoritative examples of the range of applicable sentences for particular offences based primarily on offence seriousness, then this amounts to a recognition that the role of the Appeals Chamber is to frame appropriate[33] guidance for the exercise of discretionary power in sentencing. This is a role that remains to be clarified for either the ICC or the *ad hoc* tribunals; one that is likely to remain unclear unless and until a statement of agreed purposes for sentencing in the respective international institutions emerges.

In contrast to the ICTY/ICTR Statutes, Article 78 of the ICC Statute contains a general direction regarding those factors to be taken into account in the determination of sentence according to the Rules of Evidence and Procedure; as follows:

> 1. In determining the sentence, the Court shall, in accordance with the Rules of Procedure and Evidence, take into account such factors[34] as the gravity of the crime and the individual circumstances of the convicted person …

Rule 145 of the ICC Rules of Procedure and Evidence are far more extensive in detailing the type of permissible factors relevant to the determination of sentence than the corresponding Rule 101 of the ICTY/ICTR:

> 1. In its determination of the sentence pursuant to Article 78, paragraph 1, the Court shall:
>   (a) Bear in mind that the totality of any sentence of imprisonment and fine, as the case may be, imposed under Article 77 must reflect the culpability of the convicted person
>   (b) Balance all the relevant factors, including any mitigating and aggravating factors[35]
>   (c) In addition to the factors mentioned in Article 78, paragraph 1, give consideration,

---

[30] *Supra*, note 10, paras 89–115.

[31] *Prosecutor v Furundzija* (Case No. IT-95-17/1), Judgement, 10 December 1998, paras. 198, 296.

[32] It may refuse to follow conflicting decisions on matters of law in the interests of justice.

[33] What is considered 'appropriate' depends, of course, on the accepted rationales for sentencing.

[34] As Kress (1998, p.445) points out, the most disappointing aspect of this inconclusive approach is the absence of any reference to 'applicable national standards' (cf. optional Article 78 of the Draft Statute; Bassiouni 1998, p.93).

[35] Rule 145(2) goes on to provide: 'In addition to the factors mentioned above, the Court shall take into account, as appropriate:
(a) Mitigating circumstances such as:
(i) The circumstances falling short of constituting grounds for exclusion of criminal responsibility, such as substantially diminished mental capacity or duress;

inter alia, to the extent of the damage caused, in particular to the harm caused to the victims and their families, the nature of the unlawful behaviour and the means employed to execute the crime; the degree of participation of the convicted person; the degree of intent; the circumstances of manner, time and location; and the age, education, social and economic condition of the convicted person.

A particular problematic provision is Article 80 of the ICC Statute which effectively provides that the penal regime established for the ICC does not affect the application by states of penalties prescribed by their national laws. As Zappala (2003, p.200) points out, this provision increases the likelihood of a paradoxical situation occurring where the instigators and leaders of a conflict may escape death through being tried before international courts, whilst the implementers of their orders face the death penalty having been tried at the national level.[36] This reflects the tension and perceived injustice caused by the fact that the ICTR cannot impose the death penalty where Rwandan courts are able to do so (Drumbl, 2000).

Exploring the Sentencing Paradigm

This section aims to provide a more detailed analysis of the distinctions broadly outlined in Figure 2.2 above with a view to elaborating a model that can be employed analytically for evaluation in international sentencing. The distinctions drawn are grouped together as follows for the purpose of analysis: sentencing process and evidential issues; professional and lay participation.

(ii) The convicted person's conduct after the act, including any efforts by the person to compensate the victims and any cooperation with the Court;

(b) As aggravating circumstances:

(i) Any relevant prior criminal convictions for crimes under the jurisdiction of the Court or of a similar nature;

(ii) Abuse of power or official capacity;

(iii) Commission of the crime where the victim is particularly defenceless;

(iv) Commission of the crime with particular cruelty or where there were multiple victims;

(v) Commission of the crime for any motive involving discrimination on any of the grounds referred to in Article 21, paragraph 3;

(vi) Other circumstances which, although not enumerated above, by virtue of their nature are similar to those mentioned.'

36 The Rwandan Organic Law on the Organization of Prosecutions for Offences constituting the Crime of Genocide or Crimes against Humanity adopted in 1996 provides for the imposition of a mandatory death penalty (Article 14) for cases coming within those Category 1 offences listed in Article 1 as follows:

(a) Persons whose criminal acts or those whose acts place them among planners, organisers, supervisors and leaders of the crime of genocide or of a crime against humanity;

(b) Persons who acted in positions of authority at the national, prefectural, communal, sector or cell level or in a political party, the army, religious organisations, or militia and who perpetuated or fostered such crimes;

(c) Notorious murderers who, by virtue of the zeal or excessive malice with which they committed atrocities, distinguished themselves in their areas of residence or where they passed;

(d) Persons who committed acts of sexual violence.

Sentencing Process and Evidential Issues

The most important issue to impact on sentence decision-making in international criminal trials is the structure of the process; particularly, whether there should be a distinction made between verdict and sentence and provision for a separate sentencing phase of the trial. As I will argue, the decision has fundamental evidential repercussions for the sentencing outcome. The current position is that both the *ad hoc* tribunals and the ICC have a predominantly unified structure. However, this was not initially the case with the *ad hoc* tribunals where the respective Rules of Procedure and Evidence for the ICTY and ICTR (Part Six, Section 4) implicitly provided for a system where evidence relating to sentence could only be heard once the decision as to guilt or innocence had been made:

> *Rule 100: Sentencing Procedure on a Guilty Plea*
> (A) If the Trial Chamber convicts the accused on a guilty plea, the Prosecutor and the defence may admit *any relevant information* that may assist the Trial Chamber in determining an appropriate sentence.
> (B) The sentence shall be pronounced in a judgement in public and in the presence of the convicted person, ... [emphasis added]

Early *ad hoc* tribunal cases such as *Tadic* (ICTY)[37] and *Akayesu* (ICTR)[38] even went so far as to hold separate sentence hearings, but their respective rules were later amended to remove this possibility.[39] The rationale for this was essentially the bureaucratic and administrative one of greater speed and efficiency. The new procedure ensured that the presentation of evidence and pleadings on sentencing matters occurred *before* the verdict was determined, with the result that both phases of the trial are now reflected in a single judgement based on the merits of the case. Rule 86(C) of the ICTY/ICTR Rules of Evidence and Procedure effectively provides that after the presentation of all the evidence pertinent to the trial of the issues, the closing arguments of the Prosecutor and the Defence must 'address matters of sentencing'.

The ICC Statute adopts a similar model. Article 76(1) provides that following a conviction the Trial Chamber should move on to the sentencing issue, taking into account evidence presented and submissions made during the trial that are relevant to sentence. Significantly, in Article 76(2)[40] it goes on to provide that (in contested cases only and before completion of the trial) the Trial Chamber may direct (or must, if requested by the Prosecutor or the accused) a further hearing to hear any additional evidence or submissions relevant to sentence.[41] Schabas (2001a, p.131, and 2004,

---

[37] *Prosecutor v Tadic* (Case No. IT-94-1), Sentencing Judgement, 14 July 1997.

[38] *Prosecutor v Akayesu* (Case No. ICTR-94-4-T), Sentencing Judgement, 2 October 1998.

[39] Rule 98 *ter* now provides in Rule 100 (A) 'If the Trial Chamber convicts the accused on a guilty plea, the Prosecutor and the Defence may submit any relevant information that may assist the Trial Chamber in determining an appropriate sentence.' This effectively means that the sentencing judgement is based on the merits of the case.

[40] See Rule 143 of the ICTY Rules of Evidence and Procedure.

[41] Article 76(4) confirms that (wherever possible) the sentence must be pronounced in public in the accused's presence.

p.157) suggests that this procedure creates a strong presumption in favour of a distinct sentencing hearing following conviction but this has not been the experience of the *ad hoc* tribunals. However, Zappala (2003, p.198) argues that the position regarding the ICC remains unclear as to whether there should be one decision containing both verdict and sentence, or two distinct decisions. More positively, the provision for separate hearings and pronouncement of sentences under Article 76(2) may prove a fruitful avenue for the development of sentencing jurisprudence on the appropriateness of life imprisonment (van Zyl Smit, 2002, p.14).

Clearly, evidence relating to mitigating and aggravating factors will be heard in so far as it relates to the commission of the crime. In the case of the *ad hoc* tribunals, Rule 85(A)(vi) of the respective Rules of Evidence and Procedure provides for the presentation of 'any relevant information that may assist the Trial Chamber in determining an appropriate sentence…' after all other evidence led by the Prosecution and the Defence (or otherwise ordered by the Trial Chamber) has been presented, unless otherwise directed by the Trial Chamber in the interests of justice. Significantly, since the textual amendment of Rule 100, there is no implication that the Defence should present evidence pertinent to mitigation of sentence on the basis of the accused's guilt, but that its emergence should be as part of the normal course of the trial and, therefore, directed towards assisting the tribunal to determine the relative merits of the case against the accused. Since the Rules refer to the submission of 'all relevant information' there is some doubt regarding the exact nature of the evidential material permitted and whether it may be treated as equivalent to evidence submitted in accordance with the Rules.[42] Similarly, whether trial rules on the submission and admissibility of evidence also apply to the Trial Chamber's deliberations during the sentencing phase is a matter for conjecture.

Arguments in favour of holding a separate sentencing hearing after conviction are considerable. For instance, in a mono-phase hearing, the necessary omission of mitigation evidence may prove prejudicial to the Defence when it comes to sentencing because it restricts the information concerning the individual's personal role in the commission of the crime and its immediate aftermath. The introduction of such evidence may also impact adversely on the accused's rights of silence and protection against self-incrimination. In particular, the Defence may be induced to introduce more witnesses during the trial process in order to establish the accused's good character and personal circumstances.[43] Alternatively, from the Prosecutor's point of view, a second hearing is likely to permit the introduction of aggravating factors (such as the accused's criminal record) that might be considered inadmissible for reasons of irrelevance during the trial proper (Schabas 2004, pp.157–158). In any

---

[42] Recent ICTR decisions have attempted to clarify what information relating to aggravation and mitigation is relevant to sentencing and the appropriate burden of proof. For example, in *Prosecutor v Niyitegeka* (ICTR-96-14-T), Judgement and Sentence, 16 May 2003; 'It has borne in mind that the principle according to which only matters proved beyond a reasonable doubt are to be considered at the sentencing stage extends to the assessment of any aggravating factors, while mitigating factors are to be taken into consideration if established on a balance of probabilities. This Chamber reiterates that a particular circumstance shall not be retained as aggravating if it is included as an element of the crime in consideration' (para. 488).

[43] As Zappala (2003, p.198) suggests, this is hardly likely to prove expeditious.

event, the range of admissible material for sentencing purposes is potentially considerable.[44]

A further difficulty resulting from the merging of substantive law and sentencing matters in the mono-phase approach concerns the establishment of the factual basis for sentencing. Where offences are broadly defined (as in international criminal law) the tendency for evidential matters relating to sentence to be ignored or treated superficially is accentuated. The problem is exacerbated considerably where a plea of guilty has been entered to some or all of the offences charged. The implications are considerable since the absence of substantive uncontested material relating to sentence may encourage inconsistency in sentencing and injustice in particular cases.[45] Where a guilty plea exists a dispute regarding the nature of the factual evidence contended as relevant by the defence for mitigation of sentence may need to be challenged by the Trial Chamber, either in terms that require the defence to adduce further evidence to substantiate their version of events, or through the instigation of some kind of procedural device (such as the English so-called 'Newton' hearings)[46] whereby several different approaches are adopted in order to elicit an agreed version of the facts before proceeding to sentence.[47]

Professional and Lay Participation

In this section we are essentially concerned with examining the procedural roles accorded to both professional and lay participants in the international trial process in so far as this affects the sentencing outcome. In the light of the previous discussion, it is apparent that the legal and procedural context for sentencing encompasses the entire trial (and pre-trial) process, and that the approach adopted in this book is one that favours a conceptualisation of sentencing based on integrated decision-making. Thus, sentencing is viewed as a processual and dynamic trial activity whose outcome is the product of the complex influences on discretionary decision-making operating at different decision sites within (and before) the trial. As in the preceding section, our particular interest here concerns the role and influence of trial participants with regard to the admissibility, assessment and use of evidence pertinent to sentencing.

Professional actors As regards the judiciary, the extent of the discretionary power available to members of the Trial Chamber in the determination of sentence has already been noted. In addition, international criminal trial judges possess considerable discretionary powers relating to the admissibility and relevance of

---

44 This includes the detailed consideration of expert medical, psychiatric and personal circumstances reports and witness testimony that are admitted and evaluated purely for sentencing purposes.

45 This may constitute a breach of Article 14(1) of the ICCPR. See further Kittichaisaree (2001, p.291) in connection with the ICTY and ICTR.

46 See further Ashworth (2000a, p.309).

47 Rule 69 of the ICC Rules of Procedure and Evidence provides that any prior agreement between the Prosecutor and the defence not to contest an alleged fact is subject to the overriding discretion of the Trial Chamber to order a more complete presentation thereof in the interests of justice (particularly those of victims).

evidence presented throughout the trial which may have a significant bearing on the eventual sentencing outcome. As a matter of procedure, ICC judges must be present at each stage of the trial and throughout their deliberations (Article 74(1) of the ICC Statute) and the Court can only base its decision on an evaluation of the evidence presented and discussed before it at the trial (Article 74(2)). The decision to hear any additional evidence on the question of sentence in the event of a conviction is governed by Article 76(2).[48]

Closer examination of the ICC Statute and Rules governing the form and presentation of evidence raises some important issues regarding the synthesis of rules relating to the admissibility of evidence by judges in adversarial and inquisitorial trial traditions (Findlay, 2001, p.40). For instance, Article 64(6)(b) of the ICC Statute confers important powers on judges allowing them to give directions requiring (*inter alia*) the production of documents or other evidence,[49] and, by virtue of Article 64(6)(d), ordering the production of evidence in addition to that already collected prior to the trial, or presented during the trial by the parties.[50] Additionally, whilst Article 69(3) permits the parties to submit any evidence they choose to provide, the Court has 'the authority to request the submission of all evidence that it considers necessary for the determination of the truth'. Consequently, although ICC (and ICTY/ICTR) trial procedure relies heavily on oral testimony (reflecting the adversarial tradition),[51] the obligation placed on the Court to adduce whatever evidence it regards as necessary in order to fulfil its function approximates to the instrumental role adopted by the Court evident in most civil law systems.[52]

The roles of the prosecution and the defence in international criminal proceedings with regard to the presentation and assessment of evidence relevant to sentencing are also strictly regulated by procedural norms contained in the foundation instruments. Subject to the overriding authority of the Trial Chamber to adduce and admit evidence, Prosecutors in the ICC must, as part of their disclosure obligations, ensure that any material disclosed to the Defence contains anything which they believe might serve to mitigate the guilt of the accused or affect the credibility of the prosecution evidence (Article 67(2) of the ICC Statute). The Prosecutor is also under an obligation under Rule 74(8) of the ICC Rules of Procedure and Evidence to raise issues affecting the self-incrimination of any witness and to arrange for an *in camera* hearing, or the Trial Chamber may take similar measures on its own initiative on being informed (directly or through the Prosecutor) by the accused, Defence or the relevant witness that self-incriminatory testimony may be raised (Rule 74(9)).

---

48 See further Schabas (2001a, pp.125–131).

49 The Trial Chamber also has the power to rule on the admissibility and relevance of evidence on the application of either party (Article 64(9)(a)).

50 The presiding judge has the overriding power to direct the conduct of the proceedings, including that of ensuring that they are conducted in a fair and impartial manner (Article 64(8)(b)).

51 It is important to bear in mind that for some civil law systems (such as France and Belgium) the concept of evidence tends to suggest information contained in the written dossier, whereas the term 'evidence' in a common law trial is normally reserved for that which has been heard orally at the trial (Spencer, 2002, p.21).

52 The inquisitorial tradition is for judges to be more proactive in seeking out the truth particularly as regards the examination of the accused and other witnesses. In fact, as Spencer (2002, p.627) describes, this is a primary responsibility imposed on the judiciary in France, Belgium and Germany, although they have the discretionary power to allow parties to put their questions directly.

The question of what might amount to self-incriminatory testimony in the context of sentencing depends on the extent to which the accused feels the need to expose details relating to his/her own character (and/or previous criminality) in order that what they perceive as mitigating evidence might come to the attention of the court in circumstances where that was unlikely to occur during the sentencing phase of the trial. The fairness of any procedure which might induce a decision by the accused during the trial phase proper to provide evidence that is (a) unnecessary in order to mount an effective defence to the indictments charged, and (b) may prove to be highly prejudicial to the defence, may well amount to a breach of Article 14(3)(g) of the ICCPR, which expressly provides that in the determination of any criminal charge the accused has the right not to testify against himself or confess guilt.[53] In fact, it is arguable that the nature of the inducement, and its likely prejudicial effect, is accentuated where (as with the international institutions) there is no jury and the judges may take a proactive role in questioning the accused. As Emmerson and Ashworth (2001, p.456) suggest when commenting on the Strasbourg case-law in relation to Article 6 of the ECHR, the issue is complex and requires a balance to be drawn between the degree to which a court might feel itself justified in pursuing a line of questioning because the persuasiveness of the accused's account has been thrown into doubt, and the extent to which the absence of any further verification might enable adverse inferences to be drawn upon which to found a conviction.

An unresolved issue relates to whether the Prosecutor has a duty to give the Defence due warning of any matter that might constitute a significant aggravating factor, thereby allowing the Defence the opportunity to contest the evidence.[54] In these circumstances the primary consideration must be for the Defence to be given an opportunity to contest evidence which, although not material to the substantive charge(s) before the court, amounts to aggravating material for the purposes of sentence. This may prove to be a difficult line to draw. For example, Rule 145(2)(b)(i) of the ICC Rules of Procedure and Evidence mandates the Trial Chamber to take into account (*inter alia*) as aggravating circumstances any prior criminal convictions for crimes that fall within the jurisdiction of the Court, *or of a similar nature*. However, Rule 145(2)(b)(vi) requires the Court to also take into account 'other circumstances which, although not enumerated above, by virtue of their nature *are similar* to those mentioned' (emphasis added). The point that arises is the extent of the Prosecutor's obligation to bring certain previous offences committed by the accused to the attention of the Court where those offences do not fall within the ambit of Rule 145(2)(b)(i) but attracted longer than 'normal' sentences, or were determined with specific reference to the accused's perceived dangerousness. If it is argued that the accused's dangerousness amounts to 'other circumstances' which make the offences 'similar to those' referred to, then this may be challenged on the basis that the circumstances relate, not to the gravity of the crime itself, but to the characteristics of the offender 'which are susceptible of change with the passage of

[53] In terms of inquisitorial logic this rule stems from the absence of any duty on the accused's part to contribute to the proceedings.

[54] For discussion in the European context, see Emmerson and Ashworth (2001, p.505).

time'[55] and also qualitatively, since the determination of dangerousness is highly equivocal, as is the role of the court in decision-making.[56]

The above argument is not simply a matter of technical distinction but illustrates the difficulty in deciding the extent to which the 'circumstances' surrounding the commission of previous offences are relevant to the instant offence if they disclose and confirm aggravating features that tend to establish a pattern of offending or characteristic traits of the offender. The problem for the Defence where the issue of 'dangerousness' is raised is how to draw the necessary distinction in such evidence between its effect on the Court's perceived seriousness of the present offence(s) for the purposes of conviction and its impact as an aggravating factor relevant to the sentencing decision.

These difficulties lend weight to the argument in support of a two-stage procedure where the sentencing phase of the trial takes place once the guilt or innocence of the accused has been determined. Whether the information material to sentence is presented before or after conviction is significant for the defence for reasons other than those previously indicated. For example, if the normal rules of evidence do not apply to the information submitted for the purpose of the sentencing, as Zappala (2003, p.197) suggests, does this prevent the Defence from asking the Prosecutor to provide proof as regards those circumstances which relate to the commission of previous offences, where these are alleged to be of a similar nature to those presently indicted? In adversarial systems the duty of prosecuting counsel following conviction is normally neutral in terms of the case, or any particular sentence recommendation, whereas the defence may legitimately challenge unsubstantiated material bearing on sentence, although not the substantive merits of the case. In such circumstances the court may call on the prosecution to elaborate, in which case evidence may be adduced to further substantiate details of the aggravating factors provided this has no relevance to any issue in the trial proper (Thomas, 1970, p.314).

Notwithstanding, the need for evidence to be reconstructed to serve the purposes of the sentencing phase is a phenomenon that may also take place within an integrated model where sentence is determined after verdict within a mono-phase procedure. Analogous comparative evidence from Italy appears to support this contention. In Italy specific criteria establish the boundaries for the exercise of discretionary power relevant to sentence, but it is witness testimony elicited during the trial phase that is evaluated against these legal constraints.[57] Similarly, the rights accorded to victims under Article 90 of the Code of Criminal Procedure 1989 (CCP) are directed towards the trial (verdict and sentence) rather than to sentence.[58] Such a model should also be integrated in the sense that the rationale, policy and procedure governing the exercise

---

55 These words were used in the ECHR case of *Thynne, Wilson and Gunnell v United Kingdom* (1991) 13 EHRR 666, para. 70.

56 For detailed analysis, see Henham (1997).

57 Judicial deliberations follow immediately after the close of the trial and, after considering any unresolved preliminary matter and/or procedural issues, judges must consider each issue of fact or law, *as well as the proper sentence*. Needless to say, abbreviated proceedings and procedures that facilitate bargaining for sentence distort the extent to which the facts upon which sentence is based actually correspond with those that occurred.

58 The rights of the person injured by an offence set out in Article 90 of the CCP are basically threefold:

of judicial discretion for the purposes of verdict and sentence ought to reflect and relate to one another. This has not occurred with Italian sentencing.[59] In a sense, what has transpired in Italy reflects those fundamental tensions which frequently manifest themselves in purely adversarial systems; that, ultimately, the ideology of traditional criminal law theory – certainty, predictability and consistency – is problematic for rationalisations of penality that envisage consequentialism as a major justification for the existence of the penal system. The failure of adversarial systems to integrate trial philosophy and practice has meant that questions of procedural fairness and rights protection have assumed particular significance. I would argue that these shortcomings have been replicated at the international level.

Victim participation The participation of victims in international criminal trials raises complex philosophical and ethical questions that have fundamental repercussions for the admissibility, evaluation and impact of evidence relevant to sentencing. These varying views reflect the different approaches taken towards victim participation in domestic and regional jurisdictions as represented in the debates on the foundation instruments for the *ad hoc* tribunals and the ICC.[60] These debates have been conducted in a context where restorative justice ideology has achieved increasing prominence in western criminal justice systems, and increased attention has been given to victims through the development of international human rights and humanitarian law in the 1990s.

Notwithstanding, before examining the impact of these influences on the procedural framework of the international criminal trial, it is important to clarify some misconceptions and, more particularly, the paradox that commonly exists between the rhetoric and reality of victims' rights in the criminal processes of adversarial, inquisitorial and hybrid trial forms.[61] My reason for stressing this paradox is the contention that, although the ICC apparently represents a significant step forward for victims' rights in terms of recognition and participation, such procedural advances remain symbolic and rhetorical precisely because the ideological and moral justification for their existence has not been rationalised and formulated as an integral part of the penality of international sentencing. In consequence, the normative structures of international criminal justice may not have moved much beyond the contradictions evident in many domestic jurisdictional regimes.

Some Comparative Evidence[62]

The English criminal trial process, for example, as an exemplar of the adversarial paradigm, adopts the view that the *locus standi* of the victim as a provider of factual

(1) to request a judge to commit the defendant for trial (in the case of crimes susceptible to 'private prosecution') and associated rights (principally the right to be advised in the event of a request for dismissal by the public prosecutor; the right to oppose a specific settlement of the proceedings by payment of a fine)
(2) to present defence briefs to the public prosecutor and judge
(3) to present elements of evidence.

59 See further Mannozzi (2002).

60 For useful commentary on the latter, see Amnesty International (1999).

61 The conceptual aspects of this analysis is developed in Chapter 6.

62 For detailed discussion, see Henham and Mannozzi (2003).

information relating to the circumstances of the crime is no different from that of any other witness. In essence, the victim's contribution is limited to testimony that assists in establishing the facts against which the guilt or innocence of the accused can be judged according to the onus of proof which the prosecution must discharge in a criminal case; namely, beyond all reasonable doubt. Although certain types of witnesses (for example, children and rape victims) are protected by special measures, adult victim witnesses are subject to the normal rules of examination and cross-examination applicable to an English adversarial trial,[63] and to the rules of evidence. Furthermore, witnesses may receive protection against being questioned in an intimidatory and humiliating manner,[64] and the limits of witness examination may be tested against the right to a fair trial under Article 6.1. of the European Convention on Human Rights,[65] or the ethical codes of legal participants in the trial. The victim has no civil *locus* in the English criminal trial which might jeopardise his perceived neutrality in the eyes of the judge. In circumstances where the victim is a *potential* civil claimant, the normal practice is to await the outcome of the criminal process before proceeding with the civil claim.[66] Although compensation can be awarded as an additional outcome to a criminal trial, this is by no means equivalent or meant to substitute for civil process.

Consequently, the conceptualisation of victims' rights in England reflects the present limited nature of victim participation in the English sentencing process and a marked reticence to embrace the notion of *any* victim involvement in sentencing until relatively recently (Edwards, 2001). The pace of reform has been hindered further by the narrowness of the debate. In an influential article in 1993, Ashworth drew a distinction between so-called 'service rights'[67] for victims and 'procedural rights'. Service rights might best be described as *non-participatory* victim rights, including such things as the right to receive relevant information at various stages of the court process, and the right to compensation for victims of criminal violence.[68] 'Procedural rights', on the other hand, refer to more fundamental rights to consultation and participation in the criminal process; '*participatory rights*' in a tangible sense.[69] These might include rights to consultation regarding prosecution, bail/custody, acceptance of plea, sentence and parole release decisions. As Zappala makes clear:

---

63 For a useful summary, see Sprack (2004).

64 See *Brown (Milton Anthony)* [1998] 2 Cr App R 364 at 391 *per* Lord Bingham.

65 See further Ashworth (2000a) Ch. 9.

66 There are two main reasons for adopting this course:

(1) Clearly, a finding of guilt in the criminal trial strengthens any civil claim a victim might wish to make.

(2) The burden of proof in the English civil process is discharged by establishing the elements of the claim on the balance of probabilities. It therefore makes practical sense, particularly in jury trials, to separate criminal and civil process requirements. Accordingly, the procedural and evidential requirements differ considerably.

67 These were later termed 'substantive rights' by Ashworth (2000b).

68 As Ashworth (2000b, p.499) puts it: 'These entitlements would be designed both to deal with the emotional and financial impact of the crime and to prevent or minimise any "secondary victimisation" resulting from exposure to the criminal process.'

69 For a complimentary framework, see UN Declaration of Basic Principles of Justice for Victims of Crime and Abuse of Power. UN doc. General Assembly Resolution 40/34, 29 November 1985.

> … it can be said that the *rights to 'service'* aim at addressing the need of victims for physical and psychological support, post-trauma assistance, and other forms of relief that largely depend on the crime suffered. Instead the protection of victims' interests at the *procedural level* goes through the recognition of specific rights that could enable victims to contribute to prosecution, to obtain restitution or reparation, and to obtain various forms of satisfaction (2003, p.221) [emphasis in original].

Ashworth (1993) suggests that the classification of such rights should depend, not on the wishes of victims, but on the 'nature and goals of the criminal process as a legal and social institution'.[70]

Ashworth's analysis illustrates the rather narrow context of the victim participation debate in England. It ignores those theoretical arguments concerned with the nature and function of victim participation in sentencing within the context of broader criminal justice process and social issues, as well as their implications for operationalising models of victim participation.[71] It is particularly significant that this limited conceptualisation of victim participation fails to examine the extent to which information provided by the victim prior to sentence might impact on the eventual sentencing decision.

The structure of the criminal trial in Italy (a hybridised jurisdiction) has the primary function of ascertaining the facts, not that of gaining 'knowledge' about the individual.[72] In general, the victim plays a minimal role in the Italian criminal trial, particularly as regards the phase that deals with decision-making on the length of punishment. Generally, the victim is not called upon or urged to offer information that could aid the judge in evaluating the effective consequences of the offence, and thus in deciding on the appropriate punishment.[73] Ironically, the victim does not have a real interest in spontaneously supplying such information. As *partie civile* the victim is often present at the criminal trial[74] but can only look after his or her interest regarding damages. The victim does not have an independent right to contest a sentence that has acquitted the accused and is firmly excluded from the sentence bargaining procedure (and has no right to be heard regarding its admissibility). Furthermore, compensation for damages arising from the offence is viewed as a

---

70 Ashworth deliberately restricted the scope of his analysis to an examination of the advantages and disadvantages of the procedural right for victims to submit 'victim impact statements' before sentence. Whilst acknowledging their perceived status within different conceptions of criminal justice, he concluded with a rather cautious assessment of the likely advantages of victim impact statements, suggesting that their main advantage might be in improving victim satisfaction and 'giving the court a more rounded view of the offence'. He felt that victims would gain increased respect for the criminal justice system through improvements in victim services, rather than relying on new procedural rights for victims; Ashworth (1993, pp.508, 509).

71 A point well made by Edwards (2001, p.39).

72 I am indebted to Grazia Mannozzi for information on the Italian criminal trial process. See further; Henham and Mannozzi (2003).

73 The victim nevertheless possesses independent rights within the trial procedure under Article 90 of the CCP (*supra*, note 58), even though these are rather limited.

Note that the law does not in any way circumscribe the nature and aims of participation in the trial by the injured party; the latter can take part personally in the preliminary hearing and discussion, and is not required to appoint a defence attorney to exercise his legal rights; Article 101 of the CCP.

74 See Articles 74–82 of the Criminal Code 1930 (CC).

possible source of 'falsification' of the procedural rite, which is almost totally dominated by the *public* interest of punishing the guilty party and restoring the social peace, not the *private* interest of compensating an individual for economic damages.[75]

The victim as witness is *substantially* different from other possible witnesses since the injured party is 'involved' in the criminal act – often dramatically so.[76] In consequence, the accounts of injured persons must above all contain intrinsic elements (completeness, coherence, congruity, sobriety) and in addition be accompanied, if possible, by some independent verification that supports their reliability. In the absence of elements that confirm or corroborate the reliability of the injured party, Italian judges are unlikely to reach a guilty verdict in respect of the accused. As a result, victims are moved to exercise their (potential) role in the trial with absolute sobriety. Too high a profile in the trial and the presentation of too much evidence can easily be seen as a sign of animosity or vindictiveness. This acts to the disadvantage of victims since it leads judges to regard them as hostile, and thus accord their testimony limited reliability. It is for this reason that injured parties adopt rigorous self-restraint in exercising their procedural rights. In short, the structure of the Italian trial process and sentencing phase, together with the culturally institutionalised suspicion and distrust directed towards victims on the part of those involved in the legal process, tends to marginalise the victim during the trial.

It is apparent that the narrow distinction between procedural and service rights for victims tends to approximate a pure retributivist model, where the victim is marginalised and there is little acknowledgement of victims' needs beyond their status as witnesses, or limited recognition of their potential as participants in the sentencing process apart from some restricted form of victim impact statement. Whilst this restricted view of the victim's role is echoed in the Italian model for adult sentencing based on the 1930 CC, various forms of institutional structure now exist based upon restorative justice modelling.[77] The English approach has been to endeavour to rationalise and accommodate alternative sentencing justifications within the overarching philosophy of limited retributivism and the proportionality demanded by just deserts, as creatively interpreted by judicial discretionary sentence decision-making. The Italian retributive model, by contrast, has fragmented in the sense that the rationality of the 1930 reforms does not necessarily sustain any conceptual affinity with more recently introduced models. This may be a reflection of the debate between those who argue that restorative justice does require a paradigmatic shift away from retributive concerns, and others who envisage the possibility of conceptual links between retribution and restorative concerns (Zedner, 1994), particularly through linking notions of communitarianism to retributive punishment by questioning its moral legitimacy (Cotterrell, 1999).

---

75 Such compensation is provided for in the Italian legal system essentially for reasons of 'pragmatism', or 'procedural streamlining'; to avoid as much as possible the initiation of other civil trials for compensation after the criminal trial has concluded with a guilty verdict.

76 Usually it is the victim who makes the accusation or initiates the private prosecution. Moreover, the victim often seeks compensation for damages through an attorney who, in his name, becomes the 'plaintiff'. This type of witness is viewed with 'suspicion' by the judiciary; a suspicion which can be considered institutionalised as it derives from well-entrenched judicial practice.

77 See further Mannozzi (2003a).

These apparent differences in structure and form between Italian and English sentencing are paradoxical for victims in the sense that Italian law imposes no substantive limits on the possible extent of victim participation in sentencing, whilst English sentencing law envisages no substantive rights at all, and has only recently succumbed to the notion of victim personal statements which aim to satisfy purely procedural or 'service' rights. Therefore, in both Italy and England, for what appear to be entirely different reasons, the legal and political contexts of judicial discretion have resulted in a narrow and partisan conceptualisation of the victim, and restricted the extent to which victim participation in sentencing should be promoted.[78]

I would suggest that the foregoing analysis serves to illustrate how similar process results are achieved through different penal strategies in different jurisdictional settings because of the operational effects of legal culture. Similarly, notions of lateral and upward internationalisation need to examine what appear as realignments, convergence or dissimilarities in sentencing against an awareness of their wider socio-political significance. Nevertheless, the conclusions drawn are also consistent with the general willingness on the part of both civil and common law systems to institutionalise criminal processes which are unconstitutional, or otherwise in breach of human rights norms on the grounds of managerial or bureaucratic efficiency. Such manifestations have little to do with notions of integration as models for penological change.

International Victim Paradigms

If we are to draw a lesson for international sentencing from domestic analyses of the use of judicial discretion in sentencing, it must surely be that the relationship between the philosophical justifications for punishment and sentencing outcomes is complex and, more particularly, that the conception and representation of legalistic criteria frequently has more symbolic than real significance for the choice of sentencing options. If this is true, then the achievement of consequentialist objectives such as restorative justice in different contexts will depend on the symmetry existing between philosophical justifications and procedural imperatives. However, as I shall argue, the substantive engagement of victims' concerns have not been effectively addressed either, as formal legalistic and procedural criteria, or in the social reality of sentencing practice.[79]

---

[78] Arguably, recent reforms in English sentencing will do little to further the cause of victim integration in sentencing, simply on the grounds, firstly, that they do not increase victims' procedural rights in any substantive sense, and, secondly, that they fail to address one of the main structural obstacles to the notion of integration, i.e. the strict separation of the trial/verdict and sentencing phases of the criminal process characteristic of adversarial trial forms. The reasons for arguing against the latter are not weakened by observations of the Italian experience. In Italy attempts to adversarialise trial process and the way in which the judiciary use their discretion in ordinary proceedings following the 1989 CCP reforms have been hampered by the slowness of the inquisitorial judicial culture to adapt to change and exploit the potential for addressing victims' concerns within the existing philosophical framework imposed by the 1930 CC. Consequently, any advantages for victim integration in sentencing that might be derived from a process structure which combined the verdict and sentence phases of the trial have not been fulfilled.

[79] By way of exception, the Swiss Prosecutor Carla Del Ponte has been proactive in championing the rights of victims in the international trial process. See, for example, comments made before the ICTR Appeals Chamber in *Barayagwiza*. On the dangers of manipulation of victims' interests by the Prosecutor for strategic reasons, see Jorda and de Hemptinne (2002, p.1372).

As regards the former, for the purposes of the ICC Statute and Rules of Procedure and Evidence, 'victims' are defined as 'natural persons who have suffered harm[80] as a result of the commission of any crime within the jurisdiction of the Court'; Rule 85(a). However, by virtue of Rule 85(b), the expression also includes 'organisations and institutions that have sustained direct harm to any of their property, which is dedicated to religion, education, art or science or charitable purposes, and to their historic monuments, hospitals and other places and objects for humanitarian purposes'. No such description appears in the ICTY/ICTR Statutes where a victim is simply defined as 'a person against whom a crime over which the Tribunal has jurisdiction has allegedly been committed'; Rule 2(A) of the ICTY/ICTR Rules of Procedure and Evidence. Whereas the ICC Statute and Rules of Procedure and Evidence contain copious references to victims and their 'rights' of intervention and participation, this is less apparent in the case of the *ad hoc* tribunals.[81]

Nevertheless, the treatment and protection of victims and witnesses before the ICTY and ICTR do receive special attention. In particular, Article 20(1) of the ICTY Statute and Article 19(1) of the ICTR Statute which govern the commencement and conduct of trial proceedings requires the Trial Chambers to 'ensure that a trial is fair and expeditious and that proceedings are conducted in accordance with the rules of procedure and evidence and due regard for the protection of victims and witnesses'. Article 22 (Article 21 of the ICTR Statute) goes on to provide that:

> The International Tribunal shall provide in its rules of procedure and evidence for the protection of victims and witnesses. Such protection measures shall include, but shall not be limited to, the conduct of in camera proceedings and the protection of the victim's identity.

Much attention has been devoted by the respective Trial Chambers to the clarification of issues relating to the protection of witnesses and their anonymity[82] but there has been considerable criticism regarding the lack of any comprehensive witness protection programme. In consequence, a Victims and Witness Unit for the ICTY was established under Rule 34, but this encountered practical difficulties in

[80] 'Harm' includes physical or mental injury, emotional suffering, economic loss or substantial impairment of fundamental rights.

[81] It should be noted that various pre-trial rights are provided for victims. In the case of the ICC, Article 15(3) of the ICC Statute permits victims to make representations to the Pre-Trial Chamber with respect to any request made by the Prosecutor to proceed with an investigation. Article 19(3) provides that victims may submit observations to the Court with regard to proceedings relating to jurisdiction and admissibility. Further, by virtue of Article 53(1)(c) the Prosecutor may conclude, despite having taken the gravity of the crime and the interests of victims into account, that an investigation would not serve the interests of justice. In such circumstances the Prosecutor must inform the Pre-Trial Chamber and the State making a referral or the Security Council (as appropriate) of his or her conclusion and the reasons for it; Article 54(2). See generally, Section III, Victims and witnesses, ICC Rules of Procedure and Evidence.

[82] See *Prosecutor v Tadic* (Case No. IT-94-I-T), Decision on the Prosecutor's Motion for Protective Measures for Victims and Witnesses, 10 August 1995, paras 62–6; *Prosecutor v Blaskic* (Case No. IT-95-14), Decision on the Application of the Prosecutor dated 17 October 1996 requesting Protective Measures for Victims and Witnesses, 5 November 1996, para. 41. For criticism see Chinkin (1997).

obtaining improvements[83] which have had a significant impact on the trial process. In fact, as Cockayne clearly describes, this situation provides cogent evidence of the tension existing between two models of trial process, which tends to confirm the difference between the social reality of victim participation and its symbolism:

> In one [model], represented through the rhetoric of the Prosecutor and the official spokespeople of the Tribunals,[84] victims and witnesses are central actors in the trial process. The Tribunal is, according to this model, there as a mouthpiece, a chance for their voices to be heard, for them to participate in the formation of the historical record and to ensure that these crimes are not forgotten. This model suggests a sociological role for the trial process which is not often ascribed to domestic criminal trials. The Tribunals are a tool for the *construction* of an international civil order ... In contrast, domestic criminal trials are rarely justified in these terms, as contributing to the construction of the domestic public order. Instead, they are conceived as enforcing that order. The second model for the Tribunals' trial process is more like that. It treats victims and witnesses as instruments in the Prosecutor's quest for a conviction. Protective and rehabilitative measures are not conceived as an integral part of the Tribunal's performance of their mandates, reconstructing civil order, but as instrumental measures designed to ensure victim participation and the ability of the Tribunal to function (2001) [emphasis in original].

The ICC Statute specifically provides for the creation of a Victims and Witnesses Unit within the Registry that is mandated to provide (in consultation with the Prosecutor's Office) protective measures and security arrangements, counselling and other appropriate assistance for witnesses, victims appearing before the Court and others who may be at risk because of such witness testimony; Article 43(6).[85]

Article 68 of the ICC Statute[86] provides a far more detailed account of the nature of victim and witness protection[87] and their participation in the proceedings than does Article 22 of the ICTY Statute (Article 21 ICTR Statute). For example, Article 68(1) provides that '[t]he Court shall take appropriate measures to protect the safety, physical and psychological well-being, dignity and privacy of victims and witnesses' and imposes obligations in this respect upon the Prosecutor. Significantly, the provision goes on to state that the measures taken are not to be prejudicial to or inconsistent with the rights of the accused and a fair and impartial trial. This injunction is repeated in Article 68(3), which provides that the Court has the

[83] These include problems relating to the lack of any definition of witness and when such a person might qualify for protection from the Unit, and the fact that contact is primarily with the Registry whereas the relationship of victims and witnesses with the Tribunal prior to trial is mainly through the Prosecution.

[84] See, for example, ICTY Press and Information Office, *Rule 61: The Voice of the Victims*, Information Memorandum 1, 1996.

[85] The position of victims is also strengthened by the creation of a Trust Fund to be administered according to criteria to be determined by the Assembly of State Parties. The Fund is established for the benefit of victims of crimes within the Court's jurisdiction and their families. Property collected through fines and forfeiture may be transferred to the Fund by order of the Court; Article 79 of the ICC Statute.

[86] Rule 86 of the ICC Rules of Procedure and Evidence contains a general injunction to the Trial Chamber and other Court organs when performing their functions under the Statute or Rules to take into account the needs of all victims and witnesses as directed by Article 68 especially children, elderly persons, persons with disabilities and victims of sexual or gender violence.

[87] See Rule 87 of the ICC Rules of Procedure and Evidence for details of their procedural implementation.

discretion to permit the views of victims and their concerns to be presented and considered at whatever stages in the proceedings it thinks fit, where the personal interests of victims are affected.

The detailed implementation of these provisions is to be found in the ICC Rules of Procedure and Evidence, Subsection 3 Participation of Victims in the Proceedings, Rules 89–93, but, notwithstanding the detailed procedural injunctions contained therein, there is nothing that *obliges* the Court to admit relevant victim evidence. Read in conjunction with Rule 145, which deals with the determination of sentence, the ICC provisions concerned with victims do not provide for their unconditional participation in any stage of the proceedings. Article 68 is conditional in several aspects. For example, the decision as to what constitutes 'the personal interests of the victims' is left to the Court's discretion, as is the decision whether to admit the victims' views and concerns at all. Article 68(3) simply mandates the Court to '*permit* their views to be presented and considered at stages of the proceedings *determined to be appropriate by the Court*' and then goes on to qualify that possibility further by adding that any such presentation and admission must be 'in a manner which is not prejudicial to or inconsistent with the rights of the accused and a fair and impartial trial'.[88] Rule 145 (1)(C) merely obliges the Court to '*give consideration*' to (*inter alia*) the harm caused to victims and their families. There is no right for them to lodge a victim impact statement which must be taken into account in fixing the sentence.

In short, the ICC Trial Chamber's obligations do not extend beyond immediate victims within the jurisdiction of the court and their families[89] to take on board the feelings and concerns of 'significant others' within victim communities. No attempt has been made to provide mechanisms to address what these wider concerns might be and how the Court might engage with them, or whether what is proposed has any sort of moral legitimacy in terms of the wider victim community. Furthermore, there is no apparent indication, either in any rationale discernable from the foundation instruments or any procedural mechanisms, whether what victims are allowed to put forward and its admission subject to the Court's discretion might (or should) contain information along these lines. Again, the concerns of victims and victim communities receive symbolic rather than actual attention.

In terms of Ashworth's (1993) distinction between 'service rights' and 'procedural rights' discussed earlier, I would draw a distinction in the characterisation of so-called 'participatory rights' between those rights that *allow for the possibility* of some form of participation by victims, and those rights that are tangible as a matter of social reality. Whilst I would agree with Zappala (2003, p.221) that '... in the ICC Statute an attempt has been made to increase the procedural rights for victims and expand them to the procedural dimension',[90] I would argue that this expansion has been symbolic rather than concrete in its effects and has had little (if any) impact in addressing the fundamental philosophical and structural weaknesses affecting international criminal trials and sentencing.

---

[88] This is a necessary discretion to maintain balance between the competing rights of the parties.

[89] The fact that there were multiple victims may be taken into account as an aggravating factor in the determination of sentence; Rule 145(2)(b)(iv) of the ICC Rules of Procedure and Evidence.

[90] Zappala (2003: 232) does acknowledge certain practical drawbacks pertaining to the greater procedural participation possible for victims under the ICC regime.

More than symbolism is promised by Article 75 of the ICC Statute which enjoins the Court to establish principles relating to reparations to (or in respect of) victims to include restitution, compensation[91] and rehabilitation. It is clear, however, that reparations is employed as a concept which includes something analogous to civil damages and the restitution of property, or what Retzinger and Scheff (1996) refer to as 'material reparation' in the context of restorative justice. In restorative terms material reparation suggests a specified settlement between the parties, something not contemplated by Article 75 despite the fact that, according to Article 75(3), the Court has a discretion to invite representations from 'the convicted person, victims, other interested persons or interested States which it is obliged to take account of before making any order'.

Of much greater importance[92] is the potential for 'symbolic reparation' in the context of international conflict which, as Johnstone (2002, p.117) suggests, refers to a less visible process whereby the social bond between offenders and victims is repaired and restored through a process where shame and related emotions are evoked and acknowledged by the participants. It is equally apparent that the sense in which 'rehabilitation' is used in Article 75 is a more narrow conceptualisation that envisages any improvements in the material well-being of victims and the communities devastated by armed and social conflict as a necessary precursor to any symbolic healing of such communities. At it stands, no instrumental role or even acknowledgement of this as a desirable penal objective for international sentencing is envisaged.

The implications for international sentencing of the formal legal and procedural provisions promoting victims' interests in the *ad hoc* tribunals and the ICC are profound. As Zappala points out in the following assessment of the advantages produced by the increased recognition for victims under the ICC regime:

> ... it is extremely important for international criminal justice that victims be involved in the proceedings. This increases the chances of achieving the objectives of reconciliation and the removal of injustice. Participation enables victims to feel that they are part of a mechanism designed to deliver justice. This may contribute to reducing a desire for vengeance and increasing the chances of a successful confidence-building process that may lead to national reconciliation and lasting peace (2003, p.232).

However, for these aspirations to become reality requires something more than an increased potential for change. In order to deliver sentencing that contributes to reconciliation and the removal of injustice there must be a rationalisation of purpose which makes the moral legitimacy of the process its central concern.

As I have argued, the legitimacy of the rationales that comprise the penality of international sentencing should be developed through a recognition of moral relativity and a reconceptualisation of process, whereby the sentencing process is seen as a transformative structure; a means for connecting the relative realities of justification and legitimacy. This does not involve a descent into philosophical

---

91 The issue of compensation for victims in relation to the ICTY was the subject of a working group; see further Eighth ICTY Annual Report, UN doc. A/56/352, 17 September 2001.

92 As Zedner (1994) suggests, in practice such a dichotomy may be exaggerated. Mediation, for example, may lead to practical actions making good damage done and, therefore, its impact is also material.

anarchy. It invites a reconceptualisation of the rationale and function of the international criminal trial; one that is driven by legitimacy of outcome. In legalistic and procedural terms this will involve moving beyond the possibility of increased victim participation (welcome as this may be) towards a model of proactive engagement for victims and others; towards the achievement of accountability, truth, reconciliation and justice. These arguments are developed in a broader sociological context in the following chapter.

Chapter 3

Sentencing as Social Reality

The previous chapter began by making the case for modelling the sentence decision-making process, arguing that process modelling is important for understanding the relationship between the legal and social dynamics of international sentencing. The chapter continued to develop this notion of sentence modelling by analysing the legal context of international sentence decision-making.[1]

The present chapter extends this conceptualisation of process modelling to embrace the wider sociological dimensions of international sentencing.[2] More specifically, the emphasis is on describing the social context in which the process of sentence decision-making takes place in international criminal trials. The analysis examines the form and context of sentence decision-making and sentence delivery; the interplay between legal form and discretion in sentencing, the formal pronouncement of sentence and its significance – symbolism, rhetoric and judicial style, the justifications for sentence, their presentation and relevance; and transparency in sentencing and victim participation, examining the extent to which the sentencing phase is integrated.

Introduction

The analytical focus for this chapter is the actual process of decision-making in international criminal trials – in other words, its social reality. Determining the nature (or existence) of any conception of social reality is essentially an empirical endeavour dependant upon ontological commitment. Accordingly, in this chapter information relating to the social dimensions of the international sentencing process derived from the analysis of trial narrative and expert commentary is located in terms of existing models of the sentencing process, each of which entails some degree of theoretical and methodological predisposition. The purpose is, therefore, to concentrate on deconstructing sentence decision-making as a micro-representation of reality.

In the previous chapter a number of broad distinctions characterising adversarial/inquisitorial process styles were identified as significant variables for understanding

---

[1] Chapter 7 suggests that contextual models can be developed further to provide a framework for comparative contextual analysis and illustrates how this approach can be utilised to advance our theoretical and empirical knowledge of international sentencing.

[2] It must be cautioned that the models discussed were all developed in adversarial/common law jurisdictional contexts. However, I would argue that such models are nevertheless valuable for making cross-cultural comparisons, since the extent to which such models are capable of accounting for psychologically significant variables in sentence decision-making depends on our ability to explain and understand the nature of the input variables and their relative significance in different contexts.

the existing structures and processes of international sentencing.[3] The issues raised by the subsequent legal analysis of these factors are now examined within the parameters drawn by my discussion of sentence modelling.

The Form and Context of Sentence Decision-Making and Sentence Delivery

The analysis of sentence decision-making in international criminal trials which follows is predicated on the notion that it is essential for sentence modelling to be able to conceptualise the psychological reasoning processes involved in discretionary decision-making and the relative importance to be attached to the variables which go towards informing that process as a social activity.[4]

The model for comparative contextual analysis developed by Henham and Findlay (2002) elaborated in Chapter 7 is informed by a number of different approaches to understanding the social reality of sentence decision-making. Broadly, these approaches are concerned to explain the social and psychological mechanics of sentencing, particularly how these impact on the selection of information relevant to decision-making. Although understanding the process of sentencing was initially concerned almost exclusively with the positivist search for causality, more sophisticated analyses gradually began to investigate the influence of legal and social constraints, especially how the processes of legal reasoning reflected social context. Hogarth's (1971) study was seminal in this respect, particularly in terms of the phenomenologically derived model he described:

> ... the model which finally emerged was one that viewed sentencing as a dynamic process in which the facts of the cases, the constraints arising out of the law and the legal system, and other features of the external world are interpreted, assimilated and made sense of in ways consistent with the attitudes of the magistrates concerned (1971, p.382).

I would suggest that Hogarth's findings raise some interesting but difficult questions which need to be addressed in the context of international sentencing. Firstly, Hogarth found that over half the magistrates in his study considered public opinion as an appropriate factor to take into account in sentencing and that this played a punitive role in decision-making. Arguably, for international sentencers the views of the 'global community' may be taken to represent those of public opinion. However, as in domestic contexts, it is legitimate to ask whether the concept of some externally tangible penality is a vacuous notion where societies and international relations are characterised by moral pluralism and states are often drawn together through international conflict in the defence of common interests. The cynical response to this argument is to suggest that perception is really a matter of internal attitude and,

---

[3] These included the role of the prosecution and the defence, the status of written evidence, the role of the judge in questioning witnesses and the admissibility of evidence, the distinction between verdict and sentence, the presence or absence of a separate sentencing phase, the extent of discretionary power in determining sentence and the status of the victim.

[4] It follows that the purpose of the model is to act primarily as a heuristic device for facilitating the adoption of those methodological techniques which will allow commentators to deconstruct the relevant contexts which inform important decision sites in the trial process, such as sentencing.

therefore, it is understanding the subjectification of external 'reality' that becomes important. However, Hogarth is not suggesting a methodology for understanding subjective experience. The implication is that the objective attribution of characteristics to the penality of the 'global community', or whatever other views are taken to represent the opinions of 'significant others', represent extremely influential variables in understanding the sentence decision-making processes of international judges. This conclusion would need to be recognised in any reconceptualisation of international penality.

Secondly and crucially, Hogarth found that sentencers' identification of what they considered to be 'essential' information and the importance they attached to its various categories was consistent with their penal philosophies and attitudes (cf. Hood, 1972). For example, he found that treatment-orientated sentencers were more active in looking for information that those with punitive attitudes and, when he looked at the way in which sentencers organised and integrated information, Hogarth found that it was integrated and organised in ways that minimised inconsistency; in other words, sentencers would effectively rearrange case information subconsciously to fit in with their habitual sentencing behaviour. Additionally, there were marked differences in the thought processes of sentencers, those with punitive attitudes tending to have a simple way of organising information and a stereotyped and compartmentalised decision-making approach, whilst non-punitive sentencers had more complex and flexible thought processes and a higher tolerance of conflict and ambiguity. Research by Parker *et al.* (1989, p.117) also suggests that assessment of the accused's moral character by sentencers is substantially based on personal judgement and affects their interpretation of other factors. Thus viewed, ideologies and individualism may be seen as barriers to effective justice management.

This body of work is therefore significant in that it seeks to suggest factors that are responsible for structuring sentence decision-making, although it does not purport to 'explain' sentence decisions in individual cases since that is essentially an empirical question. There are, nevertheless, three specific factors emerging from narrative analysis and commentary on the sentencing practices of the international criminal courts and tribunals that merit closer attention in the light of this research evidence.

Firstly, commentators generally agree that the international sentencing process is infused and dominated by an ideology which is primarily retributive in character (Schabas, 2001b). Whilst there is no empirical evidence to suggest that international judges and prosecutors have predominantly retributive ideologies, recent work by de Bertodano (2002) confirms their susceptibility to politicisation and, consequently, the selectively retributive ideologies of liberal western democracies. Focusing upon the ICC, she suggests that the absence of a fully independent appointments committee is likely to perpetuate the politicisation of the judiciary through the appointments system; that precondition to jurisdiction decisions under Article 12 of the ICC Statute may be effectively politicised through being blocked by the UN Security Council, and that the principle of complementarity embodied in Article 17 will result in the further subjection of the judiciary to political pressures.

De Bertodano (2002, p.429) concludes that guaranteed political independence is integral for the organs of international criminal justice. Although she equates the promotion of justice as the desirable and sole aim for the ICC, she suggests that the promotion of international peace or political harmony or social improvement are beyond its legitimate scope. I would argue otherwise, one of the principal arguments of this book being that the ideological rationalisation and repositioning of penal objectives to accommodate restorative themes can be achieved, and that the implications of this process need to be thought through for each stage where discretionary decisions are made that impact (both individually, collectively and cumulatively) on sentence outcomes. Consequently, de-politicisation and independence in appointments and decision-making will provide the pragmatic space for decision-makers, but what it will not do is to ensure that discretion is exercised in an ideologically compatible framework for the promotion of truth and justice. Put another way, rationality of purpose will not of itself ensure the selection of judges without punitive attitudes and penal philosophies but it will (at least) ensure that the normative framework within which their discretionary decisions are made does not permit them to ignore the concerns of victims and victim communities (for example, by forcing them to take into account victim information and ensuring rights of participation which have a *mandatory* effect on decisions affecting sentence outcomes).

Secondly, the international judiciary's considerable discretionary powers relating to the admissibility and relevance of evidence presented throughout the trial has a significant bearing on the eventual sentencing outcome. This observation raises the issue of the relationship between the penal philosophies and attitudes of sentencers and their selection, and the evaluation and use of trial information relevant to sentence. Is there any truth (for example) in the hypothesis that the penal orientations, legal or social backgrounds of sentencers in the international courts and tribunals have a direct bearing on the exercise of their discretionary powers? Recent research by Pakes (2001; 2004, p.160) on the styles of trial procedure adopted by trial judges in the ICTY appears to suggest that there may be a significant difference between the styles adopted by judges drawn from adversarial and inquisitorial legal cultures. Pakes hypothesises that judges from an adversarial trial tradition are likely to be less proactive than those from an inquisitorial culture in the manner in which they conduct their trials, and that this becomes significant because ICTY rules allow judges considerable discretion in the conduct of trials. Consequently, one might expect judges coming from an adversarial tradition to be more reactive in that they are more likely to leave witness examination to the prosecution and defence, ruling only on objections and other issues such as the admission of particular items of evidence. Alternatively, judges from an inquisitorial tradition might be more interventionist in the questioning of witnesses, as permitted under the ICTY rules.

Following the analysis of data relating to witness examination, cross-examinations, rebuttals and rejoinders in the cases of *Blaskic* (Judge Jorda from France presiding) and *Tadic* (Judge McDonald from the US presiding), Pakes concludes that the way in which the presiding judges ran these two trials broadly resembled the styles associated with the trial traditions from whence they came. This is not surprising in itself, since as long ago as 1962, when examining the sentencing decisions of State and Federal Supreme Court judges in the US, Nagel found a connection between judicial behaviour and legal background demographics such as previous experience as a defence or prosecution lawyer. Socio-legal studies, such as that by Dezelay and Garth (1996) examining the changing role of lawyers in international commercial arbitration amid the transformation and development of legal culture, confirms not only the importance of legal culture as received knowledge determining praxis,[5] but also emphasises its dynamism and its propensity to adapt and foster positive change. We should, therefore, expect the judiciary in the conduct of international criminal trials to reflect the ideological and normative imperatives of their respective legal traditions in a reflexive and constructive interpretation of rules and procedure.

Pakes does, in fact, support the moral injunction to 'truth-finding' implicit in the inquisitorial-style tradition as a desirable force for the gradual transformation of ICTY trial procedure that would not threaten impartiality. However, there is a broader dimension to the analysis of judicial discretionary behaviour that needs to be taken into account. This is the implicit notion that the variation and transformation of trial style is an autonomous process. In other words, Pakes treats the legal and social characteristics of sentencers and their impact on discretionary decision-making as independent rather than dependant variables. For example:

> If both parties have the opportunity to present their evidence in front of an *impartial* decision-maker, justice will emerge ... where finding the truth, rather than resolution of conflict is the objective, it makes sense to have the decision-maker much more involved in eliciting information ... [t]ruth finding, as a core objective fits better with the inquisitorial system involving an active judge who have a certain obligation to ensure that the 'whole truth' is laid bare (2001, p.9) [emphasis added].

However, sentencers (as all trial actors) utilise normative codes instrumentally as negotiatiors and transformers of factual information whereby values are attributed to factual assertions at various decision-making sites integral to the trial process. They do not operate in an ideological or normative vacuum. Consequently, it is necessary to consider the nature of the decision-making process and its significance for sentencing. In the first instance this implies an acknowledgement that discretionary decision-making is a product of the interaction of many complex variables – a unique experience, the description and explanation of which, and the extent to which conclusions can be generalised, being dependant upon the epistemological persuasion of the observer. Secondly, as soon as we accept the notion of discretionary decision-making as being instrumental (as Pakes does), it must be recognised that we are investing the notion of 'truth' with some legitimacy – we are saying that not only is the pursuit of 'truth' a desirable objective for international trial process to move towards, but also that there must exist some measure(s) whereby the 'legitimacy' of what is accepted as 'truth' can be measured. If so, it must then be asked whose 'truth' is it that is being negotiated and manufactured within the wide discretionary parameters provided by the normative codes of international trial instruments?

Arguably, it is a 'truth' negotiated within a normative framework informed by the ideology of retribution and the political imperialism of western liberal democracies. Consequently, the normative codes provided as mechanisms through which trial participants operationalise this ideology are thereby symbolically legitimated through the trial process. The question raised here, and a recurring theme throughout this book, is how to rationalise and reposition this moral justification towards the

---

[5] For a detailed consideration of the concept of legal culture, see Bell (2001, Ch. 1).

adoption of penal ideologies that allow sentencers to engage more with themes of restorative justice for victims and victim communities.

However, the macro-conceptualisation of the trial process as a structure for manufacturing discrete and partial accounts of social action must also be seen in terms of how specific structures, procedures and decisions are recursively reproduced as part of ongoing discretionary decision-making. As McBarnet concludes:

> The operation of dominant ideology must be studied not only in terms of how it is put into practice in social interaction, not only in terms of its interrelationship with the social and economic structure of society, but also in terms of its own internal form and dynamics (1981, p.168).

The complex motivations that lead social actors to negotiate and transform legal and social norms have been the subject of numerous studies in the sociological traditions of symbolic interactionism and phenomenology.[6] In his seminal work Jerome Skolnick (1966, p.27) envisaged 'law as a context for the behaviour of legal men' implying that a study of law in action (such as discretionary decision-making in sentencing) is essentially concerned with deconstructing the meaning attributed to action by social actors through studying the interrelationship and transformation of rules within legal institutions. An additional important dimension for understanding context is a recognition that it requires an appreciation of how court interaction necessarily proceeds according to norms which are characteristic of authority-permeated relationships (Emerson, 1969). For example, Goffman (1969) notes how hearings may be conducted on the basis of 'transformation rules' which enable officials to act in ways that in normal interaction would clearly violate appropriate behavioural norms.

More recently, Rogers and Erez (1999) have made significant progress in conceptualising and investigating the contextuality of meaning in their study of the cultural interpretation of 'objectivity' in sentencing among legal professionals in South Australia. Rogers and Erez found the need to contextualise this 'construct' arose from the differing perceptions which legal practitioners had regarding certain actions as either objective or subjective when asked about their experiences and opinions regarding the operation of victim impact statements. Using transcripts of interviews the authors record that objectivity 'emerged as a major across-case theme', and that applied semiotic theory was used as an analytical methodology 'to decode the symbolic references that the various legal practitioners ascribed to the linguistic, social and relational constructs of the term 'objectivity' in their particular practices' (Rogers and Erez 1999, pp.269, 270). The result was an attempt to 'explain' how definitions of objectivity are produced through the analysis of the subjective experiences of legal professionals as a constantly changing process. The significance of this approach is that it represents a rare attempt to fix the meaning or contextualise an interactive process relevant to sentencing by deconstructing the subjectivity of trial participants' subjective experiences. Hence, the methodology is

---

[6] Of particular relevance are studies by Sudnow (1965) and Cicourel (1968). Sudnow's work is significant in the trial context because it stresses how 'normal cases' in busy courts are manufactured through the stereotyping and routinisation of operations and procedures that systematically force cases exhibiting unusual or abnormal characteristics into conformity.

culturally contextual in that it suggests ways in which the objectivity of process is constructed subjectively within a particular legal culture.

Figure 3.1 attempts to suggest diagrammatically how the subjective meanings attributed to procedural norms by trial actors are rationalised and reconstructed to produce substantively legitimate outcomes through the interactive decision-making process as a recursive social activity. The application of procedural norms therefore objectifies and vindicates trial ideology recursively over time, irrespective of context, and invests it with legitimacy.[7] More particularly, the rationalisation of the subjective meanings which trial actors hold in relation to their external world is achieved through communication and interactive strategies deployed in trial process within the framework of their perceptions of procedural and situational norms. It is a rationalisation that is motivated by perceived system objectives and their strategies for achieving them.

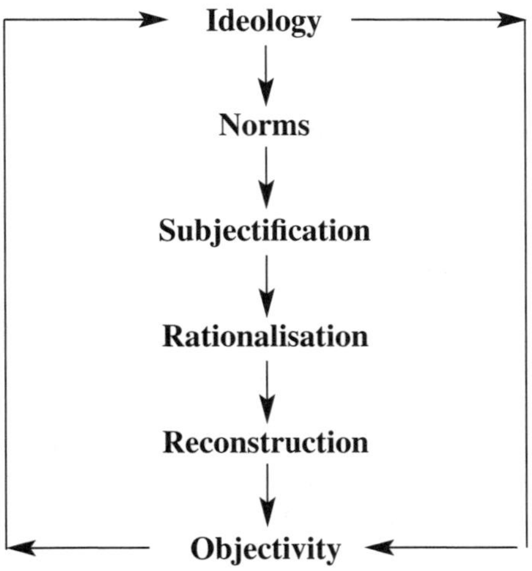

Figure 3.1 Conceptualising process as the link between legitimacy and ideology

Whilst legal and cultural demographics are significant determinants of motivation and perception,[8] it is the ideological and normative context of the process which determines its institutional and social reality and provides the structural framework within which individual participants recognise, negotiate and determine events. It follows from this that the reconceptualisation or moral repositioning of the ideological and normative imperatives that underpin trial process must recognise how external variables are perceived and influence the subjective interpretation of

[7] I am not suggesting here that this resembles a self-perpetuating, organically integral, communication system along the lines argued by system theorists such as Luhmann (1985).

[8] What Bourdieu (1977, p.193) might call the constitutive function of culture.

trial behaviour by social actors. Accordingly, it must be understood that discretionary decision-making in the trial process is a social mechanism for negotiating the relative realities of subjective interpretation and meaning and providing the normative framework for their reconciliation and reconstruction as objectivity, or contextually verifiable events.

The third factor that emerges from research on the structures of sentence decision-making which has particular relevance for international sentencing is the notion of individualisation of sentences. It was noted in the previous chapter that some confusion persists in the sentencing decisions of the *ad hoc* tribunals regarding the interpretation of 'individualisation' as a sentencing concept. In particular, I suggested that the present conceptualisation of individualisation and its potential engagement with the restorative concerns of victims and victim communities is inhibited by the retributive dynamic prevalent in international trial ideology. For example, in *Todorovic* [9] the ICTY Trial Chamber observed:

> At the outset, the Chamber observes that, while the Appeals Chamber of the International Tribunal has held that retribution and deterrence are the main principles in sentencing for international crimes, in the Chamber's opinion, these purposive considerations merely form the backdrop against which an individual accused's sentence must be determined' [footnote omitted].

In terms of individual sentencing decisions this means that the concept of individualisation is constrained by legalistic criteria. Although international sentencers have wide discretionary powers that could be used to develop sentencing principles which promote consequentialist objectives, the individualisation of sentences currently focuses on the issue of individual criminal responsibility and its clarification.[10]

The existing paradigm neglects social context and presents an incomplete account of how sentencing behaviour can transcend symbolism through the transformation of sentencing principles. Accordingly, a contextually sensitive paradigm that allows for the possibility of deconstructing sentencing decisions in terms of the meanings, purposes, motivations and intentions of trial participants, their ideological predilections and those of state parties requires a more naturalistic or holistic overview of the decision-making process. Tata (1997, p.407) suggests that most contemporary attempts to model the sentencing decision 'misrepresent decision-making as a deductive, linear, analytical and mechanical activity', preferring instead a more transparent intuitive account of sentencing involving a 'schematic-holistic' or 'whole-case' approach that conceptualises sentencing as an activity whereby

---

[9] *Prosecutor v Todorovic* (Case No. IT-95-9/1), Sentencing Judgement, 31 July 2001, para. 28.

[10] This has been consistently reinforced in decisions of the ICTY. For example, in *Krnojelac*, '... the overriding sentencing obligation considered by the Trial Chamber has been that of fitting the penalty to the individual circumstances of the Accused and to the gravity of the offences for which he has been found responsible'; *Prosecutor v Krnojelac* (Case No. IT-97-25), Judgement, 15 March 2002, para. 507; or, as in *Sikirica* (citing the *Celebici* Appeal Judgement, para. 717), '...the overriding obligation of the Trial Chamber in determining sentence is to individualise a penalty to fit the individual circumstances of the accused and the gravity of the crime'; *Prosecutor v Sikirica* (Case No. IT-95-8), Sentencing Judgement, 13 November 2001, para. 231.

decisions are constituted and reconstituted according to 'context' and 'audience'. Consequently, decisions are seen as unstructured, relative, pragmatic and situational; 'reasons' are regarded as suspect (*post hoc*) rationalisations of case stories 'largely constructed and typified by the criminal process even before they reach the judge' (Tata, 1997, p.413).

This narrative model emphasises the innate subjectivism and contextual relativity of judicial perceptions of legal and social constraints. The interplay between process and human variables is seen as crucial in shaping the discourses of sentencing. In recognising that there may be a tendency to exaggerate the process of sentencing at the expense of appreciating the unique construction of each sentencing decision, Tata's model implicitly acknowledges the pivotal significance of demographic and psychological variables in decision-making.[11] The significance of this approach lies in its identification of sentencing as a recursive activity patterned by social rules and Tata's acknowledgement that philosophical justifications for punishment do not provide interpretative categories for understanding penal process; rather that their role may well be to 'provide symbolically defensible normative accounts of how or why societies punish' (Tata, 1997, p.412).

Tata's notion of process symbolism and the instrumentality of judicial discretionary power confirms the notion of process as mediator of opposing moralities. Its function, as is the function of international criminal justice, can only be as an arbiter of the moral relativity of truth and justice. The extent to which process can be transformative and a legitimator of morally opposing justifications for action is therefore best seen in functional terms. Process mediates value conflict. International criminal justice exists (if at all) as a reflection of the legitimacy attached to the justification for performance of that function by the so-called 'global community'. It is a virtual reconciliation of truth and justice for relative consumption, just as it is in domestic contexts. It is ever-changing, depending on conflict, communities and cultures. It can be seen (promoted) as relational (or not), as a positive or negative force for peace (or not). Herein lies the link between justification, process and legitimacy.

If we accept that the rationality of international penality should be informed by adopting a relational approach to the conceptualisation of justice, rather than through the imposition of external rationales foreign to local priorities for truth and restoration, it implies that localised notions of moral legitimacy ought to be mirrored in national and international structures. Seen from this perspective, conceptualising rationales for the individualisation of sentences in international criminal trials provides an opportunity to develop a relational framework for sentencing which is driven by the need to reconcile the moral justification for process with its perceived moral legitimacy. Consequently, the context for restorative outcomes is conceived through moving beyond conventional conceptualisations that envisage 'communities' purely in terms of victimisation towards one that sees process as a context for their holistic restoration. Figure 3.2 below summarises these points.

---

[11] Further research is needed to elucidate the nature of the interactions between the psychological characteristics of sentencers and specific case material before Tata's thesis can be fully substantiated (Henham, 2000a).

Philosophical rationales provide symbolic rather than interpretative categories for understanding penal process
Discretionary process is subjective and contextually relative
Decisions are (re)constituted according to perceived context (audience)
Sentencing mediates opposing moralities
Restorative justice is an interpretative category for morality based on truth and reconciliation
Hence communitarianism becomes instrumental – rights to inclusion and participation in sentencing are (re)conceptualised in these terms
Restoration becomes a paradigm for sentencing that acknowledges moral pluralism and its relative contexts
International penality then transcends symbolism and hegemony
The moral legitimacy and justification for penality is provided and understood through context

Figure 3.2 Principles for operationalising restorative values through the establishment of morally legitimate norms

Sentencing can provide an operational context for conflict resolution or relational justice according to whatever interpretative category sentencers are asked to work with. Rationality alone, in terms of prioritising moral values and their expression as general justifications, does not qualify for this task. It provides 'ought' statements – desirable states of affairs (value principles). It is only when values are operationalised (become instrumental – as normative principles) that they have the capacity to influence individual thought and social action. In the context of international penality, the relationship between ideology and norms is likely to take the form of a definite sentencing policy (such as just deserts/proportionality) which has been predicated on rational principles derived from a modified version of retributivism. However, it might equally arise through the incorporation of a set of autonomous rights principles, whose underlying values are enshrined in a foundational statement of intent. The crucial empirical question is: how far does practice (process) actually give effect to those values which originally inspired the norms embodied in the relevant instrument or rights paradigm?[12] This implies that for restorative themes to impact on international penality, the link between moral

[12] Seen in this light, the notion of 'instrumentality' means inclusion and participation for a purpose.

justification and legitimacy must be forged through processual norms by instrumental discretionary decision-making.

The Interplay between Legal Form and Discretion in Sentencing

Henham and Findlay's (2002) comparative contextual model for conceptualising discretionary decision-making suggests that sentencers are consistently able to individualise sentences and reach beyond the justificatory rhetoric, symbolism and procedural imperatives of trial ideology through the selective appropriation and interpretation of legal and social constraints. This paradigm suggests that decision-making sites which impact on sentencing within the trial process act as regulatory mechanisms where the relative distance between the symbolism of punishment as procedural discourse and the reality of its implications is established. It challenges the conventional view that it is the autonomous effect of procedural rules which circumscribes discretionary practice. This debate is highly significant in terms of acknowledging law's normative character, since it implicates sentencers as instrumental in the justification and signification of legal and procedural norms as morally appropriate and responsible for the transformation of normative principles into normative imperatives that are regarded as morally legitimate by the relevant audience. Consequently, it becomes important to deconstruct the relative realities of symbolism and context.[13]

This section explores the extent to which discretionary decision-making is responsible for the symbolism of punishment in international criminal trials and the degree to which the norms and structures of international sentencing are implicated in this phenomenon. Thus, it focuses on sentencing and its significance in terms of symbolism, rhetoric and judicial style, especially in relation to the justifications for punishment. The significance attached to the role of judicial discretion is particularly evident in the sentencing judgements of the ICTR. For example, after detailing the applicable texts, the Trial Chamber in *Serushago*[14] went on to consider the scale of penalties applicable, concluding:

> … the Chamber will prefer … to lean more on its unfettered discretion each time that it has to pass sentence on persons found guilty of crimes falling within its jurisdiction [para. 18].[15]

However, the relationship between the moral justification for international punishment, its normative rationale and judicial discretionary decision-making is particularly apparent from a closer examination of the ICTR's approach to

---

[13] Banakar (2003, p.153) makes the important point that the sociological description of the social reality of legal decision-making need not result in reductionism. If one takes the view that the recursive reality of legal practice is essentially concerned with getting things done legally, then sociology's reflexivity can assist in elucidating the complex relationships between structure and agency and the significance of how participants' subjective interpretations of processual reality are constructed and relate to one another; cf. Rogers and Erez (1999).

[14] *Prosecutor v Serushago* (Case No. ICTR-98-39), Judgement and Sentence, 5 February 1999.

[15] The language is reproduced almost verbatim in ICTR sentencing judgements.

sentencing. The ICTR's consideration of the general principles regarding the determination of sentences is typified by the method adopted in the *Kambanda*[16] decision.[17] It can be broken down into five components:

1. A declaration of moral justification in global terms:

> 26. In determining the sentence, the Chamber has always to have in mind that this Tribunal was established by the Security Council pursuant to Chapter VII of the Charter of the United Nations within the context of the measures the Council was empowered to take under Article 39 of the said Charter in order *to ensure that violations of international humanitarian law in Rwanda in 1994 were halted and effectively redressed.* As required by the Charter in previous cases, the Council noted that the situation in Rwanda constituted a threat to international peace and security. And resolution 955 of 8 November 1994, which was passed by the Council in this connection, clearly indicates that the aim for the establishment of the Tribunal was *to prosecute and punish the perpetrators of the atrocities in Rwanda in such a way as to put an end to impunity and thereby to promote national reconciliation and the restoration of peace* [emphasis added].

Clearly, the moral justification for punishment contained in paragraph 26 is tied inextricably to the objective of ending and redressing gross violations of international humanitarian law in Rwanda, but it is expressed in such a way as to suggest that by punishing those individuals responsible, national reconciliation and peace will be promoted. Thus, the global moral injunction is both retrospective and prospective in its aspirations for criminal justice, although unclear in its implications for rationalising sentencing practice.

2. A declaration of moral justification in local terms:[18]

> 27. It will be noted that the preamble of the Rwandan Organic Law, referred to above, states that:
> 'Considering that it is vital, in order to achieve national reconciliation, to forever eradicate the culture of impunity;
> Considering that *the exceptional circumstances facing the country requires the adoption of adequate measures to meet the need of the Rwandan people for justice*' [emphasis added].

---

[16] *Prosecutor v Kambanda* (Case No. ICTR-97-23), Sentencing Judgement, 4 September 1998.

[17] Where general justifications for sentence are mentioned they are invariably unrelated to any normative framework for the determination of the penalty: 'The jurisprudence of the ICTR with regard to penalties has addressed the principal aims of sentencing, namely, retribution, deterrence, rehabilitation and justice'; *Prosecutor v Ruggiu* (Case No. ICTR-97-32), Judgement and Sentence, 1 June 2000 para. 33; and, more recently: 'In reaching its decision on an appropriate sentence to be imposed on the Accused, the Chamber has taken due consideration of the well-established principles of retribution, deterrence, and protection of society ...'; *Prosecutor v Niyitegeka* (ICTR-96-14-T), Judgement and Sentence, 16 May 2003; para. 484; 'The gravity of the offences shall therefore be reflected primarily in the Chamber's decision on the sentence to be inflicted upon the Accused, in order to serve such primary purposes as retribution, deterrence, protection of society, stigmatization and public reprobation of international crimes ... '; *Prosecutor v Ntakirutimana* (Case No. 1: ICTR-96-10; 2: ICTR-96-19-17 T), Judgement and Sentence, 21 February 2003; para. 882.

[18] This dimension does not, of course, apply in the case of the ICC.

The combined effect of paragraphs 26 and 27 is for sentencing decisions to reflect the need to end impunity, promote national reconciliation, restore peace and, to adopt measures that meet the needs of the indigenous victim community[19] for justice.

A recapitulation of the moral justification for punishment is more infrequent in the judgements of the ICTY. In *Jelisic*,[20] the ICTY's Trial Chamber approved of comments in *Tadic*[21] to the effect that the tribunal's mission of putting an 'end to the serious violations of international humanitarian law and to contribute to restoring and keeping the peace in the Former Yugoslavia' was especially relevant to determining the appropriate penalty. Again, however, the achievement of this objective was linked directly to the need for the penalty to reflect the exigencies of retribution and deterrence and, in addition, as an expression of public reprobation and stigmatisation of the offender, to reflect the international community's indignation at what had taken place and its denunciation through the imposition of an appropriate penalty. Notwithstanding, the more considered approach of the Trial Chamber in *Erdemovic*[22] was explicit in linking the use of judicial discretionary power to the achievement of restorative objectives such as accountability, reconciliation and establishing the truth. However, its reassurances that the process was 'underpinned by principles of justice, fair trial and protection of the fundamental rights of the individual' have to be evaluated in the context of the tribunal's predominant rationale of retribution and deterrence.

3. A declaration that, notwithstanding the above, the penality of the tribunal must be rationalised in terms of retribution and deterrence:

> 28. That said, it is clear that the penalties imposed on accused persons found guilty by the Tribunal must be directed, on the one hand, at retribution of the said accused, who must see their crimes punished, and over and above that, at deterrence, namely dissuading for good those who will attempt in future to perpetrate such atrocities by showing them that the international community was not ready to tolerate the serious violations of international humanitarian law and human rights.

---

19 This expression should be taken to accommodate the competing claims of a morally pluralistic society.

20 *Prosecutor v Jelicic* (Case No. IT-95-10), Judgement, 14 December 1999, para. 116.

21 *Prosecutor v Tadic* (Case No. IT-94-1), Sentencing Judgement, 11 November 1999, para. 7.

22 'The International Tribunal, in addition to its mandate to investigate, prosecute and punish serious violations of international humanitarian law, has a duty, through its judicial functions, to contribute to the settlement of the wider issues of accountability, reconciliation and establishing the truth behind the evils perpetrated in the former Yugoslavia. Discovering the truth is a cornerstone of the rule of law and a fundamental step on the way to reconciliation: for it is the truth that cleanses the ethnic and religious hatreds and begins the healing process. The International Tribunal must demonstrate that those who have the honesty to confess are treated fairly as part of a process underpinned by principles of justice, fair trial and protection of the fundamental rights of the individual. On the other hand, the International Tribunal is a vehicle through which the international community expresses its outrage at the atrocities committed in the former Yugoslavia. Upholding values of international human rights means that whilst protecting the rights of the accused, the International Tribunal must not lose sight of the tragedy of the victims and the sufferings of their families'; *Prosecutor v Erdemovic* (Case No. IT-96-22), Sentencing Judgement, 5 March 1998, para. 21.

4. References to the need for certain (aggravating and mitigating) factors to be taken into account in the determination of sentences – this is referred to as individualising the penalty, and it is seen in terms of what the relevant Statute and Rules permit to be taken into account. Hence, individualisation is conceived in terms of establishing the proper degree of criminal responsibility of the offender for the target offence. This should be reflected in variations in 'the intensity of punishment' (paragraph 29).
5. A declaration that in order for the Chamber to be able to individualise sentences correctly judges must be able to use their unfettered discretion to take into account any other factors they see fit. The *Kambanda* judgement does not delineate the ambit of 'individualisation' as a concept, nor does it provide any rationale which might justify the need to go outside the parameters suggested by the Statute and Rules (paragraph 30).[23] No declaration is therefore made suggesting that 'individualisation' could be seen as a way of bridging the gap between the rhetoric of the global and local moral justifications contained in paragraphs 26 and 27 and the needs of the victims and communities affected by international conflict. Individualisation is characterised purely in terms of individual circumstances (paragraph 34).

A number of reasons may, therefore, be suggested to explain the failure of the *ad hoc* tribunals to make the necessary connections between the contexts of criminality and the contexts of penality:

1. The Statutes and Rules of Procedure and Evidence do not provide penalty scales that are determined according to the perceived gravity of the offence.[24]
2. Conceptual confusion is caused by a failure to clarify the relationship between substantive offence elements and sentencing principles. Consequently, the conception and representation of legalistic criteria has more symbolic than real significance for the choice of sentencing options.

---

[23] The conventional approach was confirmed in *Ntakirutimana*, *supra*, note 17; 'Article 23 of the Statute and Rule 101(B) of the Rules also require that the individual circumstances of the Accused and the existence of any aggravating and mitigating circumstances in their case be thoroughly considered. Application of these principles allows the Chamber to fulfill its "overriding obligation to individualize [the] penalty", with the aim that the sentence be proportional to the gravity of the offence and the degree of responsibility of the offender' (para. 883).

[24] The current position is typified by the Trial Chamber's approach in *Niyitegaka*, *supra*, note 17, which, whilst recognising the significance of penalty scaling for sentence determination, fails to initiate the process of developing appropriate guidance; '… the Chamber has considered the principle of gradation in sentencing, according to which the highest penalties are to be imposed upon those at the upper end of the sentencing scale, such as those who planned or ordered atrocities, or those who committed crimes with especial zeal or sadism. Whether an accused is found guilty of genocide, of crimes against humanity or of violations of the Geneva Conventions or Additional Protocol II thereto, the principle of gradation enables the Chamber to punish, deter, and consequently stigmatize the crimes considered at a level that corresponds to their overall magnitude and reflects the extent of the suffering inflicted upon the victims' (para. 486). However, as pointed out in *Prosecutor v Semanza* (ICTR-97-20-T), Judgement and Sentence, 15 May 2003, the practice of awarding a single sentence for the totality of an accused's conduct made it difficult to determine the range of sentences for each specific crime. Nevertheless, the Chamber felt that it was now possible to ascertain general ranges of sentences which may provide useful guidance to the Chamber in determining the appropriate sentence in this case (para. 562).

3. There is no rationalised normative practice which establishes the need for a justificatory relationship to be established between the prescribed penalties and the practice of sentencing, beyond that demanded by the primary rationales of retributivism and deterrence.
4. International trial judges are given a broad and largely unregulated discretion in sentencing.

Initially, what emerges from analysis of the sentencing judgements of the *ad hoc* tribunals is that the expressed rationales and structures of international penality are employed as rhetorical devices by the international judiciary; that there is no tangible connection between the language of justification and the reality of judicial sentencing practice.[25] The rationality for punishment and its expression in the previous sentencing decisions of the tribunals remains disconnected from decision-making precisely because there is no need for judges to engage further with it. The rationality of international sentencing is not operationalised into a normative framework for sentencing – it is retributive and deterrent in orientation, but not instrumental in helping to direct the practice of sentencing decision-making. Neither does this philosophical orientation impose normative obligations on judges that force them to connect sentence justifications in terms of their consequences for relevant audiences such as victims or victim communities. Consequently, the rhetoric appears vacuous; symbolically directed towards satisfying the universal morality of the 'global community'.[26]

Similarly, in many domestic legal systems symbolic judicial exhortations are often made to a mythical 'moral majority'[27] in order to justify exemplary sentences. More significantly, however, the gap between rhetoric, symbolism and reality is perpetuated in many national systems precisely because the philosophical foundations for penality and their implementation through the application of sentencing norms have no relational context. In other words, the exercise of judicial discretion does not move beyond satisfying the substantive requirements imposed by procedural norms; it does not need to reach out and engage with significant others or embrace alternative moral agendas. In short, the process derives its legitimacy through adherence to formalism. Hence, procedural justice is symbolically equated with moral justice by judicial discourses of rhetoric and symbolism which apparently transcend pluralism and factionalism.

Weber's analysis of substantive and formal rationality is insightful in this context (Cotterrell, 1992, p.153). According to Weber, the legal norms which regulate punishment are founded on principles of substantive rationality in so far as they are informed by a mixture of morals and beliefs existing beyond the formalism of the legal rules themselves. However, in reality such norms are highly formalised in structure and there exists a complex balance between formal logical processes which facilitate the recursive reproduction of law as an autonomous system of rules and the

---

[25] These rhetorical devices therefore form part of what Giddens (1977) might refer to as 'practical consciousness'.

[26] As encapsulated in the preamble to the foundation instruments of the international institutions.

[27] This is often objectified for legalistic tests in terms of 'the reasonable man' or 'the average decent law-abiding citizen' in common law jurisdictions.

extent to which ideology about the moral acceptability of social action informs decision-making. The crisis in the legitimacy of criminal justice, both global and local, is perpetuated in Weberian terms by the bureaucratisation of legal rationality to the extent that the criminal process recursively perpetuates the development of internally consistent principles which tend to re-enforce dominant political ideologies. A system of formal rationality reproduced in contexts where political and moral ideologies are at odds (as in modern pluralistic states) means that legal formalism predominates and increasingly causes the alienation of the criminal process from the outcomes it produces.

In Italy, for example, where criminal procedure is also a hybridisation of inquisitorial and adversarial styles, the emphasis on procedural form and the failure of legislative or juridical attempts to rationalise contemporary punishment justifications has seriously impaired the ability of the justice system to engage with relational justice forms (Henham and Mannozzi, 2003). Although this phenomenon is shaped by complex cultural reasons, it serves to illustrate how the practice of sentencing as symbolism can simply re-enforce existing dichotomies in relationships of structure and agency. In such circumstances the instrumentality of judicial discretion remains a negative force for altering the delicate balance between form and substance, and, thus, engaging with alternative definitions of morally justified penality.

However, more insidious implications than this exist for sentencing in international criminal trials. If, as argued earlier, the actions of international judges reflect the ideological and normative imperatives of their respective legal traditions in a reflexive and constructive interpretation of rules and procedure, then it may be expected that this will include their propensity for instrumental discretionary behaviour. Recently, Bohlander and Findlay (2002, p.25) have commented on the dangers inherent in the disproportionate influence of competing legal traditions in ICTY practices and its potential for frustrating any accommodation with more pluralistic aspirations for international criminal justice. Again the Italian experience bears out this line of reasoning; there, the normative constraints of inquisitorialism have sustained a judicial culture where discretion is neither valued nor necessary in sentencing. Coupled with retributive-based sentencing justifications and a normative framework conceived during a period in history when the Italian justice system was entirely inquisitorial,[28] this has meant that procedural ideology has taken over from judicial pragmatism, instrumentality and engagement. Notwithstanding, the relatively recent hybridisation of the criminal process through the introduction of adversarial procedure and distinctive restorative paradigms for dealing with certain offence/offender categories, the relative obfuscation of rationales in Italian sentencing remains (Mannozzi, 2002).

For international sentencing, continued obfuscation and paralysis in the development of a principled sentencing jurisprudence, other than one constrained by retributive aspirations for justice, will seriously impair the ability of judges to direct their discretion towards individualisation and the possibilities for developing a procedural context for relational justice forms. It is suggested that the only way forward is to counter the potentially subversive effects of judicial behaviour

[28] In 1930 during a period of ultra-nationalistic political ideology.

rationalised from different legal traditions and the negative impact of an ideology that does not extend beyond the symbolic need to comply with procedural norms by channelling discretionary power towards the achievement of restorative goals.

Transparency and Integration

The parameters of transparency in sentencing are intimately associated with the notion of rights and their enforceability. If procedural norms to facilitate the achievement of restorative solutions are introduced into the legislative instruments of international courts and tribunals it becomes imperative that discretionary behaviour and procedural pathways to particular outcomes are identified and evaluated against paradigms that support aspirations for victim participation and engagement in sentencing.

The use of the expression 'transparency' carries with it the implication that the foundation instruments and the prescribed procedural rules for international trial practice should not be deliberately obfuscatory, nor their implementation obscured from public scrutiny and accountability. Nevertheless, it is often argued that processual rules are somehow designed to obstruct rather than facilitate the establishment of 'truth' and therefore justice. Such a presumption echoes McBarnet's (1981) astute observation that procedural law cannot simply be equated with legality. It is not apolitical, but is formulated and applied for discrete objectives that may not necessarily serve the needs of the accused or the victim or civil society, but may instead sustain a distinct moral and ideological focus for the criminal trial.

It has been argued that the retributive dynamic predominates as the rationalisation for punishment for international crimes, not only because it is undoubtedly an accurate reflection of the relationship between the protagonists in a post-conflict situation, but also because there is an absence of any coherent statement of purpose in the foundation instruments of the relevant trial bodies that goes far beyond the fulfilment of retributive aspirations for penality. This is evident from the confused attempts to rationalise punishment in international sentencing judgements (Henham, 2003b). Hence, in this sense, transparency is negated by obfuscation. Furthermore, as the public theatre of the trial is paramount in the structuration of processual activity in international criminal trials, any absence of transparency encourages the perception that lack of visibility is motivated by a deliberate desire to conceal.

At first sight, the foundation instruments of the international institutions, particularly the ICC, go much further than many domestic legal systems in providing procedural safeguards to ensure the fair trial of the accused and for the participation and protection of victims and witnesses at all stages of the criminal process. For example, Article 67(1)(a) of the ICC Statute is unequivocal in stating that the accused must be informed promptly and in detail of the nature, cause and content of the charge in a language which he/she fully understands and speaks. Yet these kinds of safeguards are largely absent when it comes to the deliberation and pronouncement of sentence. As discussed in the previous chapter, the conventional practice now adopted by both the *ad hoc* tribunals and prescribed for the ICC is that all evidence relating to trial of the issues and sentence is heard before the verdict and sentence is delivered.[29] Furthermore, although sentence is pronounced publicly and wherever possible in the presence of the accused,[30] deliberations are *in camera* and there is no obligation for the reasons or an account of the process whereby the *sentencing* decision was reached to be made public. This contrasts with the position on verdict delivery, where Article 74(5) of the ICC Statute states specifically that the decision must be in writing and contain a full and reasoned statement of the Trial Chamber's findings on the evidence and conclusions. However, only a summary of the decision need be delivered in open court. Consequently, so far as sentencing is concerned, whilst the matters the court is required to consider are set out in some detail in Rule 145 of the ICC Statute, the legislative instruments do not appear to go further than requiring that they should be taken into account during the private deliberations of the Trial Chamber, which will invariably occur in practice in any event.[31]

Although, of course, the international courts have (in many instances) delivered consistent and lengthy accounts of their reasoning in sentencing offenders, the absence of any clear obligation in this respect is nevertheless an important procedural omission, given the normal absence of a separate sentencing hearing. The existence of such hearings arguably promotes the creation and development of a coherent sentencing jurisprudence; one that encourages a culture of judicial transparency through the public reception and rational evaluation of evidence. As the International Law Commission made clear in its comments on the work of its forty-sixth session,[32] the procedural guarantees inherent in the concept of a fair trial should be extended to a separate sentencing hearing (as was then proposed) since its purpose was to determine an appropriate punishment for the *individual* as well as the crime. In the absence of any obligation to hold such a hearing, an even stronger argument for transparency in sentence decision-making surely exists. Again, the absence of any mandatory procedure for transparency in sentence decision-making can be said to stem from the major systemic weaknesses which pervade the entire international criminal trial process; namely, that procedural safeguards are more apparent than real because there is no need for them to be otherwise. The articulation of justifications for punishment do not have to extend beyond the consequences which flow from the penal philosophies of limited retributivism and deterrence.

There are, however, broader issues raised. Firstly, there is an argument for supporting separate sentence hearings for symbolic reasons; that marking out as distinct from the verdict the public deliberation and pronouncement of sentence has an enormously powerful symbolic effect in drawing attention to and dramatising the punishment, as well as promoting psychological and emotional feelings relating to atonement and closure.[33] Arguably, a mono-phase process produces obfuscation in

---

[29] Notwithstanding the ICC Trial Chamber's power to hold a further hearing on matters related to sentence under Rule 143 of the Rules of Procedure and Evidence.

[30] Article 76(4) of the ICC Statute; Rule 144(1) of the Rules of Procedure and Evidence.

[31] Such lack of clarity is also apparent in the failure to define adequately whether or not the 'decision' includes the verdict *and* sentence for the purposes of Article 74 of the ICC Statute.

[32] Comment to Article 46 'Sentencing' Yearbook of the International Law Commission, Volume II, Part 2, Report of the Commission to the General Assembly on the Work of its 46th Session (1994) *Draft Code of Crimes against the Peace and Security of Mankind*, UN Doc. A/49/10.

[33] This is, of course, entirely consistent with the perspective adopted by symbolic interactionsists such as Lemert (1972), and see King (1978).

sentence justification and, since it does not promote an alternative context for sentencing, is likely to negate and stultify arguments which explore issues relating to the constructive engagement of sentencing outcomes in favour of those that sustain the *status quo*.

Secondly, an argument can be made out for suggesting that a two-stage process serves to emphasise the qualitative distinction between the pre- and post-conviction phases of the trial by signifying that different substantive and procedural norms apply. It is significant that in the English context, where similar wide judicial discretionary powers in sentencing exist within a mono-phase process,[34] the sentencing phase of the trial is often used by judges to make what Ashworth (2000a, p.306) refers to as 'moralistic homilies', and that the systematic analysis of relevant aggravating and mitigating factors is associated with or developed within this process culture. I would argue that such a tendency is facilitated through a mono-phase trial process, particularly where, as with the *ad hoc* tribunals, the process is dominated by a predominantly retributive ideology which has not encouraged transparency and the reasoned analysis of evidence for sentencing purposes.

A further example provided by Cockayne (2001) relates to witness anonymity and the over-reliance by the ICTR on closed sessions. Cockayne suggests that this has seriously eroded the principle of transparency intended as central to the trial process and an essential element if the ICTR is to fulfil its reconciliation mandate. Reliance on witness anonymity not only threatens to undermine transparency of the trial process; it also renders witness testimony unverifiable by the relevant audience. Hence, from this perspective, the treatment of victims and witnesses raises larger questions about the principles of transparency underlying the international trial process, especially the question of *which* 'audience' the trial is directed towards.

I have suggested that the international judiciary do not have to rationalise their sentencing decisions beyond what is necessary to satisfy the symbolic manifestation of the retributive ideology attributable to international forms of punishment, the latter being insufficiently offset by procedural safeguards designed to ensure that the objectives of international humanitarian law are in fact achieved. Humanitarian objectives clearly imply that the justifications and reasons given for punishment should address the concerns of victims, and, paradoxically, reciprocal recognition that the norms of international humanitarian law are applied by institutions designed to maintain international peace and security. Such an observation emphasises the importance of processual integration; in essence, it suggests that sentence individualisation and victim accommodation should become part of the same process.[35]At present, the obligations of Trial Chambers do not extend beyond taking cognisance of immediate victims within the jurisdiction of the court and their families, and certainly do extend to taking on board the feelings and concerns of 'significant others' within victim communities.

---

[34] Despite there not being a two-stage process, the consideration of evidence for sentencing takes place *after* verdict delivery. In practice, a separate sentencing hearing does take place through adjournments, because certain evidence to be adduced for sentencing (e.g. medical or social circumstances reports) are not immediately available.

[35] I would not go as far as Duff (2003, p.187), however, in arguing that the offender should have participative rights in any negotiated sentencing process.

It may be argued that victim and communitarian interests are only going to be served if the interests of the victim/community are represented at each stage of the criminal process. If so, the ideological rationale for international criminal trial would need to be carefully redefined to reflect the aspirations of such pluralistic demands for legitimacy. Hence, the overall justification for the trial would be to provide a procedural context where the overriding objective would be to facilitate the reconciliation of competing perceptions of 'truth'. Those participants with claims for 'truth', and the determination of whose version of the 'truth' counts (and the reasons for this) would be implicated in process through the trial rationale. Such novel rationales for resolution would recursively sustain the existence and structure of the trial to promote outcomes appropriate for all parties.

I would support penal measures that focus on those areas where the most productive outcome for all parties can be forged. Conceiving of the international criminal trial as a context for constructive resolution does not necessarily imply a predominantly consequentialist penality. Ethnographic research involving tribal and transitional cultures has long confirmed the role of retributive justice in promoting positive feelings towards seeking peace and reconciliation (Bottoms, 2003). A rationale for trial justice that combined elements of retribution, denunciation and deterrence with restorative initiatives would be sustainable, provided account of all views was taken to produce a constructive rather then a symbolic outcome. Such an approach draws together and re-enforces both the local and global contexts for criminality and allows each to experience the actual and symbolic suffering inflicted through retributive punishment, whilst taking from the trial the building blocks for trust and reconstruction delivered by restorative solutions worked through by the court itself.

I therefore agree with von Oppeln (2002, p.252) in asserting that it is important to provide linkage between normative and actual reality in satisfying the needs of victims and communities in war/post-war societies, particularly in scenarios of non-international armed conflict when regulatory imperatives are weaker. More particularly, the paradox between the ideology of universal human rights protection and the inadequacies of strategic intervention should be approached from a perspective which envisages rights protection as a methodological imperative. This paradox is reflected in the failure of process rationality to accommodate the inherent conflict between punishing violators and protecting the violated. This disjunction can be conceptualised as shown in Figure 3.3:

Ideology – Rationales for the punishment of gross breaches of international humanitarian law
Process – Structures for negotiating ideologies of punishment and legitimising conflicting interpretations of truth
Methodology – Strategies for operationalising the ideology of human rights for those affected by breaches of international humanitarian law

Figure 3.3 Conflict resolution as a methodological imperative

Figure 3.3 envisages the trial process as a mediator of 'truth' tasked to determine appropriate strategies for the implementation of solutions that are cognisant of the legitimate expectations of those who have been affected by armed conflict and social disintegration. At present, the methodological imperative for peace and reconstruction in conflict societies is divorced both conceptually and practically from the process of punishment in international criminal trials. I suggest that the resolution of 'truth' through process must go further than this and implicate process itself as an integral determinant of 'legitimate' strategies for intervention. The integration of legitimate expectations for punishment and strategies for peace and reconciliation must transcend the following kinds of negative perceptions identified by Drumbl (2003):

- Criminal trials and the 'closure' represented by verdict and sanction divert attention from efforts at reconstruction and cannot address many of the causes of mass violence.
- Criminal process further politicises the dominant discourse.
- Sanctioning deviant conduct does not necessarily promote accountability.

As in the domestic context, international criminal trials represent but one facet in a range of possible political responses to a particular form of normative conflict. Whether the deviant response is individual or collective, political action is shaped by the perceived social and cultural requirements of the powerful elite. Where trial rationality and penality are predicated on reasoning and structures that promote exclusion, as is currently the case with international criminal justice, the prospects for promoting peace through reconstruction and reconciliation will inevitably remain a remote possibility. Figure 3.4 suggests modelling for international criminal trials that identifies how the concept of inclusivity can be utilised thematically to reposition the ideology and method of international penality in order to facilitate the achievement of such constructive aspirations. The key to integration is through developing the instrumental capacity of judicial discretion.

- **Structural inclusivity** – The legal and political contexts in which judicial discretion is exercised

- **Symbolic inclusivity** – The judicial reconciliation of restorative justice themes within the framework imposed by limited retributivism

- **Instrumental inclusivity** – The instrumentality of judicial discretion – this is the autonomous and purposeful channelling of discretionary power for perceived legitimate ends. It is achieved through balancing public/universal interests against individual rights. It is within this discretionary framework that the judiciary are empowered to negotiate legitimacy.

Figure 3.4 Inclusivity as a paradigm for international penality

The integrated decision-making model proposed in Figure 3.4 is, therefore, one which recognises how inclusivity exists at the ideological level through legal and political context, and at the level of process through the rhetoric of symbolic reconstruction. However, its most important feature is that it acknowledges the constructive potential of judicial discretionary power. This is instrumental power – judicial discretion is envisaged as a methodology for integrating strategies for reconstruction and peace; as a negotiator of legitimacy at the levels of ideology, process and intervention.

The adoption of an integrated modelling approach to discretionary decision-making implies a need to engage trial contexts in terms of the following variables:

- rules about participation
- how evidence becomes truth
- how truth becomes fact
- how value is attributed to fact
- how fact and value merge
- how outcomes derive from definitive truth.

These imperatives envisage that the attribution of value to fact through discretion provides the power for change. A useful analogy is provided through an examination of the relationship between law and custom in the judicial decision-making processes of tribal and indigenous societies. For example, Gluckman (1955)[36] in his account of the judicial process among the Barotse tribe of Northern Rhodesia (now Zimbabwe) states:

> When Lozi judges have to give a decision on a dispute, they draw, both during trial and in adjudication, on custom, legislation, judicial precedent, equity, the laws of nature and of nations, and good morals and public policy. They do so in a process which is controlled by publicly known logic … Morality and equity control the weighing of laws, besides being a particular source of judicial rulings … customary life – thus is a prime source of judicial decision under the guise of precedent.

The important point about this and similar accounts is that, as Gluckman suggests,[37] the judges effectively operate a kind of sociological methodology in their decision-making; they refer to and utilise their interpretation of general morality in order to control the adaptation of flexible legal concepts to novel circumstances. This judicial manipulation is facilitated, and achieves morally just solutions, because it takes place in a society where there are hierarchical customary definitions of moral behaviour derived from natural law. As Gluckman concludes:

> I do not suggest that these concepts, many of which are shared with other systems of law, exist *in vacuo*. I argue that they carry the historic, political, and economic load of their social milieu: they are permeated with a specific set of social presumptions, interests, values, etc.

Gluckman's observations are important for the present context. He is describing a judicial system where the power for change is channelled through the judges and

---

36 References here are extracted from Bohannan (1967, pp.59–91).

37 *Ibid*, note 33, p.88.

controlled by them. The judges are effectively trusted to operationalise a moral consensus,[38] but in an instrumental and creative way that draws on clear understandings of their role in forging the relationship between law, morality and justice. Of course, I am not suggesting that there are any parallels to be drawn here in terms of the inspiration for, and nature of, moral behaviour between the contexts of contemporary international justice and indigenous tribal justice. The point I wish to make is that such accounts of customary law-making argue in favour of using the instrumental power of judicial discretion to facilitate constructive processual outcomes – in other words, discretion provides a context for negotiation between moral values and normative behaviour. Such studies suggest a number of propositions:

- Law's moral power can be realised in sentencing by developing the capacity for judicial discretionary decision-making to shape social reality.
- The capacity for developing the instrumental power of judicial discretion depends on allowing maximum flexibility for decision-makers.
- This means that discretion determines the morally appropriate linkage between value and fact.
- This correspondingly implies a conceptualisation of sentencing which recognises that:
  - judicial decision-making promotes images of what the law signifies, and produces accounts of how the law impacts
  - the objectification of legal norms through recursively organised practice simultaneously engages with subjective interpretations of moral legitimacy.

Hence, the ability of judicial discretionary power to engage with morally legitimate conceptions of fact/value depends upon the extent to which an identifiable common morality can be said to influence the exercise of discretion. The notion of a common morality has two important dimensions in this context:

1. It refers to the morality of justice as it may be perceived by the victims and communities in post-conflict societies.
2. It is a shared morality because the notion of inclusiveness has been adopted as a key element of trial ideology. Hence, the normative framework becomes the vehicle for identifying competing moral claims for justice. Judges are empowered to negotiate these demands through the use of their discretionary power.

Whether ideology and process is comfortable with the notion of judges as a mechanism for flexibility and creativity can therefore be envisaged as pivotal to the recursivity of process. In this sense, human agency provides both the means and the ends for enforcing morality and justice and legitimating structure across time and space.

---

[38] In a similar way to that envisaged by the social contract theorists of the Enlightenment in pre-industrialised western European societies of the late nineteenth century.

Recognising that judicial discretion can be used instrumentally and flexibly to reflect and reinforce common strands between moral ideology and social structure is important for any reconceptualisation and repositioning of the penality of international criminal justice. Such a realisation does not, however, deal with the problems posed by moral pluralism and the relativity of international criminal justice.[39] Nor does it help to confront ideological imperialism or reconcile hegemonic power with the operation of institutions ostensibly established to ensure adherence to principles that advocate the universality of humanitarian legal norms. In Rwanda, for example, as Drumbl (2002, p.5) argues, the ICTR may not provide the most appropriate forum to reconstruct social norms or promote peace, reconciliation and justice, given its predominantly retributive ideology. He suggests that the ICTR's retributive paradigm encourages strategic interventions that fail to connect with notions of local justice, and argues that local participatory justice forms (*gacaca* tribunals) which concentrate on reintegrating offenders are much more likely to restore harmony and social justice in Rwanda over time.

Drumbl (2002, p.11) cites Sach's dichotomy between the trial as a context for microscopic/logical truth rather than to experiential/dialogic truth as a reflection of the mechanisms of accountability provided for post-conflict justice in Rwanda. He suggests that, at the very least, the latter would be better facilitated through local structures of popular justice running alongside the more restricted opportunities for truth-finding provided by international criminal trials. My argument in this chapter has been that the instrument power of discretionary decision-making in international criminal trials can (and should) be harnessed to forge rationalisations for sentencing that conform to alternative paradigms for justice; that process can be reconceptualised as enabling rather than constraining. In this way the processual activity which is sentencing should be conceived as a forum for the relative engagement of contexts, placing constantly varying demands on sentencers to devise morally acceptable outcomes that reconcile the demands for local justice with more universal aspirations for international justice. In the final chapter I go on to to suggest how this aspiration can be achieved.

---

[39] Namely, the determination of what may be the appropriate response in a particular case.

Chapter 4

Normative Constraints on Sentencing

This chapter is concerned with the systemic and structural constraints which threaten notions of fair trial within international sentencing processes, particularly procedural mechanisms for sentence reduction. The issue is explored by focusing on the nature and form of plea bargaining in international criminal trial processes, including the discretionary power of the prosecution, defence and judiciary, the nature and extent of victim involvement, questions relating to the transparency of process, proportionality and desert implications, and the broader implications for adversarial/inquisitorial trial paradigms.

Introduction

The analysis in this chapter investigates the nature of the relationship between due process principles and practice and its significance for international sentencing through an evaluation of the rationale for discounting sentences in return for guilty pleas and the status and function of plea agreements in the context of international criminal trials. It focuses on ICC sentencing rules and procedures and their probable interpretation in the light of ICTY and ICTR decisions.

The discussion is predicated on the assumption that procedural justice cannot be satisfactorily evaluated on the sole basis of the extent to which procedures conform to 'objectively' defined characteristics, since ideology and political process are invariably crucial to the development of procedural norms and the policies which inform them. Indeed, some writers have recognised the illusory objectivity of the justice concept, preferring instead to justify the inclusion of certain basic principles of due process by reference to political, libertarian or social values.[1] The paradigm of deserts theory manifestly fails to address the nature and desirability of due process beyond its commensurate concerns and, therefore, tends towards an erosion of due process in favour of crime control. Kamenka (1979) argues further that, once justice has become principle or policy, it ceases in importance and is replaced by a bureaucratic-administrative conception of justice which fosters the rational calculation of the 'proper' distribution of benefits. Since international humanitarian law clearly recognises that guarantees should exist regarding the inviolability of state institutions to protect individual rights, it is imperative that courts exercising international criminal jurisdiction should provide a balance between maintenance of

[1] See Saphire (1978); Mashaw (1987). Others, such as Matza (1964, pp.104–106) have argued that the major components of justice have an entity which is objectively verifiable, although preferring the more mundane position of equating or conceiving fairness as a synonym for justice. Bayles (1990) is closer to Matza in asserting the autonomous quality of process benefits like participation and equality.

the presumption of innocence through due process and the justification of punishment, both in its nature and extent.

In terms of trial procedure, the ICC Statute (Article 65) provides that, where the accused admits guilt under Article 64(8)(a), the Trial Chamber must satisfy itself as to the voluntariness of the admission, that the accused understands the consequences and that the admission is supported by the charges and factual evidence then available to it.[2] Article 65(3) goes on to state that, if the Trial Chamber is not satisfied that that these conditions are established, it may deem the guilty plea as not having been made and proceed to trial. The presumption of innocence is enshrined in Article 66, which also confirms that the onus is on the prosecution to prove to the satisfaction of the Court that the accused is guilty beyond all reasonable doubt.[3]

However, the ICC Statute and the Rules of Evidence and Procedure are largely silent regarding the impact of a guilty plea on sentence. For instance, Article 76(1) refers only to the Trial Chamber's obligation to 'take into account the evidence presented and the submissions made', whilst Article 78(1) points vaguely to offence gravity and individual circumstances as being relevant to the determination of sentence. Rule 145 of the Rules of Procedure and Evidence does little more than explicitly mention the relevance of aggravating and mitigating circumstances (Rule 145(1)(b)), give further examples of individual circumstances (Rule 145(1)(c)), and provide two examples of mitigating circumstances (Rule 145(2)(a)(i) and (ii)). Nowhere is there any explicit recognition or consideration of the following crucial issues:

- whether a guilty plea counts as a mitigating factor
- if so, what conditions, circumstances or principles should govern the impact that the guilty plea has on the final sentence determination.

The absence of any discussion of these matters, or their elaboration in the ICC Statute or Rules, is a matter of considerable concern.

The concept of the sentence discount in return for a guilty plea has long provoked controversy in common law jurisdictions, the fundamental due process objection being that such discounts undermine the presumption of innocence and the necessity

[2] For further detail, see Behrens (1998). Schabas (2001a, pp.124–125) supports the view that the ICC Statute achieves an acceptable pragmatic compromise in reconciling the opposing philosophical approaches to the concept of the guilty plea characteristic of common law and civil law jurisdictions. It is worth noting that in England and Wales, when the offender pleads guilty the judge does not hear the evidence, only the prosecution's statement of facts. Disagreements relating to the factual basis for sentencing may be resolved by a 'Newton hearing'. For further discussion, see Ashworth (2000, pp.308–311). The ICC Statute (Article 65(4)) goes further than this in providing that the Trial Chamber may request the Prosecutor to present additional evidence (including witness testimony) in order to satisfy itself that a more complete presentation is made in the interests of justice.

[3] In civil law jurisdictions the guilty plea may not be recognised. In France, for example, the dossier must be examined for sufficient evidence of guilt, whilst in Germany 'plea bargains' involving the judge and the accused may be made despite the absence of a formal guilty plea being entered on the record. In hybrid jurisdictions like Italy specific procedures have been introduced to facilitate forms of negotiation designed to speed up criminal procedure. For further analysis, see Jung (1997); Tulkens (2002, pp.661–673).

for the prosecution to prove its case.[4] Similarly, despite recent procedural deviations in many civil law jurisdictions, the inquisitorial paradigm remains committed to the view that matters of guilt or innocence are firmly established following an evaluation of all the accumulated evidence irrespective of plea. Nevertheless, the negotiations which preceded the formulation of the rules for the acceptance of guilty pleas in the ICC Statute were notable for the apparent misconception and suspicion on the part of civil law countries regarding the nature, effect and consequences of a guilty plea as commonly understood in common law jurisdictions (Behrens, 1998). However, as Behrens (1998, p.439) points out, whilst the original ILC Draft[5] was treated with circumspection, since it failed to specify the consequences of a guilty plea, detailed comparisons of the criteria applied by judges in both trial styles in the sessions of the Preparatory Committee revealed remarkable similarities – particularly as regards judicial checks on whether the plea was made voluntarily and in full knowledge of the consequences. Thus, the debate as to whether the procedure should be termed 'a guilty plea', 'confession of guilt' or 'admission of guilt' became superfluous, as is the provision eventually added to the ICC Statute (Article 65(5)), which states:

> Any discussions between the Prosecutor and the defence regarding modification of the charges, the admission of guilt or the penalty to be imposed shall not be binding on the Court.[6]

More important is the significance of the negotiating procedure in its broader sociological context. Clearly, a common theoretical assumption is the consensual nature of negotiation and presumed equality between the parties, yet the evidence tends to suggest that the effects of legal rules and procedures is merely to re-enforce existing structural arrangements in society. As Tulkens puts it:

> During proceedings, all the inequalities of the parties are reproduced – inequalities of condition (social origin, socio-economic level and cultural group), but also ... inequalities of position (2002, p.678).

Particularly significant in the present context is the propensity for plea negotiations to exacerbate the potential for social exclusion within cultures,[7] whether they be

---

[4] For an important discussion of the issues of principle involved in the context of the European Convention on Human Rights, see Ashworth (1998, pp.286–292). It is interesting to note that early forms of adversarial trial militated strongly against guilty pleas since this resulted in the loss of any opportunity for mitigating evidence to be presented to the court; Langbein (2003, p.20).

[5] ILC Draft, Article 38, para. 1 lit.d) (UN-Document A/49/10, p110 ff.). As Behrens (1998, p.459) interestingly observes, the Appeals Chamber in *Erdemovic* (decided during this phase of the negotiations) were forced to reopen the proceedings following the revelation by the accused that his guilty plea had been entered under duress and he had not been informed precisely about the nature of his plea.

[6] Schabas (2001a, p.125) suggests that this provision was forced because of a general misconception on the part of certain civil law countries that undertakings between the prosecutor and the judge were binding at common law.

[7] An example of this phenomenon in the English context is the fact that a greater proportion of black defendants plead not guilty than whites (Hood 1992, p.87). Consequently, fewer black defendants can take advantage of sentence discounts, which contributes to the disproportionately longer prison sentences imposed upon them by the courts due to the so-called 'trial penalty'. Not only does this practice threaten due process, failure to address causes and consequences re-enforces negative attitudes and contributes to social deprivation.

transitional cultures or cultures fragmented by conflict, as is their failure to recognise the demands for justice resulting from cultural pluralism. Consequently, negotiating procedures are potentially counterproductive for the fulfilment of rationales that promote peace and reconciliation. The following aspects may be listed:

- the relative weakness of the accused's negotiating position as citizen of a subjugated state or social group
- the absence of clear guidelines concerning the appropriateness of plea negotiations for the most serious crimes
- cultural misunderstandings regarding the procedure and its effects
- the extent to which victim communities should engage in negotiations
- the fact that the procedure is conducted within the constraints of a retributive ideology
- whether procedures based on expediency can engage with issues of social justice
- obfuscation and lack of transparency regarding the nature of the process and its effects on the calculation of sentence.

However, there are many other specific concerns relating to the recognition of any principle which rewards guilty pleas with sentence reductions. Some of the arguments are summarised[8] below, and then evaluated in the context of the existing jurisprudence of the *ad hoc* tribunals:

1. There are due process concerns as to whether evidence has been effectively reviewed in pre-trial stages where pressures exist to encourage defendants to plead guilty as early as possible in the proceedings.[9]
2. There may develop a practice whereby there is a significant difference in sentence severity for a defendant who pleads guilty compared to the sentence imposed for a similar case where the defendant was convicted after a trial.[10] Although usually referred to as a guilty plea discount (or sentencing or confession reward), it may also be regarded as a 'trial penalty' to emphasise its coercive aspects. However, sentencers may justify the trial penalty on the basis that it is often prompted by the egregious nature of the crime as revealed in evidence given at the trial, and this would otherwise be concealed by a sterile guilty plea (McCoy, 1994). Indeed, some may argue that certain defendants do not deserve discounts under any circumstances, even if they are pleading guilty.
3. Notwithstanding, the guilty plea discount is frequently justified by sentencers on the basis of its remorse rationale.[11] It may be argued that a truly remorseful

---

[8] For a detailed analysis see McCoy and Henham (2004).

[9] In this respect Zappala's (2003, p.78) suggestion that (in theory) the guilty plea process should take place spontaneously following the formulation of charges seems somewhat superfluous.

[10] For research which evaluates the practice of rewarding guilty pleas with sentence discounts in the English courts, see Henham (2001).

[11] Bagaric and Amarasekara (2001) have recently argued that the doctrinal basis for the recognition of remorse as significant in sentencing is untenable. Certainly, remorse does not fit easily into philosophical categories. For example, just deserts theorists, such as von Hirsch (1993, p.72), argue that punishment must be assessed objectively on the basis of the degree of harm and offender blameworthiness, with remorse becoming relevant (if at all) at the post-sentencing stage. On the other hand, the notion of a

offender would be prepared to accept any just punishment and, therefore, should plead guilty without expectation of any sentencing concession. Remorse may also be seen as a rationalisation used by sentencers to conceal the true nature of the transaction being undertaken, i.e. bargaining away, or buying-off the defendant's due process[12] rights in return for the economy of a low trial rate, and/or absolving victims and witnesses from the ordeal of oral testimony.

4. There are important considerations regarding the extent to which victims should participate in the decision to accept a guilty plea in return for a sentence discount. Victims (actual and potential) clearly have an interest in seeing a true offender convicted, and many victims may be prepared to face the ordeal of a court appearance rather than seeing the offender receive a significant sentence reduction in return for a guilty plea (Fenwick, 1997; Henham, 1999a).

Existing ICTY and ICTR Practice

These considerations drawn largely from the common law adversarial tradition provide pertinent contexts for assessing the approach taken to these issues by the *ad hoc* tribunals. More specifically, as predictors of international procedural justice, they focus attention on significant issues against which to evaluate the relevance of existing fair trial and access to justice paradigms. As evidence of internationalisation, they also point to the potentially subversive influence of processual concerns as determinants of judicial practice in any international arena where the politics of retribution are allowed to flourish at the expense of ideology and principle.

A considered evaluation of the guilty plea as a basis for conviction and its significance as a mitigating factor in sentencing is evident from the ICTY's judgement in *Todorovic.*[13] After pointing out that Todorovic was only the third accused before the ICTY to have been convicted on the basis of a guilty plea, the Trial Chamber examined previous case-law, including decisions of the ICTR,[14] where guilty pleas had been considered as factors in mitigation of sentence. In particular, the Trial Chamber in *Todorovic* placed great emphasis on the following passage from the *Erdemovic*[15] sentencing judgement:

> An admission of guilt demonstrates honesty and it is important for the International Tribunal to encourage people to come forth, whether already indicted or as unknown perpetrators. Furthermore, this voluntary admission of guilt which has saved the International Tribunal the time and effort of a lengthy investigation and trial is to be commended.

---

sentencing or confession reward corresponds closely with utilitarian considerations designed to prevent future crime by adopting a humane approach to the offender. Remorse may even be seen as punishment in itself and, therefore, justifying mitigation of sentence on the basis that the net cost in suffering would equal that of the non-repentant offender serving a longer sentence; McCoy and Henham (2004).

[12] Other supporting normative paradigms might reflect constitutional or human rights concerns.

[13] *Prosecutor v Todorovic* (Case No. IT-95-9/1), Sentencing Judgement, 31 July 2001.

[14] In particular, *Prosecutor v Kambanda* (Case No. ICTR-97-23), Sentencing Judgement, 4 September 1998; *Prosecutor v Serushago* (Case No. ICTR-98-39), Judgement and Sentence, 5 February 1999.

[15] *Prosecutor v Erdemovic* (Case No. IT-96-22), Sentencing Judgement, 5 March 1998, para. 16 ii.

Again, quoting at length from *Erdemovic*, the Trial Chamber in *Todorovic* went out of its way to express its agreement with remarks made *obiter* in *Erdemovic*[16] by Judge Cassese in which he recognised the significant contribution made by the guilty plea to the work of the ICTY. Such is their import that they are reproduced here at length:

> It is apparent from the whole spirit of the Statute and the Rules that, by providing for a guilty plea, the draftsmen intended to enable the accused (as well as the Prosecutor) to avoid a possible lengthy trial with all the attendant difficulties. These difficulties – it bears stressing – are all the more notable in international proceedings. Here, it often proves extremely arduous and time consuming to collect evidence. In addition, it is imperative for the relevant officials of an international court to fulfil the essential but laborious task of protecting victims and witnesses. Furthermore, international criminal proceedings are expensive, on account of the need to provide a host of facilities to the various parties concerned (simultaneous interpretation in various languages; transportation of victims and witnesses from far-away countries; provision of various forms of assistance to them during the trial etc.). Thus, by pleading guilty, the accused undoubtedly contributes to public advantage.[17]

The *Todorovic* Trial Chamber[18] also indicated that the timing of the guilty plea was crucial in securing the economic, managerial and bureaucratic advantages to be derived, whilst continually re-enforcing and equating with this the notion that the guilty plea is intrinsically concerned with the pursuit of 'truth'. Naturally, there should be some scepticism surrounding the claim that unequivocal and genuine pleas of guilty are consistent with crime control considerations and justifications. Certainly, the experience of common law adversarial procedure has been that the process by which courts have come to endorse and normalise the trial penalty has been a contingent response to the ascendance of crime control ideology and managerial approaches to justice (Feeley and Simon, 1992). The threat to due process principles inherent in this insidious process has been largely ignored by some commentators, who appear to condone its crime control rationale (Schabas, 1997, p.18). Accordingly, it is arguable that the repeated affirmations of the primacy of the presumption of innocence, equality between the parties and the protection against self-incrimination to be found in the ICC Statute and Rules may amount to nothing more than rhetoric of dubious validity if the Court were to adopt the justifications espoused in the judgements of the *ad hoc* tribunals.

It is also significant that 'remorse' was dealt with as a separate mitigating factor in *Todorovic*, unconnected with rationales which might justify the guilty plea discount.[19] Yet this reveals some confusion in the approach of the ICTY, and the need

---

[16] *Prosecutor v Erdemovic* (Case No. IT-96-22), Appeals Judgement, 7 October 1997, para. 8.

[17] The *Todorovic* Trial Chamber went on to add the important factor that 'by pleading guilty, an accused relieves victims and witnesses of the necessity of giving evidence with the attendant stress this may incur'. *Supra*, note 13, para. 80.

[18] *Supra*, note 13, para. 81.

[19] *Todorovic*, *supra*, note 13, paras 89–92, and 114. The Trial Chamber accepted the defendant's remorse as genuine, and appeared particularly impressed by his expressed desire to 'channel his remorse into positive action to reconciliation in Bosnia and Herzegovina', although this was expressed more by way of sentiment than intended action on the part of the defendant (paras 90 and 91).

for further debate regarding the purported relationship between the guilty plea discount and remorse, since it is clear from *Jelisic*[20] that the ICTY acknowledged some connection between remorse and the accused's guilty plea by suggesting that its relative weight as a mitigating factor was attributable to the fact that the accused had failed to demonstrate any remorse for his crimes.[21] Such lack of clarity is compounded by Schabas (1997, p.18), when he asserts that a guilty plea is 'a sign of remorse that is germane to sentencing'. Nevertheless, the notion that remorse should be considered separately from the guilty plea as mitigation is consistent with aspects of both inquisitorial and adversarial criminal procedure, since it is often absent from the former, and of little relevance to the latter (Henham, 1999a).

McCoy makes the following comments concerning the complex relationship between remorse and guilty plea discounts which should also be borne in mind in the present context:

- It is undeniable that some offenders do indeed accept responsibility for their crimes, and many actually feel deep remorse. But the inherent subjectivity in knowing whether this is truly so, and how much if any credit an offender should receive for being remorseful, are thorny questions not answered by the knowledge that remorse is sometimes real.

- The argument about remorse has several facets. The American federal system explicitly states that defendants who plead guilty *may* receive credit for 'acceptance of responsibility', but not necessarily. Does a defendant accept responsibility because he is remorseful or because he accepts the fact that the prosecutor can prove he committed the crime? 'Acceptance' is not necessarily the product of remorse.

- Another facet is an assumed link between remorse and rehabilitation. It is said that a remorseful offender has taken the first step towards reform and rehabilitation, and in a sense has thus already served some portion of sentence and should receive a lesser term. However, remorse does not necessarily lead to rehabilitation. In short, the remorse rationale is less satisfying than thoughtful judges, upon reflection, might be willing to acknowledge (McCoy and Henham, 2004).

As Schabas (1997, p.18) acknowledges, the practice of discounting sentences in return for guilty pleas is intimately connected with forms of 'plea bargaining' in many common law jurisdictions.[22] Here again, however, Schabas appears to condone

---

20 *Prosecutor v Jelisic* (Case No. IT-95-10), Judgement, 14 December 1999, para. 127.

21 Jelisic's appeal on the point that the Trial Chamber had failed to give him any credit for his guilty plea floundered because he did not demonstrate that the Trial Chamber had erred in exercising its discretion regarding how much weight to accord the guilty plea; *Prosecutor v Jelisic* (Case No. IT-95-10), Appeals Judgement, 5 July 2001, paras 119–123. Furthermore, the ICTY Trial Chamber in *Blaskic* refused to recognise any mitigating role for remorse where the accused had command responsibility for the crimes in question. Indeed, the Trial Chamber held that command responsibility should operate to 'systematically increase the sentence or at least lead the Trial Chamber to give less weight to the mitigating circumstances'; *Prosecutor v Blaskic* (Case No. IT-95-14), Judgement, 3 March 2000.

22 Technically, in common law jurisdictions a plea bargain occurs only where there is a change of plea from not guilty to guilty but no charge or fact bargain is involved. In such circumstances the 'bargain' relates to the defendant exchanging his right to trial and possible acquittal for the certainty of a lower sentence than he would otherwise have received upon conviction.

a view he asserts is generally held by judges that, even where plea bargains are not binding upon the court, such practices make a valuable contribution to 'the smooth operation of criminal justice'. He does, nevertheless, recognise the extreme pressures which may be placed on the accused to bargain in cases where the prosecution seeks life imprisonment.[23] Certainly, the most compelling arguments in favour of such bargains usually relate to crime control considerations involving prosecutorial certainty of conviction where evidence may be weak or non-existent in relation to the more substantive charges, or a saving of court time, expense and inconvenience in not having to prosecute a large number of charges.

Although there is no recognition or provision for such agreements in the Statutes and Rules of either the ICTY or the ICTR, they have come before both tribunals on a number of occasions, the first being the ICTY in the *Erdemovic*[24] case. The plea agreement made in *Erdemovic* was expressed to be for the purpose of clarifying the understanding of the parties as to the nature and consequences of the accused's guilty plea, and to assist in ensuring its validity (para. 18).[25] However, it is apparent that the agreement contained two significant elements:

1. A charge bargain, whereby the Prosecutor agreed not to proceed with an alternative count of a crime against humanity, provided the defendant pleaded guilty to the lesser charge of a violation of the laws and customs of war, the factual basis of which was agreed.
2. A sentence bargain, whereby, whilst acknowledging the Trial Chamber's unfettered discretion to determine the sentence, the Prosecutor agreed to recommend a sentence of seven years' imprisonment in recognition of the mitigating circumstances.

By contrast, the plea agreement recognised by the ICTR in *Kambanda*[26] appears[27] to record in a straightforward manner the unequivocal nature of the defendant's guilty plea, and his professed motivation for tendering it, although there is passing reference to whether it contained matters constituting 'substantial cooperation' on the part of the convicted person with the Prosecutor, such as to amount to mitigation within the meaning of Rule 101(B)(ii) of the ICTR's Rules. Furthermore, the plea agreement in *Todorovic*[28] was explicit in recording the fact that the defendant had undertaken to provide full cooperation with the Prosecutor 'in relation to information and evidence known to him regarding the events surrounding the armed conflict in the former Yugoslavia from 1990 to the present'. The plea agreement also went further than that accepted in *Erdemovic*, since the defendant acknowledged that by pleading guilty he voluntarily undertook to waive significant procedural rights.[29]

---

[23] As evidenced in some US states where bargains may effectively result in the substitution of life imprisonment in capital cases; *Alford v North Carolina* 400 U.S. 25 [1970].

[24] *Supra*, note 15, para. 19.

[25] *Supra*, note 15, para. 18.

[26] *Supra*, note 14.

[27] Since the full text is not reproduced in the Judgement and Sentence.

[28] *Supra*, note 13, para. 10.

[29] According to the Plea Agreement, para. 4 (cited in the Sentencing Judgement, *supra*, note 15, para. 10), these included the right to plead not guilty, the right to be presumed innocent until guilt has been

The virtues of cooperating with the Prosecutor were clearly recognised in *Krnojelac*,[30] it being acknowledged that this enabled the Trial Chamber 'to complete the trial in much less time than it would otherwise have taken. It is interesting that, in a footnote,[31] the ICTY suggested that such mitigation in sentence should not be taken as any endorsement of the reciprocal principle that non-cooperation might be taken as an aggravating factor; however, it is very difficult to see how such an outcome could be either detected or prevented. Similarly, in *Plavsic*,[32] where the accused pleaded guilty pursuant to a plea agreement[33] following negotiation on counts, the result was unequivocally endorsed by the Trial Chamber on the basis that it obviated the need for victims and witnesses to give evidence, and could save considerable time, effort and resources.[34]

However, the *Plavsic* case represents an important attempt on the part of the ICTY to elaborate more fully the rationale for establishing some connection between the guilty plea and reconciliation, and the difficulties of achieving this within the context of serious breaches of international humanitarian law having been committed by the accused. Arguments were put forward by the prosecution on the basis of *dicta* from the *Todorovic* and *Erdemovic* sentencing judgements supporting the notion that the guilty plea is intimately connected to reconciliation since it is important in establishing 'truth', and 'truth' is fundamental to reconciliation. The defence submission was based on its interpretation (and suggested applicability for the accused) of the specific grounds where ICTY jurisprudence had supported a sentence discount following a guilty plea; namely:

a) it demonstrates honesty;
b) it contributes to the fundamental mission of the International Tribunal to establish the truth in relation to crimes within its jurisdiction;
c) it provides a unique and unquestionable fact-finding tool that greatly contributes to peace-building and reconciliation among the affected communities: individual accountability leads to the return of the rule of law, reconciliation and the restoration of peace across the territory of the former Yugoslavia;
d) it contributes to public advantage and the work of the International Tribunal by saving considerable resources for investigation, counsel fees and trial costs; and
e) it may relieve some victim witnesses from the stress of giving evidence.[35]

Notwithstanding, the Trial Chamber chose to focus on two specific matters relating to the accused's guilty plea concerning expressions of remorse and steps towards reconciliation.[36] The Prosecution accepted that the accused's remorse was full and unconditional, expressing the hope that it would assist the reconciliation of her

---

established at a trial beyond a reasonable doubt, the right to a trial before the International Tribunal, the right to confront and cross-examine witnesses against the accused, the right to compel and subpoena witnesses to appear on the accused's behalf, the right to testify or to remain silent at trial and the right to appeal a finding of guilty or to appeal any pre-trial rulings.

30 *Prosecutor v Krnojelac* (Case No. IT-97-25), Judgement, 15 March 2002, para. 520.

31 *Ibid*, footnote 1536.

32 *Prosecutor v Plavsic* (Case No. IT-00-39&40/1), Sentencing Judgement, 27 February 2003.

33 Under Rule 62, ICTY Rules of Procedure and Evidence.

34 *Ibid*, para. 67.

35 Defence Sentencing Brief, para. 41.

36 *Supra*, note 32, para. 70 *et seq.*

people with their neighbours, and that it was noteworthy from someone who had formerly occupied a leadership position. The Trial Chamber accepted statements made by the accused to this effect at the sentencing hearing and earlier, considering the issue of remorse as intimately connected to the mitigating circumstances associated with the initial tendering of the guilty plea, coupled with the substantial saving in time and expense. Thus, the accused was, on this basis, entitled to a discount in the sentence which would otherwise have been appropriate, although no further details were specified.

This aspect of the Trial Chamber's reasoning does little to clarify the relative positioning of remorse and the guilty plea. The issue raised is whether remorse is integral to the guilty plea, or a separate mitigating factor which, although closely connected to the decision to plead guilty, is not crucial to its existence. Certainly, as a general principle, there is no empirical evidence to suggest that entering a guilty plea is necessarily a remorseful act on the part of the accused, or that the plea itself is explicit evidence of remorse.[37] The point is that, if remorse (or any other matter personal to the accused) is absent from the rationale for the guilty plea, there is no individual mitigation of sentence based on the plea *per se*; the mitigation is purely for bureaucratic, administrative crime control considerations. Although the balance is relative, it is nonetheless important where, as in *Plavsic*, there is a suggestion that the entering of the guilty was an open and free acknowledgement of remorse made as a positive gesture towards reconciliation. In this respect, the acceptance of responsibility for grave crimes was (as with Truth and Reconciliation Commissions) a necessary first step towards peace and reconciliation.

The Trial Chamber went much further than previously in considering the relationship between a guilty plea entered in such circumstances and its meaning and implications for reconciliation. It heard expert evidence,[38] assessing the significance of the plea for the prospects of reconciliation in the region; stressing particularly the fact that it came from a prominent political leader; that it was a crucial acknowledgement of the true criminal nature of the acts; that it sent out a powerful message regarding the legitimacy of the ICTY and its functions; that it was an acknowledgement of the personal suffering of victims; and was likely to provide a degree of closure for victims. The crucial point was the central role of victims in dispensing justice and the need for sufficient judicial and non-judicial processes to recognise their pain and suffering as a result of gross violations of human rights.

The implications of this reasoning were not worked through, yet remain crucial for understanding the rationality of international sentencing and in determining its future direction. The Trial Chamber in *Plavsic* accepted that:

> ... acknowledgement and full disclosure of serious crimes are very important when establishing the truth in relation to such crimes. This, together with acceptance of responsibility for the committed wrongs, will promote reconciliation.[39]

---

[37] The author's own research on the operation of sentence discounts in the English Crown Court found that the significance of the variables normally associated with the guilty plea discount (particularly remorse) was far outweighed by other factors (Henham 2001, p.24).

[38] Dr. Alex Boraine, Former Deputy Chairperson of the South African Truth and Reconciliation Commission.

[39] *Supra*, note 32, para. 81.

Consequently, it concluded that the accused's guilty plea and acknowledgement of responsibility should carry significant weight in mitigation as a 'positive impact on the reconciliatory process'. The Trial Chamber therefore accepted that the guilty plea and other expressions of remorse contributed towards establishing the 'truth' of what took place. However, it raises the important issue of whether such a procedural mechanism operating in the context of a (predominantly) adversarial trial paradigm is best placed to determine 'truth',[40] and indeed, raises questions about the context in which this particular version of 'truth' is being produced, and for whom. This observation highlights the paradox for sentencing in international criminal trials; how to produce sentencing outcomes which can engage with victims and victim communities whilst concurrently satisfying retributive demands for punishment. It might be argued that it is impossible to envisage an international trial paradigm that could reconcile the aspirations of both positions, or that this can only be achieved through some accommodation with non-judicial means. Alternatively, as I argue, a complete reconceptualisation of the trial paradigm is necessary to facilitate engagement with restorative themes.

These difficulties were illustrated by the outcome in *Plavsic* itself. Despite acknowledging that it would give significant weight to the accused's plea of guilty, especially her expressions of remorse and their positive impact on reconciliation, the Trial Chamber was eventually swayed by the heinous nature of what had taken place and its effects. The prosecution was criticised for giving insufficient weight to (*inter alia*) the accused's guilty plea and her post-conflict conduct, yet there was a distinct lack of clarity in the Trial Chamber's determination of exactly what the effect of the mitigation (described as 'very significant') should be on the sentence. Such an outcome tends to support Zappala's (2003, p.89) suggestion, based on the Appeal Chamber's unwillingness to entertain a sentence discount in *Kambanda*, that it may not be appropriate to allow plea bargaining and plea agreements for crimes of extreme gravity.[41] It is clear that the parameters and the balance between crime seriousness and expediency have yet to be drawn, but the apparent absence of any willingness on the part of the international tribunals to preclude such practices, or lay down guidelines for sentencing practice, indicate their increasing acceptance as institutionalised procedural mechanisms designed to save time and resources at the expense of due process rights.

Further justifications for the increased and continued use of plea agreements by the ICTY were provided more recently in the related cases of *Obrenovic*[42] and *Momir Nikolic*.[43] The latter contains a principled discussion of the issues wherein the Trial

---

40 Zappala (2003, p.89) makes the important point that the determination of 'truth' where a guilty plea is entered is neither judicial nor pedagogical, and therefore appears to contradict the mission of international criminal courts to take account of victims' interests. However, it may be argued, for example, that Article 65, para. 4 of the ICC Statute (*supra*) counters this effect.

41 Zappala's reasons for supporting the practice are not totally convincing. He appears to advocate the pragmatic use of guilty plea discounts and plea agreements, on the basis of their advantages to the Prosecutor in shortening investigations, and that it may be in the public interest to shorten the trials of minor participants on the basis of cost.

42 *Prosecutor v Obrenovic* (Case No. IT-02-60/2-S), Sentencing Judgement, 10 December 2003.

43 *Prosecutor v Momir Nikolic* (Case No. IT-02-60/1-S), Sentencing Judgement, 2 December 2003.

Chamber addresses many of the arguments for and against the use of plea agreements for serious violations of international humanitarian law.[44] Passing reference is made to the varying reasons for their widespread adoption in common law jurisdictions and the importance of juridical context and culture in determining the emphasis that might be given to specific justifications, such as the level of consideration accorded to victims, the public interest and the administration of justice. However, the rationalisation offered for the explicit institutionalisation of plea agreements in the ICTY remains unconvincing, and indeed illustrates the paradoxical nature of the ideological justification for international penalty.

The Trial Chamber in *Momir Nikolic* was at pains to stress the dual conception of trial ideology for the ICTY; that of putting an end to impunity for those who perpetrate gross breaches of international humanitarian law, on the one hand, and contributing to peace and reconciliation, on the other.[45] It used this ideology to distinguish its mandate from national criminal justice systems by arguing that the principled use of plea agreements actually made a constructive contribution towards full accountability, and distanced itself (implicitly) from the remarks of Judge Cassese in *Erdemovic*,[46] supporting their use for (*inter alia*) reasons of bureaucratic and administrative expediency. In so doing, the Trial Chamber again stressed the argument that guilty pleas can often make a significant contribution to peace and reconciliation,[47] particularly when coupled with sincere expressions of remorse. Procedural safeguards would ensure that the interests of 'justice' were not compromised.

Nevertheless, I would argue that there is an inherent philosophical contradiction in the argument advanced in support of the restorative capability of plea agreements in international criminal trials. Firstly, the ICTY cannot effectively divorce itself from the administrative efficiency argument. Essentially, what the Trial Chamber in *Momir Nikolic* tries to argue is that the trial ideology of the ICTY forces a reconceptualisation of plea agreements. We are asked to suspend belief in those rationales and implications that do not sustain the ICTY's professed search for 'truth' (such as control of process, suppression of evidence, exclusion from participation, denial of process, erosion of rights, absence of public accountability) in return for a vision of plea agreements as procedural mechanisms that nurture the ideological thrust of international penality towards the constructive ideals of reconciliation and reconstruction. Without denying that this may be one effect, such a conception of plea agreements conveniently ignores the substantive reasons for their increased use in common law jurisdictions in recent years, and tries to impose a rationale for their continuation and expansion which attempts to redefine the underlying rationale for the existence of plea agreements as procedural devices.

The ICTY Trial Chamber in *Dragan Nikolic*[48] referred to its decision in *Momir Nikolic* for detailed discussion on the appropriateness of plea agreements in cases

---

[44] *Ibid*, para. 43 *et seq.*

[45] *Ibid*, paras 58 to 62.

[46] *Supra*, note 15.

[47] *Supra*, note 43, para. 72. This was a significant finding in the judgement itself; para. 145.

[48] *Prosecutor v Dragan Nikolic* (Case No. IT-94-2-S), Sentencing Judgement, 18 December 2003, paras 57–73. See also comments by Meron (2004, p.524).

involving serious violations of international humanitarian law. The former case is important in a number of respects, not least for its reaffirmation of the principled use of plea agreements and, additionally, for its admission and consideration of comparative research evidence on sentence law and practice commissioned from the Max Planck Institute for Foreign and International Criminal Law in Freiburg, Germany (Seiber, 2003).[49]

The Introduction to the Trial Chamber's sentencing remarks suggest that, in pleading guilty and admitting the factual details of his plea agreement, the defendant helped further a process of reconciliation;

> He has guided the international community closer to the truth in an area not yet subject of any judgement rendered by this Tribunal, truth being one prerequisite for peace [para. 3].

The Trial Chamber also confirmed[50] that additional evidence emanating from the sentencing hearing, describing in greater detail the defendant's conduct and its impact on surviving victims and their relatives, would be taken into account in the discussion of aggravating and mitigating factors as relevant, but could not be considered as constituting new crimes not alleged in the indictment forming the basis for the plea agreement. Consequently, Dragan Nikolic was convicted on the basis of the Trial Chamber's acceptance that pleading guilty to certain cumulative counts in the indictment could justify entering a single conviction for persecutions, a crime against humanity, as agreed under the terms of his plea agreement.[51]

The Trial Chamber discussed the general significance of entering a guilty plea,[52] re-enforcing the previously expressed view that a guilty plea undoubtedly tends to further the process of reconciliation, preventing witnesses from having to give evidence or re-opening old wounds by having to relive their experiences. It also mentioned in a somewhat disingenuous fashion:

> As a side-effect, albeit not really a significant mitigating factor, it also saves the Tribunal's resources.

In its discussion of principles and purposes,[53] no real attempt is made to take the issue of rationality further than in previous cases. The Trial Chamber's analysis provides a very circumscribed and one-dimensional view of its penality, dominated by the perception that the objectives of punishment are somehow achievable through simple enforcement of the rule of law. This is most apparent in its discussion of deterrence:

> One of the main purposes of a sentence imposed by an international tribunal is to influence the legal awareness of the accused, the surviving victims, their relatives, the witnesses and the general public in order to reassure them that the legal system is implemented and enforced. Additionally, the process of sentencing is intended to convey the message that

49 *Ibid*, para. 22.

50 *Ibid*, para. 105.

51 *Ibid*, para. 119.

52 *Ibid*, paras 121–122.

53 *Ibid*, paras 127–140.

> globally accepted laws and rules have to be obeyed by everybody. 'All persons shall be equal before the courts and tribunals.' This fundamental rule fosters the internalisation of these laws and rules in the minds of legislators and the general public [para. 139].

The passage implicitly acknowledges the symbolic importance of denunciation as an aspect of deterrence, invoking the Durkheimian notion that the universally accepted morality of the tribunal's mission (and its underlying rationality) is sufficient to justify punishment in terms capable of identifying, reconciling and satisfying demands for global and local justice.

However, this assumption is flawed and raises some fundamental questions regarding the legitimacy of international criminal justice. For example, is it realistic to suggest that law (or more specifically punishment norms) effectively influence the internalisation of morals? Similarly, can universally accepted moral principles be transformed into normatively effective principles for action through sentencing? The answers to these questions are by no means clear. What does seem certain, however, is the need for legal and processual norms to be perceived as legitimate by those who are significantly affected by their operation. The fact that such norms exist to give effect to universally held moral principles may be sufficient for both to be regarded as legitimate in the eyes of the wider international community. However, it is important to distinguish the fact that, for victims and others affected by social conflict, legitimacy also depends on whether international punishment actually resonates with understandings of local penality.

Discussion by the Trial Chamber of the plea agreement and the guilty plea's effects in *Dragan Nikolic*[54] includes the interesting observation by the Defence[55] that there was no plea bargain because the defendant did not seek to plead to anything less than the entire indictment or contest his guilt. Speaking of the Defence, the Trial Chamber states:

> It argues that although the indictment was reduced from 88 counts to four, 'the gravity of the offences is equally contained within those four counts as it was within the original 88'.

Of course, the point is that the agreement is in itself a bargain. More importantly, can we really believe that the magnitude of Dragan Nikolic's crimes were reflected in the specimen counts?

Although the expert and country reports prepared by the Max Planck Institute and ICTY/ICTR jurisprudence on the guilty plea issue were considered,[56] no attempt was made to draw upon any contextual reasons for areas of synthesis and difference, nor was the domestic context of the Former Yugoslavia explored. Neither was any attempt made to evaluate this material in terms of the relationship between local and global justice. For example, there is no discussion of the interesting findings[57] which suggest that in relation to the model cases used for the country reports there was a tendency for the guilty plea to have a lesser effect where the scenarios were seen as international crimes committed as acts of war rather than ordinary (general) crimes. It

[54] *Ibid*, paras 218–237.

[55] *Ibid*, para. 224.

[56] *Ibid*, paras 227–230 and para. 231.

[57] Seiber (2003), Section 4.1.2.4, Expert Report.

was also interesting that the highest discounts were given for crimes of torture. One important factor was the ability of judges for general offences to see aggravating or mitigating factors in concrete terms as circumscribed by criteria included in the model code/established principles, whereas, for the war scenarios the criteria were uncertain.[58] The Max Planck report speculates that this resulted in judges falling back on those criteria where there was certainty (e.g. criteria explicitly approved, or the fact of the plea itself). Unwillingness to include the latter may again have reduced the significance of the guilty plea in war cases. According to the report,[59] offender-related factors dominated decision-making followed by act-related factors, with victim factors being regarded as the least important.

The Trial Chamber's conclusion notes[60] how the possibility of considering the mitigating effect of a guilty plea in national systems is usually limited to less serious crimes. Its attempt to reconcile differences in the application of the guilty plea in national jurisdictions is limited to the observation that the reasons for mitigating a punishment on the basis of a guilty plea for international crimes is more pragmatic:

> ... the mitigating effect of a guilty plea in this Tribunal is much broader, including the fact that the accused contributes to establishing the truth about the conflict in the Former Yugoslavia and contributes to reconciliation in the affected communities.

This begs the question of establishing how proceedings that are circumvented through the use of a plea agreement (even one agreed late on as here) can deconstruct events sufficiently to provide truths which make positive contributions to peacemaking beyond those resulting from the professed acceptance of responsibility, contrition, shame, etc., of the offender. Relying heavily on the expert testimony of Dr Nancy Grosselfinger, the Trial Chamber accepted the defendant's guilty plea as an expression of his honesty and readiness to take responsibility.[61] Coupled with his expressions of remorse and his cooperation with the Prosecution this contributed towards reconciliation in the Vlasenica municipality. Remorse was therefore accepted as one mitigating factor,[62] and it seems that the Trial Chamber were prepared to accept the Defence's suggestion that Dragan Nikolic expressed remorse:

> ... not only 'in the narrow sense' by admitting his personal guilt, but that he attempts to give effect to the process of co-operative reconciliation which is an essential prerequisite for the fuller remorse.

However, the most illuminating aspect of the judgement concerns reconciliation.[63] The case of *Dragan Nikolic* raises the issue of legitimacy in a specific and very significant way by linking its discussion of plea agreements with the potential for reconciliation. The Trial Chamber explicitly accepted that acceptance of responsibility by admitting guilt is an important factor in the process of

---

[58] *Ibid*, para 4.1.2.6.

[59] *Ibid*, para. 4.1.3.

[60] *Supra*, note 48, para. 232.

[61] *Ibid*, para. 237.

[62] *Ibid*, para. 242.

[63] *Ibid*, paras 243–252.

reconciliation, particularly the notion that it could lead to a more widespread acceptance of responsibility among others who had been involved in breaching the norms of international criminal law during social conflicts. Nevertheless, while otherwise unequivocally endorsing the important role of plea agreements in truth finding,[64] the Trial Chamber also cautioned:

> Neither the public, nor the judges themselves come closer to know the truth beyond what is accepted in the plea agreement. This might create an unfortunate gap in the public and historical record of the concrete case, although, when coupled with an accused's substantial co-operation with the prosecution, an agreement grants more insights into previously undiscovered areas. However, while treating plea agreements with appropriate caution, it should be recalled that this Tribunal is not the final arbiter of historical facts. That is for historians. For the judiciary focusing on core issues of a criminal case before this International Tribunal, it is important that justice be done and be seen to be done (para. 122).

A significant issue raised by these comments, however, is whether justice 'as seen to be done' in the terms described actually *is* justice. This inevitably returns us to the issue of legitimacy, and the question of whose 'truth' is being constructed through trial process, and for whose consumption. Is it in fact a truth that can be regarded as consistent with global and/or local demands for justice?

Such conjecture is re-enforced by the importance attached to the fact of the defendant's substantial cooperation with the Prosecution.[65] Additional information (recorded interviews) was requested from the Prosecution by the Trial Chamber to establish the extent to which the cooperation provided by Dragan Nikolic could be described as substantial. There appeared to be an implied threat that his early release prospects would be directly affected by his continued cooperation with the ICTY and domestic war crimes prosecutors (when established). The importance attached to facilitating the ICTY's fact-finding mission is important in creating a perception that the guilty plea mechanism is essentially a prosecutorial tool for securing the maximum number of convictions in return for minimum resource input.

These attempts to redefine or reposition plea agreements compound the obfuscation already apparent in the model for justice delivery underwritten by the international criminal institutions as personified by the trial and the ideology of trial justice. As has been argued, the moral legitimacy of the international trial form and its ideological justification, although symbolised by a universal appeal to humanitarian principles, is, nevertheless, grounded in the penality of retributivism and deterrence. Particularising ownership of the universal requires a paradigm shift in trial ideology through the recognition that legitimacy must have concrete (i.e. contextual) significance, and, that it is largely communitarian in significance. Consequently, procedural norms are context-specific in that their legitimacy can only be assessed within the ideological framework in which they operate. When the ICTY (or any other trial institution) asserts that plea or other processual negotiation can contribute to the processes of peace and reconciliation,[66] it does so within a particular

64 *Ibid*, para. 248.

65 *Ibid*, paras 253–260.

66 An excellent example is provided by *Obrenovic*, *supra*, note 42. See especially the comments of Emir Suljagic, a Bosnian Serb, cited at para. 112.

ideological context. This is not to deny the reality of what is asserted; rather, it simply recognises that normative behaviour is controlled and legitimised by ideology and policy.[67]

Notwithstanding, the fact that guilty pleas are capable of making a contribution towards restoring peace and promoting reconciliation forces us to examine the existing international trial paradigm more critically, precisely because it illustrates a paradox in the ideology and practice of plea bargaining within the predominantly retributive context of international penality. We have seen how the foundation instruments of the *ad hoc* tribunals and the ICC, coupled with the wide discretionary powers given to international judges in sentencing matters, allow international sentencers (albeit largely eclectically) to promote utilitarian as well as retributive penal justifications for punishment. A repositioned trial ideology would focus on maximising the instrumental capacity of discretionary decision-making for accommodating retributive and reductivist considerations at important decision sites in the trial (such as sentence). Such an ideology recognises that the legitimacy of international penality depends on the integration of victims and victim communities, and that this should be ideological and normative. If judicial discretionary power were enabled to pursue legitimate restorative outcomes beyond those that follow from the determination of guilt or innocence, plea agreements and other forms of processual negotiation would become marginalized as unnecessary.

Finally, a more specific criticism illustrating the distorting effect of plea agreements and their capacity for downgrading the 'truth' in terms of how the trial marks the seriousness of what has taken place through punishment concerns the factual basis underlying the conduct charged. This difficulty was particularly evident in *Momir Nikolic* where the defendant was originally charged with numerous crimes, including genocide. Following an amended plea agreement the defendant eventually pleaded guilty to the lesser charge of persecutions (a crime against humanity), and all remaining counts on the indictment against him were dropped. In considering Rule 62 *bis* of the ICTY's Rules of Evidence and Procedure,[68] the Trial Chamber observed that it was satisfied that the factual basis upon which the charge of persecutions was based reflected the totality of the defendant's criminal conduct.[69] Whilst the

---

[67] A specific example of how such control might be exercised is through the principle which asserts that no accused should be penalised for exercising the right to go to trial and have the prosecution prove its case. As suggested earlier, experience from common law jurisdictions confirms that trial ideology controls the operation of this principle to the disadvantage of those opting for full trial through the so-called 'trial penalty'; see, McCoy and Henham, *supra*, note 8.

[68] Rule 62 *bis*: If an accused pleads guilty in accordance with Rule 62 (vi), or requests to change his or her plea to guilty and the Trial Chamber is satisfied that:

(i) the guilty plea has been made voluntarily;
(ii) the guilty plea is informed;
(iii) the guilty plea is not equivocal; and
(iv) there is a sufficient factual basis for the crime and the accused's participation in it, either on the basis of independent indicia or on lack of any material disagreement between the parties about the facts of the case,

the Trial Chamber may enter a finding of guilt and instruct the Registrar to set a date for the sentencing hearing.

[69] *Supra*, note 43, para. 51.

sufficiency of the factual basis for the crime eventually charged, and the accused's participation in it, is not in doubt, the application of this rule ignores the fundamental capacity of plea and other forms of negotiation for manipulating evidential 'truth' to suit processual goals. Not only does the plea deny the possibility of testing the evidence in open court, the acceptance of a charge as reflecting the totality of the accused's criminal conduct effectively denies the court the opportunity to give full expression to the whole of that criminality through the imposition of a penal sanction which adequately reflects the seriousness of the crime(s) and the culpability of the offender. In effect, the effectiveness of international penality in terms of its undoubted capacity for symbolic public expression and denunciation of past breaches of international criminal law is seriously compromised if the magnitude of the punishment is not seen to be proportionate to the totality of the defendant's criminal conduct.

The Problem of Accountability

A vitally important legal issue is whether breaches of human rights norms associated with the operation of the guilty plea and plea agreements in international sentencing might provide grounds for appeal or review. The position is not encouraging. Although appeals relating to the operation of guilty pleas were considered by the ICTR in *Kambanda* and the ICTY in *Erdemovic*, there are no specific provisions contained in the foundation instruments of any international criminal trial institution which deal with the possibility of what is to happen when the sentence it imposes infringes human rights norms which fall outside the ambit of its rules as presently interpreted. As Zappala (2003, p.171) points out, some protection is provided under Article 14, paragraph 5 of the ICCPR, which provides that everyone convicted of a crime shall have the right of review of his or her conviction and sentence by a higher tribunal.[70] Notwithstanding, disagreement persists on narrow doctrinal issues, such as whether the right to appeal is limited to matters of law or mixed law and fact.

Although Zappala (2003, p.193) concludes that the ICC provisions dealing with rights of appeal and revision are 'far more balanced and in conformity with human rights standards than the provisions governing these proceedings before *ad hoc* tribunals', there seems to be no alternative avenue available where the operation of an institution's procedural norms breaches the human rights of the defendant.[71] One possibility, suggested by Cockayne (2001, p.20), might be for recourse to the UN Human Rights Committee. Under Article 2 of the ICCPR, an individual could (in theory at least) bring a claim against all those State Parties to the ICC Statute who are also party to the ICCPR and its First Additional Protocol on the basis that the following provisions of Article 14(1) of the ICCPR are relevant to the operation of plea agreements and sentence discounts in international sentencing:[72]

---

[70] A similar right is provided in regional instruments such as the ECHR by Article 2, Optional Protocol 7.

[71] Zappala (2003, p.194) suggests an important interpretative role for ICC provisions where *ad hoc* Tribunal provisions are silent or ambiguous on certain issues, including the interpretation of provisions against international human rights law standards.

[72] Ashworth (1998, p.291) identifies the right to a 'fair and public' hearing (Article 6(1)) and the right to be treated fairly and without discrimination (Article 14, ECHR) as particularly relevant to the operation of the guilty plea discount in England and Wales. Note, however, that the procedure whereby an individual

> All persons shall be equal before the courts and tribunals. In the determination of any criminal charge against him ... everyone shall be entitled to a fair and public hearing by a competent, independent and impartial tribunal established by law.

Although the Committee might issue a non-binding recommendation should a claim prove successful, it is unclear what its effect might be since the State Parties to the ICCPR do not, except through the Assembly of State Parties, have the capacity to revise sentences, and the ICC, although having international legal personality, is not a party to the ICCPR. Alternatively, an appeal may be possible on the basis that a sentence was in violation of Article 21(3) of the ICC Statute:

> The application and interpretation of law pursuant to [Article 21 Applicable law] must be consistent with internationally recognised human rights, and be without any adverse distinction founded on grounds such as gender ... age, race, colour, language, religion or belief, political or other opinion, national, ethnic or social origin, wealth, birth or other status.[73]

Notwithstanding, the dangers posed to human rights (particularly defendants' rights) by supranational organisations such as the ICC are considerable, driven as they are by a punitive dynamic and developing outside any institutionalised mechanisms of accountability. Further, if human rights norms at the local and regional level are more likely to reflect their development at the international level as the internationalisation of trial process increases, the question of governance and accountability becomes more acute. For example, consider the nature of the relationship between international mechanisms which will act as the authoritative source of these norms (such as the ICC), and the extent of control which State and non-State Parties will have over the development of procedural norms in the ICC (Cockayne, 2001). An important distinction between the ICC and the *ad hoc* tribunals in this context is the fact that the ICC operates within a framework of complementarity rather than jurisdictional primacy. Thus, an ICC process which allowed local procedural norms to factor into international trials might not only have increased chances of legitimacy in the affected communities, but could also play a highly significant role in developing comparative criminal procedural jurisprudence (Cockayne 2001, p.27).

---

may plead guilty without trial or examination of the evidence has been held not to be in breach of Article 6 by the Commission irrespective of the availability of the procedure under national jurisdictions; *X v United Kingdom* (1972) 40 CD 64, 67. In *Deweer v Belgium* (1979-80) 2 EHRR 439, the Court even went so far as to hold that the payment of a penalty in exchange for the right to a hearing is not necessarily inconsistent with Article 6 provided there was no duress. The extent to which the willingness of the prosecution to accept a plea of guilty to a significantly less serious charge exerts undue pressure on the accused remains a moot point. See further Emmerson and Ashworth (2001, p.506).

[73] Regarding the principle of equal treatment generally see Article 26 ICCPR. By way of comparison, Article 14 ECHR provides: 'The enjoyment of the rights and freedoms set forth in this Convention shall be secured without discrimination on any ground such as sex, race, colour, language, religion, political or other opinion, national or social origin, association with a national minority, property, birth or other status.' As Emmerson and Ashworth (2001, p.110) point out, the anti-discrimination provision in the ECHR may only be invoked in conjunction with a substantial convention right.

Assessing the Implications

Although Jung (1997, p.116) has drawn attention to the changing contexts of plea bargaining as evidence of 'consensus' or 'democratisation', there is no doubt that its continued existence in both common law and civil law jurisdictions threatens to disturb the balance between state, individual and society implicit in social contract theory, and exemplified in notions of fair trial (Tulkens, 2002). As such, beyond the potential for undermining process already described, plea bargains in the international context may similarly be seen as unconstitutional in implicitly contravening the principles of legality established by relevant Statutes and Rules of Procedure. Despite reserving unfettered discretion in sentence decision-making to the tribunals, recent practice in the *ad hoc* tribunals has established the paradox of tacit acceptance of plea agreements for various reasons largely associated with crime control considerations. Whilst eschewing judicial complicity such practices are, nevertheless, hostages to the system interests of the prosecution and dependant on the bargaining competence of the defence. They also exist to marginalize the judiciary in a context where the theatre of the trial is paramount. On this point, the international trial becomes so much more relatively significant as the theatre for justice than trials may be in other jurisdictions. Justice, therefore, becomes negotiated and not imposed.

More generally, plea bargains in the international arena symbolise a repressive and coercive function of international tribunals. Pressures to convict and utilise effectively scarce resources by rewarding substantial cooperation and complicity by defendants with sentence discounts are re-legitimised as compatible with legal rationality in the rhetoric of international tribunal discourse.

As previously indicated, there exists a distinct lack of harmony between victim interests and the crime control interest of encouraging and rewarding guilty pleas, suggesting the need for entrenched rights of consultation and participation by victims in plea agreements and sentence discount decisions before the ICC. At present, Article 65.4.(a) of the ICC Statute contains a general injunction to the Trial Chamber in connection with proceedings where an admission of guilt has been made, whereby it may request the Prosecutor to present additional evidence (including witness testimony) if it 'is of the opinion that a more complete presentation of the facts of the case is required *in the interests of justice*, in particular in the interests of victims' [emphasis added]. Schabas (2001a, p.149) suggests that this provision appears aimed at situations where some kind of plea bargain is made between the Prosecutor and the defence such that the rights and interests of victims may not otherwise be fully taken into account.[74] Another general injunction occurs in Article 68.3, which is designed to ensure that the Court permits the 'views and concerns' of victims to be presented and considered at any stage in the proceedings where the 'personal interests of the victims' are affected, provided these are not inconsistent with notions of fair trial.

---

[74] More generally, as Findlay (2002) suggests, access to justice at the international level fails to reflect that accorded to victims in several common and civil law jurisdictions, where direct access is given to the sentencing process. Certainly, in the case of the ICC it does not extend much beyond protection for victim witnesses and victim compensation; see ICC Statute, Articles 43(6), 68(2), (3) and (4), 75, 79.

No doubt the sentiments embodied in these Articles are laudable, but one remains sceptical regarding the extent to which crime control considerations will override any perceived need to obtain additional evidence in the interests of justice for victims. After all, as we have seen, the primary rationale of crime control is clearly evident in the sentencing judgements of the *ad hoc* tribunals, where plea bargaining has taken place. Therefore, it cannot be stated with any degree of conviction that victims' rights in the ICC are likely to be a paramount consideration. A more realistic assessment suggests that the *interests of justice* are more likely to be equated with notions of retributive justice than victims' rights and reparation. As Zedner (1994, p.239) remarks, whilst reparative goals of criminal justice possess no intrinsic penal character, thus rendering them apparently incompatible with retributive considerations, a broader conception of reparative justice recognises the communitarian aspects of victims' rights.[75] The point is well made by Fenwick (1997, p.327), who reminds us that a victim who does not testify at the trial has no interest in the notional 'balancing' which occurs where a lenient sentence given in return for a guilty plea is justified on the basis that victims may be spared the ordeal of giving evidence.[76] Further, from the victim's point of view, sentence discounts resulting from guilty pleas *and* plea bargains are particularly unsatisfactory, since both sentence and offence fail to reflect the degree of harm actually suffered by the victim (Fenwick 1997, p.327). The factors are especially pertinent for the legitimacy of international sentencing in victim communities. Aside from the personal impact,[77] wider considerations should include the need for the 'community'[78] to pursue the consequentialist objectives of rehabilitation, reparation and reconciliation where socially harmful actions have been perpetrated on a catastrophic scale.

Past support for plea discounts and the ideology of crime control in common law jurisdictions, with its emphasis on financial expediency, speed and finality of conviction, has been on the basis that it is broadly in the interests of victims because it spares victims the ordeal of giving evidence whilst recognising that some due process rights may be infringed. Nevertheless, Fenwick's (1997, p.330) conclusion is surely apposite; that the perceptions of victims towards these processes is extremely complex and that there is a substantive case for establishing rights of consultation and participation in these decisions, particularly for victims of serious offences.

Whilst accepting the overwhelming case for safeguarding victims' rights and ensuring their legitimate participation in trial proceedings, alternative fair trial paradigms are not encouraging in this respect. For example, neither the 1985 Council of Europe recommendation on 'The Position of the Victim in the Framework of Criminal Law and Procedure', nor the 2000 EU Council's 'Draft Framework Decision on the Standing of Victims in Criminal Procedure', recommended any specific role for victims in the sentencing process, although, as Emmerson and

75 This theme is developed further in the conclusion.

76 More generally, as Tochilovsky (1998, p.59) points out, there is a certain irony in the fact that many of the procedural rights made available to victims for trials conducted by the *ad hoc* tribunals are absent from the criminal procedures of those countries where the crimes charged were perpetrated.

77 Such as the removal of uncertainty of conviction. As Fenwick (1997, p.26) also points out, the distorting effect of charge bargaining and sentence discounts on an offender's record has significant repercussions for potential victims.

78 This expression is not used here in any definitive sense.

Ashworth (2001, p.557) explain, they constitute evidence of a positive commitment and flexibility towards the issue. Notwithstanding, in the English context there has been strong judicial objection to the notion that victims' representations should form part of the sentence decision-making process.[79] As far as Article 6 of the European Convention is concerned, whilst the European Commission accepts the fact that Article 6 applies to sentencing decisions, it does not recognise Article 6 protection where a defendant pleads guilty since there is no trial *per se*. However, a plea bargain involving a charge, fact or sentence bargain would presumably be covered by Article 6 in circumstances where a defendant later changed their mind. Again, recent English decisions appear to have fallen well short of sustaining an adequate balance between victims' rights and those of the defence in the case of plea bargains on the grounds of abuse of process at common law.[80]

More broadly, these arguments illustrate the apparent failure of existing rights paradigms to provide a principled basis for addressing the iniquitous prospect of negotiated justice in the ICC. If generalised notions of justice are to be developed which transcend process constraints and are tolerant of representative participation and communitarian objectives, then the wider role of the victim in the penality of international justice must be elaborated.

[79] See further Emmerson and Ashworth (2001, pp.559–560) for possible forms of representation from victims. It is interesting to note the limited form of participation advocated by the Practice Direction, 16th October 2001; on the role of victim personal statements in sentencing in England and Wales, see further Edwards (2001); Sanders, Hoyle, Morgan and Cape (2001).

[80] One of the worst examples is *Attorney General's Reference (No 44 of 2000)*; *sub-nom R v Peverett* [2000] TLR 739.

Chapter 5

Philosophical Issues in International Sentencing

Introduction

The purpose of this chapter is to provide a reasoned assessment of the relevance and applicability of conventional notions and justifications for punishment as they relate to institutionalised forms of international sentencing.[1] Recent analyses have revealed consistent obfuscation in the penal justifications advanced by sentencers in the ICTY and ICTR (Beresford, 2002; van Zyl Smit, 2002; Henham, 2003). In particular, I have argued that some ideological and theoretical accommodation and the rationalisation of process is necessary in order to forge meaningful concepts and practices of internationalisation in sentencing (Henham, 2003a). There is common agreement that current international sentencing praxis is characterised by tension at the levels of ideology, policy and structure. Failure to rationalise philosophical justifications for international sentencing, the politicisation of process and an absence of accountability limit not only the potential for the rational development of sentencing jurisprudence at the international level, but also constructive engagement with alternative sentencing justifications and paradigms.[2]

The analysis provided in this chapter sets out to describe and evaluate the significance of philosophical justifications for punishment through forms of internationalised sentencing by drawing upon the jurisprudence of the *ad hoc* tribunals, and the foundation instruments of the ICC. The discussion is conducted within an analytical framework which recognises that the phenomenon of punishment (global or local) must, as Garland (1990) acknowledges, be contextualised by engaging with the social meanings attributed to the complex of ideas, institutions, rules, practices, relationships and discourses which together constitute the penality of internationalised sentencing. The specific interrogation of the relationships between the modes and purposes for internationalised punishment and the complex set of interrelated processes and institutions which constitute international penality produces a reasoned basis for critiquing the existence and nature of overarching (or underlying) sentencing principles and practices.

---

[1] On the need to relate philosophical justifications for punishment to their practical context, see Duff and Garland (1994).

[2] For particularly instructive accounts of alternative paradigms in the context of the Rwandan genocide, see Alvarez (1999); Drumbl (2000); Drumbl (2002).

Further, the analysis does not simply critically reflect internationalised sentencing philosophy against accommodations and rationalisations of principle which are jurisdictionally focused, using localised sentencing philosophy as a referent for conclusions which suggest that there are some inadequacies with internationalised sentencing philosophy. The intention is to explore the underlying rationality of international forms of sentencing against its diverse contexts, both global and local, rather than any paradigmatic model. Such an approach recognises the possibility that the development of international sentencing is predicated on alternative (or new) paradigms wherein philosophy and principle are either not yet enunciated, or perhaps devalued as important legitimating ideology.

As discussed earlier, a key conceptual underpinning to the arguments proposed herein is in the notion of *context*. It has been emphasised that this concept is crucial to understanding how individuals interpret and transform principles and associated rules within legal institutions. In a wider sense, context also requires an appreciation of the forces of power and domination which shape the organisational and institutional imperatives that produce the social behaviour that is sentencing at the local and global level. It is, therefore, concerned with revealing interconnections of power and domination as they are developed in the interactive processes of the criminal trial. In short, context is concerned with how social, cultural, political and economic factors relate to institutional processes, relationship patterns and individual variation in the criminal trial.

The approach adopted in relating the discussion of philosophical justifications for international punishment to sentencing practice in the international institutions is one firmly grounded *in* context. In this I follow Tamanaha's (1997) exhortation to relate moral and normative subjectivity and its relative forms to existing states of affairs.[3] It is a position that serves to relate the transformation of the ideological to the normative by deconstructing the meanings which relevant participants attribute to *process*, thereby revealing how the nature of objectivity is understood as subjective experience (Henham and Findlay, 2002). I suggest that this approach is an essential prerequisite for any meaningful examination of the philosophical discourse of international punishment, since it provides for an understanding of penological justifications at different levels of social reality;[4] from a position which favours philosophical pragmatism through to a consideration of how these principles and precepts can provide guides to social action in the context of international

---

[3] By this I imply that the reliance on grounding in social context should prevent the abstraction of institutions and functions of punishment from their essential legal, moral and political supports. In this regard, context itself provides the domain for analysis and identifies and suggests explanations of social reality.

[4] In this context referring to establishing an understanding at different levels of conceptual abstraction. Thus, within our conceptualisation of international forms of sentencing, legal (jurisdictional/system); organisational (institutional/structural) and interactional (behavioural/structuration) factors demand such explanatory differentiation. In concrete terms, for example, we can argue that comparative contextual analysis recognises the possibility of viewing sentence decision-making from several contextual dimensions enabling different levels of analysis. This might entail modelling sentencing as a decision-making process within the international criminal trial, through to the examination of trial sites for decision-making which contribute to the formulation of sentencing decisions, down to the ethnography of sentence decision-making as a micro-activity. See Chapter 7 for further elaboration.

sentencing.[5] Here the potency of comparative contextual analysis allows us to reach beyond mere regressive comparison with the local contexts of sentencing philosophy and practice by providing the basis for understanding and evaluating the mechanisms which directly sustain the rationales for sentencing operating in international criminal trial processes.

It is a truism to suggest that the particular contexts of internationalised sentencing reflect particularly dominant cultural forms and modes of social control which have temporal and relative effects on punishment practices. Hence, contemporary notions of criminality, acceptable forms of punishment and concepts of justice determine important aspects of the penality of internationalised punishment that are mediated through the penal practices of the international criminal tribunals. However, Garland's (1990, p.253) point regarding the signifying nature of penality has special resonance in the notion that international forms of punishment should be reflective of generally understood cultural meanings of crime and punishment. This, in consequence, leads us to consider the *significance*[6] of the transformative capacity of law, and as Cotterrell (1998a) argues, to reflect on law's *moral* worth and its implications for penality in terms of its institutionalisation and the forms of punitive control exercised over citizens within the international context. It also recognises that the determination of power relationships within and between states may serve to marginalise the universality of human and minority rights in victim communities and de-contextualise punishment administered internationally.[7] Hence, internationalised forms of penality must be cognisant of relative contingency in the practical implementation of universally recognised human rights norms (Henham, 2001). These considerations are reflected in the chapter's examination of the fundamental rationales for international forms of punishment in the context of globalised notions of penality.

In summary, therefore, the two key aspects of the overall approach adopted in the following analysis are the contextual and moral emphases. By this is meant, firstly, an emphasis on the need to interpret and justify sentencing policy in relation to the specific contexts in which that policy arises and has to be applied, and in relation to which it is understood; and, secondly, an insistence that penal policy in sentencing must have moral resonance (not just efficiency) so that there needs to be far more clarity as to its moral meaning in specific contexts. Throughout it is argued that current approaches to international sentencing are confused and unclear in this respect and that the predominant retributive approaches are inadequate to meet this need for moral resonance.

The chapter is divided into three parts: the first examines the nature and significance of the philosophical justifications for punishment as reflected in the sentencing decisions of the international criminal tribunals and suggests reasons for challenging the legitimacy of current justifications and practices; the second part

---

5 The need to integrate philosophical, theoretical and methodological insights in our evaluation of *context* is also a vital exercise for understanding the development of future context; it is an ongoing, recursive process; Henham and Findlay (2001).

6 Both in terms of its implications for legal theory, and its social significance.

7 See further Drumbl (2000). For analysis of this phenomenon in the context of international law theory, see Polat (1999).

focuses on clarifying some fundamental philosophical questions raised by internationalised forms of sentencing and explores the relevance of existing philosophical justifications for punishment in the international sentencing context; the chapter concludes by considering arguments for the adoption of philosophical and institutional paradigms for international sentencing which are responsive and reflective of the contexts of criminality.

The Penality of International Sentencing

This section sets out to examine the penality of international sentencing within the context of the internationalised criminal trial. In so doing it is concerned with the deconstruction of meanings and justifications for international process by engaging with the broader dimensions associated with punishment as a social phenomenon. As Garland suggests:

> ... penality communicates meaning not just about crime and punishment but also about power, authority, legitimacy, normality, morality, personhood, social relations, and a host of other tangential matters (1990, p.252).

Hence, the deconstruction of international sentencing praxis provides the key to understanding the novel and different dimensions of international penality. For this it is necessary to engage with the ideological, jurisdictional, institutional and relational significance of the practice of international sentencing in its various forms.

The intention, therefore, is to explore philosophical justifications for punishment in the sociological context of internationalised sentencing praxis.[8] This does not imply any acceptance of the naturalistic fallacy suggested by Finnis (1980) by suggesting that propositions relating to the principles which should govern international sentencing can be derived from the analysis of existing normative practice. On the contrary, the present approach is complementary, since the objective validity[9] of morally significant propositions can only be tested against empirical fact and the operation of those social processes which they hope to influence. Therefore, the extent to which normative propositions in international sentencing actually dictate, or are reflected in empirical fact, is an essential endeavour for social theorisations of international sentencing praxis. A recognition of the legal, social and political contexts in which international sentencing takes place is necessary not only to identify and understand the manifestation of competing interests in process, but also to provide validity to any assessment of competing moral justifications for punishment.

In Chapter 1 it was argued that a significant paradigm for conceptualising the activities of international criminal institutions is to regard them as structural

[8] Thus recognising that understanding international sentencing praxis requires that the things being researched cannot be removed from their social world. In fact it is this social world that gives them their meaning and is as much an essential issue for research and comparison as the thing itself. The key concern in the application of context in comparative research is which contexts are crucial, and how considerations drawn from different contexts (and various levels of context) should be weighed against one another.

[9] The meaning of this expression remains ontologically conjectural (Roberts 2002, p.547).

mechanisms concerned with the legitimation of hegemonic power, authority and control. As such they provide modalities which permit members of the international community to dispense a morally relative form of justice[10] through legitimised repression. Further, as Schabas (2002) suggests, a unifying point between the internationalised tribunals relates to the 'process of encroachment by the international community on national processes with a view to ensuring criminal prosecution of human rights abuses'. This emphasises that the internationalisation of criminal trial process is also intimately connected to issues which relate to global governance and accountability. These may include, more particularly:

- the universal criminalisation of behaviour irrespective of context[11]
- the right to assert modalities and techniques for penal repression
- the determination of the means for allocating responsibility for criminality irrespective of the different historical, social and cultural contexts in which punishment norms are applied
- the relative autonomy of internationalised trial processes which have developed outside institutional mechanisms of accountability.

Within the context of the hegemonic paradigm, philosophical justifications for international punishment may be perceived as *ex post facto* rationalisations that obfuscate the application of sentencing principles grounded in rules and procedural structures reflective of political compromise. For instance, as illustrated by the ICTR in *Kambanda*,[12] where sentences fall short of the retributive expectations of the victim community they may be rationalised for international consumption in terms of vaguely articulated alternative penal justifications such as rehabilitation and deterrence.[13] The ICTR Trial Chamber in *Kambanda* also compounded this failure for the victim community by not capitalising on the accused's confessions and admissions of guilt through encouraging the process of reconciliation at the local

---

[10] A form of justice presently dominated by a punitive ethic.

[11] As Howland and Calathes (1998, p.157) suggest in the case of Rwanda: 'The major reason justice systems fail to respond adequately to crime is that we inadequately think about crime by defining crime only as law-breaking. We then concentrate solely on the resulting adversarial relationship between government and the criminal offender. This existing pattern of thinking fails to address, or even recognise, the other dimensions involved. A human rights crime is not merely an offence against the state. Likewise, justice is more than punishment and incapacitation.'

[12] *Prosecutor v Kambanda* (Case No. ICTR-97-23-S), Judgement and Sentence, 4 September 1998.
'... the penalties imposed on accused persons found guilty by the Tribunal must be directed, on the one hand, at retribution of the [said] accused, who must see their crimes punished, and over and above that, on the other hand, at deterrence, namely dissuading for good those who will attempt in future to perpetrate such atrocities by showing them that the international community was not ready to tolerate the serious violations of international humanitarian law and human rights' (para. 28).

[13] Kambanda, the former prime minister of Rwanda, pleaded guilty to genocide. The Rwandan Organic Law on the Organisation of Prosecutions for Offences constituting Genocide or Crimes against Humanity committed since 1 October 1990 advocates the death penalty for the masterminds of the crimes (planners, organisers), persons in positions of authority, persons who have exhibited excessive cruelty and perpetrators of sexual violence.

level.[14] As Cockayne (2001) points out, such isolationism in the ICTR's approach serves only to undermine the educative and reconciliatory purposes of the trial process, and its legitimacy.

Moreover, as discussed in the context of the *ad hoc* tribunals, retribution in international criminal justice has been more readily equated with the concept of victor's justice; vindication and western exculpation (Bassiouni and Manakas 1996, pp.228–231); the symbolic manifestation of hegemony. The tribunals have been unequivocal in confirming the *moral* legitimacy of retributive punishment derived from the authority vested in them by the United Nations Security Council, Chapter VII, to ensure that serious violations of international humanitarian law are prosecuted and punished. However, the need to put an end to impunity is normally driven by a desire for communal vengeance and retribution on the part of successful nation states immediately following the resolution of conflict. It may, therefore, be erroneous to presume that internationalised principles of criminal justice based on retribution and ideological imperialism will remain anything other than partial, relativistic and profoundly undemocratic.[15]

In *Furundzija*,[16] the ICTY was unequivocal in its assertion that the notion of punishment itself was an infallible tool for the achievement of retribution, stigmatisation and deterrence. Elsewhere, in the judgements of the *ad hoc* tribunals there has been a developing recognition that international principles of punishment may also include consequentialist objectives such as rehabilitation and reconciliation. In *Erdemovic*,[17] for example, the ICTY Trial Chamber stated:

> The International Tribunal, in addition to its mandate to investigate, prosecute and punish serious violations of international humanitarian law, has a duty, through its judicial functions, to contribute to the settlement of the wider issues of accountability, reconciliation and establishing the truth behind the evils perpetrated in the Former Yugoslavia. Discovering the truth is the cornerstone of the rule of law and a fundamental step on the way to reconciliation: for it is the truth that cleanses the ethnic and religious hatreds and begins the healing process.

The ICTY clearly envisaged its contribution towards reconciliation as a counterbalance to the need to inflict retributive punishment against those accused of violating international humanitarian law, yet beyond asserting that alternative justifications might be directed towards satisfying the needs of victims and their families, no further elaboration was forthcoming.[18]

---

[14] In this the ICTR may be accused of having failed to place sufficient emphasis on its statutory 'reconciliation' mandate.

[15] The concept of democracy is invoked here to imply principles which sustain and protect individual liberty and communitarian interests against state hegemony. The recognition and development of such principles was seriously threatened following 12 July 2002 when the UN Security Council voted unanimously to exempt peacekeepers in UN-established or UN-authorised missions who do not support the court from investigation and prosecution by the ICC for a year in the face of US threats to UN missions around the world.

[16] *Prosecutor v Furundzija* (Case No. IT-95-17/1-T), Judgement, 10 December 1998.

[17] *Prosecutor v Erdemovic* (Case No. IT-96-22-T), Sentencing Judgement, 29 November 1996, para. 21.

[18] A further objection may be raised on the basis that, as in *Kambanda*, *supra*, note 11, para. 50, confessions and declarations in procedural mechanisms such as plea agreements were taken as

Similarly, in *Ruggiu*,[19] the ICTR Trial Chamber merely referred to its jurisprudence as having 'addressed the principal aims of sentencing, namely retribution, deterrence, rehabilitation and justice', without further explanation or justification (para. 33). Regrettably, the *ad hoc* tribunals have consistently failed to define such sentencing aims, or explore their meaning in the international trial context. Nor have they intimated exactly how particular sentencing purposes might be linked to guidance in determining punishment. The tribunals have, instead, continued to synthesise and contextualise their discussions of appropriate punishment objectives within a predominantly retributivist paradigm.

As suggested in Chapter 1, the evidence of confusion and obfuscation on the part of the *ad hoc* tribunals relating to the possible scope and meaning to be accorded to penal justifications is incontrovertible. For example, in *Erdemovic*[20] the ICTY suggested that clear distinctions could be drawn between 'general prevention (or deterrence), reprobation, retribution (or "just deserts"), as well as collective reconciliation', and intimated that these purposes would provide guidance in determining the appropriate punishment for crimes against humanity. Unfortunately, no attempt was made to explore the meaning of these purposes in the context of international criminal justice, or how they might be interpreted through the development of appropriate guidance in determining punishment. Similarly, in *Rutaganda*[21] and *Tadic*,[22] unsubstantiated retributive and deterrent claims were made for punishment, whilst the Trial Chamber in the latter case went further in claiming incapacitation of the dangerous and rehabilitation as desirable objectives. In *Todorovic*,[23] the ICTY simply acknowledged that deterrence may be considered as an important general justifying aim for sentencing international crimes, whilst affirming the appropriateness of retributivism as the relevant paradigm for punishment. Again, in *Kunarac*,[24] the Trial Chamber of the ICTY noted the various and interchangeable use of such expressions as 'objectives, purposes, and principles, functions or policy' in previous decisions of the Trial and Appeals Chambers[25] and went on to suggest that:

> What appear to be justifications for imprisoning convicted persons, or theories of punishment, actually are treated as or resemble sentencing factors, in the sense that these considerations are consistently said to affect, usually in an unspecified manner, the length of imprisonment.

In addition to its failure to distinguish or overtly articulate the crucial distinction between the general justifications for sentencing and their specific relevance as guides

---

unequivocal manifestations of truth which would automatically contribute towards the restoration of national unity and reconciliation.

[19] *Prosecutor v Ruggiu* (Case No. ICTR-97-32-I), Judgement and Sentence, 1 June 2000.

[20] *Erdemovic, supra*, note 17, para. 58.

[21] *Prosecutor v Rutaganda* (Case No. ICTR-96-3), Judgement and Sentence, 2 February 1999.

[22] *Prosecutor v Tadic* (Case No. IT-94-1-S), Sentencing Judgement, 14 July 1997, para. 61.

[23] *Prosecutor v Todorovic* (Case No. IT-95-9/1-S), Sentencing Judgement, 31 July 2001.

[24] *Prosecutor v Kunarac* (Case No. IT-96-23-T & IT-96-23/1-T), Judgement, 22 February 2001, para. 836.

[25] For detail, see *Kunarac, ibid*, footnote 1430, 263.

to principled sentencing practice in particular cases,[26] the ICTY effectively capitalises on the confusion by appearing to relegate the issue to one of semantics.[27] It entrusts the future significance and legitimacy of the decisions themselves to the vagaries of judicial discretion, thereby increasing the legitimate authority and power of tribunal judges.[28]

Van Zyl Smit (2002, p.15) suggests that, particularly in the case of the ICC Statute, the undeveloped nature of the penal justifications for international sentencing largely reflect the difficulties encountered in establishing credible processes through international consensus, and that the constraints of international human rights law should in future ensure sentences which are 'neither inhumane nor grossly disproportionate to the seriousness of the offence or the culpability of the offender'.[29] However, as van Zyl Smit acknowledges, the elaboration of rationales for sentencing are desirable specifically for structuring international sentencing process, and, more generally, in focusing the objectives of the international criminal justice system. Whilst the impact of international human rights norms on the development of international sentencing principles undoubtedly depends on the exercise of judicial discretion, consistency[30] and fairness of approach demand accommodation and

---

26 The justification for the general practice of punishment is a normative question, generally distinguished from the specific aims of punishment in concrete cases (Hart, 1968). A useful distinction is that drawn by Morris and Tonry (1990) between the purposes *of* sentencing, and the purposes *at* sentencing.The crucial relevance of philosophical theories for the practice of punishment is that practical aims and objectives are consistently tested against the moral justification for punishment.

27 Significantly, the Trial Chamber in *Kunarac*, *ibid*, para. 842) specifically stated that it was inappropriate for it to have recourse to United Nations Security Council Resolution 827 for guidance as to what general sentencing factors should be considered.

28 This is supported by the Trial Chamber's decision not to consider any 'principles' other than those submitted by the prosecutor, and the following generalised assertion: 'By whatever name they go, these considerations are of *real and considerable* importance. Which of them may *legitimately* be considered as factors ... deserves *careful* consideration' [emphasis added].

29 He also suggests that this will facilitate an interpretation which recognises 'the essential humanity of the offender'.

30 The need for consistency and the development of appropriate regulatory mechanisms is discussed by Beresford (2002). The issue also received particular attention from the ICTY Appeals Chamber in *Prosecutor v Delalic* (Case No. IT-96-21-A), Judgement, 20 February 2001, paras 756–758 and subsequently in *Prosecutor v Krnojelac* (Case No. IT-97-25-T), Judgement, 15 March 2002, para. 526. In *Delalic* the Appeals Chamber went out of its way to emphasise the strategic significance of consistent sentencing (para. 756), whilst in *Krnojelac* the Trial Chamber reiterated the current position of the ICTY regarding the status and development of sentencing jurisprudence: '... In most jurisdictions a range or a pattern of sentences has been built up over the years. A court in such circumstances is obliged to have regard to that range or pattern, without being bound by it, in order to ensure that, in the exercise of that discretion, the sentence which it imposes in the particular case does not produce an unjustified disparity which may erode public confidence in the integrity of the administration of criminal justice. No such range or pattern of sentences presently exists in this Tribunal, but with time one will necessarily emerge. At the present time, it is possible for a Trial Chamber to have regard only to those sentences which have been imposed by the Tribunal in *generally* similar circumstances as to both offences and offenders' (para. 526) [emphasis in original; footnotes omitted].

It is worth noting that the preferred approach is virtually identical to that which operates in England and Wales; see, generally, Ashworth (2000a). It is also important to point out that the need for consistency is implicit in conceptions of retributivism, and regarded as a necessary precondition for the existence of democratic principles of justice in those countries where retributivism is accepted as the predominant rationale for punishment.

balance between the rationales for punishment and their effective promotion through judicially controlled sentencing principles. There are several reasons for this:

- The principled implementation of humanitarian norms in international sentencing will require a level of international cooperation and consensus equal to that evidenced in the creation of the human rights structures. If hegemony, dissensus and compromise have characterised the creation of international criminal trial structures, why should their strategic implementation be any different?[31]
- Rationality of purpose is necessary for the resolution of conflict at the most basic level, for instance between retribution and rehabilitation, particularly to prevent the disproportionate deprivation of liberty.
- The specification of a primary rationale(s) facilitates the delineation of alternative spheres of operation for other rationales, thus promoting consistency of approach.
- Rationality in approach contributes towards the reduction of discriminatory practices and differential impact.
- Sentencing rationales can be formulated and reviewed to take account of wider issues relating to penal policy and practice, particularly restorative justice paradigms.
- As I have discussed elsewhere (Henham 2000b, p.245), the development of local and global sentencing norms may conflict with the normative imperatives demanded by transnational rights agendas. More particularly, in failing to provide rationale(s) to promote the development of a coherent sentencing jurisprudence, the normative interpretation attributed to key concepts may not accord with the distinct moral and normative meanings attributed to them by state jurisdictions. The problem may be compounded if praxis develops against notions of fair trial demanded by rights paradigms such as the European Convention on Human Rights.

The punitive dynamic of international criminal justice raises other significant questions regarding the legitimacy of the international sentencing process exemplified by the *ad hoc* tribunals. Schabas (2001b) notes that the recent focus on prosecution and victims' rights and punishment in the international trial process has been at the expense of defendants' rights; a 'culture of conviction' appears to have replaced the 'culture of acquittal' at the expense of fair trial norms. This reflection of the international community's emphasis on retributive punishment (rather than protection and deterrence) is clearly evidenced in the development of substantive and procedural norms. Again, providing rationality of purpose would forestall the tendency for international sentencing to be subverted towards discriminatory procedural practice.

In addition, international criminal tribunals exist independently of any legitimation that may be derived from being embedded in the liberal democratic frameworks typical of national courts in western democracies. If it is argued that the semi-anarchy

[31] In this, judicial demographics, particularly political allegiances and penal philosophies of tribunal judges, are paramount considerations.

of the international community of states sustains and propagates a penality of western exculpation and selective retribution, it may also be pertinent to suggest that the criminalisation of behaviour characterised as war crimes, or otherwise in breach of principles of international criminal law, represents a particularised contextualisation of deviance (Akhavan, 2001). The argument may be taken further by suggesting that the behaviour itself is performed in a context where deviance has, in fact, become the norm. Hence, it becomes relevant to consider on what basis the punishment process is to be legitimated. Should punishment be regarded as transformative, in the sense that exacting retribution on the body of the perpetrator somehow rehabilitates the deviant act and the responsible social group? Again, the issue returns us to the question of legitimacy and the context in which the process of criminalisation occurs. However, although the norms against which the deviance of crimes tried by international tribunals are measured are those authorised by the international community, as has been argued, the penality of particular institutions is also influenced by local procedural norms. This complex reality further emphasises the need to appreciate the relative contexts of penality and its manifestation in the processual characteristics of international sentencing.

Reconciling the difference between the context of criminality and the context of criminalisation is fundamental to the legitimation of international sentencing law. If, as is argued, a moral basis for legitimation is necessary, then the present fall-back retributive justifications of international sentencing appear too confused and tendentious to provide this. As Cotterrell (1999) suggests, a Durkheimian sociology of morality might regard retribution (or other approaches to punishment) as justifiable up to a point as an expression of the moral character of society as a whole.[32] However, the problem for international sentencing is ultimately the conundrum of what 'international society' can be taken to represent morally. Clearly, this must, in Durkheim's terms, extend beyond the 'cult of the individual' to provide a sociologically justifiable moral basis for regulating transnational social relations. In addition, as discussed later, the increasing polarisation between citizen and state has further strengthened the retributive position. Nevertheless, I would argue that the concept of citizenship should be reconceptualised in the internationalised context of criminal justice to envisage law as a technique for recognising and regulating the moral limits of acceptable behaviour between human beings (as victims and offenders) on a global basis, whilst also appreciating the contingencies inevitably imposed by local context.[33] In this way, international sentencing law and practice must strive for legitimacy through developing its capacity to provide for the humanitarian and tranformative regulation of breaches of international criminal law.

The foregoing comments on the sentencing practices of the *ad hoc* tribunals and possible reasons for questioning the legitimacy of praxis in international sentencing raises some fundamental questions regarding the nature and significance of

---

[32] As emphasised, how that value system plays out in any penal practice depends largely on local context.

[33] For arguments supporting the recognition of such a connection, see Honore (2002). Of particular relevance to the current argument are Honore's following assertions: 'The critical or rational morality to which law-makers implicitly appeal will comprise certain values inherent in law irrespective of the particular legal system concerned. Law seeks to supplant unregulated violence, both within societies and between them, by fostering the values of co-operation and peaceful co-existence. The critical morality to which the law-maker implicitly appeals relates to these values…' (2002, p.492) [footnote omitted].

competing philosophical justifications for sentencing in the international sphere. The first part of the following section attempts to crystallise these concerns before the analysis turns to explore the extent to which conventional western liberal justifications for punishment[34] are capable of addressing such questions and providing moral and normative imperatives which resonate with paradigms of international justice and infuse them with foundations of substantive rationality.

Fundamental Issues and Philosophical Justifications

The Need for Rationality

The preceding discussion has illustrated a significant lack of clarity on the part of the *ad hoc* tribunals in addressing issues that are fundamental to any sentencing system. These concern the significance of punishment, the reasons for its imposition and its signification. Although the predominant rationale for imposing punishment in these international criminal tribunals appears to be retribution, the justification remains unclear beyond exhortations that the selected punishment is a necessary response on the part of the civilised world to gross violations of international humanitarian law. On this basis certain states have therefore assumed the *moral right* to inflict punishment on perceived wrongdoers, offering the foregoing rationale as a general justification for the creation of institutions for international criminal trials, and the infliction of retributive punishment. Notwithstanding, the judicial process of sentencing in the *ad hoc* tribunals is characterised by pragmatism; constructing and offering alternative or complementary rationalisations in individual cases. These distributive justifications generally appeal to utilitarian rationalisations for punishment such as deterrence or reconciliation which may find some expression in the relevant foundation instruments.[35] Furthermore, as a communicative enterprise, the infliction of punishment in the *ad hoc* tribunals appears to have failed at both the retributive and utilitarian levels.[36]

If it is then argued that competing purposes for punishment must be clarified for international sentencing to engage with its perceived audience of offenders, victims, communities or states, it becomes necessary to clarify concepts and provide mechanisms or structures for this transformative enterprise. This raises some critical questions regarding the relationship between citizen and state and how this impacts on the globalisation of penality. As suggested, for the liberal theorists of the Enlightenment, the moral authority for state punishment was derived from the desire of citizens for protection against the tyranny of social and political inequality (Radzinowicz, 1966, Ch. 1). The continued legitimation of penality depended on the appropriate balance being achieved between individual rights and the continued affirmation by the state of principles of equality embodied in democratic principles for the administration of justice. More recently, Murphy's (1979) elaboration of

34 The question can be equally directed at alternative philosophical traditions.

35 As in the case of the Rwandan tribunal.

36 An example is the failure to distinguish between concepts of 'victim' and 'community', with its resultant implications for the development of restorative justice paradigms.

social contractarianism sought to justify retributive punishment by asserting that this stated equilibrium should be achieved through the state maintaining the balance of advantage in favour of law-abiding citizens. To sustain either position, certain assumptions are made regarding the instrumentality of the state, particularly its capacity to translate moral into normative imperatives.

These assumptions are suspect. As Garland (1996, p.445) suggests, through the process of 'responsibilisation', where certain state functions such as crime control have become unattainable, the state/citizen relationship is reconfigured through policy objectives designed to shift accountability.[37] Similarly, Pratt (1998) describes how the relationship of mutual dependence and trust built up between citizens and state during the nineteenth century gradually diminished through the centralisation of penal authority in the state, the institutionalisation of penality and the concomitant restriction in individual autonomy (Shearing, 2001). Pragmatism has replaced welfarism as the predominant rationale underscoring the penality of western industrialised societies.

Paradoxically, this realignment in penal accountability has increased individual and group resolution of crime problems in areas of criminality ceded (deliberately or otherwise) by the state. Further, the state has reciprocated by increasingly instigating penal policies based on the principle of 'less eligibility' (Sparks, 1996), whilst simultaneously promoting human rights paradigms. In the sphere of international law theory, Polat (1999) has suggested a parallel trend in the historical development of the relationship between notions of state sovereignty and justice, noting in particular the exclusionary character of mediating frameworks for the resolution of international disputes and the promotion of human rights. As Garland succinctly puts it:

> The image of the State as a rational moral agent, dispassionately dispensing justice in the name of everyone, looks increasingly hard to sustain in the face of high levels of individuation and moral diversity (MacCormick and Garland, 1998, p.14).

However, whether the relationship between citizen and state might be reconfigured in pluralistic terms that merit the continued consent of citizens is problematic (MacCormick and Garland, 1998, p.29). The immediate consequences for liberal democracies is that the state's punishment apparatus exists merely as a symbolic focus for social control, the *moral* basis upon which it legitimately exercises the power of punishment (the state's consideration for the powers citizens have autonomously ceded to it as part of the social contract) having diminished. Thus, the morality and symbolism that is accorded to the international criminal trial forum derives from the need to relate citizenship and victimisation to the values and norms of international humanitarian law and, by implication, those states exercising global power and authority.

In consequence, the reconciliation of conflicting rationales for international sentencing must recognise that individual states may abrogate their responsibility to protect citizens equally against certain consequential aspects of criminality, and exclude significant minorities from participating in the processes of criminal justice.[38]

---

[37] See Pratt (1995) for analysis of how this has been achieved in relation to protective sentencing.

[38] The redefinition and colonisation of conflict situations are crucial determinants of the relationship between citizen and state; see Christie (1977).

This exclusion extends to participation in the creation of structures and processes which are instrumental in the protection of human rights.[39] In systems where judicial discretion continues to flourish, the judicial elite may therefore play a crucial role in asserting principles of non-discriminatory justice and balancing state interests against individual rights. Consequently, the pragmatic reconciliation of rationales for punishment must be achieved through the *process* of discretionary judicial decision-making.[40]

The incremental polarisation of citizen and state has significant ramifications for the rationalisation of punishment at the international level. Existing international criminal trial structures and procedural codes reflect a democratic deficit in the accountability of international institutions which not only hinders the prospects for the development of universal standards of international criminal sentencing process, but also undermines locally negotiated settlements. This deficit is manifest in the failure of international norms to account for discrete cultural contexts and a concomitant failure to integrate international mechanisms and procedural standards providing the source of such norms (such as the ICC) with those of democratic (i.e. state/non-state) governance. This structural weakness facilitates further the promotion of the international community's focus on retribution over utilitarian objectives, and the general obfuscation of trial process at the expense of defendants' and victims' rights.

Thus, consistency and parity in the development of international principles for sentencing based on articulated purposes is identified with legal formalism; analysis of mechanistic issues concerned with the technical interpretation and deviation from norms which themselves exist as consolidations of current retributivist practice (Beresford, 2002). Accordingly, concerns regarding the relevance and impact of concepts such as proportionality, complementarity and amnesty (Gavron, 2002) are addressed without reference to the wider purposes and contexts of international sentencing.

The Relevance of Philosophical Justifications

The foregoing analysis suggests several aspects of international sentencing where there exists an urgent need for a rationalisation of the philosophical justifications for penality. More particularly, sentencing structures and practices in the *ad hoc* tribunals and the ICC are legitimated by the assumed *moral right* to inflict retributive punishment on those convicted of gross violations of international humanitarian law.

---

[39] As Gardner implies, this may involve a breach of the state's duty of humanity towards its citizens: 'For punishment to be a morally acceptable alternative to protection, the State has to assure itself not only that the measure of punishment controls retaliation while stopping short of becoming a mere institutionalisation of the retaliator's excesses, but also that the act of punishment affirms, rather than denies, the punished person's status as a thinking, feeling human being' (Gardner, 1998, p.35).

[40] Note, however, that the relationship between the theory and practice of sentencing is not that straightforward; see Tata (1997, p. 419, footnote 103). 'Of course, the cultural question concerning how societies attempt to justify the "need" to punish and the empirical question of how the sentencing decision is processed are interrelated not least at the point where judges attempt to justify their decisions publicly. However, as I argue later, this should not lead us to assume that the reasons given in court are the obvious category for explanation of "why" the judge passed the sentence s/he did.'

The question to be explored here relates, not to the validity of competing moral claims to punish,[41] but rather the degree to which particular philosophical justifications might validly be utilised to promote competing moral claims for punishment in the international sphere.[42]

In the context of retributivism[43] a distinction may be drawn between the reason or rational justification for punishment and its moral justification (Dolinko 1991; 1997). The distinction is particularly significant for understanding conceptualisations of retributivism in international sentencing. Hence, it may be rational to assert that individuals who have perpetrated the most egregious crimes known to humankind are deserving of severe punishment, but it does not necessarily follow that the application of retributive punishment in such cases is morally justified.[44] Indeed, the morality or otherwise of retributive punishment in terms of deserts may well be overridden by extraneous factors (Feinberg, 1970, p.60), which may relate to matters peculiar to the individual concerned, the morality of social and criminal justice policy, or the fundamental nature of the state's relationship with its citizens.

In the case of international tribunals the connections between retributive punishment and moral justifications are more tenuous against the effects of globalisation. These effects concern the extent to which international criminal justice policy is morally relative and the extent to which international penal structures are capable of facilitating the development of democratic principles of justice. In essence, these difficulties stem from the Rawlsian injunction that moral imperatives should be derived from rationality, since the parameters for establishing a rationality for internationalised punishment premised upon the maintenance of any kind of collective international rational will are profoundly unclear.

Where international humanitarian norms are concerned the criminal trial process is normally called upon to adjudicate on actions which the international community designates as having breached the acceptable moral limits for the conduct of war (Nagel, 1972). Thus, the slaughter of innocent civilians may be regarded as a morally justified incidence of what is regarded as a morally just cause. It may, therefore, be argued that it is difficult to envisage an international criminal trial forum as dispensing anything other than a selective form of moral justice. However, it is also possible to argue that the point of retributive punishment in this context might be to reassert or counter alternative moral claims (Hampton 1988). Indeed, Hampton (1988, pp.125–126) proposes the notion that retributive punishment 'is the defeat of the wrongdoer at the hands of the victim … that symbolizes the correct relative value of wrongdoer and victim'. Unfortunately, this position is in itself morally judgmental, notwithstanding the doubtful validity of the means offered to effect a reconciliation of the victim's moral justification for acting as against that of the perpetrator, or conjecture regarding the nature of the audience to which any retributive condemnation is directed.

---

[41] This being a study in moral relativity.

[42] The word 'valid' is used to connote inclusivity and equal relevance for all moral claims.

[43] The nature of retributivism remains conjectural; see, for example, Cottingham (1979).

[44] Hart (1968) seems to equate the 'general justifying aim' of punishment as the moral justification for penality.

In the Kantian tradition, Michael Moore (1987) attempts to relate the moral culpability of offenders to the need for retributive punishment, and further asserts that society has a *duty* to punish culpable offenders:

> As a theory of a kind of justice, it *obligates* us to seek retribution through the punishment of the guilty. This means that officials have a duty to punish deserving offenders and that citizens have a duty to set up and support institutions that achieve such punishment (Moore 1993).

Nevertheless, as Dolinko (1991, p.557) maintains, a significant problem with Moore's approach concerns his apparent insistence that the duty to act arises, not because the act is morally bad *per se*, but that it is legally prohibited. Moore's position does not then assist us in making the correct moral judgment as to which human behaviours should be labelled as 'bad', criminalized and thereby made the subject of retributive punishment.[45] A possible response to this argument might be to assert that the egregious nature of some forms of human behaviour (particularly those labelled as genocide, crimes against humanity and war crimes) suggests that retribution is intrinsically deserving. However, this does not overcome the argument that Moore ignores the social, political and historical contexts of criminalized behaviours, particularly the long-term impact of repressive, discriminatory and authoritarian regimes in societies with significant rival ethnic divisions. Hence, Moore's thesis that retribution delivers 'a kind of justice' fails to provide a rational justification for the development of a democratic conception of justice for international sentencing.

Notwithstanding, more recently Moore (1993), and others,[46] have proffered the notion that retributive punishment is somehow intrinsically good, thereby investing retributivism with some consequentialist or utilitarian credentials. Moore in particular takes issue with definitions of retributivism as deontological in asserting that, since the punishment of the guilty is a categorical duty,[47] to maximise the beneficial effects of this state of affairs justifies the occasional punishment of innocent citizens. As Dolinko (1997, p.514) suggests, this kind of approach gives rise to a widening of possible alternative beneficial effects, and presumably that the relative benefits of retributive punishment should only be measured against some comparative ranking of perceived beneficial consequences.[48] Ultimately, Dolinko (1997, pp.518–528) argues that there is no rational or moral justification for basing the institution of punishment solely on the basis of the view that punishing the guilty is intrinsically good.

---

[45] As Duff (2001, p.25) suggests: '... it does not tell us *why* they [the guilty] should suffer, or why guilt should generate the judgment that I ought to suffer, or *what* they ought to suffer, or why it should be a proper task for the *state* to inflict that suffering.'

[46] See further, Dolinko (1997) and references cited therein.

[47] Deontological retributivists would argue that since retributivism justifies punishment of the guilty the rightness or otherwise of any particular punishment is not in issue; this is a function of agent-relative norms.

[48] Dolinko (1997) points out that this position does not accord with Moore's expressed view that the beneficial consequences of punishment should 'form no part of what makes punishment just'.

More significant in the present context is the implicit imperative that there exists a moral obligation for states to create institutional structures for international penality capable of bringing about the perceived beneficial consequences of retributive punishment. It may be argued that it is precisely this form of reasoning which has shaped the creation of international criminal tribunals and become evident in the retributive rhetoric contained in so many of the sentencing judgments of the ICTY and ICTR described earlier. A significant example is to be found in the ICTY's judgment in *Furundzija*:[49]

> It is the *infallibility* of punishment, rather than the severity of the sanction, which is the tool for retribution, stigmatisation and deterrence. This is particularly the case for the International Tribunal; penalties are made more onerous by its international stature, moral authority and impact upon world opinion, and this punitive effect must be borne in mind when assessing the suitable length of sentence [emphasis added].

As employed in this passage, the expression 'infallibility of punishment' implies that the infliction of punishment for either retributivist or consequentialist justifications *necessarily* entails specific benefits[50] in the context of international sentencing. Moreover, these intrinsic benefits are intimately connected to the notion of retributive punishment as a distributive principle. However, as suggested, such factors alone do not imply any *moral validation* of the institution and justification of retributive punishment in this context. Furthermore, the potential reconciliation of retributivist and consequentialist claims through sentencing is neither rational nor sufficient justification for the practice of punishing international criminals.

Nevertheless, the moral worth of retributive punishment in international criminal trials is frequently justified on the basis of the *moral obligation* which exists on the part of the international community to put an end to the culture of impunity as regards the breach of principles of international humanitarian law. In this sense, the moral and rational justifications for retributive punishment are intimately connected and, therefore, asserted as equally valid. However, what was (and is) being asserted on the part of the 'international community' is a *moral* case for action. As suggested earlier, the moral validity and the rational justifications for international punishment have been conceptually collapsed, so that the moral and the rational case for action and its justification are envisaged as one and the same. Hence, the moral case was translated into the creation of institutional structures for international punishment that were not predicated on rational reasons for their maintenance and development beyond those retributive aspirations implicit in the implementation of the moral obligation to end the culture of impunity. Consequently, on the one hand, the retributive justification embodied in the notion of victor's justice has been invoked by the sentencing tribunals explicitly to extol the intrinsic moral virtues of retributive punishment in this context, whilst in other cases retributivist punishment has been conceptualised as having consequentialist benefits. The problem is that these perceived consequential benefits for retributivist punishment are connected by sentencers to the moral case for action through arguments which cannot be sustained in terms that recognise the ideological and political realities of international conflict resolution.

---

[49] *Furundzija*, *supra*, note 13, para. 290.

[50] The exact nature of these benefits is not made clear.

Although apparent consequential benefits cannot provide the *moral* justification for retributive punishment in the international arena there is less difficulty in envisioning links between retributivism and denunciation, and the *ad hoc* international tribunals have not been reticent in advancing such a justification. For example, the ICTY in *Aleksovski*[51] suggested that retribution was:

> Not to be understood as fulfilling a desire for revenge but as duly expressing the outrage of the international community at these crimes ... A sentence of the Tribunal should make plain the condemnation of the international community was not ready to tolerate serious violations of international humanitarian law and human rights.[52]

Nevertheless, as Bagaric and Amarasekara (2000) suggest, denunciation does not imply communicative aspirations. On the contrary, the real extent of community abhorrence is secondary to the judicial perception of informed public opinion. However, where national and international punishment norms fail to coincide, victim communities may well perceive this denunciatory aspect of retributive punishment as remaining unfulfilled, thereby undermining any *morally* justifiable claim for retributivism to have satisfied public opinion and restored public confidence in the punishment process. Paradoxically, the potential educative role attributed to retributive punishment as a denunciatory process may have more coherence at the level of serious violations of international humanitarian law than for lesser criminality in postmodern pluralistic western liberal democracies. Notwithstanding the moral relativity of the justifications espoused for retribution, there is no doubting the symbolism of the international forum as an effective platform for publicising what are perceived as acceptable moral values and norms and to express feelings of revulsion, indignation and condemnation on behalf of the international community.

Von Hirsch's (1993) justification of punishment as censure is a form of limited retributivism that relies heavily on such consequentialist considerations, and has been criticised for failing to explain why the amount of punishment necessary to achieve censure is morally justifiable without recourse to utilitarian reasoning.[53] Von Hirsch argues that it is the moral quality of the conduct, in particular the offender's blameworthiness, which determines the appropriate penal response in terms of deserts:

> One is entitled to condemn only if one has reason to believe that the conduct is wrong, and only to the degree of its wrongfulness ... The decision to visit conduct with censure needs to be supported by a judgement on the merits that the conduct is reprehensible, and is so to the degree to which it is visited with blame (1993, pp.24–25).

---

[51] *Prosecutor v Aleksovski* (Case No. IT-95-14/1-A), Judgement, 24 March 2000, para 185.

[52] As Frulli (2001) points out, one of the most important functions of the sentencing judge in the international tribunals should be to give effect to the degree of wrongdoing expressed in international criminal law. A difficulty lies in reconciling the relative differences in gravity accorded to crimes against humanity and war crimes in national and international courts.

[53] See further Bagaric (2001, p.72). Other difficulties with von Hirsch's theory concern its inability to distinguish convincingly between different degrees of responsibility, or quantify harm. Establishing the relationship between the relative seriousness of behaviour (cardinal proportionality) and the relative severity of sentence (ordinal proportionality) is particularly problematic where national and international disagreement persists about the relative seriousness of crimes which breach international humanitarian law and the penalties which should attend them.

Particularly significant in the present context is the notion that the application of retributive punishment through censure is at once expressive of society's moral opprobrium, the need to redress the moral balance between the accused and the state, and an acknowledgement that the victim has been wronged through the public attribution of fault. Von Hirsch does not, however, suggest that censure by the state should seek to change moral attitudes in the sense of Feinberg's (1984) moral paternalism, but rather that the communicative function of censure is one of deterrence.

Despite the unsubstantiated nature of deterrent claims for censure, the ICTR in *Rutaganda*[54] was unequivocal in its description of the relationship between these justifications:

> ... it is clear that the penalties imposed on accused persons found guilty by the Tribunal must be directed, on the one hand, at retribution of the said accused, who must see their crimes punished, and over and above that, on the other hand, at deterrence, namely to dissuade for ever, others who may be tempted in the future to perpetrate such atrocities by showing them that the international community shall not tolerate the serious violations of international humanitarian law and human rights.

Such an approach encapsulates perfectly von Hirsch's (1993, p.11) view that an appropriate sanction '... expresses blame, this conveys the message that the conduct is reprehensible, and should be eschewed'. However, as Norrie (2001, p.211) and Ashworth (1989a, p.354) both argue, modern just deserts theory fails to take account of context, particularly the impact that social and political factors may have on individual and collective forms of blameworthiness and the legislative policies which states devise to operationalise proportionality. This dichotomy between legal and social equality (and its implications for justice) crucially undermines the *morality* of desert theory's conceptualisation and allocation of responsibility (Hudson, 2003). At the international level this implies a need to go beyond the reconciliation of national and international sentencing norms to address the realties that produce and sustain conflict and social breakdown. Whilst these concerns are external to retributive sentencing practice,[55] they remain crucial to the development of relevant consequentialist justifications for international sentencing praxis.

Nevertheless, despite frequently being accorded supremacy over retribution,[56] it seems doubtful whether utilitarian justifications attributed for international punishment by the *ad hoc* tribunals deal adequately with this criticism. Whilst

---

[54] *Rutaganda, supra*, note 21, para. 456. This view is echoed by the ICTY; see *Kunarac, supra*, note 24, para. 841, endorsing comments by the Appeals Chamber in *Aleksovski, supra*, note 51, para. 185.

[55] As Ashworth (1989a) suggests, deserts sentencing is essentially concerned with developing mechanisms for the legal quantification of blame.

[56] For example, in *Prosecutor v Delalic* (Case No. IT-96-21-T), Judgement, 16 November 1998, para. 1234, the ICTY went so far as to suggest that deterrence '... is probably the most important factor in the assessment of sentences for violations of international humanitarian law. Apart from the fact that the accused should be sufficiently deterred by the appropriate sentence from ever contemplating taking part in such crimes again, persons in similar situations in the future should similarly be deterred from resorting to such crimes.' As Beresford (2002, p.42) points out, individual deterrence has not been widely supported as a rationale for punishment by the ICTY; see *Kunarac, supra*, note 24, para. 840.

retributivists like von Hirsch (1993, p.11) take issue with the notion that compliance with morally acceptable norms of behaviour requires inducements beyond those understandings conveyed by an appropriate condemnatory sanction, utilitarian justifications are predicated on the notion that there exists a *moral* duty to maximise the utility of punishment through measures designed to reduce the incidence of targeted criminality.[57] Although the beneficial effects claimed for punishment by the *ad hoc* tribunals include the utilitarian rationales of deterrence, incapacitation and rehabilitation,[58] the moral imperative to maximise the utility of punishment in terms of the justifications given remains ideological, eclectic and rhetorical. In other words, there is an intrinsic failure to move beyond the symbolism and the individuation of sentences to recognise that there exists a *contextual reality*[59] which the process of international punishment must address as concerned with the constructive engagement of internationalised forms of punishment within victim communities.

In this respect Akhavan (2001) makes a significant observation when he argues that the central role of the international criminal trial process is not the definition of deviance or the transformation of deviant acts and rehabilitation of the social group through the application of retributive punishment; it is deterrence. International criminal justice only makes sense if we understand it as a project targeted at those powerful elites which harness destructive social forces for their own individual ends. Akhavan goes further, claiming that international criminal trials should play a dual deterrence role; the first involving the specific deterrence of powerful elites, and the second a broader 'socio-pedagogical' deterrence, involving the creation of a flow of moral propaganda creating subliminal deterrence. However, Akhavan presents a limited conceptualisation of deterrence for these purposes. In the context of the ICC, for example, the source of the authority for the norms against which the deviance of crimes within its jurisdiction are measured is a combination of universal and localised national norms[60] which suggests particular expectations of victim communities. Secondly, the deterrence-based approach is based on unproven assumptions about perpetrator rationality in the context of armed conflict, genocide and crimes against humanity. Most important, however, is the fact that the concept of 'socio-pedagogical' deterrence focuses attention on the need for ICC sentencing to engage directly with victim communities.

This leads us to a relevant (but more complex) conceptualisation for deterrence theory which involves consideration of issues that cross the self-imposed intellectual boundaries of legal theory and legal sociology; namely, the extent to which moral

---

57 For a general overview, see Ashworth (2000a, pp.62–78). The relationship between utilitarian theories, rights and international criminal justice is examined in Chapter 6.

58 It should be noted that these rationales for punishment are discussed as 'principles of distribution' rather than 'general justifying aims'; Hart (1968).

59 This is essentially an acknowledgement that context requires that international punishment must engage with the social world that gives it meaning and provide the means for reconciling and weighing different contexts (and various levels of context) in ways which have *moral* resonance. For instance, if one were to analyse the role of the international judge in delivering sentence it would be important to inject the influence of the victim and the part his/her suffering plays in the calculation of appropriate penalties from perceptions of the structure and function of international punishment which resonate with those of victim communities.

60 Because of the notion of complementarity.

justifications for punishment[61] actually provide rational principles for action in sentencing. As suggested earlier, the purpose here is not to conflate moral and normative considerations, but to explore interpretations which might allow us to make the link between the recognition of sentencing law and principles as representations of morality[62] and the existence of forms of expressed morality in civil society that might exist in notions of communitarianism.[63] On this view the expressive force of legal punishment is determined by the extent to which the infliction of punishment itself is capable of conveying to citizens the notion that the behaviour with which it deals is morally blameworthy, and that in consequence its effectiveness is not based on deterrence through fear but on a widely held perception that it is morally legitimate.[64] The link between moral legitimacy and social constructs such as culture and community is necessarily dependant on *context*.

Before pursuing the significance of that observation for international punishment, however, it is important to note the pivotal role of discretion in sentence decision-making. It is through process that judges are required to justify and signify the moral appropriateness of sentencing norms; consequently law's moral power as a transformative mechanism is determined by its capacity to shape social reality through recursively organised practice (Figure 5.1). The transformation of normative principles as morally significant (as an aspect of social reality) necessitates an understanding of law's capacity to achieve this end.[65]

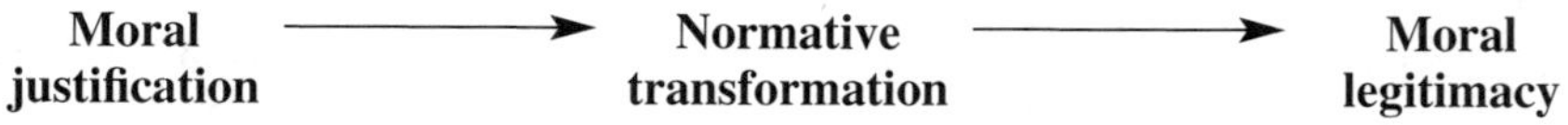

Figure 5.1 Sentencing as transformation

The deficient relationship between utilitarian theory and context is evident in conceptualisations of rehabilitative and incapacitative justifications for international sentencing. More particularly, the context[66] in which behaviour comes to be labelled as deviant is especially relevant for conceptions of rehabilitation[67] developed in international settings. The conventional focus of rehabilitative ideology is primarily

---

61 For example, for utilitarianism – to maximise its utility.

62 I.e. as derived from postulates that are representative of particular philosophies of punishment which claim some *moral* justification.

63 These are likely to remain contested in post-conflict societies.

64 Note Norrie's (2000) relational theory of blaming which seeks to allocate the responsibility for wrongdoing between individual citizens and the community. In this context judicial discretion is pivotal in determining the appropriate balance between the rights of the accused and communitarian interests in achieving justice.

65 For further exploration of these issues, see Henham (2001). As Honore (2002, p.494) points out, however, the mandate for judges is to apply the law (i.e. do justice) in accordance with legal norms which are taken to be morally defensible.

66 The notion of 'context' refers to the many analytical levels of rehabilitative praxis in a given local or global setting.

67 A point emphasised long ago by Becker (1973). It should be noted that rehabilitation may be used in the sense implied by Akhavan (2001) to describe some beneficial consequences of retributive punishment.

one which accords primacy to the needs of the offender and is delivered through supportive communities (von Hirsch and Ashworth, 1998, Ch. 1). As Rex (1998) argues, a largely unexplored notion in contemporary rehabilitative theory is that of the *moral authority* of the state. This point is highly significant for conceptualising rehabilitation in the postmodern context where, as Garland (1990, p.186) points out, moral judgments as determinants of rehabilitative ideology have been displaced and substituted by administrative imperatives. Thus, rehabilitation has been subsumed within the panoply of institutional practice and become symbolic of state interests, losing sight of communitarian ideals of social justice and moral education. In the international context, the schism between ideological justifications and institutional practice is accentuated, admitting the possibility of coercion and indeterminacy in sentencing (Lewis, 1971), and a return to positivist rationalisations for treatment. Clearly, the necessary treatment programmes, cooperation and moral commitment necessary to maximise the social utility of rehabilitation in an enforcing state following sentence by an international tribunal remains highly conjectural (Beresford, 2002, p.45, footnote 43).

The conceptual and moral objections to the ideology and policy of incapacitative rationalisations for sentencing are well-documented.[68] The possibility that selective incapacitation might be appropriate where individuals have 'the propensity to commit violations of international humanitarian law, or, possibly, crimes relevant to such violations, such as "hate" crimes or discriminatory crimes' was canvassed by the ICTY in *Kunarac*.[69] Beresford (2002, p.45) appears to suggest that, although the *ad hoc* tribunals are unlikely to adopt preventative or protective justifications on this basis, they may be encouraged to 'adopt some form of incapacitative sentencing' in response to criticism[70] of unduly lenient sentences. In rightly drawing attention to the need to balance the rights of offenders and victims where such decisions are taken, Beresford (2002, p.46) then seems to countenance the moral acceptability of incapacitative sentencing as long discretionary judicial decisions on predictive dangerousness can be justified through third-party expert (medical/psychiatric) opinion.

Beresford's observations raise some interesting philosophical points in the international context, not least of which is that concerned with the possible justifications for protective sentencing. As regards selective incapacitation, views range from pure utilitarianism to undiluted retributivism.The former holds that it is justifiable for sentencers to order precautions to be taken against those offenders who seem likely to commit harmful offences in the future, even when these precautions added to the penalty exceed what is regarded as commensurate to the offence. This is in fact both a reductivist and a utilitarian approach, since it adopts the view that the perceived social utility to be derived from protective sentencing in terms of crime prevention outweighs the humanitarian cost to a small minority of offenders and their families (Tonry, 1992, pp.165–180).[71] For the committed retributivist, precautionary

---

68 For an overview, see Henham (1997).

69 *Kunarac*, *supra*, note 24, para. 843.

70 A significant factor here is surely the source of the criticism.

71 Floud and Young (1981, p.60) have argued that protective sentencing is morally *un*objectionable since dangerous offenders, having forfeited their right to be presumed harmless, must inevitably carry the burden of accepting the principle of just distribution of risks.

sentences are always unjustifiable, since they consist of punishment for crimes as yet uncommitted.[72] This view therefore holds good against both selective and collective forms of incapacitation. In relation to the latter, Crocker (1995) has argued, that the only basis for its justification relies on the notion that the defendant, having failed to serve previous sentences in full has not had *full* retribution extracted from him and therefore it is his moral culpability that merits more severe punishment. Owens (1995) goes so far as to suggest that collective incapacitation is more ethically acceptable than selective incapacitation on the basis that the former does at least reflect previous serious misconduct rather than a presumed tendency towards it.

These contrasting views regarding the morality of protective sentencing in reality represent ethical assumptions which form the moral basis for justifying the ascription or derogation of individual offender's rights[73] in a situation where they are adjudged dangerous. This notion provides a measure of their relevance and acceptability as justifications for international sentencing contexts. Bottoms and Brownsword (1982), for example, argue that preventative detention is always a wrongful violation of detainees' rights, but justified in the case of a *vivid danger* (i.e. when serious harm is likely to be perpetrated in the near future).[74] However, two important questions remain unanswered; first, who is to determine the distinction between a 'vivid' and 'something less than an imminent danger' in predicting whether individuals may commit serious breaches of international humanitarian law in future social conflicts, and, secondly, are these taxonomies in any event adequate or relevant frameworks for the analysis of such contexts? Surely, the unconditional nature of any potential aggressor's actions is more difficult (if not impossible) to predict where societal breakdown and armed conflict persist. It is also legitimate to question whether the conventional bases upon which the relationship between predicted harm, commensurability and culpability are determined in western domestic sentencing systems are appropriate foundations for punishment in the context of international conflict.

Some obfuscation is apparent in the ICTY's deliberations in this respect. More particularly, the Trial Chamber in *Kunarac*[75] appears unconvincing in reasoning that the 'propensity to commit violations of international humanitarian law, or, possibly crimes relevant to such violations' can be discerned only on the basis that an offender might have a record of previous criminal conduct '*relevant to those committed during the armed conflict*',[76] since, 'in practically all cases ... the convicted persons would be first-time offenders *in relation to international crimes*'.[77] The Trial Chamber concluded:

> Violations of international humanitarian law, by their very nature, can be committed only in certain contexts which may not arise again in the society where the convicted person, once, released, may eventually settle.

---

72 For an attempt at reconciliation of the two extremes, see Wood (1998).

73 The significance of rights for international sentencing is addressed in Chapter 6.

74 The concept of 'vividness' includes seriousness, temporality, immediacy and certainty.

75 *Kunarac*, *supra*, note 24, para. 843.

76 Emphasis in original.

77 Emphasis in original.

However, it might equally be asserted that the reasons for conflicts of the kind which arose in the former Yugoslavia and Rwanda are deeply rooted in the historical and cultural fabric of those societies. Consequently, returning offenders who discover upon release that the moral justifications for their previous involvement in armed conflict remain surely have a propensity to commit further violations of international humanitarian law, more particularly so in their desire to seek revenge against those seen as responsible for committing acts in furtherance of a policy of ethnic cleansing. The approach of the ICTY in *Kunarac* is one which relates propensity solely to the immediate circumstances surrounding an offender's participation in the instant conflict, whilst ignoring the past and future context of conflict situations.

The moral basis for any predictive detention is further weakened where the legitimacy of the decision-making body may be impugned, or charged with an institutional bias towards retributive punishment, as has been the case with the *ad hoc* tribunals. The suggestion that international criminal tribunals may be encouraged towards preventative detention in response to perceived public reaction against inadequate or unduly lenient sentences may prove a dangerous threat to individual rights and a guise for the further abuse of retributive punishment exacted against citizens of 'punished' states. It is also worth noting that since sentence lengths for international crimes are necessarily high the scope for additional preventative margins are correspondingly reduced, albeit that the concept of a 'preventative margin' *per se* is highly conjectural.

Christie (2000, p.189) raises some interesting issues for the notion of preventative sentencing and dangerous states.[78] Whilst not directly addressing this relationship in the context of international sentencing, he suggests factors which (I would argue) are pertinent for international criminal tribunals in developing rational justifications for sentence. Christie's focus is on the potential criminality of a state and the effects on its citizens, which, he suggests are far more diverse and difficult to predict than at the individual level.[79] Christie's (2000, p.192) final plea in seeking to influence such states is one for the analysis and clarification of *context*. These questions are important for international punishment because they raise the issue of the position of individual citizens and the state in ways which attempt to link the behaviour of states with notions of civility in the institutions of penal law (for example, the moral climate in which the police operate). Again, for international punishment these insights signal the need for sentencing rationales which are tolerant of communitarian and localised systems of penality. The dichotomy between individual autonomy and globalised systems of penal law is artificially encouraged by the failure to implicate concepts of state and corporate control in the formulation of international punishment rationales.

Before moving to the final section of this chapter, I propose to explore further the complex relationship between retributive rationales and communitarian aspirations for punishment in the international sentencing context by assessing the relevance of Duff's (1986, 1996, 2001) communicative theory of punishment.[80] Duff's thesis

---

78 It should be noted that those international criminal tribunals so far established are concerned with the punishment of individuals rather than states or corporations.

79 Examples signalled by western liberal governments in recent years have included Zimbabwe, Libya and Iraq.

80 For another argument which sees punishment as a form of moral communication, see Nozick (1981).

essentially claims that the main aim of punishment should be to reintegrate individual offenders into the community through a process of reconciliation. Duff believes that this reconciliation is brought about through the process of punishment which induces repentance and aims to alter the moral sentiments of the offender.[81] Thus, punishment is perceived as non-coercive and aimed to communicate to the offender the condemnation of his conduct. In particular, Duff contends that hard treatment punishment:

> … should be understood as a secular species of *penance*. A penance serves several, closely interrelated, purposes. It aims to focus (indeed, to force) the wrongdoer's attention onto his wrongdoing … It aims to communicate to him not merely the judgement that he did wrong, but a symbolic portrayal of the character and implications of that wrong (1998, p.164) [emphasis in original].

Although Duff's theory appears consequentialist, he insists upon its retributive credentials since it relies on the notion of the individual as a rational moral agent whose rehabilitation is achieved through internal reasoning and moral choice, rather than through coercion and the instrumentality of the state. Nevetheless, Duff's account remains ideological and conjectural (Bagaric, 2001),[82] particularly in its insistence that punishment is primarily communicative rather than expressive. His suggestion that coercive measures are necessary in order to induce moral development is controversial, and, indeed, von Hirsch (1993, p.73) has opined that the state is not entitled to use its coercive powers to endeavour to induce moral sentiments. Furthermore, as Hudson (1996, p.51) suggests, communicative theory is deficient as a general justification for sentence, since it fails to offer reasons for moral education and reconnection with communitarian values. Nevertheless, Duff's thesis seems to resonate intuitively with the notion of the international trial as transformative and rehabilitative within the context of a predominantly retributive rationale. Certainly, it might be argued that retributive punishment administered as a morally educative process may be both internally and externally consistent with rehabilitative themes.[83] However, the fundamental weakness of this position stems from its inability to reconcile the moral and social justifications for hard treatment.[84]

Having considered the nature and relevance of conventional punishment rationales in the context of the existing sentencing practices of the *ad hoc* tribunals, it is evident that the disjunction between the moral and the rational justifications for punishment at the international level is unlikely to be satisfactorily addressed through conventional

---

81 In this it moves beyond von Hirsch's emphasis on the censuring aspects of punishment. Von Hirsch (1999) recognises that censure provides the offender with the opportunity to make a rational moral choice to desist from crime, but not on the basis of the kind of moral repentance envisaged by Duff. For further comparison, see Bottoms (1998).

82 Mackie (1982) develops Hume's observation that moral distinctions are founded on sentiment rather than reason by suggesting how genetic and social considerations are responsible for shaping both individual and collective retributive emotions, and thus the ways in which moral thinking is rationalised.

83 As Cavadino and Dignan (2002, p.44) suggest, it fits in well with the ideas and practices of reparation and reintegrative shaming.

84 As Mathiesen (1990, Ch. 2) argues, historically this has not always been the case. See also Narayan (1993).

western liberal approaches to penality. Whatever the instrinsic moral arguments that might be claimed for particular rationalisations, the internationalisation of penal law renders the cultural relevance of moral claims more tenuous. The reason for this is to do with the moral and functional significance of punishment across cultural contexts and the concept of equivalence. In other words, the issue is not simply one of relativity – of recognising that rationalisations for punishment and their moral resonance differ according to cultural context – it is to do with the very notion of punishment and penality itself; that the function and the morality attaching to the labelling of behaviour as deviant and the forms of collective action taken in response are not equivalent in moral or functional terms. In fact, conventional western moral justifications and their rational implementation through the apparatus of state-sponsored punishment may be entirely inappropriate conceptions in certain cultural contexts.

It is for these reasons that I now propose to conclude the chapter by exploring the potentially more reflexive and constructive rationales offered by various restorative justice themes and assessing their significance for international sentencing.[85] The themes of restorative justice are engaged in the first instance because they are felt to offer the best chance for different cultural contexts to seek meaningful engagement with the morality and rationality of international punishment practices. Despite arguments to the effect that notions of truth and justice are more likely to be achieved for particular communities through alternative structural mechanisms, the need to find measures of equivalence for international penality in the enduring presence of international criminal trial structures such as the ICC is incontrovertible. Thus, the engagement with restorative themes is not simply to do with empowering victims and victim communities; it goes to the core of what is an adequate cultural response to gross breaches of international humanitarian law in terms of appropriate moral judgments made and actions taken against perpetrators and collaborators. The task for international structures of penality is to provide the conceptual and practical means to recognise and give effect to differing cultural interpretations of equivalence and relevance in sentencing.

International Sentencing and Restorative Justice Ideology

I would argue that there are several significant reasons for examining the relationship between restorative justice ideology and the rationales for punishment in the international criminal tribunals.

1. At the theoretical level, if we accept Cotterrell's (1992, p.71) notion that law exists as an integrative mechanism, this suggests a need for international sentencing to provide interpretations and adopt practices that might allow us to make the link between the recognition of law as a representation of morality and

---

[85] It is acknowledged that the nature and scope of the restorative justice paradigm is conjectural. Nonetheless, it is normally accepted that it includes elements relating to the humanitarian treatment of offenders, elements of compensation, restitution, reparation and possibly reintegration, diversionary and mediatory processes and victim participation. For an excellent overview, see Johnstone (2002).

the existence of forms of expressed morality in civil society which exist in notions of communitarianism.[86]

2. Restorative justice ideology implies an approach to punishment which is tolerant of the diverse contexts of criminality and capable of accommodating and realising its implications.
3. More pragmatically, if we accept that the largely unfettered judicial discretion pertaining in international tribunals is a powerful authoritative mechanism for legitimating judicial power and rational justifications for retributive punishment, then we must also recognise that the international judiciary are equally pivotal in resolving the tensions between the rights of the accused and those of victims and victim communities which concern reparation and reconciliation.
4. Although the language of restorative justice ideology has featured significantly in the discourse of the *ad hoc* tribunals[87] and receives some attention in the foundation instruments of the ICC,[88] some fundamental issues remained unresolved. More particularly, these relate to what is meant by restorative justice in this context, and how the linkage between rehabilitative aspirations and reconciliation might be conceptualised.
5. Whilst it is necessary to consider exactly how (and on what basis) restorative aspirations beyond reparation or compensation can be integrated into the existing predominantly retributive framework for international punishment (Ashworth, 2002b), I would argue that there is a strong *moral* imperative for punishment to, at the very least, engage constructively with communitarian needs. As Morris suggests:

> ... Uniformity or consistency of approach (as opposed to uniformity or consistency in outcomes) is what is required and this is achieved by always taking into account the needs and wishes of those most directly affected by the offence: victims, offenders and their communities of care (2002, p.610).

Within the consequentialist agenda of restorative justice ideology exist certain basic philosophical assumptions regarding those moral principles which should govern human action or conduct in sentencing offenders. The use of the word 'restorative' intrinsically implies notions of 'rebuilding', 'repairing', 'reinstating'; 'replacing', 're-establishing'; and, similarly, component themes such as reparation or

---

[86] As I suggest elsewhere: 'Thus, the moral legitimacy of the international penal regime is constituted through its capacity to reflect socially meaningful (i.e. pluralistic) conceptions of morally unacceptable behaviour. This in turn requires an acknowledgment that it is the international sentencing *process* itself which provides the transformative mechanism and supplies linkage between moral purpose, legal norms and social behaviour. It follows, therefore, that these purposes (if they are to include reconciliation) must be articulated' (Henham 2003a, p.91) [emphasis in original].

[87] In the case of the ICTR it is explicitly stated that the United Nations Security Council's objective in creating the tribunal pursuant to Article 39 of the Charter is to prosecute and punish the perpetrators of the atrocities in Rwanda to put an end to impunity, *and thereby to promote national reconciliation and restoration of peace* [emphasis added]. This language clearly envisages an instrumental role for the ICTR in this process. Nevertheless, as emphasised in *Prosecutor v Sherushago* (Case No. ICTR 98-39), Judgement and Sentence, 5 February 1999, para. 20, retribution and deterrence remain the primary objectives.

[88] See further, the ICC Statute and Rules of Procedure and Evidence, Section III.

reconciliation are all concerned with conceiving of the discretionary sentence decision-making process as an opportunity for 'harmonisation', 're-engagement', 'healing', or even 'purification'.[89] These moral imperatives have been developed within the context of punishment theory by Braithwaite and Pettit (1990),[90] whose form of utilitarianism is concerned to maximise the notion of dominion; that punishment should promote liberty and be applied only in circumstances where individuals have violated the rights of others.[91] The implications for the pursuit of criminal justice include favouring a socialising rather than a coercive institution to re-enforce the shamefulness of crime:

> ... the socializing institution will do two things at once: it will present crime as wrong and therefore as something of which people ought to be ashamed; and it will present it as a sort of activity actually disapproved of in the society and therefore as something of which people are likely to be made ashamed if they choose it (Braithwaite and Pettit, 1990, p.89).

The implications also favour the presumption that the criminal justice system should pursue strategies of reintegration in the community, particularly the restoration of dominion, and Braithwaite and Pettit (1990, p.91) consider that this is most effectively achieved through reprobation of the offender and the promotion of restorative rather than punitive responses to crime. However, critics have doubted the viability of Braithwaite's insistence that modern societies possess so-called micro-communities of care to shame and reintegrate offenders, or that there is sufficient community support to facilitate restorative justice goals through popular justice.[92]

Notwithstanding particular criticisms of Braithwaite's thesis, there is no doubting its significant influence on penal thought and policy development. Its attractiveness in the international context lies in its capacity to conceptualise the notion of institutional punishment as a process which is firmly anchored in context; in this instance accommodating and providing the linkage between the context of the international trial as a symbolic forum for international public retribution, and the context of the offender as citizen and perpetrator of actions with profound social significance within particular communities. Hence, the promotion of reintegrative policies within the victim community is seen as intimately connected to reprobation of the offender. Forging a conceptual framework between structure and function is an essential prerequisite for Braithwaite's approach, and also sits comfortably with Norrie's (2000) relational theory of blame allocation. It possesses considerable potential for developing sentencing rationales and constructs in international fora which resonate with the needs of victim communities,[93] rather than the dichotomous model that currently exists.

---

[89] These definitions are those contained in the Concise Oxford Dictionary.

[90] For criticism, see von Hirsch (1993, Ch. 3).

[91] We are not concerned with the validity of this position in this chapter.

[92] Braithwaite (1994) is clearly suspicious of the capacity of judicial discretionary power to formulate restorative solutions.

[93] Clearly, any assertion that international punishment must reflect socially meaningful conceptions of morally unacceptable behaviour must also recognise the relativity of context, and the fact that purposes (however developed and principled as legal norms) may be judged morally indefensible by different factions (for instance, where a sentence is designed to deter certain actions which are considered politically

This need extends further than mere clarification of the philosophical justifications for sentence in international tribunals. It is necessary to develop such rationalisations with a firm commitment to ground rationality in context; to relate the justifications for punishment within a unitary paradigm which connects the global and local. An illustration of the need for such an inclusive paradigm is provided by the sense in which utilitarian rationales in the *ad hoc* tribunals have remained disconnected; for instance, part of the obfuscation that exists is precisely because of a failure to engage with the notion that individual and collective rehabilitation are fundamentally interrelated. Traditional postmodern conceptions regard rehabilitation as essentially reductivist in promoting crime reduction; the ethos of the justification is that it suggests the provision of 'curative' or 'healing' disposals. Furthermore, as suggested by the Trial Chamber of the ICTY in the *Delalic* [94] case, in order to achieve facilitate this objective:

> The factor of rehabilitation considers *the circumstances of reintegrating* the guilty accused into society ... so that they can become useful members of it and enable them to lead normal and productive lives upon their release from imprisonment [emphasis added].

In the Appeals Chamber,[95] the Tribunal, whilst acknowledging its significance reaffirmed that rehabilitation could not 'play a *predominant* role' in the decision-making process (para. 806) (emphasis in original), and was clearly subordinate to deterrence and retribution as the main purposes of sentencing in the *ad hoc* tribunals. In their deliberations the Appeals Chamber refer to the primacy accorded to rehabilitation in many national jurisdictions and certain international and human rights instruments, such as the International Covenant on Civil and Political Rights, Article 10(3) of which states that: 'The penitentiary system shall comprise treatment of prisoners the essential aim of which shall be their reformation and social rehabilitation.' The *ad hoc* tribunals have clearly failed to connect with the notion of rehabilitation in the wider context of the potential for its conceptualisation as an individual and collective endeavour.

Mathiesen (1990, p.29) makes an important point relating to the relative moral influence of rehabilitative ideology within the prison system, and more particularly, that the rationality of this ideology has been maintained to fulfil the demands of *system interests.* I would argue that these observations are equally pertinent to the characterisation of rehabilitation in international penality through its failure to exploit the nexus between individual and social rehabilitation within a more far-reaching and inclusive paradigm for punishment which is tolerant of process *and outcome*. In so doing, the relationship between rationalisations supporting

---

legitimate). Since the primary function of the trial process remains that of blame allocation, more constructive and transformative sentences depend on the explicit identification of needs and the nature of particular communities. As Cotterrell (2002a) suggests, these communities may be of shared beliefs or interests, extending beyond the boundaries of the nation state. Much depends on the extent to which international tribunals are able to legitimise law's authority through sentencing practices which are sensitive to the communities regulated by international criminal and human rights law.

94 *Delalic*, *supra*, note 58, para. 1233.

95 *Prosecutor v Delalic* (Case No. IT-96-21), Appeals Judgement, 20 February 2001, para. 806.

rehabilitation and those supporting the institutions of hegemonic power cannot be ignored.[96]

On the basis of Dignan and Cavadino's (1996) attempts to construct a typology of victim-based contexts for evaluating criminal justice, the current limited conceptualisations afforded by international criminal tribunals for rehabilitative and restorative justice themes are undoubtedly circumscribed by the tribunals' adherence to a traditional retributive model. To progress beyond this philosophical and institutional limitation would require both a philosophical reorientation which favours the moral utility of achieving reparative justice through reconciliation, and further, the reintegration and empowerment of victims by adopting a more communitarian model (Cavadino and Dignan, 1996, p.156). The latter, however, is largely envisaged as dependant on institutional change, whereas the traditional court process[97] is seen as an inappropriate locus for reintegrative ceremonies and popular forms of justice. Further, as Zedner (1994) suggests, prevailing notions of reparative justice and retribution tend to 'ignore the structural imperatives of deprivation and disadvantage under which many offenders act' whilst more developed conceptualisations of reparative justice might be capable of addressing communitarian ideals of social justice (Zedner 1994, p.250). Zedner advocates a vision of reparative justice predicated on the utility of all criminal justice practices as sharing responsibility for social inclusion and control and the equal distribution and enforcement of rights.

The possibilities of furthering the interests of restorative justice within a communitarian framework in the international context also raises some fundamental questions regarding the meaning of 'truth' and 'justice'. At the decision-making level, there is no doubt that within the *ad hoc* tribunals and the ICC the overriding determinant of what constitutes 'truth' (or in Tamanaha's terms, the value added to facts and the determination of what constitutes fact *ab initio*) is the existence of largely unfettered judicial discretion. However, the potency of the discretionary variable is equally significant (if not more so) for alternative resolution mechanisms. Moghalu (2001) therefore makes a significant point when he suggests that a holistic approach to the resolution of conflict is required; meaning that prosecutions and alternative mechanisms should *not* necessarily be regarded as mutually exclusive. In the light of the Rwandan experience, Drumbl (2000) concludes more pragmatically that policy responses and institutional form should be grounded in *context* in order to obviate the imperatives of globalised or legalistic agendas. Drumbl (2000, p.1317) considers that the western response of retributive and punitive justice as universally implemented could effectively eliminate the discretion necessary to assess the nature of affected post-genocidal societies. In a later paper he also advocates the introduction of 'a new blended paradigm' which will facilitate the combination of contextually derived retributive and restorative justice themes, although this is not developed conceptually (Drumbl, 2002, p.301).

---

[96] As exemplified by Article 33 of the Socialist Federal Republic of Yugoslavia (SFRY) Criminal Code which includes the following as two of its three reasons for the imposition of sentence: '(1) preventing the offender from committing criminal acts *and his rehabilitation*; (3) strengthening the moral fibre of a socialist self-managing society and influence *on the development of the citizens' social responsibility and discipline*' [emphasis added].

[97] Whether adversarial, inquisitorial or hybrid.

The contemporary relationship between truth and justice and the prospects for developing fused, holistic or blended paradigms which reconcile competing justifications for punishment is further complicated by the relative validity accorded those interpretations produced by institutional mechanisms developed and charged with determining the balance between fact and value. On the one hand, the *ad hoc* tribunals appear unequivocal about their mission:

> Discovering the truth is a cornerstone of the rule of law and a fundamental step on the way to reconciliation: for it is truth that cleanses the ethnic and religious hatreds and begins the healing process.[98]

Similarly, the ICTR Trial Chamber in *Kambanda*[99] found itself the arbiter of the truth of the former Rwandan prime minister's protestations of remorse and repentance as expressed in his plea agreement[100] in which it was alleged that:

> ... his prime motivation for pleading guilty was the profound desire to tell the truth, as the truth was the only way to restore national unity and reconciliation in Rwanda.

Whilst clearly doubting the genuineness of Kambanda's contrition the Trial Chamber accepted the characterisation adopted in many civil criminal law systems of the guilty plea as a demonstration of honesty to be equated with truth and justice. However, as discussed, the interpretation of truth forced by the institutionalisation of penality through the structures of international criminal tribunals is shaped predominantly by retributivism and crime control considerations.

On the other hand, alternative structures and processes, such as Truth and Reconciliation Commissions (TRCs) in their various forms, provide alternative relative interpretations of truth and justice that are drawn from (and rooted in) *context*, and, therefore, it is claimed, nearer to historical truth (Cohen, 1995; Osiel, 1995). However, whether TRCs provide a more relevant[101] form of truth is conjectural since it is arguable that international criminal justice may have a more enduring impact on victims, because trials contribute to the deconstruction of myths that surround notions of collective responsibility. International criminal trials also provide a symbolic, and historically definitive version of truth with legal consequences which assists in achieving closure and a refocusing of efforts on the reconstruction of broken communities. Internationalised courts and tribunals created to exist alongside domestic processes of accountability (including TRCs), as in Sierra Leone, East Timor and Serbia (Bohlander, 2001; Linton 2001a, 2001b; Strohmeyer 2001), also appear to operate within different criminal justice parameters, reflecting the failure to develop standardised norms of criminalisation to underpin international criminal justice practice (Schabas 2002).

Notwithstanding, a more significant conceptual issue for reconciling penal justifications concerns the transformative capacity of international sentencing law

---

98 *Erdemovic*, *supra*, note 17, para. 21.

99 *Kambanda*, *supra*, note 11, para. 50.

100 For discussion of the impact of such crime control mechanisms on international process, see Henham (2003a, pp.100–109).

101 Relevant in the sense of victims or communities.

and the relationship between transformation and context; in effect, law's relationship to notions of truth, reconciliation and justice. Although TRCs have provided alternative paradigms for the reconciliation of victim communities, their relative capacity to integrate retributive and restorative imperatives may be limited for both conceptual and pragmatic reasons. For example, Christodoulidis (2000) questions the capacity of legal rules to bring about reconciliatory functions such as 'mercy' through the process of the South African Truth and Reconciliation Commission.[102] He argues that law is overdeterministic and incapable of proceeding beyond the categorical abstractions imposed by the reductive nature of legal rules:

> ... there can be no *legal* judgement over appropriateness of the application of law. There can be no decision *within* a context as to the appropriateness *of* the context (Christodoulidis 2000, p.189) [emphasis in original].

Thus, Christodoulidis suggests that essentially complex reflexive ethical decisions cannot be reached solely within a legal context, nor can it address the phenomenological connections between conflict and social identity necessary to produce reconciliation. These themes are continued in more recent contributions, particularly du Bois's (2001) notion that, whilst reconciliation is about transcending differences, truth depends on emphasising the distinction between perpetrators and victims, and van Roermund (2001), who suggests further that truth actually depends on the desire for reconciliation and amounts to a recognition of the humaneness of the perpetrator.

These insights could be equally well directed at international trial process, or indeed, particular forms of criminal process. In the case of the former, as we have seen, the search for truth is delineated by retributive concerns which condition the form of punishment and shape those discretionary interpretations which determine the distance between guilt and truth. Yet the perceived legitimacy of the structures which are designed to test competing versions of truth is a separate issue from that which envisages the notion of law as a moral code that possesses a transformative *capacity*, as has been argued earlier in this chapter. The former is merely an acknowledgement that structure, form and decision-making are patterned by social rules, whilst the latter focuses on the essence of the operation of law within social contexts. In this lies the resolution of the debate between Nelken and Cotterrell concerning the extent to which sociological insights are relevant to the interpretation of legal ideas, and the validity of Cotterrell's assertion that legal contexts should only be interpreted sociologically (Nelken, 1998; Cotterrell, 1998a; Banakar, 2000).

As I have argued elsewhere (Henham 2001, p.267), analysis of the law and process of sentencing is necessary in order to explain the transformation of sentencing law's narrative principles into morally significant reasons for action. Consequently, the transformation of law into normative guides to conduct requires an appreciation of the relationship between legal reasoning and punishment both analytically (as legal formalism) and sociologically (as process). Acknowledging the relativity of context

---

102 The route to reconciliation through amnesty offered by mechanisms such as the South African Truth and Reconciliation Commission was rejected by the *ad hoc* tribunals as incompatible with the primary purpose of prosecution and the willingness of a state to bring the perpetrators of atrocities to justice.

and process also recognises the plurality of legal interpretations and the temporal and cultural relativity of conventional accounts (Rogers and Erez, 1999). Philosophical justifications provide the moral context for developing the normative potential of sentencing law through the process of discretionary decision-making. The legitimacy of process depends on the capacity of international sentencing law to connect with pluralistic notions of morality within conflict societies, thereby investing internationalised punishment with a sense of moral security; a context of meaning rooted in communities (Cotterrell, 1998b). The recursivity of international process will also ensure that as its sentencing jurisprudence develops exponentially the moral bases of law's authority and its reflection in punishment will widen and draw increasing attachment between global and local conceptions of truth and justice.

Summary

The following propositions have been argued and elaborated in the preceding analysis:

- The examination and grounding of the philosophical rationales for international punishment must relate to global and local contexts.
- Rationality and consistency of approach are not mutually exclusive aspirations for international sentencing praxis.
- The pragmatic reconciliation (or otherwise) of punishment rationales is achieved through the discretionary decision-making process.[103]
- The potential reconciliation of competing claims for punishment through sentencing is not a rational or sufficient justification for the practice of punishing breaches of international humanitarian law.
- Moral justifications and normative practice in international sentencing must address the forces that produce and sustain conflict and social breakdown.
- International punishment should convey to citizens the notion that the behaviour with which it deals is morally blameworthy.
- International punishment adopts a paradigm based on the relative autonomy of states and citizens that ignores the forces of globalisation and its consequences.[104]
- There is a need to appreciate the transformative capacity of sentencing and the connections that are made through punishment between moral justifications and moral legitimacy.
- The only way to justify the morality of international sentencing is by providing rationalisations for punishment which facilitate the convergence of notions of truth with justice.
- The relative realities of truth and justice are revealed where structure and process are grounded in context.

[103] The issues of judicial regulation and accountability are particularly relevant.

[104] The impact of international human rights norms has no effect on these processes.

Chapter 6

Access to Justice and Rights

Introduction

There is no doubt that the influence of the human rights paradigm on the domestic legal systems of western liberal democracies in the late twentieth century has been substantial. These forces have correspondingly informed the debates and substantive content of the foundation instruments of more recently created international criminal trial institutions such as the ICTY, ICTR and the ICC (Findlay, 2002). However, as suggested, the rules and procedures to support and develop international criminal law and sentencing have been driven in equal measure by multinational political imperatives (Dennis, 1997). As discussed, this paradox raises some fundamental questions about the true nature of the justifications which form the basis for rationalising the 'justice' of punishment in international sentencing decisions and, more specifically, the conceptualisation and role for human rights envisaged within this context. It is the latter which provides the focus for this chapter.

In particular, I argue that the incorporation of human rights norms into the rules and procedures of international criminal trial fora is merely symbolic, driven by the need to provide a veneer of legitimacy to the hegemonic ambitions of Western Europe and the US.[1] Against this argument is the notion of the universality of the values such rights are meant to protect. As Cassese (1999) suggests, for the ICC, a humanitarian mission provides the rationale for its existence rather than national adversarial systems where the primary justification for courts is to provide order and stability for civil society. In short, the notion of international criminal justice is inextricably linked to the fate of the victims of crimes against international humanitarian law.

So portrayed, these arguments present a simplistic and false dichotomy for the purposes of analysis, since they make no distinction between ideology and pragmatism. I would argue that the conceptualisation and analysis of international criminal justice implies a need to collapse the distinction between principle and

[1] For an excellent discussion of politicisation in the ICTY's sentencing practices, see Alvarez (1998); for example: 'Throughout the opinion, from its preliminary findings through the specific factual and legal findings against Tadic, it is hard to escape the conclusion that the judges' target is not merely Tadic, but Serbian nationalism, and that the judges' tacit endorsement of community values in favor of an integrationist ethic is also incidentally an endorsement of the Dayton formula for peace. Because of this, the tribunal's solid legal case for criminal liability under international humanitarian law itself poses risks that the tribunal will continue to be perceived as the political tool of those states who were most instrumental in establishing it.' See also Alvarez (1999, p.479), where the supposed impartiality of ICC judges is questioned.

practice; more particularly, the recognition of certain crimes as breaching the human rights of victims and the process rights relating to trials of such crimes (Henham, 2000b). In other words, the description and evaluation of rights against standards of procedural fairness must determine and explain the socio-historic conditions of their creation *and* the social reality of that existence for significant actors (both individual and collective).

Accordingly, as throughout this book, the analytical theme of this chapter is the contextualisation of rights in international sentencing, in the sense of providing what Tamanaha (1997, p.54) describes as a pragmatic understanding of the fact/value distinction. The principal implication of this perspective for distinguishing and understanding conceptions such as access to justice, fair trial and rights in the context of international sentencing is fundamental in suggesting that they are only meaningful if we examine their social reality.[2] The aim of this chapter is, therefore, to evaluate the significance of this position for furthering our understanding of the theoretical and empirical dimensions of international sentencing process.[3]

The chapter is divided into three main parts. The first draws attention to key issues for the conceptualisation of rights in the context of international sentencing. Secondly, the analysis examines the relationship between process values, rights and the legitimacy of international sentencing praxis, and goes on to explore some theoretical concerns relating to our understanding of rights in postmodernity and their implications for the conceptualisation of international penality. Thirdly, the analysis considers the nature of conceptions of access to justice and rights for victims in international sentencing. The chapter concludes that the differences between the symbolism and relative reality of process rights for victims and victim communities reflect a more fundamental need to re-conceptualise the notion of victims' rights in the wider context of international penality.

The Internationalisation of Sentencing and Rights

The Relational Context

In his recent Hamlyn Lectures, Ashworth (2002a, p.3) suggests that the sort of egregious crimes which constitute gross breaches of international humanitarian law

[2] For an example of the significance of context relating to the significance of the trial in constructing a common legal culture, see Alvarez (1998): '... the nature of legal narratives matters: legal storytelling is, after all, constructed within a "culture of argument" whose goal is to persuade. Accordingly, trials may elicit a kind of solidarity premised on civil engagement in disagreements by way of procedures entailing display of respect for one's adversary, respect that may be entirely procedural (and a matter of rules-following) at the outset but that often tends to grow into something more substantive – if not between the most unreconstructed of antagonists, then among the larger numbers of their more moderate sympathizers. There is a kind of solidarity, in other words, in continuing exchanges that result in the mutual recognition that agreement on a question of common concern is strongly desirable and ultimately possible, even if only at some uncertain point in the future.'

[3] For further elaboration of the theoretical and methodological foundations for comparative contextual analysis, see Henham and Findlay (2001).

can be condemned without reference to human rights, but recognition of them *as* violations of human rights lends a further layer of objectivity to the condemnation. Ashworth considers that this layer comes, not from the fact that rights in relation to criminal procedure for international criminal trials can be measured against paradigms such as the European Convention on Human Rights (ECHR), but rather from the idea of human rights violations being associated more with grave atrocities than with the rights of defendants and suspects.

This observation highlights the dialectical nature of this conceptualisation of human rights norms and its relationship to international sentencing practice. The normative objectivity of international humanitarian law and the complexities of legal justice do not resonate with the subjectification of punishment in the international community (especially victim communities) and does not, therefore, enable significant psychological connections to be made between law and action – in short, law, process and rights operate at a relative distance. More particularly, this realisation re-enforces the need to construct a meaningful model of justice for international sentencing which recognises the relational quality of rights norms; one which appreciates the fact that process rights must relate to the legal and moral context of criminal action and punishment. As Norrie (2000) suggests, a relational model of justice is concerned to examine the connections between responsible individuals and communities so that punishment is envisaged as part of that shared experience. Rights conceived in these terms implies a sharing of the justice process; namely, that rights should no longer be conceived as a distinct set of normative constraints on process, but rather as an integral and inseparable component of relational justice. In effect, for international penality this conceptualisation envisages a meaningful connection between the universality of rights and their application in context.

However, to what extent are these notions of relationality relevant for contemporary conceptions of international penality? One way to explore this question is to examine the focus of rights and international penality in the context of the relationship between states, offenders and victims. Garland (2001, p.110) has argued that, in Western European domestic systems of penality, the state's claim to sovereignty in terms of crime control and punishment is a myth. Since it is politically unacceptable for the state to withdraw from the promise to protect its citizens, this results in limited institutional reform together with adaptations taking the form of either politicised/pragmatic reactions to new threats, or what Garland calls 'expressive mode'; a sort of acting out of the anger and outrage that crime provokes. This scenario emphasises the exclusory nature of the dialectical connection between formal justice and popular justice; the fact that so-called rational formal law as a mechanism of organised social control is supportive of selected moral and political norms, whilst 'popular justice' is misrepresented as supporting the social and political interests of individual citizens and the rule of law (Norrie, 1996b, p.395).

For international penality the links between states and citizens are even more tenuous. The claim to penal sovereignty is universal (Amann, 2000); it exists in the capacity of certain nation states united as a multilateral entity (such as through the UN) to act collectively and proactively against a perceived threat to protect citizens, or, reactively, to punish what has been done as a breach of international criminal law. Universal human rights norms are deployed in order to perpetuate the notion that the institutions of international punishment exist to promote these claims by upholding principles of justice and fairness which command universal allegiance.

However, the penality of international sentencing is not predicated upon rational principles derived from these universally claimed justifications to act. The point is well illustrated by Alvarez when referring to the absence of community sentiments on which to base notions of closure for the ICTY:

> As this implies, a basic flaw in the model of closure as applied to the Balkan conflict is that such cases of mass atrocities in fact arise ... because there are few shared community sentiments and therefore little on which tribunals can draw ... at least to elicit a shared emotional response. There is also the problem that the prospects for the restoration of some shared values may depend, at least when the effort involves international tribunals, on a broad consensus that if political acts are condemned as crimes because they violate fundamental values, international efforts to convict should apply to all members of the international community (Alvarez, 1998).

Consequently, punishment is played out 'at a distance'. It is shaped by the international political context. Also reflective of western domestic penality is the tendency to diminish offender status in preference to victim status, which facilitates the widespread acceptance of repressive punishment (Schabas, 2001b).

The practical reality is that the application of human rights norms are subject to similar forces. As embodied in structure (rules of procedure and evidence), protective devices are interpreted in ways that re-enforce the predominant political ideology informing the international criminal process. They are also subject to situational perceptions of the trial and its participants which are grounded in political and social contexts.

Symbolism and Rights

It is also important to note how the symbolism and reality of rights for international sentencing processes parallel and extend domestic paradoxes. A useful illustration relates to the balance between the assertion of victims' rights and conceptions of the public interest. For example, in the context of England and Wales, Ashworth (1993, 2000a, 2002, p.77) argues that victims' interests should count for no more than anyone else's when considering in whose interests the criminal justice process is being carried out. Notwithstanding that such a restrictive conceptualisation of victims' rights is controversial, the issue of victims' rights and the public interest also raises other difficult questions. These include defining the nature of the public interest; whether public interest arguments are contrary to the intrinsic nature of fundamental rights; how conflicts between fundamental rights and the public interest (or conflicting public interests) might be resolved. These debates reflect that, whilst it may be in the public interest that fundamental rights are upheld, there is an absence of any meta-principle to guide rational choice and so provide for the principled development of human rights norms (Douzinas, 1996, p.128). The paradox therefore exists at two conceptually distinct levels: first, that there is no rational basis for reconciling public interests and fundamental rights, and, secondly, that state discourse espouses a rationale for supporting victims' rights for public interest reasons which is obfuscatory, designed to conceal the progressive alienation of citizen and state in matters of criminal justice.

At the international level, the concept of 'public interest' is clearly inadequate to convey the nature of the relationship between citizens and the institutions and mechanisms of punishment. Furthermore, as discussed earlier, there is no rational basis upon which to explore the relational contexts of international punishment without recognising the social reality of power and social control in the new international world order. Consequently, although several 'interests' might be identified as relevant (for example, multinational economic and political interests; the interests of victim communities; offenders' interests), arguments for balancing basic rights and interests depend, ultimately, on our perception of how the goals of international punishment come to be defined and resolved. If the aims and solutions are perceived as partial or repressive, then it becomes appropriate to challenge the basis upon which particular rights are secured and upheld in international criminal trials.

At present, it is questionable whether the assertion of fundamental human rights for citizens of victim communities is seen as a primary rationale for the existence of internationalised penal structures alongside the punishment of gross human rights violations under international humanitarian law.[4] It may, therefore, be argued that, if for western liberal democracies the state's punishment apparatus exists merely as a symbolic focus for social control, the institutions of international punishment provide a symbolic focus for the political management of international risk (Shearing, 2001).

The Notion of Balance

Returning to what may be regarded as the correct balance between the interests of victims and others in local criminal process systems, Ashworth's position has been convincingly challenged by Cavadino and Dignan (1997, p.237), who suggest that, although the premise for the 'public interest' argument is essentially valid, the conclusion Ashworth draws from it does not automatically follow. They suggest that, as long as there is some sort of officially administered 'state veto' of the behaviour, what the judge chooses to do to satisfy any reparative requirements of the victim should be accommodated. Whilst recognising that victim satisfaction and empowerment constitute an aspect of the 'public interest', Cavadino and Dignan concede that victim allocution should be limited to reparative rather than retributive considerations. However, they advocate that restorative themes are more likely to be maximised through the adoption of an 'integrated restorative justice' model which allows for a principled compromise between retributive and reparative/restorative justice themes based on Dworkinian rights theory (Cavadino and Dignan, 2002, p.54).

For international sentencing, the idea that the balance between victims, offenders and ordinary citizens might be achieved more equitably if criminal justice was concerned to maximise personal autonomy through participation in offence resolution is an attractive one. Braithwaite (2002, p.202) has recently argued,

---

4 Defining the legal relationship between international crimes and human rights violations is difficult; see Roht-Arriaza (1999).

however, that this is more likely to be achieved through restorative and responsive regulation within combatant states than by selective criminal enforcement which 'creates incentives to invest in setting up scapegoats' rather than in complying with the law. Since, realistically, such aspirations will be largely pursued through alternative resolution mechanisms, the pursuit of restorative themes in international sentencing is destined to remain severely constrained by the limited scope for victim participation provided by the conventional retributive model adopted by international criminal tribunals and its systemic weaknesses.[5]

The Retributive Dynamic

The primacy of the retributive dynamic in international sentencing clearly has a direct impact on rights. As Schabas (2001b) suggests, the focus on the rights of the prosecution, victims and punishment in international criminal trial process is evinced by the fact that a 'culture of conviction' rather than a 'culture of acquittal' now predominates. The latter, which protected the rights of defendants, and ensured fair trial standards, has been overtaken by a zeal for the elaboration of new enforcement and punishment mechanisms; in effect, the system of international criminal justice oppresses the accused.[6] Equally, the international community's focus on punishment, rather than protection or deterrence, has reflected the expenditure on *ad hoc* tribunals rather than human rights protection mechanisms. There are also broader questions raised about the legitimacy of international trial processes which lack any institutionalised mechanisms of accountability, thereby increasing the danger of violations of human rights (such as defendants' rights) by supranational organisations (such as the ICC). Again, this kind of 'democratic deficit' serves to distance the structures of international penality from national domestic contexts and communitarian values. As Ashworth (2002a, p.83) suggests, processes incompatible with human rights violate the integrity principle and cannot claim moral standing.

It should also be noted that the predominance of the retributive dynamic in international penality exists notwithstanding the fact that common law/civil law models of criminal procedure as reflected in international sentencing process have influenced the conceptualisation and recognition of rights. If we take as an illustration the presumption of innocence, as Chiavario (2002) notes, this is deeply entrenched in Western European judicial culture, and whilst its form and significance varies between countries, there is general recognition that its existence is related to the 'right to a judicial process' for the accused. The presumption of innocence is similarly enshrined in the ICC Statute (Article 66). Overcoming the presumption is a

[5] An example is the so-called 'public advantage' to be obtained through the encouragement of guilty pleas; see dissenting opinion of Judge Cassese in *Prosecutor v Erdemovic* (Case No. IT-96-22), Appeals Judgement, 7 October 1997, para. 8.

[6] Schabas (2001b) further suggests that, while the provisions relating to due process and fair trial are very strong within the ICC Statute, the institutional structure and inevitable questions as to the equality of arms constrains the defence in its role. The prosecution bias is exacerbated by the lenient rules on heresay, corroboration and a general bending of admissibility rules. Similarly, the tightening of many substantive norms, such as those relating to command responsibility, has made the task of defence counsel even harder. Judicial interpretation also takes the bias further. The national security issue is another perceived threat to defendants' rights.

necessary precondition for a non-arbitrary conviction. However, in both domestic and international jurisdictions, fundamental rights remain theoretical to the extent that they are readily sacrificed for procedural, managerial and bureaucratic advantage. One way to reconcile these apparently competing forces is to suggest, as Tulkens (2002, p.652) does, that for Western European systems of criminal procedure, negotiated justice represents a move away from notions of the universality of the criminal law towards a more civil law oriented model that recognises its facilitative function in the reconciliation of public/private interests.

There are interesting parallels here for internationalised justice and rights. Clearly, fundamental objections to the functionalist paradigm of consensual justice are inequality between the parties, discriminatory practice and lack of transparency. These arguments tend to suggest that rights protection will increase if the normative practice of criminal procedure is more effectively regulated. However, such technical adjustments are unlikely to sever the link between ideology and praxis.[7] In particular, for international sentencing the ideology and structures of punishment are closely aligned to maintaining the economic and political integrity of western liberal democracies. Conceptualisations of criminal law and procedure as facilitative of consensual forms of justice provision therefore fail to recognise cultural relativism and the predominantly authoritarian and undemocratic function of international criminal trials.

In reality, although the ideological precepts of international criminal law and the need to punish and prevent gross violations of human rights are universally acclaimed, their manifestation as principles of administrative justice is not suggestive of how to balance individual rights against the apparatus of partisan political power since that is not their object. The declared philosophical rationale (or in Hart's (1968) terms, the 'general justifying aim') for the creation of international penal processes remain predominantly retributive and marginally deterrent. Thus, the principles for distributive justice also remain imprecise and unarticulated (Beresford, 2002; Henham, 2003a). Arguably, this state of affairs reflects the partiality and localised nature of human rights provision, and, as Fitzpatrick (2001, p.190) suggests, merely serves to illustrate that we are a long way from any utopian universalist vision for human rights provision of the sort advocated by de Sousa Santos (1995, p.330). It also emphasises the tenuous nature of the links often drawn between globalisation and the realisation of a democratic and human rights culture (Steiner, 1999). These insights in turn force a re-examination of the relationship between human rights and democratic principles in the context of internationalisation (Loughlin, 2001).

Finally, it is important to note that, just as common law/civil law models of criminal procedure as reflected in international sentencing process (Cassese, 1999, p.484) are relevant to the conceptualisation and recognition of rights (Findlay, 2001), so the development of these paradigms are likely to reflect back on domestic jurisdictions in their assessments of what constitutes acceptable trial practice. Further, for the ICC, as Roht-Arriaza (1999, p.484) suggests, states may take more positive steps than in the past to ensure compatibility with internationally affirmed

---

[7] As Frase (1998) suggests in another context: '... mere procedural guarantees are an inadequate safeguard against political and governmental oppression ... if human rights are to serve as an effective bulwark against government oppression, they must be extended beyond procedure ...'

rights, and the principle of complementarity is also likely to provide a powerful incentive for compliance.

To summarise, the foregoing analysis has drawn attention to the significance of lack of autonomy and global governance as major factors in the conceptualisation of rights for international sentencing. If we accept the premise that the rationales adopted by states for the redistribution of economic and political risk are the true motivators for the reconfiguration of criminal justice, both domestically and internationally, then it follows that institutional structures for punishment are key symbolic mechanisms for sustaining power and control. Whilst the relative autonomy of citizens and the state in conventional liberal democracies is reflected domestically in recognised principles for the administration of justice, international penal processes and rights norms have to date had no direct involvement with citizens within victim communities. The perception that retributive punishment is appropriate for the commission of gross violations of human rights, and the need for prevention have, therefore, determined the nature of the conceptual linkage between process norms and values rather than any relational context.

Theorising Process Values and Rights

Process and Legitimacy

The rights dimensions of international trial practice and their reflection in domestic sentencing regimes pose difficulties in their conceptualisation and evaluation. Their conceptualisation might be achieved against theoretical models of the international criminal justice process, but we are far from developing credible models for domestic jurisdictions, let alone international ones (Frase, 1998, p.111; Henham, 1998). Clearly, there are perceived policy advantages to be gained through the evaluation of criminal justice processes (including the recognition and operation of human rights norms) against appropriate models, but the issue is far from straightforward. To begin with, as suggested in Chapter 2, there is a failure among analysts to distinguish the ontological commitments implicit in certain forms of modelling (Henham and Findlay, 2002); for instance, the traditional heuristic function of theoretical models in social science illustrated by Packer's (1968) seminal crime control/due process dichotomous model of the criminal process as compared with the normative modelling of Ashworth's (1996, 1998, Ch. 2) rights-based approach.

It is certainly true that adversarial/inquisitorial and crime control/due process models focus too narrowly on trial procedures and the identification of value systems, but, as I have argued elsewhere (Henham, 1998), rights modelling must also draw a firm distinction between *identification* and *prescription*. In other words, in conceptualising and modelling the criminal process it is important to distinguish the processes of normative identification and normative prescription (Henham, 2001, p.267). Another way of approaching this difference is to consider it as reflective of the perennial fact/value dichotomy. Essentially, normative identification refers to the capacity of models to collapse fact/value by possessing the capability to conceptualise and identify the objective and subjective meaning of social action – in this instance, rights protection in court process. Objective understanding of fact relates to what rights law signifies and how it impacts, whilst subjectification concerns our ability to appreciate the moral content of law and the transformation of moral reasons for action into normative behaviour through the operation of law. Normative prescription is concerned with the evaluation of criminal process and policy-making the results of which (in turn) inform theory.

I would argue that our understanding of the role of human rights norms in the criminal trial process has been hampered by failure to develop a model which is sensitive to the fact/value dimensions of social process. Although Ashworth (1998, p.29) is clearly correct in suggesting that his rights-based approach is normative rather than descriptive, it is also prescriptive since it is concerned to identify not only the aims of the criminal process, but also the nature, foundation, ambit and relative importance of rights in their wider social context (Ashworth, 1996, pp.229–330). However, Ashworth's approach does not move beyond moral prescription and address how conflicts between normative principles might be worked out as empirical reality (Henham and Findlay, 2002).

The significance of these observations for rights modelling are intensified when analysing the international sentencing process. In general terms, the core issues for understanding are the transformation of moral principles into moral reasons for subjective action through the process of sentencing and the application of punishment, and the ability of sentence modelling to provide a conceptual vehicle for understanding both the normative and the empirical reality of process. More specifically, these issues are crucially important in the context of the operation of human rights norms in international sentencing for the following reasons:

1. As an exercise in legal positivism, it is necessary for us to be able to delineate the 'objective' boundaries of rights law. As with any other form of transplanted law and hybridised process, one aspect of comparative analysis must include the capacity for understanding the significance of particular practices. As Frase (1998, p.114) suggests, traditional models are incapable of appreciating such conceptual nuances as, for example, with plea bargaining, which may be viewed as either adversarial *or* inquisitorial in character. Another example concerns victim participation – what is the significance and possible effect of permitting (as does the ICC) a degree of victim participation in the proceedings? Does it, akin to civil law systems where civil process designed to claim reparation for injuries caused are merged with criminal proceedings, impact adversely on judicial attitudes to victim testimony during the trial (Henham and Mannozzi, 2003)?
2. Even more complex is the requirement for modelling which is capable of interpreting and translating competing versions of social reality into commonly accepted definitions of rights principles. It is in this sense that we are concerned with the 'subjectification' of process, or how the relationship between legal reasoning and punishment in sentencing can be conceptualised and explained as a form of social reality which is capable of accounting for the transformation of law's normativity into morally significant reasons for action. Essentially, understanding must proceed at the levels of inference and meaning to produce accounts of how rules, procedures and processes are conceptualised and understood by trial participants in the daily interaction of sentencing. As Rogers

and Erez (1999) suggest, the social reality of sentencing for trial participants is revealed by exploring the 'objectivity' or common experience of process whilst also deconstructing its 'subjectivity'.

These theoretical and methodological imperatives are compounded for understanding international process where there must be some comparable[8] definitions of what participants in the sentencing process understand by a particular event and its significance. If we return to our earlier example of the presumption of innocence, Chiavario (2002, p.553) suggests the general connection of this principle to the 'right to a judicial process'. However, enshrined in the foundation instruments of international criminal tribunals this fundamental right falls to be interpreted in the context of novel hybridised processes which contain procedural imports and compromises, such as the procedure relating to the admission of guilt under Article 65 of the ICC Statute. The relationship between theory and context is complex here because what is required of rights modelling is the capacity to appreciate how the subjective experience of process in domestic jurisdictions is connected to its objective existence in international fora.

The objectivity of process exists to the extent that we are able to identify the criteria whereby relevant participants recognise external reality, i.e. the reality of objects, events or states. The connections between subjective experience and objectivity exist in so far as there are common definitions of process as objective reality. The interaction between normative principles such as the presumption of innocence and procedural rules relating to the admission of guilt will be conditioned by legal culture. As Bell suggests:

> ... categorisation depends on what the various legal actors think is happening in a legal situation ... Although the participant has a personal perspective on legal events, culture is a collective phenomenon where groups use the same language and have a common identity despite other differences ... assignment of meaning to natural facts depends on collective intentionality ... the community acting creates the institutional reality, which individuals can then use to explain events. But it is clear that this institutional system and practice precedes them (2001, Ch. 1).

However, in our interpretation of legal culture[9] we must, as Hodgson (2000) observes,[10] be mindful of the fact that legal language exists within the *context* of legal culture, and that mere categorisation and comparison does not equate with objectivity. These difficulties become clearer if we pursue our example of the relationship between the presumption of innocence and admissions of guilt in international sentencing process.

---

[8] Not only within, but across cultural traditions. As Ewald (1998) suggests: 'If one's aim is to understand the ideas that lie behind (the) foreign legal system ... what we want ... is a grasp, from the inside, of the conscious reasons and principles and conceptions that are employed by the foreign lawyers – a grasp of the styles of legal thought ... in interpreting a foreign legal system, "the law" is best understood as a style of conscious thought: what we should be seeking to understand is not law in books or in action but law in minds.'

[9] In the case of the ICC, possibly conflicting interpretations.

[10] For Crawford (2000, p.225) this means developing 'ways of understanding *contrasts* and *differences* without slipping into cultural relativism'.

Although making provision for the admission of guilt on the part of the accused at some stage in the proceedings, the instruments of international criminal tribunals are generally silent regarding their effect. For the purposes of description and evaluation there needs to be some agreement regarding the nature of the issues against which we might wish to evaluate the relevance of existing fair trial and access to justice paradigms. Clearly, a general perception that the presumption of innocence implies some right to judicial process does not provide a method for contextual understanding at either the global or local level.

Although the present analysis cannot offer ethnographic or interactive verification, comparative normative analysis of this issue as between England and Wales and Italy illustrates the difficulty of providing a convincing account of what internationalisation in this context might actually signify (Henham and Mannozzi, 2003). On the surface it seems perfectly obvious that the notion of a 'bargain' implies some sort of negotiation or agreement. Coupled with the common law notion of 'plea', the implication is that the defendant is exchanging his right to a trial (and possible acquittal) by bargaining for a lower sentence.[11] Yet, the English adversarial process fails to acknowledge the existence of any bargain since no negotiation or bargaining with the judge is officially permitted.[12] The so-called Italian procedural innovation in the form of a negotiated sentence ('application of the penalty upon the request of the parties') under Article 444 of the Code of Criminal Procedure 1989 (CCP) is a sentence bargain in the sense that the Italian system is characterised by the principle of mandatory prosecution, so that any 'bargaining' can only exist in relation to the degree of punishment rather than the charge. Furthermore, under the Italian process, there is no formal express acceptance of guilt; the defendant implicitly accepts guilt by requesting a negotiated sentence and by virtue of Article 445 the penalty is regarded as 'comparable to a judgment of guilty'.[13] In theory, since there is no actual plea it remains open for the judge, after reviewing the record, to disapprove a sentence bargain under Article 444 and find the defendant 'not guilty'. In addition, in an important decision of the Italian Constitutional Court[14] it was held that the CCP's plea bargaining provisions were unconstitutional as a violation of the constitutional presumption of innocence, to the extent that no provision existed for judicial review of the 'bargain' to ensure proper balance between the crime and the bargained sentence. Arguably, the decision effectively increased the judicial role in reviewing negotiated sentences in the special proceedings, thus indicating an unwillingness to see sentencing discretion pass from the judge, as under the traditional inquisitorial model, to the parties themselves under the new system.

The significance of this illustration for our understanding of plea bargaining in international courts goes far beyond highlighting the inadequacy of traditional criminal justice modelling for providing appropriate contextual explanatory

---

11 Known as a 'sentence discount' in England and Wales. The statutory conditions governing their use are contained in S144 of the Criminal Justice Act (2003).

12 *R v Turner* [1970] 2 WLR 1093.

13 According to Pizzi and Marafioti (1992), the guilty plea requirement was omitted because the Code's drafters feared an admission of guilt would undermine the presumption of innocence guaranteed to all defendants by the Italian Constitution.

14 Judgment No. 313, 3 July 1990, Corte. Cost. 35.

frameworks. Empirically, it challenges the possibility that there can exist any 'accepted' or 'traditional' or 'commonly understood' descriptions of 'plea bargaining' in international courts.[15] In effect, the differing reciprocal pathways of cultural transmission which contribute the constituent elements of processual reality at the international, regional and local levels are so complex as to render comparative generalisations meaningless. Cultural definitions may move upwards or downwards, vertically or horizontally as between international, regional and domestic sentencing regimes thereby restating, modifying or rejecting original contextual understandings. Instead, contextual descriptions of process, or component elements such as rights within process, need to acknowledge both the complexity of process influences, and the significance of this for determining any claims for its legitimacy.

Conceptually, these issues highlight additional weaknesses in conventional ways of modelling process in failing to appreciate the different levels of abstraction implicit in *context* and its global, regional and domestic dimensions. In addition to reflecting these factors, credible models and methodologies of the international criminal sentencing process must be capable of distinguishing and analysing:

1. *Proposed process values* – those values regarded as fundamental for the criminal process which international instruments are designed to protect.
2. *Proposed categories for rights* – those principles which are designed and incorporated in international criminal procedures to give effect to the values specified in point 1.
3. *The reality of rights in practice* – the institutionalisation of rights; the degree to which practice in international sentencing actually gives effect to the rights specified in international instruments.
4. *The nature of the process values attaching to rights in practice* – the degree to which the process values which reflect actual practice correspond to those which originally inspired the conceptualisation of rights for the international process.

In consequence, providing convincing accounts of the procedural practices relevant to international sentencing (such as plea bargaining) is problematic. In relation to the ICC, for instance, Schabas states:

> There were difficulties in circumscribing the rules applicable to guilty pleas because of differing philosophical approaches to the matter in the main judicial systems of national law ... Under the Rome Statute a 'healthy balance' has been struck between the two (common law/civil law) approaches (2001a; p.124) [words in brackets added].

This analysis, although perfectly accurate as far as it goes, further illustrates the serious limitations of legal positivism as a methodology for supplying justifications for the legitimacy of process. In these statements Schabas concludes that the reconciliation of difference is legitimised through procedural rules, although his reading of context does not extend beyond this. In short, evaluative judgements about the balancing of

[15] As Nelken (2002) implies, this concerns issues that are wider in scope than the distinctions drawn between the 'internal' or 'external' perceptions of legal culture and its specific components; 'What is at stake here is the need to pay more attention to the relationship or fit between law and society, and to develop methods for seeing how this varies culturally.'

different values implied by different procedural traditions once crystallised in legal form are invested with an appearance of procedural reality. This kind of analysis fails to consider that an examination of the social reality of process is required in order to appreciate what actually 'counts as facts' within a particular context.

Broader Theoretical Concerns

The difficulties illustrated above in finding ways of relating process values and legitimacy within existing paradigms of the criminal process when applied in comparative contexts raises some significant theoretical issues, in particular, the analysis of rights and internationalisation as a phenomenon of postmodernity. More specifically, Cotterrell (2002b) has recently identified a number of issues which have particular relevance for the present discussion:[16]

1. Regarding the ontological problems of comparability, Cotterrell questions the basis on which notions of culture, system, style, etc., can be compared. I would argue that, for each layer of comparison, we should examine common conceptual themes such as societal values, moral action, citizenship, community, reintegration and exclusion on the basis that this will facilitate an understanding of how concepts of justice translate from one location to another. Hence, the significance of rights-based paradigms for international criminal justice (particularly victim communities) will become apparent through examination of these themes. In short, ontological commitment should be needs-driven.[17]
2. Cotterrell makes the important point that the integration and differentiation of law involves a continuum of comparisons. Whereas, in conventional legal interpretation the rational meaning of legal doctrine and structures derives from law's politically guaranteed authority, this is not the case for comparative law since there is no such authority. This raises the issue of what should form the basis of worthwhile comparative analysis. Again, I would suggest here that the answer to this question should be a matter of function. There exists a need for legal rationality and political stability to give effect to pluralistic interests within the context of the nation state, and give some meaning to the notion of 'community' in so far as it represents a collective accommodation reached between the interests of citizens and the exercise of state power. International criminal tribunals effectively deny or compromise pluralism within and beyond nation states for the sake of confirming a collective conscience which is untroubled by the pluralist moral orders of nations, religions and legal traditions. The question then focuses on what (whose interests?) should constitute the moral basis of authority and accountability for international punishment.
3. Finally, Cotterrell suggests that for comparative law the differentiation of authority is normally instrumental rather than legal, such as an appeal to shared

[16] Although Cotterrell's essay is primarily directed towards the development of comparative law theory, the epistemological and ontological issues posed by the globalisation of crime and criminal process reflect the need for comparative analysis against international, regional and local contexts.

[17] Naturally, this does not address the identification and proper reconciliation of needs, nor their socio-historic and political contexts.

beliefs or values. He also recognises that the universalisation of human rights is a matter of the export, reception or transplanting of fundamental values and beliefs in legal form, and that law should be seen as a means of protecting and symbolising collective identity in various ways (such as developing and distinguishing concepts of 'community').

> We need to identify different aspects or regions of the social – that is, the environment in which legal doctrine finds its meaning and to which it refers and relates (2002b, p.47).

The fundamental point, however, to be made in relation to these issues is that they implicitly recognise the need for the development of some conceptual linkage between theory and praxis where rights norms are recognised as socio-legal phenomena. The secularisation and insularity of legal ideology in postmodernity reduces theorisation as an epistemological exercise to the level of the rhetorical and precludes any engagement with the possibility of theoretical reflexivity through empiricism. For the development of *socio-legal* theory the latter signals an imperative that the verification and generation of knowledge about rights must reach beyond their symbolic existence. Consequently, I would argue that any theoretical proposition which maintains that the universality of human rights values is challenged by cultural relativism implicitly contains a theoretically relevant methodological imperative – the need to find epistemologically acceptable ways of appreciating difference – which returns us to the theoretical question of having to explain cultural relativism. Hence, the relationship between rights as a universal concept and rights in context is a classic manifestation of the action/value dualism in sociological theory. It is not sufficient to suggest, as does Douzinas (1996), that any attempt to reconcile the notion of the universality of human rights with the relative reality of rights recognition and practice is futile; that we must somehow recognise the symbolism of rights and, paradoxically, the open-ended nature of their determination in concrete terms at some future time. For example:

> Postmodernity recognises the exhaustion of the exalted attempts to ground action upon cognition, reason or some other *a priori* conception of the good and marks the beginning of a new ethical awareness ... in their paradoxical linkage of symbolic openness and ethical determinacy, human rights can become the postmodern formulation of the principle of justice.
>
> ... the community of human rights is universal but imaginary; it does not exist empirically and has limited value as a transcendental principle.
>
> Rights are symbolic entities that develop relationally within social and legal networks: this is what makes their full definition impossible and opens them to continuous expansion and proliferation (1996, pp.117, 119, 128).

The grounding of rights in concrete terms is a contingent and necessary recognition of the operation of rights law as partiality which challenges ideology and the drawing of ethical boundaries. Moral absolutism and moral realism must have some linkage as social reality. This is provided through the recursivity of the relationship between structure and process and the transformative action of process facilitated through human agency. Process essentially produces outcomes which signify something beyond symbolism. The symbolic and the actual must, therefore, connect as *social reality*. Otherwise, conceptualisation of the symbolic means nothing – symbolism must represent something real in the mind of individuals to generate meaningful consequences for social processes – if rights symbolise desirable human values, their conceptualisation must also reflect the relative reality of their existence. This means that our theoretical conceptualisation of rights must be capable of suggesting ways in which values are transformed through processes such as international punishment beyond symbolism to connect with the relative realities of 'victims' or 'communities' or 'significant others'. As suggested earlier, whilst rights law and the ideology of rights are regulatory principles for human behaviour, their theorisation as a phenomenon which has social meaning – the linkage between values, norms and action – is driven by the need to understand the relationship between ideology and legitimacy.

As Figure 6.1 illustrates, a theoretical conceptualisation of rights which recognises their relative reality through *process*[18] serves to relate the transformation of the ideological to the normative by deconstructing the meanings which relevant participants attribute to *process*, thereby revealing how the nature of objectivity is understood as subjective experience. I would argue that this approach is an essential prerequisite for any meaningful examination of the rights discourse of international punishment, since it provides for an understanding of how process collapses the distinction between fact and value at different levels of social reality; from ideology and principle to a consideration of how these provide guides to social action in the context of international sentencing. In this way theoretical connections between ideology and legitimacy at the abstract and the concrete levels can be described and explained.

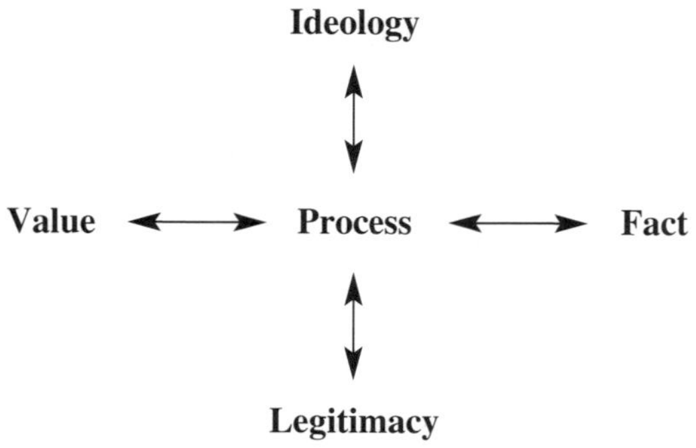

Figure 6.1 Collapsing fact/value in process

As Salter (1996, p.46) suggests, postmodern scholarship has consistently suppressed notions of human subjectivity and those concepts of self-determinism and rational choice which form the basis of the ideal of universal human rights. Ideology, power and social justice appear elevated beyond human subjectivity and human rights are

[18] This follows Tamanaha's (1997) exhortation to relate moral and normative subjectivity and its relative forms to existing states of affairs.

treated as 'the conditioned effects and determined products of the autonomous play of discursive formulations'. As I argue elsewhere (Henham, 1999b, p.172), however, an appreciation of the subjectivity of legal justice is far removed from providing a coherent theoretical account of its consequences for a principled normative framework for human rights. In this, Norrie's (1996a, p.546) suggestion that 'liberal theories of subjective right and justice need to be supplanted by premises of a more social or communitarian kind' is important in directing our attention to the existential nature of relations between individuals and communities. Norrie (1996b, p.392) considers that the dialectic connection between notions of formal and popular justice is exclusory, since so-called rational formal law is supportive of selected moral and political norms, whilst 'popular justice' is incorrectly portrayed as representing the social and political interests of abstract individuals and the rule of law. Clearly, it is also necessary for communitarian concepts to recognise the effects of socio-political constraints on individual autonomy and appreciate how moral and legal norms interact in pluralistic societies. Postmodern legal scholarship tends to diminish these imperatives. As Cotterrell (1995, p.316) argues, the balance and interplay between justice and order should 'determine the level of legitimacy accorded to legal doctrine and the agencies involved in their institutionalisation'. This implies that an understanding of the moral context of law's implementation is a fundamental prerequisite for theorising the ideology and legitimacy of rights principles and rights practice.

Elsewhere, I have argued that criminal justice theory appears unable to conceptualise how the cross-jurisdictional recognition and enforcement of particular rights paradigms (such as the European Convention on Human Rights) produces morally relative imperatives that determine moral priorities and normative behaviour for state institutions and individual citizens which may be irreconcilable (Henham, 2000b, p.245). For sentencing, as with any other social process, these effects must be understood in their socio-historic context. However, globalised legal paradigms of international sentencing law and rights protection are grounded in moral symbolism; they represent moral absolutes that have morally and culturally relative understandings for 'victims' and 'victim communities', and whose impact is compromised by conflicting ideologies and political realities.

Conceptualising Access to Justice and Rights for Victims

The irony of the last point is well illustrated by Tochilovsky (1998, pp.55, 59) who acknowledges the fact that many of the procedural rights made available to victims for trials conducted by the *ad hoc* tribunals are absent from the criminal procedures of those countries where the crimes charged were perpetrated. For as Findlay suggests,

> The consideration of access to justice as exemplified through trial participation has not much ventured outside the 'rights foundation' of international criminal procedure. This in turn is primarily conceived as applying to the accused. For instance, little is said at the international level about the access by victims to justice within the trial context, beyond peripheral concerns such as protection for victim witnesses and victim compensation (2002, p.253) [footnotes omitted].

These observations raise fundamental issues concerning the conceptualisation of access to justice and rights in international sentencing. Findlay's paradigm (2002, p.256) is instructive in this respect as it envisages access to trial justice at three levels; namely, access to trial, access by those within the trial, and access to the community by the trial. Findlay concludes by suggesting that the institutional features of trial access are best analysed against principal sites for decision-making such as sentencing where particular issues (including victims' procedural rights) may be identified and evaluated. Drawing on existing trial structures, I therefore propose to explore the significance of this model for understanding the nature and significance of victims' rights within the international sentencing process and the wider local and regional contexts beyond the trial itself.

An important aspect in conceptualising the reality of access and the impact of normative controls such as rights for sentencing is to view sentence decision-making as reflective of a recursive process of discretionary decision-making occurring throughout the trial process that is determined primarily by lay/professional interaction. Consequently, it is important to stress in connection with the concept of integrated judicial decision-making as it relates to sentencing that all participants should participate fully, and have a significant input in those decisions which impact on the sentencing process, as well as the sentencing decision itself. Further, for international penality the notion of integration should not only encompass the integration of lay and professional interests in trial decisions, but also engage with local and regional contexts.

Access to justice and rights for victims in international sentencing processes can be evaluated against the theme of integration in terms of the following paradigm:

- *Access to sentencing* – pre-sentence factors which either preclude trial and sentence, or have a fundamental impact on sentence determination. For international trials these include:
  - the ability of victims to determine or participate in pre-trial process (for example, regarding authorisation to proceed with investigations; challenges to jurisdiction or admissibility; presence and participation at pre-trial chamber deliberations)
  - influence of the prosecutor; the significance of plea agreements (participation and relevance of guilty plea for victims)
  - the permissible extent of victim intervention and participation in Trial Chamber deliberations (for example, as witnesses)
  - establishing the facts which are relevant for sentence (separate sentence hearings).
- *Access to sentencing by those within the trial* – victim participation in sentence determination. It includes:
  - victim impact statements (discretionary effect on sentence)
  - determining gravity/aggravating circumstances (possible submission of additional evidence)[19]
  - determining mitigating circumstances (expressions of remorse, effect of admission of guilt).

---

[19] For example, the ICC must consider (*inter alia*) the extent of the damage caused, especially the harm suffered by victims and their families (Rule 145(1) (c)).

- *Access to the community through sentencing* – factors which identify or connect with 'victims', 'communities', 'significant others'.
  - punishment justifications (symbolism and reality)
  - relevance of existing sentencing practice
  - significance of reparation and compensation
  - specific units/trust funds for victims.

In addition to the existence of specific issues, the ICC Statute (Article 68 3.) contains a general injunction to take into account the views and interests of victims throughout the trial and allow them to make representations at any time. Although Cassese (1999, p.167) hails this as 'of great significance' and 'a great advance in international criminal procedure' because 'for the first time in international criminal proceedings the victims are allowed to take part in such proceedings by expounding in court their "views and concerns" ... on matters relevant to the proceedings', it is questionable how real these effects are. I have argued elsewhere (Henham 2003a, p.108) that the need to obtain additional evidence in the *interests of justice* for victims, or take their views into account may be largely overridden by crime control and system considerations:

> ... it cannot be stated with any degree of conviction that victims' rights in the ICC are likely to be a paramount consideration. A more realistic assessment suggests that the *interests of justice* are more likely to be equated with notions of retributive justice than victims' rights and reparation.

Regrettably, the same sentiment applies to the other factors identified above in terms of their significance for victims' access to justice in international sentencing. There is no sense in which the integration of victims into the international criminal process can move beyond form to substance because the identification and degree of importance attached to victims' views is largely dependant upon the exercise of judicial discretionary power. The evaluation of victims' concerns and interests is therefore driven by the ideological dynamics of the trial process itself, and the extent to which judicial decisions determine the context for the individualisation of sentences in international sentencing, and what that context *actually* signifies. As suggested in the previous chapter, these limitations have led some commentators to question the appropriateness of the trial paradigm as a mechanism for negotiating links between ideology and legitimacy for victims and victim communities. Notwithstanding, the retributive ideology of international penality remains a significant obstacle to any valid understanding of relativity and comparability in the relationship between access to justice and victims' rights.

Conclusion

It has been argued that victims' rights cannot simply be viewed against the provision of minimum procedural standards for each stage of the international sentencing process, or as guarantor that existing procedures are consistent with the symbolic purposes of international punishment articulated in the foundation instruments and sentencing practices of international criminal tribunals. Conceiving of access to justice implies that the moral integrity of process can only be protected through rights which equate with fundamental notions of truth and justice. I have suggested that the role of theory in this context is to facilitate our understanding of how the sentencing process is pivotal in negotiating the ideology of international punishment and, consequently, its legitimacy. It is evident that adherence to rights cannot help promote notions of truth and justice for victims and victim communities where:

1. The moral integrity of the process they are designed to protect is in issue.
2. The process is not conceived as transformative in the sense of relating moral values to moral action through sentencing outcomes.
3. Ideology and practice make it impossible to identify and connect with 'significant others' and draw them into the process.
4. No accommodation appears possible between reformative rationales and the existing punishment dynamic.

Developing concepts of participation and integration reaching beyond symbolism in international sentencing ultimately depend on how the dynamics of ideology and power are played out through process as relative realities for victims and victim communities. Principal institutional features of this process dynamic include the domination of victims by trial professionals and transparency; namely, the connections between what arises in sentencing, its consequences and how it is presented. Understanding rights and access to justice in the context of this dynamic is, therefore, concerned with the idea of victims competing against conflicting moral ideologies; where fact and value are negotiated within structures and processes whose symbolism is rooted in ideological conflict and partiality.

Chapter 7

Theoretical and Methodological Issues for International Sentencing

Introduction: Theoretical Challenges

It is widely acknowledged that the contextual appreciation of law and legal processes within different legal cultures and across legal jurisdictional boundaries is problematic, and that, as Hodgson (2000, p.141) puts it, may create only 'an illusion of understanding'. Whilst theoretical postulates and their methodological imperatives are never value-free, the balance between phenomenology and social reality (i.e. what counts as an epistemologically valid explanation) must lie in the extent to which there is agreement as to what constitutes 'objective fact' or 'objectivity'.[1]

The absence of rationality in international sentencing discussed in earlier chapters also emphasises the fundamental need for social theorisations of such processes to address particularly the legal, socio-historical, economic and political contexts of processual interaction. Such a recognition also entails an appreciation of the multi-layered nature of the relationship between moral imperatives and social theory for international sentencing process. These relationships can more readily be described as dimensions of theoretical explanation (Figure 7.1). The focus is deliberately on theoretical explanation rather than description, not in the sense of declaring any particular allegiance to the epistemological concerns of modernity, but rather to stress that the approach taken to theoretical interpretation in this chapter regards theoretical analysis and empiricism as intimately connected.[2] Neither is the purpose to emphasise dualism and diversity, but instead, continuum and relativity; in effect, each dimension represents an aspect of context for international sentencing.

These theoretical dimensions have been described comprehensively by Henham and Findlay (2001) in elaborating theory and methodology for the comparative contextual analysis of trial process.[3] More specifically, they have argued that Giddens's (1979, 1984) structuration theory has significant explanatory potential for understanding the social reality of process comparatively because it recognises structural, organisational and interactional levels of analysis as interconnected aspects of the same social practice, offering three levels of understanding depending

---

[1] As Roberts (2002, pp.546, 547) suggests, one answer to this conundrum might be simply to acknowledge the moral relativity of all empirical data, and consider much more carefully what meanings concepts such as validity, objectivity, truth, and justice actually invoke.

[2] See Tamanaha (1997) for arguments supporting the integration of theoretical and methodological concerns in socio-legal research.

[3] For earlier discussion of structuration theory and its relevance to sentencing, see Henham (1998; 2000a).

on context. Rather than drawing a conceptual distinction, these analytical levels are designed to reveal the multifaceted context of social interaction as it is practiced and sustained in processual activity. They are, therefore, regarded as essential theoretical preconditions to understanding which necessarily precede the comparative analysis of social interaction in international sentencing. The key factor is the recognition that structuration theory provides a set of organising or interpretative constructs which allow us to identify the crucial elements and processes concerned in the recursive nature of the application of rules and resources by social actors (Layder, 1994, Ch. 8).

Macro	**Spatial**	Micro
Structural	**Processual**	Interactional
Global	**Jurisdictional**	Local
Postmodern	**Temporal**	Modern

Notes:
(i) The processual dimension emphasises not only the analytical continuum from structural to interactional, but also the different dimensions of structure and human agency involved in the manufacture of process.
(ii) More generally, the dimensions represent different levels for analysis and understanding both in their own terms and in terms of their interrelationship as components of decision-making.

Figure 7.1 Dimensions of theoretical explanation

Henham and Findlay (2001) have also argued that utilising a reflexive theoretical framework facilitates the construction of models[4] which can be tested and refined against specific contexts to produce meaningful comparative generalisations. This work suggests that the solution to comparative understanding rests in the development of theoretical modelling capable of conceptualising the significance of social structure, process and action and its normativity in ways that are sensitive to

[4] Existing criminal justice paradigms display several weaknesses:

(1) an inability to accommodate the different levels of abstraction required by different levels of analysis
(2) an inability to support methodologies which may have applicability to a number of theoretical approaches
(3) a failure to represent trial decision-making as an interactive social process
(4) an inability to provide the reflexive capacity to facilitate theory generation
(5) a failure to reflect the relationship between the processes of legal reasoning and discretionary decision-making
(6) a failure to provide adequate mechanisms for representing the meaning of social action across time and space and both within and across cultures at all levels of comparison (Henham and Findlay, 2001).

cultural diversity and moral pluralism. The first step towards this is to elaborate the link between action and value as manifested in descriptions of process through contextual analysis.[5]

In later writings Henham and Findlay (2002) have developed such a *contextual model* for the comparative contextual analysis of trial process which allows for consideration of particular aspects of different (possibly conflicting) theoretical positions to be identified within the explanatory framework provided by Giddens's structuration theory.[6] In particular, they have argued for a contextual model that facilitates the integration of the theoretical and methodological postulates of positivist, ethnographic and grounded theory approaches. This model focuses on the context of trial decision-making as a micro-representation of penality[7] (with its specific audiences, players, processes, institutions, power relations and symbolic structures) and lends itself to reconstruction at various analytical levels which are relevant from culture to culture, vertically or horizontally (from local to global) and holds good for analysis of the temporal contexts of discretionary decision-making.

The comparative contextual model proposes a conceptual distinction between the notion of *evaluators of context* and *evaluation in context* that is dependant on the nature of the theoretical (evaluative) paradigm chosen to explore the different

---

[5] As I have argued elsewhere (Henham, 2001, p.267), objective normative identification of criminal process consists in the description and explanation of what the law signifies, and how the law impacts in a functional sense. Such legal positivism tends to invoke notions of closure from an analytical perspective, since it is concerned only with developing criteria by which we can judge the existence and nature of law *per se*, and what it appears to do. Of course, how we judge the reality of law itself and its signification is epistemologically conjectural; the point is that we can postulate (depending on our theoretical persuasions) some *a priori* principles by which to measure/evaluate whether the phenomenon 'objectively' exists. Subjective normative identification, on the other hand, is concerned with such issues as the moral integrity of law, its subjective impact on behaviour; for example, how (in a cognitive sense) law is transformed through sentencing into normative guides to action. This might also, as Matza (1964, p.106) postulates, lead us to develop a set of evaluative principles by which we can capture the essence or 'feeling tone' involved or invoked by morally relative expressions like 'justice'. In other words, I would suggest that *both* law and the objective/subjective aspects of its normativity are equally susceptible to testing against the postulates of a theoretical model of international sentencing process which resonates with the differing contexts within which decisions are made.

[6] Structuration theory distinguishes analytical levels for the purpose of comparison and seeks to go beyond a consideration of influences over agency in order to explain decision-making. It is also interested in what influences the moment of interaction as well as that moment. It suggests that dualism and dichotomy (such as between agency and structure) have no relative reality in context and, that abstraction is necessary in order to deconstruct the mechanisms of structuration for comparative analysis. Nevertheless, applying levels of analysis or components of context for analysis does not endorse their autonomy within social action. Within certain contexts and across contexts in transition there is no reason why the macro and the micro, or indeed structure, human action and 'practical consciousness', should not be extracted and abstracted for the purpose of analysis. It may be the outcome of their interaction within particular contexts which becomes the legitimate focus for comparative analysis. Contextual boundaries such as instantiation may therefore be employed as components for comparison.

[7] The focus on the concept of 'penality' is chosen intentionally to reflect, as Hudson suggests (2003, p.194), 'the complex of ideas, institutions, rules, practices and relationships' pertaining to punishment. This implies the need to establish the existence of an inclusive universe of concrete ideas, relationships, rules and structures through which particularised notions of punishment are promulgated.

contexts of discretionary decision-making. In short, the role of the contextual model is to ensure that possible sentencing outcomes are evaluated *in context and across contexts* in ways which remain sensitive to the social reality of process within and across different legal cultures (Henham, 2001, p.272).

The twin components of the contextual modelling approach can be summarised as follows:

- *Evaluators of context* – these are theoretical propositions selected for testing on the basis that they are likely to provide some conceptual insights that will contribute to our understanding of the particular social phenomenon chosen for analysis. The focus is on *process*, or, more specifically, the construction of process in a comparative context.
- *Evaluation in context* – this refers to the *practice* of comparative contextual analysis; utilising those interpretative methodologies which have been dictated by the theoretical positions chosen on the basis of the problem posed.

Hence, *evaluators of context* may be regarded as consisting of 'accepted knowledge' which is tested against 'reality' and becomes modified by the 'emerging knowledge' produced through the recursive process of *evaluation in context*. The latter gradually allows us to modify (and/or confirm) accepted knowledge through theory verification, whilst the process of theory generation may suggest confirmation, integration and postulation of new evaluators. Essentially, the model, initially at least (or at the formulation stage), must follow on from a deconstruction of context(s) (Henham and Findlay, 2002).

Such a notion of modelling and comparativism proposes that the incorporation of particular evaluators should follow on from an examination of context and speculation as to which particular evaluative paradigms are relevant for understanding specific social interactions. The model is designed to facilitate the adoption of methodologies derived from paradigms based on theory verification (deductive) or developed through theory generation (inductive) processes.[8] Accordingly, in terms of the postulates chosen as a basis for analysing the penality of international sentencing, these are dependant on the identification of specific themes for analysis drawn from the international jurisdictional and procedural contexts deemed capable of evaluation against the model.

In summary, the initial formulation of the comparative contextual model derives from a deconstruction of context(s) against an application of insights from existing

---

[8] Whichever of these analytical approaches is preferred will depend on a determination of the initial reasons for the analysis, which may be to:

(1) test hypotheses regarding law, procedure and policy
(2) apply a normative paradigm as the preferred ideological framework for 'knowing' the trial
(3) provide some validation for pre-conceived notions about the trial and make meaningful comparative generalisations about the process of the trial (and thereby explore differences in different processes)
(4) impose some objectivity onto the consideration of more subjective (or value-oriented) evaluators of trial context
(5) move from higher to lower levels of abstraction, getting closer to individual decisions in order to understand the inclusive levels of decision-making within the site, their different contexts and outcomes (Findlay and Henham, 2001, p.74).

theory which are thought likely to have the potential to infuse the analysis with meaningful comparative conclusions.[9] Although the selection of theoretical postulates for modelling is necessarily predetermined, their verification and modification, and the ultimate content of the model, are, therefore, dependant on contextual analysis.

Furthering our understanding of the penality of international sentencing will also depend, therefore, on an appreciation of the lateral and vertical contexts of comparative analysis which are implicit in the different dimensions of theoretical explanation (Figure 7.2). Thus, for example, the processual dimension may be represented laterally as a context concerned with deconstructing the constituents of process (i.e. legal, organisational and interactive) at two levels (global to local) each of which impacts reflexively on the other. In other words, the processual dimension relates conceptually at the global and local levels in terms which may reflect degrees of similarity and/or difference (for example, as to their correspondence with particular process styles), and emphasises the developmental relationship between these two levels.

However, the contexts of process also demand evaluation against higher and lower order theoretical propositions, as indicated by the vertical axis shown in Figure 7.2. The reason for this stems from the need to expose and deconstruct the different levels of generality which are implicit within the sentence decision-making process at the

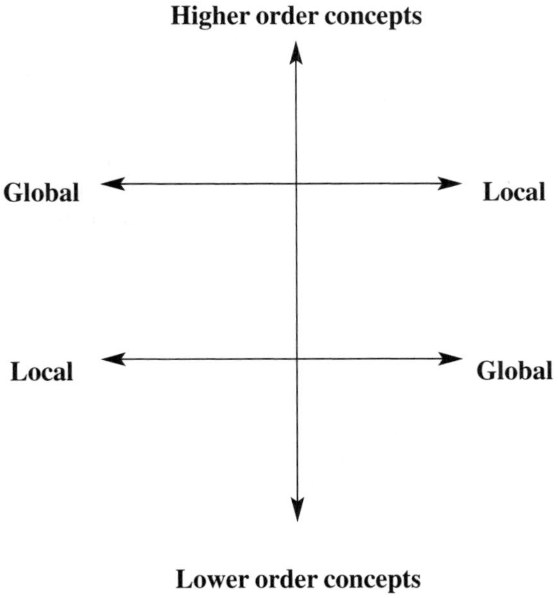

Figure 7.2 Contextualisation and theoretical abstraction

---

9 This is not the same as theoretical determinism since the outcome is dependant on the independent variables generated through the deconstruction of context.

international level. For example, a higher level of theoretical abstraction may be necessary to appreciate the cultural equivalence of process forms and the symbolic and hegemonic characteristics of discretionary decision-making, rather than to facilitate our understanding of the procedural significance of victim impact statements on sentence.

Such a conceptualisation also accommodates a linear and incremental approach to the analysis of sentencing process, since it permits an examination of those relationships which influence the sentencing dynamic within a trial and influence the eventual sentencing outcome. The sentencing dynamic can therefore be envisaged in terms of a series of interrelated decisions and relationships (or pathways of influence) which aggregate into the sentence and thereby allow for its understanding (Findlay and Henham, 2004).

As mentioned earlier, the theoretical and modelling components of comparative contextual analysis depend on the identification of specific evaluative paradigms considered to be relevant to our understanding of a particular aspect of social interaction. In this instance, we are concerned with the penality of international sentencing as expressed in praxis. This, for present purposes, is taken to incorporate those variables included in my earlier description of international penality as expressed or represented by the sentencing practices of the ICTY, ICTR and the ICC.

This remainder of this chapter is devoted to developing and evaluating this approach to theoretical modelling in the context of international sentencing. In so doing, contextual modelling is utilised heuristically in order to facilitate the deconstruction of specific contexts and dimensions of international penality, whilst at the same time providing a more instructive means than mere description for identifying the broader theoretical and methodological difficulties presented by the phenomenon of internationalisation in sentencing. This is achieved by focusing initially on what has become a particularly problematic issue for the penality of international sentencing, namely, alleged penal partiality. Recognising that theoretical accounts of international punishment as biased and unjust are underdeveloped in the literature on criminological (and social) theory,[10] it is selected as an area which appears susceptible to analysis and evaluation against the postulates of a comparative contextual model.

The second phase of the analysis develops this approach by selecting a core theme against which to examine and evaluate the issue of penal partiality in international sentencing; i.e. the nature of the relationship between judicial discretionary decision-making and the prospects for restorative justice.[11] The suggested components for the contextual model are provided by identifying and synthesising a number of potential theoretical insights into propositions to act as *evaluators of context*. The final part of the chapter explores the extent to which the contextual modelling approach enhances our understanding of bias in international sentencing as an empirical reality, and

[10] A notable exception is the work of Stan Cohen (1993, 1995).

[11] This is consistent with the argument developed by the author in this book and elsewhere (Findlay and Henham, 2005) that international punishment needs to move beyond symbolism and retribution by engaging more with the justice demands of victims and post-conflict societies in order to sustain its claims to moral legitimacy.

thereby advances our ability to conceptualise and comprehend the penality of international sentencing.

Deconstructing the Penality of International Sentencing

This section identifies several important themes relating to the penality of international sentencing discussed earlier in the book and assesses their implications for theory.

As I have emphasised, a fundamental and recurrent criticism found in recent analyses of international sentencing praxis suggests that it sustains and propagates a penality of western exculpation and selective retribution (Bassiouni and Manakas, 1996, pp.228–231), and that the criminalisation of behaviour characterised as war crimes (or otherwise in breach of principles of international criminal law) represents a particularised contextualisation of deviance (Akhavan, 2001). A significant theoretical point at issue here, therefore, concerns the extent to which we are capable of providing relevant and coherent frameworks for understanding the nature and operation (as process) of this manifestation of penal partiality that will permit coherent alternatives to be rationalised and implemented in the future sentencing practices of international criminal trial processes.

As Cohen (1995, p.10) points out, the traditional concerns of criminological theory have centred on producing paradigms that envision normatively unacceptable threats to the rules and norms of states rather than those of interstate or globalised authorities. Neither has theory generally considered how the contextualisation of deviance changes where the threats to civil society are legitimated by state authorities themselves, as where the behaviour in question is performed in a context where deviance has become the norm (Drumbl, 2000). Cohen (1995, p.44) also reminds us that the traditional paradigm for punishment in state systems of justice and social control remains the retrospective criminal law model. This is evidenced by the continued development of desert-based sentencing systems founded largely on offence criteria for determining proportionality between deviant action and reaction through retributive punishment. Significantly for the development of international paradigms, within state systems, justifications for social control outside the punitive model (such as reconciliation) have tended to remain anchored to this temporal dimension. However, the notion of closure or transformation of the past rather than the need for accountability may provide equally persuasive rationales for the creation of effective paradigms for social control. More specifically, as Findlay (1999, p.195) suggests, a reconceptualisation of the connections between crime control and community expectations (including reintegrative strategies) is necessary in order to facilitate the creation of sympathetic forms of globalised control.

These theoretical lacunae therefore throw into sharp relief the importance of developing alternative conceptualisations of key concepts such as 'citizenship' in the context of international criminal justice, particularly as regards the relationship between citizen, state and community and the intended audience for international penality. As seen in Chapter 6, there is also an increasing need to take account of the changing nature of access to justice for victims and the rights paradigm. This phenomenon invites a consideration of how the implementation of international human rights norms in internationalised forms of criminal trial relate to parallel developments at the local level in terms of their horizontal and vertical effects (Henham, 2000b; Henham and Mannozzi, 2003).

Reconceptualisation must also draw upon the changing contexts of governance and social control within state entities. As Garland (1996) suggests, through the process of 'responsibilisation', where certain state functions such as crime control have become unattainable, the state/citizen relationship has been reconfigured through policy objectives designed to shift accountability. Similarly, Pratt (1998) describes how the relationship of mutual dependence and trust built up between citizen and state in western democracies during the nineteenth century has gradually diminished through the centralisation of penal authority in the state, the institutionalisation of penality and the concomitant restriction in individual autonomy. The consequences for liberal democracies is that the state's punishment apparatus exists merely as a *symbolic* focus for social control, the *moral* basis upon which it legitimately exercises the power of punishment (the state's consideration for the powers citizens have autonomously ceded to it as part of the social contract) having diminished. Similarly, Shearing (2001), when considering the reconfiguration of state and inter-state governance of security in postmodernity, describes how the tensions within retributive ideology have conditioned the moral framework for developing risk strategies.

Analogous shifts in the contexts of penality within states subject to international criminal jurisdiction (such as the ICC) may not necessarily be paralleled globally, yet their relevance for theorising globalised notions of penality must be considered against the rationales and institutional structures established to effect principles of international criminal justice. This is in order that our understanding of the relationship between local and global sentencing contexts is couched in terms which are sensitive to the realities of process within and across jurisdictions. Thus, informed links between theory and policy may be expected to provide a reasoned basis for the development of international sentencing principles which take into account the global and local consequences of punishment and its enforcement.

In consequence, it is necessary for theory to consider the conceptual bases upon which the penality of international punishment might be accorded legitimacy. However, this is far from being a straightforward matter, since legitimacy, being an essentially relative concept, is loaded with fundamental moral and socio-cultural imperatives for criminal justice. For example, legitimacy might be conceptualised in terms which accept the notion of law as transformative in the sense that retributive punishment is necessary to rehabilitate the 'deviant' act and the responsible social group; in other words, that expurgation through public retribution is a necessary prelude to closure and the re-establishment of moral order. Alternatively, the transformative or expressive force of legalised punishment may be conceived as a measure of the extent to which the infliction of punishment goes beyond censure in its capacity to convey to citizens that the behaviour with which it deals is morally blameworthy. This approach is dependant on directing the development of theory away from the notion of legal closure (Nelken, 1998; Cotterrell, 1998a; Banakar, 2000) by permitting interpretations which might allow us to make the link between sentencing law and principles as normative representations of moral principles, and the existence of forms of expressed morality in civil society as they exist in notions of communitarianism (Henham, 2001).

Thus, the issue of penal partiality in international sentencing poses difficult theoretical challenges that centre around the inability of existing theoretical frameworks to conceptualise the significance of globalised punishment in terms of linkage between moral values, the transformative capacity of sentence decision-making and the normative regulation of behaviour, both locally and internationally.

Synthesising Theoretical Insights

To summarise, the overall theoretical focus is concerned with understanding the reality of context and suggesting ways in which social interaction within specific contexts of the criminal trial, and the components of those contexts, may become the legitimate focus for comparative analysis. Given the inadequacy of existing theoretical approaches, the analysis is concerned to satisfactorily explain and evaluate the underlying reasons for penal partiality in international sentencing decisions. As suggested earlier, this issue is addressed by exploring the potential for refining and synthesising some specific theoretical propositions within a contextual model concerned with elucidating the nature of the relationship between judicial discretionary decision-making and the prospects for restorative justice in international sentencing.

In addition to its ideological significance in conceptualising the moral legitimacy of trial justice, restorative justice is selected as an emotive context within which to examine the use of judicial discretionary power. This is because it is precisely at the moment of sentencing that tensions are likely to arise between the retributive dynamic of the international criminal trial process and the discretionary possibility of engaging with consequentialist objectives, such as those contemplated by restorative interventions. Clearly, the engagement of restorative justice themes through sentencing requires both a normative capacity for discretionary action which facilitates such outcomes and formal signification and identification with 'significant others' (those individuals who may be expected to implement the ideology) through the actual use of discretionary power. Hence, discretionary sentencing decisions where restorative justice considerations beyond rhetoric are seriously contemplated must be able to engage with its consequences.

Consequently, the modelling emphasis is on *process* and *interaction* – i.e. how the sentencing dynamic in decision-making is constructed[12] and recursively organised to form particular sentencing justifications; how these justifications relate to the wider contexts of international criminal justice, and, more particularly, communitarian concerns associated with restorative justice themes. The theoretical challenge is how best to envision these complexities by proposing a contextual model which contains the kinds of theoretical evaluators considered capable of effectively deconstructing this aspect of the international sentencing process.

---

[12] As Tata (2002, p.7) reminds us; 'Both "rules" and "discretion" are used by actors in the sentencing process as resources for negotiation which are governed by social-organisational and ideological frameworks.'

The choice of contextual evaluators for this analysis is dependant, in the first instance, on a *preliminary* identification of the relevant processual dynamics of international sentence decision-making. Conceptualisations of decision-making as process must also acknowledge the need for paradigms which are capable of operating at different levels of abstraction, and have the capacity to accommodate temporal and spatial dimensions (Henham and Findlay, 2001). We can, therefore, hypothesize that our theoretical evaluators will need to address the following major dimensions of international sentence decision-making:

- the conceptualisation of process
- the relationship between law and moral action
- the nature and significance of judicial discretionary decision-making as social interaction
- the symbolism of process
- the relationship between power and sentencing.

The evaluators suggested for inclusion in the contextual model are (and remain) contingent in the sense that such theoretical propositions may be refined, modified or reconsidered by inductive reasoning through the process of evaluation *in* context. At this stage, however, the evaluative paradigm is predicated on the identification of theoretically relevant issues arising from contemporary narrative analyses of international sentencing *practice*, as reflected in the sentencing decisions of the *ad hoc* criminal tribunals. As we have seen, these suggest the predominance of a retributive dynamic and a significant level of obfuscation and inconsistency in rationalising sentencing decisions (Schabas, 2001b; Beresford, 2002; Henham, 2003a).

Conceptualising Process

In selecting a paradigm or conceptualisation of process for the purpose of modelling sentencing in international criminal trials we are guided particularly by the need to conceptualise:

1. The recursivity of the activity – the fact that human agency is crucially implicated in the reproduction of sentencing structure;
2. Its processual nature – in the sense that sentencing outcomes are influenced by the outcome of several decision points within (and before) the trial;
3. Its interactive quality – the fact that the contexts of judicial/professional/lay interaction are crucial determinants of decision-making.

Based on Henham and Findlay's (2001) development of structuration theory,[13] the

[13] The attractiveness of structuration theory as a theoretical framework with which to underpin comparative contextual analysis lies in its ability to provide a set of organising or interpretative constructs which facilitate the identification of elements and processes involved in the recursive nature of the application of rules and resources by trial participants. In this sense, the exercise of discretionary power in sentencing is patterned through the activities of trial participants who recursively create the meaning and social reality of discretion (as both action and structure).

following theoretical propositions have been selected as evaluators *of* context for inclusion in a heuristic model[14] of the international sentencing process:

- that there are identifiable relationships between communication structures, social interaction and sentencing outcomes which function as part of a system of regular reproducible sentencing practices
- that some patterning exists in the exercise of discretionary power as part of this regularly reproduced social practice which impacts on the recursive activities of trial participants, thereby influencing the meaning and social reality of discretion.

Conceptualising Law and Moral Action

The argument at this level has been conducted on the basis that legal thought and decision-making must be conceptualised as a *process* in order to appreciate the moral power of law (Cotterrell, 1998a); that sociological interpretations do not require law's reality to be subsumed or distorted but, rather, are capable of providing conceptual settings which facilitate the deconstruction of different legal discourses (and systems) and enable us to understand how each discourse constructs 'inside' and 'outside' from the internal points of view of both law and sociology (Nelken, 1998, p.419).

As I have suggested elsewhere (Henham, 2002), Garland's (1990, p.253) point regarding the signifying nature of penality has special resonance in the notion that international forms of punishment should be reflective of generally understood cultural meanings of crime and punishment *and*, consequently, the boundaries of morally acceptable behaviour. This, in turn, forces us to consider the significance of the transformative capacity of sentencing law and, as Cotterrell (1998a) argues, to reflect on law's *moral* worth and its implications for international penality.

However, arguing in favour of a moral basis for the legitimacy of international sentencing law entails not only establishing the case for change (Henham, 2002), but also poses a potentially much more difficult question relating to the extent to which international sentencing can be taken to represent any kind of international moral order. As I suggest, the issue to be explored relates, not to the validity of competing moral claims to punish,[15] but rather to the degree to which the capacity exists to conceptualise and promote competing moral claims for punishment in the international sphere. In this respect, Durkheim's (1982, 1984) assertions relating to the 'normality of crime' and the nature of 'collective sentiments' appear pertinent, and might lead to us to reflect upon the proposition that the function of punishment as expressed in sentencing praxis is to promote social solidarity through the recursive reaffirmation of societal values – in particular, to reflect and re-affirm society's moral opprobrium regarding particular acts or omissions defined as crime or deviance.

However, the crucial point about international forms of punishment concerns the nature of the paradox between the symbolic and the actual. The Durkheimian analogy

---

[14] It is important to emphasise here that this modelling is designed to provide a set of theoretical constructs which may be modified or verified (in whole or in part) following the comparative contextual analysis of international sentence decision-making (see further Henham and Findlay, 2001).

[15] Essentially a study of moral relativity.

is patently unsustainable in an international or comparative context without further elaboration, because it implies that the conceptualisation of international punishment should be concerned to establish linkage between individual morality and the manifestation of a collective conscience, as represented by some form of global penality. Such linkage may exist in form and rhetoric,[16] but not in substance. This is because there is no *actual* 'significant other', either in terms of 'victim' or 'community', which can be the focus of any kind of constructive engagement between individual morality and punishment beyond retributivism. It is also because the creation and operational reality of international regulatory structures reflect legal pluralism and cultural diversity. Although the foundation instruments of international trial institutions embody common goals there is disagreement on rationalising these objectives in practice. Consequently, aspirations for pluralism, compromise and reconciliation are reversed. This is because the structures are facilitative, they are not integral to everyday social life, as domestic law maintains civil society. There is no mutual dependency or social integration – no *actual* bond between universal aspirations and relative reality.

As Roberts (2002) cautions:

> Durkheim's characterisation of legal prosecution and punishment, as society's 'collective conscience' responding to criminality's symbolic assault on the normative order, retains considerable contemporary resonance. The reaffirmation of a symbolic penal community, generating public allegiance to a system of norms and popular acceptance of coercive measures for their enforcement, may be significant ingredients in the legitimacy and long-term stability of a criminal justice system. Yet in the international setting, a global community of penal sentiment is elusive and probably, at this time, illusory.

The limitations of Durkheim's theorising are well known (see Garland, 1990); in particular, his apparent failure to account for the pluralistic nature of the moral order; that law and state action is a function of political domination rather than an expression of collective sentiments and, consequently, represents a limited consensus for the basic regulation of social order. Yet the significance of Durkheim for present purposes concerns his attempt to theorise the functional significance of moral consensus as expressed in law's normative characteristics, and the suggestion, therefore, of a moral justification for their enforcement.[17] However, this has to be set against the fact that pluralism is a reality of the new world order. In Durkheimian terms, the notion of the collective sentiments as representing a united morality is clearly irrelevant for postmodern liberal democracies, which are predominantly secular, pluralist and individually autonomous. Even at this level, what the state purports to do in terms of social control through punishment is largely symbolic. This is much more evident at the global level, where the only collective sentiments are symbolic and rhetorical.

An interesting and relevant aspect of this theorising concerns Durkheim's notion of individualism (Cotterrell, 1999, p.202), and its implication that individual

---

[16] For example, the Preamble to the ICC Statute evokes the notion of a 'global community' – 'Conscious that all peoples are united by common bonds, their cultures pieced together in a shared heritage ...'.

[17] Elsewhere (Henham 2000a, p.254), I have suggested that a reciprocal theorisation might envisage rights principles as deriving their moral authority from some collective expression of communitarianism.

collective concern for others *as a moral imperative* is a significant legitimation for national and international human rights movements. Cotterrell maintains that the value system of individualism envisaged by Durkheim can be conceptualised as sustaining a shared moral culture which transcends national boundaries. The difficulty remains in envisaging the moral basis upon which law's authority is claimed to rest in terms of shared beliefs or sentiments; how to identify the transnational values of individualism in forms of international regulatory power such as structures designed for the implementation of international penal norms purporting to be grounded in principles of fairness and justice.

Nevertheless, the important theoretical insight which Durkheim's sociological positivism provides is one which clearly does acknowledge law as a regulatory mechanism, and the need for pluralistic structures to 'provide moral meaning in conditions of modern social complexity' (Cotterrell, 1999, p.226). Hence, although, as Roberts suggests, we may be far from realising the aspiration of a shared global moral consensus to underpin international principles for criminal justice, the significance of Durkheim's theorising for the development of a theoretical model of international penality lies in its potential to suggest a conceptual framework for the evaluation and analysis of law and moral action in context.

Developing these ideas as a basis for modelling, it may be argued that the functional significance of international sentencing's normative characteristics is as an expression of some notion of international moral consensus about the appropriate aims and penalties for international crimes, and that there exists, therefore, a moral justification for their imposition and enforcement. Thus, at this level, the process of discretionary decision-making may be seen as *transformative* of moral values.

Conceptualising Judicial Discretionary Decision-Making

Modelling the sentencing process and the nature of discretionary decision-making in a broadly domestic context has proved a fertile ground for sentencing scholars (for an overview, see Henham, 2001). For present purposes, it is important to recall the distinction between the mechanistic or legal positivist approach typified by the work of Thomas (1979), which does not extend beyond the doctrinal analysis of sentencing law, practice and procedure, and broader sociological approaches. The latter are wide-ranging and include theoretical writing within the traditions of legal sociology and mainstream sociological approaches.

Particularly relevant to the notion of sentence modelling as an exercise in legal sociology is Weber's typology of legal decision-making, developed in the sentencing context by Hutton (1995). Essentially, Weber suggested that the mechanisms of power by which conflicting interests are regulated and compromised are considerably more significant than morality in understanding the characteristics of legal authority and the reasons for its maintenance and enhancement. In his application of Weber's typology, Hutton characterises sentence decision-making as a substantive-irrational process since there is a consistent failure to follow formal systematic rules, although he does not address questions relating to the broader socio-political context of rationality (Henham, 2001, p.257). A particularly interesting, and, as yet, untested issue, is the contention that ideal type substantive irrationality, in the Weberian sense of there being little or no relationship between procedural rules and situational outcomes with sentencing decisions based primarily on a consideration of extra-legal factors, occurs relatively infrequently.

Sentence modelling as a wider sociological enterprise which seeks to understand the nature of sentence decision-making as an interactive social process has generally reflected broader epistemological trends. The positivist search for causality (Green, 1961) gradually gave way to the more phenomenonologically sensitive conceptualisations of Hogarth (1971) and Hood (1972), yet, with the notable exception of Tata (1997), commentators have consistently failed to provide a conceptualisation of sentence decision-making which is sensitive and reflective of context. Thus, theoretical and methodological imperatives have seemed incapable of deconstructing sentencing decisions in terms of the meanings, purposes, motivations and intentions of trial participants, their ideological predilections and those of relevant state or international structures of penality.

Tata's more naturalistic or 'holistic' conceptualisation of sentence decision-making seeks to understand how sentencing behaviour is recursively constructed and deconstructed rather than causally determined on the basis of participants' perceptions of the social reality of the process. Hence, the ethnography of sentencing behaviour consists of devising methodologies to access the subjective experiences of social actors. Regrettably, the transition from 'description' to contextualisation has yet to materialise, and there has been a general failure to fulfil an important criteria of ethnographic research; namely, a commitment to cultural interpretation. However, Rogers and Erez (1999) have provided a rare attempt to contextualise sentencing process by suggesting a methodology capable of deconstructing the ways in which the 'objectivity' of process is constructed 'subjectively' by trial participants.

Henham and Findlay (2002) utilise a combination of Hogarth's 'human process' approach, and Tata's 'narrative' approach in modelling sentencing decision-making for comparative contextual analysis, including postulates which they regard as appropriate for a contextual model of discretionary decision-making that accommodates comparativism. Within such a framework it is regarded as crucial to describe and analyse the psychological appropriation and assimilation of relevant information as an objective (external) process, and consider the extent to which trial participants appear to share similar, uniform and comparable images of relevant case material and legal rules in the context of perceived audience expectation. Comparative contextual modelling is, therefore, seen as the methodological precursor to deconstructing the contextuality of decision-making as a processual activity, both in terms of its objectivity (conceptual and concrete), and subjective accounts of that objectivity (its phenonomenological content).

A synthesis of the Hogarth/Tata approaches for conceptualising sentence decision-making within the terms of a contextual model would suggest that judicial discretionary sentence decisions are individualised through the selective appropriation and interpretation of legal and social constraints in which sentencers *appear* to share similar, uniform and comparable images of relevant case material and legal rules in the context of perceived audience expectation. For international sentencing the decision-making model is complicated by the fact that the judges are drawn from a wide variety of jurisdictional backgrounds. This inevitably affects their perception and interpretation of information and therefore weakens the extent to which they can be regarded as sharing comparable understandings and expectations.

Nevertheless, since judges in the *ad hoc* tribunals and the ICC have wide discretionary power, the potential exists for the judiciary to individualise sentences and reach beyond the justificatory rhetoric, symbolism and procedural imperatives of retributivism and deterrence and engage with alternative justice paradigms within the constraints of the normative framework in which they operate. The challenge for sentence modelling lies in providing a conceptual vehicle for understanding the relationship between judicial background variables and sentencing behaviour in a comparative context where the influences of national and international legal culture impact directly upon processual activity.

Conceptualising Symbolism

There are some important, although as yet unexplored, connections to be made between interactionist accounts of punishment and the internationalisation of sentencing (Lemert, 1972; King, 1978). As far as the criminalisation of behaviour is concerned, there is no doubt that criminological analyses relating to the role of the media in creating and perpetuating moral panics in the context of international crime are important (Roberts, 2002). The notion of deviancy amplification is also illuminating in this context, since it is arguable that the use of the international stage to consistently re-enforce through symbolism and rhetoric particular accounts of the power relations of domination in situations of international conflict promotes stereotypes and misconceptions about such conflicts and the motivations of those alleged to have committed international crimes. However, in the present context the focus is on identifying those aspects of interactionist theory which might enable us to understand more clearly the significance of symbolism in the processual activity of international sentencing.

The symbolic significance of the international sentencing process for individual defendants *may* lie in its conceptualisation as a ritual of denunciation and degradation, whereby offenders might conceivably internalise the global sentiments of moral condemnation and denunciation expressed by the relevant tribunal to the extent that their own moral sentiments in this respect are altered irrevocably (Lemert, 1972). In this sense, the symbolism of punishment in international criminal courts rests in its perception as a personification, conduit or transmitter of international sentiment; a message intended equally for the condemnors as the condemned. However, because international punishment is relative in its symbolic and real effects, and these do not normally coincide, it is suggested that any conceptualisation of symbolism in this context needs to be developed against notions of 'community' which take full account of the demands for justice of post-conflict societies as well as those of the so-called 'international community' of nation states represented by western liberal democracies.

Despite its ambivalence, interactionism remains a useful sensitising paradigm or construct for analysis. It is particularly valuable, as Sudnow (1965) and Cicourel (1968) showed in their seminal analyses of trial processes, for drawing attention to the possibilities for stereotyping and the ways in which procedural rules are systematically redefined in order to satisfy systemic pressures for conformity. Similarly, Skolnick (1966, p.27) saw legal rules as 'a context for the behaviour of legal men', so that the study of law in action (such as discretionary decision-making) is essentially concerned with the deconstruction of the meanings attributed to action by social actors, and the interrelationship and transformation of legal principles and rules within legal institutions.

Interactionism is, therefore, concerned with understanding the contexts for transformation of the law and process of sentencing, and engages theoretically with the construction of individual and collectively shared experience at different levels and layers of meaning. In practical terms, as King (1978, p.218) points out, this suggests a focus on those variables that might influence instrumental behaviour by individuals within the court process; for example, wider contextual reasons for delay, inconvenience and disruption to the defendant's case.

For international sentencing we can speculate that an appreciation of symbolic interactionism could help to expand our understanding of the forces which shape the differential impacts of the international punishment process. Such enhanced understanding might be obtained by adopting a theoretical position derived from interactionism that sought to account for apparently discriminatory or prejudicial treatment of victims within the international sentencing process. In terms of the present analysis, for example, an interactionist perspective may assist us in identifying points of control within the process where legal rules and procedures actually operate against victims' interests, although procedural discourse appears to affirm the opposite. Hence, whilst this approach might not allow us to draw specific (empirically grounded) conclusions, its focus on the relationship between the symbolism of structured processes such as punishment and their psychological appropriation by trial participants would facilitate our appreciation of the impact of international court process. It might permit some informed speculation about the extent to which judicial decisions on sentence are structured by procedural rules designed to obfuscate the reality of discriminatory practice, or prejudiced against particular penal orientations which favour restorative justice alternatives.

Consequently, a speculative theoretical proposition for inclusion in a contextual model developed from an interactionist perspective is one suggesting that the functional significance of international sentencing process is obfuscated by its symbolism and discourse. This implies that discretion in judicial sentencing decisions is instrumental in constructing symbolic images of relevant case material, legal rules and punishment justifications for participants and spectators of criminal trials, and, that the structural mechanisms for conducting international trials are implicated in this phenomenon. The proposition also suggests that the relative realities of symbolism and context (international, regional and local) are significant obstacles to any constructive engagement with alternative penal justifications or mechanisms.

Conceptualising Power and Sentencing

Postmodern conceptions of law have consistently challenged claims that its ideological and normative functions might be compatible with notions of justice within western democracies (Fitzpatrick, 1992; Hunt, 1993). In the sentencing context, Pratt (1995) has described how, utilising Foucault's notion of 'technologies of power', the relationship between state moral authority and law is reciprocally created and maintained through the state's control of that body of knowledge which both defines the criminal law and determines the characteristics of those who are labelled as criminal. However, although Foucault may have explored the spatial dimensions of social regulation, as Cohen (1995, p.44) suggests, there has been little work on the temporal dimensions of social control; in other words, how states establish the continuity of social control. Further, Cohen (1993) has also invoked Sykes and Matza's (1957) theory of neutralisation to analyse government denials of complicity in state crimes, suggesting ways whereby this conception could be further explored to explain how those participating in mass violence and gross human rights violations are able to rationalise their behaviour with their moral conscience.

An important issue arising from these analyses in the present context concerns the relationship between social control and accountability – 'the notion that it is necessary to discover the truth about the past in order to achieve justice in the present'. Cohen (1995, p.47)[18] posits the possibility that structures of international punishment provide a form of social control which is instrumental in negotiating and defining what becomes known as truth and counts as justice. Although alternative structures and processes (such as Truth and Reconciliation Commissions) might provide alternative relative interpretations of truth and justice drawn from different contexts, all purport to achieve a historically definitive version of truth. In the case of international criminal tribunals, findings of truth are accompanied by legal closure and legal accountability.[19]

Postmodern or critical legal scholarship also tends to suppress concepts such as self-determinism, rational choice and autonomy so that power and social justice are perceived 'as conditioned effects of the autonomous play of discursive formulations' (Salter, 1996, p.46). However, Norrie (1996b, p.395) makes an important distinction between notions of formal and popular justice in suggesting that so-called rational formal law is a mechanism of organised social control supportive of selected moral and political norms, whilst 'popular justice' is incorrectly representing the social and political interests of an abstract individual subject and the rule of law. Norrie appears to be arguing that, in order to understand the relationship between power and social justice we need to appreciate the reasons for the dialectical connection between the rationale for social control and the phenomenology of individual moral action; in other words, the reasons for the apparent disjunction between the rationales of formal systems (such as punishment structures), the rhetoric of populism, and, the experiences and concerns of individual citizens subject to the rule of law.

The apparent lack of autonomy on the part of individual citizens is re-enforced by the shifting contexts of state and inter-state governance (Shearing 2001, p.207). In particular, governance is seen as intimately connected to the management of political and economic risk in postmodernity. Penality is a crucial factor in sustaining particular forms of governance and, therefore, in managing such risks, because the structures for punishment are used to support the rationales for control. The implications for punishment are significant in that the conceptualisation of governmentality does not concern itself with the phenomenology of moral actions, or the possibility that its

18 Cohen (1995, p.48) goes on to develop a paradigm of regimes of continuity.

19 Christodoulidis (2000) questions whether such reflexive ethical decisions can be reached within a legal context.

institutions and procedural rules might take generalised notions of individual intention, motivation or blame into account.

International forms of governance reflect these characteristics, especially the notion that international structures for punishment are instrumental in sustaining the rationales for control, even if these might include maintaining the economic interests of liberal capitalist states, or supporting global imperialism. Hence, from this perspective, international criminal tribunals cannot be regarded as impartial arbiters between rational formal law and popular justice; rather, they are implicated in the hegemony of international governance and manufacture a selected form of truth and justice.

Therefore, in the light of the foregoing analysis of power-related variables, an appropriate theoretical proposition for inclusion in a contextual model might be one asserting that the structures of international punishment are implicated in sustaining particular rationales for control and global governance on behalf of certain nation states which bear no relationship to notions of popular justice within victim communities.

Evaluating the Contextual Model

The conceptual rationale underlying the integration of the theoretical propositions specified in the preceding section within a heuristic model of sentence decision-making for international trial process can be summarised in the following terms. Structuration theory provides the macro-conceptual framework for analysing the process of decision-making as a recursive activity; within this construct, the Hogarth/Tata paradigmatic synergy suggests variables against which to test the nature of the decision-making process as a cognitive interpretative exercise; the wider sociological context of the international sentence decision-making process is explored in terms of the power relationships of postmodern penality, the capacity and significance of moral values for transforming behaviour through sentencing, and the symbolism of the international punishment process and its relative reality in context.

A Case Study Analysis

It is not possible within the scope of this chapter to fully explore the heuristic capabilities of this model since, evidently, the theoretical propositions included as evaluators *of* context characterise aspects of social reality ranging from higher to lower levels of abstraction which depend for their evaluation upon a wide variety of possible methodological techniques.[20] Nevertheless, particular aspects of sentence decision-making within international trials are explored as verification of the contextual model and an assessment provided of the perceived advantages to be gained from synthesising theoretical insights for modelling in the manner proposed.

In order to pursue these objectives, narrative accounts of the sentencing jurisprudence of the ICTY and ICTR are analysed against the postulates of the

[20] These might range from conventional doctrinal analysis of legal rules and principles to ethnographic or grounded theory approaches (Findlay and Henham, 2001).

contextual model of judicial discretionary decision-making in international sentencing already developed herein. As mentioned earlier, the focal point for this analysis is to investigate the relationship between the exercise of judicial discretion in international sentence decision-making and the prospects for its engagement with restorative justice themes. In order to facilitate the analysis the issue is considered in the context of the procedural rules and trial practice of international sentencing.

The analysis therefore concentrates on the following areas:[21]

- the form and context of sentence decision-making
- the significance of restorative justice
- negotiated justice and system rationalisations.

The Form and Context of Sentence Decision-Making

This factor is a crucial determinant of judicial discretion in any sentencing system. For international tribunals, such as the ICTY and ICTR, the original presumption in favour of a separate sentencing phase for the trial after conviction was effectively abandoned, whilst the ICC is mandated to establish the appropriate sentence in a distinct sentencing phase (Schabas, 2004, p.157). The implications for the presentation of evidence relevant to sentencing are significant since, where sentence follows directly upon conviction, evidence relating to mitigating and aggravating circumstances will be restricted to that which forms part of the trial record.[22] Hence, judicial discretion to admit evidence relevant to sentence is circumscribed by the rules of evidence which apply to the trial of the issues. In terms of theory, this provides an important example of how judicial discretion in sentencing is recursively patterned by procedural rules applicable to the trial.

Article 78(1) of the ICC Statute states that in fixing sentence the ICC must take factors such as the gravity of the crime and the individual circumstances of the offender into account, in accordance with the ICC Rules of Procedure and Evidence. The latter's Rule 145 is reasonably detailed in its description of relevant aggravating and mitigating circumstances, and suggests (*inter alia*) in Rule 145(1)(c) that the harm caused to victims and their families needs to be considered alongside those factors mentioned in Article 78(1). Similarly, conduct following the act on the part of the convicted person, such as efforts to compensate victims, must be taken into account as mitigation.[23]

As for the determination of sentence, the ICC Statute establishes some maximum terms in Article 77,[24] but effectively leaves sentencing in individual cases to be

---

[21] These areas are analysed in depth in earlier chapters.

[22] Article 76(1), ICC Statute.

[23] Rule 145(2)(a)(ii)).

[24] Subject to any review under Article110, Article 77(1) permits the Court to impose one of the following penalties on any individual convicted of a crime within its jurisdiction under Article 5: (a) Imprisonment for a specified number of years, which may not exceed a maximum of 30 years; or (b) A term of life imprisonment when justified by the extreme gravity of the crime and the individual circumstances of the convicted person. In addition fines and forfeiture of proceeds, property and assets are provided for under Article 77(2)(a) and (b) respectively.

determined through the exercise of judicial discretion, as with the ICTY and ICTR. This considerable discretion is exercised without the existence of any significant statement or guidance about what should be the purposes of sentencing (Beresford, 2002; Henham, 2003a). In theoretical terms, therefore, there is a distinct absence of any structural patterning of judicial discretion as regards justification and, consequently, between purposes and outcomes.

The absence of such considerations in the formal substantive law and procedural rules of the ICC is problematic for several different reasons. One of these is concerned with the nature of the relationship between law and moral action. The Preamble to the ICC Statute contains vague affirmations and statements of intent regarding the aims of the ICC, particularly a determination to put an end to impunity for the perpetrators of 'the most serious crimes of concern to the international community as a whole' and 'thus to contribute to the prevention of such crimes'. This oblique reference to deterrence coupled with the declaration that such crimes must not go unpunished is not linked to any specific guidance concerning what Hart (1968) would call the principles of distribution; namely, in what circumstances it might be appropriate to use rehabilitation, deterrence or retribution as rationales for punishment in individual cases.

Another difficulty with this position concerns the basis upon which any conceptual linkage can be established between the moral positions individual citizens of the 'international community as a whole' might hold regarding the appropriate principles for punishment in international tribunals. Certainly, the Durkheimian notion of individualism lends itself to conceptualising a shared moral basis for the internationalisation of human rights norms (Cotterrell, 1999), but this is insufficient to suggest a unifying morality which might support globalised forms of moral action such as punishment. Perhaps, as Cotterrell (1999, p.227) himself speculates, there is a need to further develop Durkheim's ideas within conceptualisations or taxonomies of community (such as Weber's), in order to comprehend the complex subjectivities of social action and their significance. However, it is difficult to see how individualism as notions of fairness and justice can be transformed at the level of international penality into principles for punishment. The reason for drawing this conclusion rests on Durkheim's implicit failure to address the moral imperatives of international pluralistic structures of regulation such as those now provided by international sentencing systems. Although the foundation instruments of such structures appear to reflect a moral consensus in the pluralistic new world order of modern states, regarding the need to put an end to impunity for gross breaches of international humanitarian law, this aspiration remains rhetorical rather than real. This is because the moral imperative is not transformed into a coherent normative framework for sentencing.

Nevertheless, whilst the foundation instruments and institutional structures of international sentencing fail to suggest mechanisms for the transformation of moral values into imperatives for punishment, this has not prevented judges sentencing in international criminal trials from claiming the existence of such connections. For example, in *Furundzija*[25] the ICTY Trial Chamber asserted its belief in the 'infallibility of punishment' as being largely due to the fact that:

---

[25] *Prosecutor v Furundzija* (Case No. IT-95-17/1), Judgement, 10 December 1998.

> ... penalties are made more onerous by its international stature, *moral authority and impact upon world opinion*, and this punitive effect must be borne in mind when assessing the suitable length of sentence [emphasis added].

The implication here is not only that the tribunal has the moral authority of the international community, but also that this moral authority is instrumentally transformed into morally justified action (i.e. punishment) through fulfilling the purposes of retribution, stigmatisation and deterrence in sentencing. Similarly, the ICTR has frequently implied, as in *Serushago*,[26] that a direct causal link exists between the United Nations Security Council's declared Chapter VII objective of punishment to put an end to impunity and the moral justification for retributive and deterrent sentencing.

Notwithstanding both the ICTY and ICTR are mandated to take the general practice regarding the imposition of prison sentences in the former Yugoslavia and Rwanda respectively into account, these are regarded as merely indicative of the appropriate sentence (Kittichaisaree, 2001, p.315). In the case of the ICTR, it is significant that the relevant Rwandan Organic Law stipulates in its preamble that the enumerated penalties are justified 'in order to achieve national reconciliation, to forever eradicate the culture of impunity'. This differs in its emphasis from the UN Security Council's resolution 955 of 8 November 1994, which suggests that punishment of the perpetrators of the atrocities in Rwanda in such a way as to put an end to impunity will thereby promote national reconciliation and the restoration of peace. This subtle difference in emphasis belies significant differences in the perceived moral purpose regarding the penality of the ICTR between the United Nations and the Rwandese, thereby undermining any assumed moral consensus (Alvarez, 1999; Drumbl, 2000).

Clearly, as is the case with all kinds of public manifestation of penal sentiment, viewed objectively, judicial justifications for punishment in the internationalised sentencing process of the ICTY and ICTR appear to have particular symbolic resonance for trial participants and the perceived audience, but their relative meanings may require the use of ethnographic methodologies to reveal their subjective effects.

Similarly, the fact that judicial sentencing pronouncements in the *ad hoc* tribunals stress the moral authority of punishment and claim particular (consequentialist) effects in terms of the justifications that are employed when imposing punishment (such as the link made between putting an end to impunity and national reconciliation) lends support to the social control/power thesis; i.e. that the structures of international punishment are implicated in sustaining particular rationales for control and ignore notions of popular justice.

Whilst notions of popular justice within particular victim communities (such as Rwanda) may be determinable (Drumbl, 2000), the rationales for control that are instrumental in the creation of penal structures are not necessarily discernable in the justifications for punishment utilised in international sentencing. However, the point to stress is that judicially administered punishment and its avowed justification is pivotal to the future interpretation of what actually took place; it provides a vehicle for negotiating both fact and value. Since this transformative process is central to the

---

[26] *Prosecutor v Sherushago* (Case No. ICTR 98-39-S), Sentence, 5 February 1999.

construction of meaning for punishment in international penality, it is a crucial purpose for international sentencing.

The Significance of Restorative Justice

In general terms, any conceptualisation of restorative justice themes in international sentencing invokes a paradigm that includes the humanitarian treatment of offenders; compensation, restitution, reparation (possibly reintegration); victim participation; and diversionary and mediatory processes. Ashworth (2002b) usefully characterises restorative justice process in terms of empowerment, dialogue, negotiation and agreement, with stakeholders as victims, offenders and communities, and restorative outcomes envisaged in Braithwaite's terms (1999, p.6) as 'whatever dimensions of restoration matter to the victims, offenders and communities affected by the crime'. Restoration frequently implies the reintegration of individuals and communities and outcomes assessed against measures of stakeholder satisfaction, rather than legal criteria relating to consistency and proportionality. It is also important that the residual role of the state where restorative justice approaches are adopted should be as a guarantor of principles supporting human rights standards (United Nations, 2000) seen against an essentially communitarian backdrop.

But what are the implications of these observations for international sentencing and the context of the 'international community' which it represents? How can concepts concerned with the philosophy and practice of restorative justice be related to the institutional norms and decision-making practices of international criminal trial structures? As regards the former, the foundations instruments of the ICC are instructive. With the exception of diversion and mediation, restorative justice themes are already evident in the ICC Statute and the Rules of Procedure and Evidence, Section III. Nevertheless, despite vague assertions that legal accountability contributes to rehabilitation of the victim's dignity and the reconciliation of opposing factions (Wexler, 1996, p.711), the documentation remains notably silent on a singularly vital issue, i.e. how might the formal legal rules and procedures of the ICC actually provide a guide towards the achievement of a communitarian philosophy of punishment through the discretionary decision-making process of international sentencing, and through what mechanisms?

In terms of the relationship between law and moral action, if we accept the notion that law exists as an integrative mechanism (Cotterrell, 1992, p.71), this must imply an acknowledgment that legal norms reflect notions of justice compatible and supportive of ideology at several levels.[27] However, it also implies a Durkheimian imperative which suggests a need to provide interpretations and adopt practices that might allow us to make the link between the recognition of law as a representation of morality and the existence of forms of expressed morality in civil society which exist in notions of communitarianism. Thus, the moral legitimacy of the international penal regime is constituted through its capacity to reflect socially meaningful (i.e. pluralistic) conceptions of morally unacceptable behaviour. This in turn requires an acknowledgement that it is the international sentencing *process* itself which provides the transformative mechanism and supplies linkage between moral purpose, legal

[27] Namely, global or regional, but also as suggestive of a morality of sanctioned punishment.

norms and social behaviour. It follows, therefore, that these purposes (if they are to include reconciliation, or provide linkage between rehabilitation and reconciliation) must be articulated. However, as noted previously, a fundamental problem with this conceptualisation is the fact that there is a disjunction between international sentencing's depiction of a 'one culture' world community and reality; that this represents the antithesis of plurality.

Turning now to the sentencing jurisprudence of the *ad hoc* tribunals, it was acknowledged in *Erdemovic*,[28] for example, that, whilst the ICTY has a clear mandate to investigate, prosecute and punish violations of international humanitarian law, the exercise of its judicial functions must contribute to the resolution of wider issues such as accountability, reconciliation and the establishment of the 'truth'. As the Trial Chamber put it:

> Discovering the truth is the cornerstone of the rule of law and a fundamental step on the way to reconciliation: for it is the truth that cleanses the ethnic and religious hatreds and begins the healing process ... On the other hand, the International Tribunal is a vehicle through which the international community expresses its outrage at the atrocities committed ...

Such observations would seem to illustrate and re-enforce the need for international sentencers to balance retributive and reconciliatory demands through the development of appropriate sentencing norms based on articulated purposes. However, precedent and judicial authority cannot reconcile such fundamental contradictions in penal philosophy.

Notwithstanding, in terms of the contextual model, what do these observations tell us about our conceptualisation of judicial discretionary decision-making in international sentencing? Is it consistent to argue in the international context that sentencing decisions are 'situational, pragmatic and individualised' in the sense that, within the wide parameters set for the exercise of judicial discretion, judges transform and particularise procedural rules in the service of individualistic goals? Further, are generalised images of case material, offender stereotyping and the psychological attribution of particular values to perceived facts by sentencers phenomena occuring within this context? Although it is not possible to make informed comments about the psychological process of decision-making on the basis of the restricted analysis undertaken in this chapter, it is apparent from any close examination of the sentencing narratives in international criminal trials that notions of individualisation articulated by judges are clearly balanced against what they perceive to be a clear mandate to favour retributivism and deterrence as the predominant rationales for punishment.

Unlike the position pertaining in some common law jurisdictions such as England and Wales, there exists no legal provision or constitutionally accepted convention sustaining a culture of judicial independence in international penality. Consequently, there can be no similar unifying rationale or other agenda for those sentencing the perpetrators of international crimes based on the principle that the fundamental integrity of judicial independence lies in the fact that the judiciary act as the

---

[28] *Prosecutor v Erdemovic* (Case No. IT-96-22), Sentencing Judgement, 5 March 1998.

mediators of just punishment between citizens and the state, or as defenders of a 'rational' sentencing policy; rationales which often underpin the individualisation of sentences in national jurisdictions. Rather, despite their differing jurisdictional backgrounds, international sentencers are *symbolically* united by a declared moral imperative to put an end to impunity through punishment that is linked in unarticulated ways to notions of accountability and reconciliation for victim communities. The need to reconceptualise the rationale for punishment in this context implies that the notion of individualisation should not be seen purely as an exercise in ensuring proportionate and commensurate punishment, but as one that is intimately connected to wider communitarian concerns that embrace restorative justice themes.

If it is accepted that sentencing in the international tribunals must include retributive considerations, but go beyond them to include mechanisms supportive of reconciliation, then notions of restorative justice should be developed to facilitate the achievement of this objective through sentencing praxis. These mechanisms should be predicated on principles which are concerned to re-establish recognised conduct norms and the rights and obligations existing between citizens, and citizens and the state in victim communities. However, they must be transformative at both the local and global level, a process which has often failed in the *ad hoc* tribunals because the essential roles for restorative justice process were not evident. In most restorative scenarios it must be made clear who are the 'offenders', who are 'significant others', and exactly what 'community' is being restored.

Moreover, conceptions of restorative justice, whilst being more suggestive of non-adversarial procedures, are not necessarily at variance with deserts-based retributive sentencing. However, Zedner (1994) also cautions that, although reparation and retribution are predicated upon notions of individual autonomy, both philosophies ignore the impact of structural inequality, power and social control variables. A further problem lies in the fact that, whilst retribution equates proportionality with an objective assessment of offender culpability (and harm), reparative justice is proportionate to victim harm.

Again, in theoretical terms, notions of popular justice that are consistent with the experiences and moral values of citizens in victim communities are misrepresented in the discourses of international sentencing. This is partly due to the absence of any rational links between the retributive and restorative aspirations of international penality, but also a wider phenomenon concerned with international governance, control and the management of risk. In a certain sense, the rhetorical commitment to reconciliation in sentencing and the dichotomy between this discourse and the concerns of individual citizens in victim communities can be seen as emanating from the need of hegemonic states to control both the process which manufactures the 'truth' of events and its reintegration in compatible form into victim communities. In other words, the international sentencing process may be viewed as complicit with the desires of the most powerful nation states in sustaining particular (distorted and partial) conceptions and images of 'victim' and 'community' for political reasons. Consequently, the aspirations and concerns of victim communities are generalised in trial discourse to conform to the dictates of hegemony and dominion.

Although cautioning that restorative justice invites social intervention going beyond the normal boundaries of conventional crime prevention, it is precisely the need to address significant structural and ideological matters that characterises those crimes of the magnitude with which we are concerned. Thus, notions of criminality as reflective of destruction, disintegration, conflict and breakdown go beyond traditional models which equate crime with social injustice. Instead, they lead directly to imperatives for reconstruction and reparation compatible with restorative justice principles aimed at increasing understanding, empowering victims and citizens and increasing their potential for participation and the resolution of conflict (Bush and Fogler, 1994). Certainly, in the arena of conventional crime, restorative justice principles are seen as potentially capable of re-empowering citizens and a force for social cohesion (Garland, 2001).

More recently, Braithwaite (2002, p.202) has acknowledged the potential force for restorative justice in the context of international criminal law enforcement, recognising that it provides the opportunity for institutional renewal through a 'bottom-up' process which seeks to engage civil society in structural regeneration, whilst providing a 'valuable philosophy of diplomacy' which facilitates the cultural transition from peace to war.

Whatever the potential for restorative justice, its value and relevance in the present context is its capacity to challenge conventional notions of the relationship between retributivism and other conceptualisations of penality in international sentencing. This includes a recognition that restorative objectives are *necessary* for the resolution of social conflict, and that notions of reparation and reconciliation should be achievable aspirations for sentencing, rather than accommodated by retributive practices so inconsistent and lacking in any coherent philosophical justification as to threaten their legitimacy. Ultimately, this is a question about whether (and to what extent) the international sentencing paradigm should be reconceptualised as essentially inclusive or exclusive.

Negotiated Justice and System Rationalisations

The notion of negotiated justice seems at first sight to be an anathema for international sentencing. The idea that the bureaucratic, managerial or economic imperatives of international criminal justice should somehow take precedence over the declared objective of ending impunity for those who have committed grave breaches of international humanitarian law appears rather perverse. Nevertheless, whilst, superficially, that appears to be the case, there are several complex reasons for existing sentencing practice. These issues are evaluated against the propositions included in the contextual model described earlier.

Let us concentrate firstly upon actual trial procedure and the foundation instruments of the ICC. As described earlier, the ICC Statute (Article 65) provides that, where the accused admits guilt, the Trial Chamber must satisfy itself that the admission is voluntary, that the accused understands the consequences, and that the admission is supported by the charges and factual evidence then available to it. The presumption of innocence is enshrined in Article 66, which also confirms that the onus is on the prosecution to prove to the satisfaction of the Court that the accused is guilty beyond all reasonable doubt. Unlike the position in England and Wales (for example), where the judge does not hear the evidence, only the prosecution statement of facts on a guilty plea, the ICC Statute (Article 65(4)) provides that the Trial

Chamber may request the prosecutor to present additional evidence (including witness testimony) in order to satisfy itself that a more complete presentation is made in the interests of justice.

This is a particularly important issue in terms of the context of sentence decision-making, since it affects both the factual basis for sentence and the question of transparency. The ICC approach is reflective of inquisitorial systems where the verdict and sentencing phases are conflated and the judiciary adopt an instrumental role in determining relevant evidence for both issues. An adversarial approach, such as exists in the US or England and Wales, militates against transparency since judges are either unwilling or unable to provide cogent reasons based on full factual evidence when determining sentence following a guilty plea. Such evidence would only emerge following a full trial of the issues. Again, this is an important example of how legal culture and procedural norms influence the meaning and significance of the sentencing phase.

However, a particular difficulty with the ICC Statute and Rules of Evidence and Procedure is that they are largely silent regarding the impact of the guilty plea on sentence.[29] There is no explicit recognition or explanation of (for example) whether a guilty plea counts as a mitigating factor, and, if it does, what conditions, circumstances or principles should govern the impact that the guilty plea has on final sentence determination.

This phenomenon can be examined further in terms of the propositions included in our contextual modelling for the role of judicial discretionary power in international sentencing decisions. For instance, we may question whether conceptualisation of the relationship between law and moral action suggests any insights which might assist us in understanding the reasons for (and implications of) the absence of procedural guidance or principle on what will (or should) be the impact of the guilty plea in ICC sentencing decisions. If the relationship between law and moral action is conceptualised as transformative in the terms described earlier, this would suggest that certain issues relating to guilty pleas bear closer examination; more particularly, whether negotiated justice in the wider sense effectively precludes any possibility of trial justice ever engaging with the legitimate demands of victims in post-conflict groups and societies. In short, negotiated justice is justice compromised, not justice transformed.

Particularly important is the extent to which victims should participate in the decision whether to accept a guilty plea in return for a sentence discount. Conventional adversarial rationales would suggest that victims (actual or potential) have a clear interest in seeing a true offender convicted following a full trial of the issues, and many victims may be prepared to face the ordeal of a court appearance rather than seeing the offender receive a significant sentence reduction in return for a guilty plea (Fenwick, 1997; Henham, 1999a). Where the Trial Chamber requests additional information following a guilty plea under Article 65(4) (see above) in the *interests of justice*, the provision explicitly refers to the relevance of victims' interests, yet it may be questioned whether actions furthering the interests of retributive justice are more likely to predominate, rather than conceptions of reparative justice that are compatible with communitarian concerns such as reconciliation, reintegration and social regulation. Paradoxically, however, as

---

[29] See Articles 76(1) and 78(1) and Rule 145.

Tochilovsky (1998, p.59) points out, there is a certain irony in the fact that many of the procedural rights made available to victims for trials conducted by the *ad hoc* tribunals are absent from the criminal procedures of those countries where the crimes charged were perpetrated.

The paradox of what constitutes justice in the context of the operation of the guilty plea in international sentencing clearly illustrates weaknesses in the Durkheimian notion that law's authority is derived from morality. Since it is impossible to assert convincingly that international penal norms uphold values of universal moral authority, the transformative capacity of sentencing law cannot be sustained on the basis of this argument. As Cotterrell argues:

> But nowhere in his [Durkheim's] work does he recognise adequately the interpretative tension, ... between two values the law serves: the value of rule-governed consistency or predictability and the value of moral responsiveness to the particularity of circumstances (1999, p.211).

However, this does not mean that that law's authority and transformative capacity cannot be derived from pluralistic moral positions. Durkheim's insight here is to suggest that the challenge for law is in terms of its relevance and meaningfulness for citizens. Nevertheless, his analysis falls short in failing to grasp the significance of subjectivity in establishing the meaning of social action and, therefore, in fully understanding both dimensions implicit in the transformative capacity of law; namely, its ability to influence moral action as well as to reflect moral principles. A context which legitimates plea bargaining viewed from a Durkheimian perspective might, therefore, be one which enables individual citizens to connect in a subjective (morally meaningful) way with the criminal process in all its manifestations. This can be expanded to relate to Durkheim's approach for connecting notions of morality to collective action by associating cooperation with the pursuit of needs based on principles of justice and fairness. Durkheim's analysis might therefore only allow us to assert that, at the international level, the moral interests of victims and victim communities are subjugated by *negotiated* legal process in its purported moral authority and the social function assigned to that process.

The nature of that moral authority is evident from the emphasis placed in the sentencing judgements of the *ad hoc* tribunals on particular justifications for negotiation. For example, a detailed evaluation of the guilty plea as a basis for conviction and its significance as a mitigating factor in sentencing is evident from the ICTY's judgement in *Todorovic*,[30] in which great emphasis was placed on remarks made earlier in *Erdemovic* to the effect that an admission of guilt is important (*inter alia*) because it encourages individuals to come forth, whether or not already indicted, and saves the tribunal the time, effort and expense of a lengthy investigation and trial, especially the laborious task of protecting victims and witnesses. Further, the Trial Chamber in *Todorovic* went on to add the important factor that, by pleading guilty, an accused relieves victims and witnesses of the necessity of giving evidence 'with the attendant stress this may incur'.[31] As Judge Cassese put it in *Erdemovic*: 'Thus, by pleading guilty, the accused undoubtedly contributes to public advantage.'

---

30 *Prosecutor v Todorovic* (Case No. IT-95-9/1), Sentencing Judgement, 31 July 2001.

31 *Ibid*, para. 80.

There is no doubt from these and other statements that sentencers in international tribunals regard the timing of the admission of guilt as a crucial factor in securing economic, managerial and bureaucratic advantages, whilst constantly re-enforcing and equating with this the notion that the guilty plea is intrinsically concerned with the pursuit of 'truth'. In this way the endorsement and normalisation of the sentence discount process is made to appear consistent with the moral imperative of the trial process. Furthermore, it is arguable that the symbolic affirmations regarding the primacy of the presumption of innocence, equality between the parties, and protection against self-incrimination contained in the foundation instruments of the international criminal tribunals are merely rhetorical.

What the Durkheimian approach does not do, however, is to make significant connections between discriminatory process and its ideological and political significance as a form of social control which ignores notions of popular justice. In particular, procedural justifications for accepting guilty plea discounts and their implications are frequently designed to neutralize their reality. An example is the justification of sentence discounts on the basis of expressed remorse (Bagaric and Amarasekara, 2001), which conceals the true nature of the *transaction* being undertaken. This can be seen as bargaining away, or 'buying-off' the defendant's due process rights for crime control reasons and, in Matza's (1964, p.174) terms, as a denial of the victim; where international criminal process is invoked without the permission of victims or victim communities. In both senses, the criminal process is invoked for ideological reasons which support the rationale for control rather than as evidence of consensus or democratization (Jung 1997, p.116); the latter being rarely identified beyond the symbolic in the international arena.

Assessing the Paradigmatic Approach

The Need for an Integrated Model

Before considering this issue it is necessary to preface what follows with some cautionary remarks. Firstly, it is acknowledged that the analysis pursued in this chapter can only be regarded as a tentative first step towards establishing the validity of the contextual modelling approach, and, secondly, that the analysis is incomplete in the sense that only a limited number of methodological techniques were available. Hence, the extent to which theoretical verification and generation were capable of complementing one another was strictly limited.

Notwithstanding, the analysis does suggest ways in which the integration of theoretical insights in a contextual model demonstrates a potential for enhancing our understanding of particular aspects of the international sentencing process, and, more generally, the relationship between domestic (regional) criminal justice agendas and the globalisation of criminal justice.

International Sentencing Process

It was argued earlier that the impetus in favour of an integrated model for contextual analysis is grounded in the need to understand *process* comparatively, particularly to emphasise the multi-layered nature of our inquiry and its different levels of abstraction. The ontological commitment is, therefore, driven by the need to find a set of organising and interpretative constructs capable of identifying and analysing elements and processes identified as implicated in the particular aspect of the trial process under investigation. The assumption is that, in order to be in a position to deconstruct the empirical reality of process in a coherent and meaningful way, theoretical formulations and concepts must be related through their integration within the parameters of a heuristic model (Henham and Findlay, 2002). In this sense, the function of the model is seen in conventional sociological terms: to facilitate the emergence of new 'knowledge by providing a holistic conceptual framework which has the heuristic capability to promote methodologies designed to test theoretical postulates' (Ryan, 1970).

Initially, it is important to consider the extent to which the propositions contained in the contextual model relate to the relevant dimensions of theoretical explanation. In reality, whilst particular theoretical propositions appear only to offer explanations at certain levels of abstraction, they can in fact be conceptualised in ways that relate to different degrees of abstraction and, in addition, particular theoretical conceptions will overlap at different levels of abstraction providing insights at different levels of meaning. If we take the relationship between law and moral action as an illustration, as with any form of contextual analysis, this requires the consideration and adoption of theoretical positions on issues ranging from higher order epistemological controversies regarding the nature of law and the conceptualisation of legal process right down to discrete analyses concerning particular sentencing outcomes.[32] Recognition of the existence of the relationships between levels of abstraction and using theory as a means for their deconstruction is an essential task of contextual analysis. It is also apparent that specific aspects of issues chosen for analysis – in this case, the relationship between judicial discretionary decision-making and restorative justice in international sentencing – have similar levels for understanding, and that component parts of an analytical model developed from a particular perception of empirical reality overlap one with the other at different conceptual levels. Consequently, a view has to be taken about the nature of the judicial discretionary decision-making process which correspondingly relates to how the law/moral action issue is perceived at different levels of abstraction. As such, theoretical and contextual understanding depend upon an integrated analytical approach.

We now turn to assess the extent to which the theoretical conceptualisation of the law/moral action issue in international sentencing and its integration into the

---

[32] The theoretical dimensions and debates surrounding the nature and scope of the relationship between law and moral action in international sentencing might include:

(1) legal closure v socio-legal analysis
(2) representing the social reality of process
(3) international sentencing as reflective of moral consensus
(4) decision-making as a transformative enterprise
(5) justifications for sentence and communitarian morality
(6) discretionary decision-making and moral attitudes
(7) private/public conceptions of morality in decision-making
(8) individualised sentencing practice
(9) issues of relevance and outcome.

contextual model developed for judicial decision-making and restorative justice advances our understanding of the phenomenon under investigation. The analysis suggests the following observations relevant to each aspect chosen for more detailed evaluation:

Sentence decision-making: The absence of any coherent statement of the justifications for sentencing in the foundation instruments and sentencing judgements of international criminal tribunals, together with the wide-ranging judicial discretion available to sentencers, were analysed utilising Durkheim's notion of individualism as a basis for arguing that there is a shared moral consensus which underlies international penal practice. However, the analysis was limited by the absence in Durkheim's theorising of any conceptualisation of 'consensus', 'sharing' and 'community' beyond the nation state which could be taken to connect with notions of individualism. The notion of the 'collective sentiments' as representing a unified morality with international punishment and a particular functional re-enforcement of that morality was clearly insufficient. Nevertheless, Durkheim's theorisation was invaluable in highlighting the problematic nature of international punishment as a concept which can be justified on behalf of the 'global community'.

Restorative justice: The relative absence of any mechanisms for transforming the rhetoric of restorative aspirations contained in the ICC's foundation instruments into realistic expectations was analysed by further exploring the Durkheimian notion of a linkage between punishment as a form of expressed morality and communitarian aspirations for penality. It was argued that the international sentencing process is in this sense transformative. By this I mean that, because the wide discretionary power available to sentencers in international criminal tribunals allows them to justify and signify rules as morally appropriate, judges effectively operationalise policy-justified principles of punishment by investing the normativity of penal law with moral imperatives through the application of appropriate sanctions. Durkheim's insight was therefore key to illuminating aspects of the linkage between legal reasoning and punishment in sentencing. What it failed to provide, however, was any theoretical insight into the linkage between rhetoric and reality for punishment in such a pluralistic environment as international penality.

Negotiated justice: This phenomenon was analysed in terms of the Durkheimian insight that the challenge for law is in terms of its relevance and meaningfulness for individual citizens. In its perception of the *reality* of negotiated justice, Durkheim's approach was again seen as incomplete in failing to satisfactorily explain the significance of subjectivity for moral action, or accommodate notions of power and social control. In the absence of any universal moral authority for law, it was difficult to envisage how process could reconcile pluralist aspirations for punishment (and their negotiation) in ways which would actually correspond to notions of 'justice' and 'fairness' for the significant audience of international trial process. The most important difficulty remains that of understanding how the transformative capacity of international legal process can connect in a morally meaningful way with the consciousness of individual human beings.

Taking all three aspects examined together, I would argue that following a Durkheimian approach to analysing the relationship between law and morality in society (imperfect as it may be) provides an important conceptual framework for deconstructing particular dimensions of judicial decision-making in international criminal trials at different conceptual levels; namely, the jurisdictional or structural context of the trial institutions themselves and their legal and procedural rules; the institutional, organisational or system contexts of their operation; and, the local or empirical reality of decision-making itself and its *actual* significance for victim communities. It is also apparent that Durkheim's notions regarding the relationship between law and morality are integrally linked to other theoretical propositions included in the contextual model, and at different levels of abstraction and understanding; for example, those concerning the nature of the judicial decision-making process. Thus, the theoretical propositions chosen were integrated to the extent that each was designed to address particular components of an identified social reality at different levels of meaning – the exercise of judicial discretion in international sentencing.

Domestic and International Sentencing Practice

A further reason why the contextual model provides an integrated approach to comparative analysis is that it is able to draw *meaningful* comparative conclusions which relate to issues of difference and the possible harmonisation of trial procedures (Henham and Findlay, 2001). For international sentencing, this requires comparable understandings of trial process and their significance at the domestic (local) and international levels. This does not involve a descent into subjectivity and moral relativity (Hodgson, 2000), but rather a recognition that, for comparative analysis to progress, methodologies for providing common definitions of process (however imperfect) must be developed and refined.

A useful starting point provided by the contextual model is the notion that the 'objectivity' of the trial process can only be described and explained through understanding the criteria and means by which human agents subjectively construct common definitions of objective reality (Rogers and Erez, 1999). The next step is to explore common definitions of process within and across cultures in context. Essentially, what is being sought are models which will support methodologies for identifying points where subjective consensus appears to exist regarding meaning and function in the sentencing process. The degree of consensus in terms of difference and synthesis can be examined for particular decision-making sites, such as judicial discretionary decision-making in sentencing.

A comparative analysis of local and global trial justice as represented in international penality is further complicated by the peculiarly hybrid nature of international criminal trial process, reflecting, as it does, a blending of jurisdictional ideologies and trial traditions and a process of negotiation and compromise between adversarial and inquisitorial trial forms. This merging of structure and process is administered and operationalised by human agents drawn from equally diverse legal cultures. Whilst it is also true that certain national jurisdictions also possess hybridised trial processes forged through compromise and negotiation (such as Italy or Spain), these differ from international process forms because, once implanted, such processes grow and develop indigenously in the first instance, from within the existing legal culture.

However, it is important to recognise the broader significance of the concept of 'context' rather than 'culture' in comparative analysis. As Henham and Findlay (2001) suggest, the notion of 'context' suggests a universal and unifying construct for conceptualising the wider social, cultural, political and economic determinants of trial process. Within context, legal culture constitutes a crucial component of praxis (Nelken, 1997). In this respect Bell (2001, p.4) recognises that the reality of practice is central in shaping context; the meaning of facts is determined by an account of their significance for local actors; and, a common language and identity shape collective reality.

Bell (2001, p.6) utilises Searle's conception of an 'institutional fact'[33] to convey the notion that collective intentionality is ultimately responsible for the creation of institutional reality, since 'institutional facts are necessarily embedded within the language of a particular community'. However, whilst indicative of the reflexive nature of the relationship between ideology and praxis within specific local contexts, Bell's (2001, p.22) model for deconstructing legal culture falls short of providing a heuristic tool for comparative purposes; a tool that would enable us to test the degree of congruence between the meanings attributed to criminal process by human agents across contexts at the global and local level (both horizontally and vertically).

I suggest that the contextual model developed in this chapter enhances our ability to deconstruct and mediate the meaning of the discretionary sentence decision-making process for both national and international jurisdictions at several levels of comparison. Reconceptualising the penality of international criminal trial process presents a significant challenge in this respect. The relationship of sentencing decisions to perceptions of what constitutes appropriate penal censure in post-conflict societies provides important insights into the linkage between law and morality at the following comparative levels: justifications and principles of punishment; policy and system objectives; nature of the sentence decision-making process; integration of sentencing process; and opportunities for negotiation and diversion.

Theorising International Penality

To summarise, I suggest that the advantages of utilising the comparative contextual paradigm as a basis for modelling international sentencing process are as described below.

Understanding the Transformative Capacity of Law

This is potentially crucial to understanding the relationship between the ideologies which might inform international penal structures and their relevance to victim (or target) communities. Unless we adopt a purely cynical view of international punishment as a vehicle for vindictiveness, retribution and exculpation, we must

33 'An institutional fact is a fact which we invest with meaning within a particular set of social relations because it performs a particular function' (Searle, 1995, p.26).

assume that, as with other penalities, some constructive engagement with consequentialist objectives is imperative for the development of normative practices which resonate with the concerns that produce and sustain conflict and social breakdown in victim communities. The modelling of this issue and the recognition of its moral dimensions requires the evaluation of theoretical insights to develop punishment rationales that facilitate the convergence of notions of truth with justice. Particularly relevant is the notion of law-making as a transformative enterprise and its susceptibility to evaluation within any proposed model.

Grounding Theory in Context

By this I mean the need to acknowledge in modelling the significance of *process* to comparative analysis. If it is accepted that this can only be achieved through developing our understanding of how meanings are attributed to process, and what these actually signify in terms of collective experience, then we must ensure that future modelling addresses this issue. More particularly, the model developed in this chapter has followed Tamanaha's (1997) assertion that fact and value are integrated in the constitution of process itself and, that our understanding of what actually counts as fact depends on the extent to which we can generalise about subjective accounts of what a fact is and means. It is a position which relates the transformation of the ideological to the normative by deconstructing the meanings which relevant participants attribute to *process*, thereby revealing how the nature of objectivity is understood as subjective experience. The crucial point is that the relative realities of fact and value are merged in process. I would argue that this approach is an essential prerequisite for any meaningful examination of the praxis of international punishment, since it facilitates an understanding of the relationship between normative prescription and practice at different levels of social reality (Henham and Findlay, 2002). Contextual modelling takes the view that the best chance for understanding process comparatively is to generalise from contexts in which the analysis of process is approached on this basis.

Collapsing Dualisms

Although the fact/value issue is clearly relevant to this notion it has wider significance for modelling the penality of international sentencing process. In particular, the development of structuration theory implicitly recognises the conceptualisation of structure as recursively reproduced through human agency, but does not preclude, as Vaughan (2000) suggests, the objective existence of structure (Henham and Findlay, 2001). Structuration theory is therefore employed to provide a sensitising framework for deconstructing the manufacture, significance and meaning of process for human agents, whilst also recognising that generalisations regarding the existence and meaning of process provide 'evidence' of its 'objectivity'.

Further, the theoretical grounding for contextual modelling also collapses the macro/micro dualism through its capacity to accommodate theoretical constructs which relate to different analytical levels and, therefore, levels of understanding. Finally, dualistic conceptions of the individual and society are also countered by the focus of contextual modelling on how and why penal structures are created and sustained through process. This is because the study of process in context represents a site of reflexivity for human agency where interpretation, creativity, meaning and definition is given to the social expectations and commitments which go towards forming a particular societal view of penality. At the international level, it becomes crucial to challenge preconceived notions of penality by evaluating current theoretical propositions against the emerging reality of globalised punishment. Again, the Rwandan genocide provides a perfect example of the need for theory and modelling to accommodate differing interpretations of important aspects of penal culture in context; namely, the ideological justification for the trial process and the implications for justifying penal sanctions.

Theory and Practice

My final and most important comment on the potential for contextual modelling of the international sentencing process is concerned with the issue of reconciling normative prescription and processual reality. It is essential for any heuristic model that might be developed to provide the theoretical means whereby *real* inconsistencies between the political and ideological imperatives of international criminal justice and the reality of the discretionary decision-making processes which produce sentencing outcomes are revealed and understood before any meaningful evaluation for policy development can follow. I suggest that the approach provided by comparative contextual analysis discussed herein can make an important contribution to that process. The relative realities of truth and justice are revealed where the analysis of structure and process are grounded in context.

Chapter 8

Conclusion: Reconceptualising International Penality

The preceding chapter argued that the instrumental power of judicial discretion for determining the form and significance of decision-making in international criminal trials should be harnessed to forge rationalisations for sentencing that facilitate the reconciliation of competing paradigms for justice. This proposes a conceptualisation of sentencing that is reflexive, possessing the capacity for dynamic and creative resolutions and strategies that address the consequences of social conflict and breaches of international humanitarian law. So conceived, international punishment and process would no longer be as a symbolic forum for acting out the rhetoric of positivist law; it would instead be socially responsive, morally sensitive and culturally relevant. Thus, sentencing as a processual reality would facilitate the relative engagement of contexts, placing constantly varying demands on sentencers to devise morally acceptable outcomes to reconcile the demands for local justice with more universal aspirations for international justice.

I would argue that, in order to exploit the instrumentality of discretion in this way it is necessary to:

- Reposition the rationalisation of international punishment within a conceptualisation of penality that focuses on the functionality of the trial and sentence in terms of its mission to contribute to peace and reconciliation.
- Operationalise the newly realised capability for instrumental decision-making by addressing the difficult issues of consistency and appropriate mechanisms for the regulation of discretion.
- Conceptualise rights differently. Rights must not simply be conceived as norms of regulation and accountability; as measures of the relative distance between ideology and practice. Thus, rights must become integrated as a processual reality; rights law and procedural law should be synthesised through/by discretionary decision-making. Accountability must be seen in terms that measure sentence outcomes against paradigms/strategies for peace and reconciliation rather than abstract normative frameworks.

This chapter argues for a new paradigm for international penality that addresses these issues and suggests how current debates over punishment and penal philosophy, consistency and discretion, access to justice and rights should be reconceptualised in terms that resonate with the competing demands for justice that follow international conflict and war.

Reconstructing the Model

Rethinking Rationality

When arguing for a new or modified ideology for international penality, we proceed from an ontological position which accepts that it has an identifiable ideology; a set of ideas which informs the characteristics of international trial structures. Recognising that the international criminal trial may not have legitimacy also means that we have applied some measure whereby a true understanding of the meaning of legitimacy in its comparative dimensions can be ascertained. In this book, penal legitimacy has been examined from perspectives measuring international penal norms against political ideology, communitarian values, universal rights paradigms and models of justice. The theoretical stance adopted by comparative contextual analysis argues that fact and value are merged in process. Thus, process represents the crystallisation of ideological values at different levels of abstraction (macro/micro discretionary decision-making). To have reached a judgement about legitimacy therefore requires us to consider the nature of this fusion. We must understand the construction of objective and subjective reality and the nature of its external and internal perception at the levels of ideology, morality and normativity. The connection between ideology and praxis as understood comparatively allows us to make informed speculations that inform the debate about legitimacy. In recognising need(s) for change we make value judgements regarding the deficiency of international criminal justice in some aspect of ideology and praxis.

This book has argued that the rationality of punishment and the function of process are intimately connected. In fact, it has been argued that reason and action are collapsed when the capacity for discretionary decision-making is exercised; both crystallise in the sentencing decision itself. Consequently, values are attributed to the 'facts' that constitute decisions where, as Tamanaha (1997) argues, fact and value merge. Viewed thus, the decision represents a synthesis of fact/value. Reasons for action are matters of influence and motivation for trial actors that encompass system concerns and broader cultural variables. The semantic significance of the synthesis which the decision represents is a function of the control exercised by procedural norms. Procedural norms are themselves informed by ideology and policy and may represent competing claims for moral legitimacy. The extent of this depends on the plurality of moral claims and the degree to which competing groups exert power to assert what they perceive as morally legitimate claims. The sentencing decision is the corollary of ideology and process. Within the framework for rational action permitted by its ideology, the exercise of such discretionary power determines outcome. Thus, discretion merges fact and value to correspond with a rational objective for action. For sentencing, this is a strategy which attributes value to fact for consequential reasons (see Figure 8.1).

The recursivity of ideology and legitimacy is perpetuated through the synthesis of reason and action as facilitated through the exercise of discretionary power.[1] So described, penality can be conceptualised in terms of either an *exclusive* or *inclusive*

---

[1] This is consistent with the application of structured properties by social actors suggested by structuration theory.

Ideology	**Structure**
Moral	**Social**
Value	**Norm**
Reason	**Action**
Legitimacy	**Strategy**

Figure 8.1 Dualities merged through process

paradigm. Paradoxically, viewed as an *exclusive* paradigm, penality corresponds to Hudson's (2003) idea of a more inclusive (i.e. system-bound) universe of ideas, norms, structures and processes through which the dominant ideology of punishment is promulgated. Garland (1990), on the other hand, suggests an *inclusive* (i.e. socially determined) paradigm for penality; one that invites us to go beyond the semantics of crime and punishment to engage with pluralities in terms of morality, philosophy and sociology. In other words, Garland invites us to address those moral and social issues that determine the form of the inclusive universe which is penality. In order to achieve this, any reconceptualisation of international penality needs to reconcile the relativism of justice with the semantics of process; in other words, reconcile diverging realities.

Relative reality reflects the legitimacy attached to sentencing outcomes as functional reality. Throughout this book I have argued for a reconceptualisation of international penality which is grounded in a proper appreciation of the function of sentencing and its significance in the context of international criminal trial process. We might, therefore, begin the process of reconstructing international penality by deconstructing international sentencing in terms of the following questions:

- What facts are regarded as 'truth' for sentencing purposes?
- What does the sentencing process represent in terms of power and symbolism; is international punishment merely a crude exercise in domination or ideological imperialism?
- Does sentencing by international courts and tribunals re-enforce particular definitions of morally acceptable behaviour?
- Does international punishment serve the needs of identifiable international or collective communities of justice?

There are several interrelated aspects to the construction of 'truth' through sentencing. Firstly, there is procedural truth; where procedural norms and mechanisms provide a framework for determining what information is relevant for sentence and how it is processed, so that 'truth' consists of what the system regards as an acceptable factual basis for sentence. In this sense, sentencing is literally processual – it produces an outcome; a social reality that is shaped by a pre-determined normative control structure that determines what can count as 'true facts'. This distortion is compounded through the exercise of discretion; here decision-makers selectively attribute significance to items of information to construct a definitive version of the 'truth' as both verdict and sentence.

Functionally, international criminal trials may be seen as arbiters of moral diversity and the relativity between conceptions of truth and justice; as regulators of the extent to which process can be transformative and a legitimator of morally opposing justifications for action. Process mediates value conflict. International criminal justice exists (if at all) as a reflection of the legitimacy attached to the justification for/performance of that function by the so-called 'global community'. It is a virtual reconciliation of truth and justice for relative consumption, just as it is in domestic contexts. It is ever-changing, depending on conflict, communities, and cultures. It can be seen (promoted) as relational (or not), as a positive or negative force for peace (or not).

It has been argued that structures which accommodate themes of restorative justice facilitate the reconciliation of opposing moralities and provide a forum for mediating relationships and encouraging reconstructive strategies. To reflect processes of restorative justice in the global context of the international criminal trial envisages process as a mechanism for engaging, resolving and producing strategies for particular communities of justice, drawn together to confirm (and resolve) specific problems to produce what is collectively accepted as a moral legitimate/just outcome that will contribute towards peace and reconciliation. Punishment and process therefore attains moral legitimacy by ensuring that the exercise of discretionary power and its effects are conducted in a context which favours the advancement of community interests and the protection of humanity.

The forging of justice as a collective interest may require the integration of retributive and restorative themes. This would consequently necessitate a theoretical reorientation and accommodation towards the social distribution of harm and the extent to which that calculation can integrate with retributive notions such as culpability and desert. As Zedner (1995) suggests, such a broader conception of penality recognises that the rights infringed by criminality (or social deviance) reach beyond the immediate victim and are held in common socially. It also argues against the exclusivity of international criminal process as the only appropriate response to gross breaches of international humanitarian law, favouring the involvement and promotion of community interests.

Notwithstanding, it is important not to lose sight of the fact that repositioning international penality in pursuit of collective forms of justice resolution produces a rationale and potential for integrating retributive and restorative concerns, rather than one promoting ideological hegemony. This implies a recognition that, whilst restorative justice can be seen as possessing the transformative power to change the nature and dynamics of trial decision-making, it is, nevertheless, an ideological commitment, albeit one that is undertaken with the object of integration rather than division and social conflict. It should also be recognised that discretionary decisions which favour collective forms of justice themselves reflect power exercised within an ideologically and normatively structured environment. Consequently, the task of balancing the interests of offenders, victims and communities (global and local) cannot be reconciled in terms which promote peace and reconciliation without norms of access to sentencing being promulgated and adhered to, and norms of guidance for sentencing being developed based on the new rationality.

Controlling Discretion

Whilst consistency and proportionality reflect retributivist aspirations for justice, they are at least identifiable parameters for the regulation of judicial discretionary power. However, as has been argued, their manifestation as normative regulators for sentencing in international criminal trials has proved largely symbolic and supportive of their underlying retributive penality. The restructuring of rationales for international sentencing to accommodate and integrate responses to communitarian demands for justice increases rather than diminishes the need for normative principles to inform sentencers. Thus, principles for sentencing should contain normative indicators designed to assist international judges in their role as facilitating just outcomes which satisfy collective interests emerging from social conflict and war. However, the development of an evaluative paradigm for sentencing which delivers outcomes that resonate with collective forms of justice remains problematic. There are two major reasons for this:

1. The normative framework needs to be developed from comparative understandings of the social world.
2. Understandings of the nature and significance of collective and individual claims for justice in different social contexts must be capable of being re-cast as norms in terms which are capable of guiding sentencers in international criminal trials to achieve constructive restorative sentencing outcomes.

One approach to the task of designing an appropriate mechanism for ensuring consistency in the sentencing practices of international judges is to identify those variables which determine judicial discretionary decision-making in any given sentencing context and examine how these relate (if at all) to the measures which distinguish between sentence levels[2] within that context. Hence, this approach focuses on how judicial discretionary decisions and commensurate penal severity relate to one another in different settings. However, this is a very limited exercise because it seeks to extrapolate the significance of discretionary power by assessing its relationship to past outcomes rather than through a sympathetic appreciation of existing needs for punishment, reparation and reconciliation. Neither does this approach question the ideological commitment of the process it seeks to observe. In other words, the analytical focus is devoid of context; the rationality and the concomitant normative framework for discretionary power is neither described nor analysed.

---

[2] Sentencing levels refers the relationship between sentence decisions and penalties in two senses:

(1) ordinal proportionality – how offences are ranked according to seriousness and the commensurate penalties allocated

(2) cardinal proportionality – what determines the overall severity of penalty scales.

Research which seeks to discover whether there is any commonality in the reasons and structures which regulate the ordinal proportionality of sentencing decisions across different jurisdictional contexts is necessarily an exercise in comparative analysis.[3] It is seeking to draw out areas of synthesis and difference between different sentencing contexts and reach certain conclusions about what are appropriate mechanisms of sentencing regulation. This objective gives rise to a number of difficulties and questions which can only be resolved through comparative contextual analysis.

The most obvious limitation is that quantitative data on measures of penal severity and judicial practice from different jurisdictions are not comparable. Several scholars, notably Albrecht (2001, p.294) and Frase (1998, p.119), have pointed to the fact that the comparative analysis of quantitative data on the effect of penal processes in different jurisdictions is suspect because it ignores legal and cultural context.[4] Consequently, statistical comparisons tell us little (if anything) about the socio-political forces that determine the interactions which statistics purport to represent, nor the nature of those interactions. As has been argued, comparative contextual analysis reaches beyond the observations of symbolic interactionists such as Cicourel (1968) and Sudnow (1965) regarding the symbolism of social statistics by suggesting a methodology for deconstructing the *actual* processes which constitute the dynamics of trial decision-making in terms of relationship structures and influences, and their relationship with sentence outcomes.

Comparative sentencing statistics may be manipulated for ideological and/or political purposes. For example, they may purport to show a relationship between judicial practice and apparently low levels of sentence severity for particular types of offences across jurisdictions. There is a danger that this information could be taken as an indication that rigid control of sentencing discretion was imperative in the construction of sentencing guidelines for international criminal trials. Such errors would be avoided through utilising comparative contextual analysis as a methodology, since it would reveal the reasons for contextual variability in judicial practice and provide explanations of their subjective reality within each context nominated for comparison. Consequently, any conclusions drawn from comparison of these variables would form a methodologically valid basis to inform policy.

These understandings mean that issues of parity and consistency (if politically promoted as desirable) can in practice be enhanced with the support of understandings that can arise from knowing more about the way sentence decision-making arises. This might mean the possibility of a very general policy matrix which predicts the broad influence of one major decision variable against another. Comparative contextual analysis possesses the capacity for deconstructing process and meaning, which suggests that it can provide important information about the way judges approach the more subjective aspects of discretionary decision-making, such as the individualisation of sentences.

---

[3] Essentially a socio-legal study that examines the relationship between structure and agency in the context of the criminal trial.

[4] For a practical illustration of the difficulties in compiling comparative criminal justice statistics see; European Sourcebook of Crime and Criminal Justice Statistics (http//www.europeansourcebook.org/esb/index.html) especially Chapter 3.

Comparative work by Henham and Mannozzi (2003) on victim participation and sentencing in England and Italy tends to confirm the hypothesis that context informs the instrumentality of judicial discretion rather than structure and form. If this is correct, then it may prove fruitless to impose mechanisms to control discretion without considering the broader issues of sentence justification and trial purpose argued for in this book. This observation is particularly significant in the light of experience from the *ad hoc* tribunals where (as we have seen) narrative analysis indicates some confusion in the tribunals' interpretation of 'individualisation' as a sentencing concept. For example, assuming restorative justice were to be embraced as a desirable justification, the present conceptualisation of individualisation and its potential engagement with restorative concerns and collective demands for justice is inhibited by the retributive dynamic prevalent in international trial ideology. In terms of individual sentencing decisions this means that the concept of individualisation is constrained by legalistic criteria. Although international sentencers have wide discretionary powers that could be used to develop sentencing principles which promote consequentialist objectives, the individualisation of sentences currently focuses on the issue of individual criminal responsibility and its clarification in the context of the need for proportionality.[5] Comparative contextual analysis will therefore enable us to inform policy by gauging the potential effects of control mechanisms on the judicial capacity to implement particular sentencing strategies through discretionary decision-making.

The fact that certain scholars take the view that law is distorted through socio-legal analysis is also problematic. The debate between Cotterrell (1998a) and Nelken (1998) regarding the extent to which sociological insights should be used in the interpretation of legal ideas has significant epistemological and methodological repercussions (Banakar, 2000). Although there is broad agreement between Cotterrell and Nelken regarding the need for legal sociology to address the socio-legal contexts of legal decision-making, Nelken distances himself from Cotterrell's suggestion that legal contexts should only be interpreted sociologically. However, for comparative contextual analysis the key issues are, firstly, the need to understand the moral power of the law and, secondly, the methodological implications of the related demystification of the internal/external distinction in conceptualising legal thought and decision-making processes. Correspondingly, both are vital for developing sensitive and flexible contexts for decision-making that accommodate differences in collective notions of justice.

Comparative contextual analysis supports the proposition that the discretionary character of sentence decision-making requires judges to justify and signify legal rules as morally appropriate because sentencers effectively operationalise policy

---

[5] This has been consistently reinforced in decisions of the ICTY. For example, in *Prosecutor v Krnojelac* (Case No. IT-97-25-T), Judgement, 15 March 2002 '... the overriding sentencing obligation considered by the Trial Chamber has been that of fitting the penalty to the individual circumstances of the Accused and to the gravity of the offences for which he has been found responsible' (para. 507); or, as in *Prosecutor v Sikirica* (Case No. IT-95-8-S), Sentencing Judgement, 13 November 2001 (citing the *Celebici* Appeal Judgement, para. 717) '...the overriding of the Trial Chamber in determining sentence is to 'individualise a penalty to fit the individual circumstances of the accused and the gravity of the crime' (para. 231).

justified principles of punishment by transforming law into appropriate sanctions through the criminal (punishment) process.[6] Therefore, law's moral power in sentencing is achieved by its capacity to shape social reality through the recursively organised practice of the criminal process. In order to appreciate the transformation of normative principles as morally significant components of social reality, it consequently becomes necessary to understand law's capacity to achieve this, and this can only be addressed by examining the epistemological and methodological questions raised by conceptualising 'social reality'. Hence, comparative contextual analysis proceeds on the assumption that the relationship between legal reasoning and punishment in sentencing must be systematically and empirically explained as a form of 'social reality'.

Further difficulties arise when deciding how discretionary decision-making should be analysed in any given context. As pointed out in the previous chapter, contemporary forms of sentence modelling have largely been one-dimensional and lacking in social context. Comparative contextual modelling advocates an approach to the deconstruction of discretionary decision-making that accommodates comparativism. Such an approach sees it as crucial to provide evaluators that are capable of analysing and evaluating the psychological appropriation and assimilation of relevant information for sentencing as an objective (external) process. In addition, comparative contextual modelling also considers the extent to which trial participants appear to share similar, uniform and comparable images of relevant case material and legal rules in the context of perceived audience expectations for justice.

For comparative analysis, the simple juxtaposition of conclusions drawn from research carried out in different jurisdictional settings is inadequate. This highlights a fundamental debate regarding the viability, nature and purpose of comparative analysis (Nelken, 1997, 2000; Nelken and Feest, 2001; Harding and Orucu, 2002; Legrand and Munday, 2003). The comparative contextual analysis of normative frameworks requires methodologies capable of deconstructing the contexts in which legal decisions are made. It is, therefore, a socio-legal inquiry that focuses on *actual* decision-making practice, and what this signifies for individuals and communities (reference groups) within a particular jurisdiction. Whether jurisdictions share similar juridical foundations and styles of trial process (as evidenced by the adversarial/inquisitorial distinction), or represent hybrid or transitional forms, there are common issues and themes which arise in analysing the social function of the trial form and the jurisdictional response to it. Where meaningful descriptions[7] of social action within the trial context are extracted in terms that reveal *real* understandings of decisions and procedures, I suggest it is appropriate to draw implications for policy from cross-cultural analyses of process.

Comparative contextual analysis facilitates the drawing of meaningful connections between comparative and international contexts. Accordingly, where structures and social agents from different trial styles and legal cultures are transplanted into novel jurisdictional forms (such as the ICTY, the ICTR and the ICC), it is legitimate to take

---

[6] This argument supports the contention that it is the international sentencing *process* itself which provides the transformative mechanism and supplies linkage between moral purpose, legal norms and social behaviour.

[7] 'Meaningful' to those individuals within a particular context.

particular accounts and understandings of the trial contexts from which these transplants have come in order both to comprehend what they historically and currently represent, and to speculate how they might develop in the future from a sound empirical foundation.

In effect, by utilising comparative contextual analysis as a methodological technique to deconstruct trial decision-making in any particular jurisdictional context, it is possible to expose the pathways of influence that operate at particular decision sites within the trial and reveal the true nature of the meanings which trial participants attribute to processual activity. Modelling the conclusions drawn from different contexts can then provide evaluators for deconstructing other jurisdictional contexts. As described elsewhere, such modelling allows for a wide range of methodological techniques to be adopted within a framework tolerant of inductive and deductive theorising (Findlay and Henham, 2005).

Relationships between comparative analysis and the analysis of international criminal trials are suggested on the basis that it is legitimate to look for areas of commonality and difference between local and global trial forms. This is justified because comparative contextual analysis allows us to identify how trial relationships and decision processes operate to produce what is regarded as trial justice in different contexts. It is therefore seen as legitimate to draw comparisons between jurisdictional trial forms (local, regional or global), where, despite differences in legal and cultural context, there are cogent reasons to examine how and why the quality of justice is constructed in certain ways. For example, where trial justice is measured in terms which suggest the integration of retributive and restorative aspirations, our knowledge of how trial relationships in different trial contexts accommodate these tensions in trial decision-making and the reasons for this provide a legitimate platform for examining how these experiences relate to the processes and purposes of international criminal justice.

Conclusions distilled from research conducted in different contextual settings are therefore important for identifying and understanding which variables are implicated and how they impact on discretionary decision-making in different socio-legal contexts. Thus, developing knowledge about trial dynamics – how relationships and influence determine trial decision-making in different contexts – provide important indicators of how the purposes chosen for sentencing in international criminal trials will find expression and what potential exists for their transformation.

I would therefore argue the importance of utilising comparative contextual analysis as a methodology to explain the significance of certain themes of discretionary decision-making (e.g. victim/judge relationships; judicial culture; judicial independence) across jurisdictions and extrapolate from this knowledge to provide exploratory guides (evaluators) for understanding international criminal justice process and, more particularly, improve the capacity for decision-makers to make informed policy choices.

A useful illustration is provided by Henham and Mannozzi's (2003) comparative work on victim participation in England and Italy mentioned earlier. This research focuses particularly on the social construction of victim participation by investigating victim/judge relationships. It examines the cultural context in which the influences of the judge and victim are created and merge to determine the exercise of discretionary power at significant decision sites for sentencing in the trial process. In this way it identifies how different pathways of influence produce different configurations of fact/value whose practical effects are manifested in greater or lesser participation for victims in those aspects of the trial process that are relevant for victims and sentence.

Henham and Mannozzi (2003) identify and elaborate crucial aspects of sentencing as a site of decision-making and explore their significance for the English and Italian jurisdictional contexts. These emphasise the importance of the following variables:

- the role of judicial discretion
- evidence relevant to sentence
- dichotomy between verdict delivery and sentence
- relationships between judges and other legal professionals
- relevance of the victim
- communitarian concerns in sentencing
- transparency in sentencing
- impact of legal principle and normative guidance
- processural abuse.

The conclusions so far reached in this work indicate that:

- The legal and political contexts of judicial discretion have resulted in a narrow and partisan conceptualisation of the victim in England and Italy, and have restricted the extent to which victim participation in sentencing is promoted.
- There has been failure to develop rational justifications for sentencing which address reparative or restorative justice concerns other than through reaching some accommodation with the predominant philosophy of limited retributivism and the framework of proportionality it imposes.
- The normative content of the criminal trial paradigm is not the main influence on judicial practice regarding the exercise of discretion which affects the extent of victim participation. The crucial determinant is the socio-legal context which informs the instrumentality of judicial discretion.
- Changes in structure and form (without a corresponding re-evaluation in the overall purposes of prosecution, trial and sentence beyond a basic need to remedy procedural deficiency) produce penal structures whose philosophical justifications are impossible to reconcile within the existing stated aims of punishment and the legislative model which embodies them.

Whilst these findings have considerable implications for determining the future direction of penality in England and Italy, they go much further because they raise questions about the relationship between criminal trial structures and human agency that are also relevant for understanding the trial contexts of international criminal justice. Moreover, the research suggests certain propositions for modelling victim participation that may be relevant to understanding the nature and significance of victim inclusion/exclusion in international criminal trials.

Comparative contextual analysis of victim participation in English and Italian trials helps us to understand why and how perceptions of victims are reflected in contexts of procedural similarity and difference, and actual significance determined by legal and socio-cultural context. For example, in procedural terms, both the English and Italian jurisdictions are characterised by the fact that victims do not have the right to participate in the negotiation of sentencing decisions; but what does this imply for the notion of negotiated justice in cultural terms? Does it mean that victims who do not testify are content for the criminal process to 'balance' their personal and communitarian interests as victims against ideological and system interests in speed, certainty, and finality that are driven by economic and managerial agendas? In the international context, the resolution of such issues is crucial for the pursuit of reparative and restorative goals in communities where socially harmful actions have been perpetrated on a catastrophically large scale.

The paucity of evaluative research on the sentencing practices of the *ad hoc* tribunals and the ICC has been noted (Beresford, 2002; Henham 2003a), that which exists being largely doctrinal rather than empirical. Consequently, those conclusions which have been reached regarding the impact of internationalised forms of sentencing process have not been tested against outcomes based on methodologies other than those involving the mechanistic analysis of legal norms and particular sentencing decisions along conventional positivist lines. I would argue that the knowledge obtained from comparative empirical work such as that carried out by Henham and Mannozzi (2003) can be used to inform international sentencing policy regarding the role of victims in sentencing and the likely consequences of particular outcomes for victims and communities because comparative contextual analysis allows meaningful generalisations to be made about discretionary decisions through the analytical deconstruction of specific sites of discretionary decision-making in the sentencing process in different contextual scenarios where tensions between rule governed behaviour and alternative value positions are resolved. However, much additional international and comparative research is necessary to further increase our understanding of what determines the nature and content of fact and value in discretionary decisions made in criminal trials, and how best to capitalise on the instrumental power of judicial discretion as a force for developing reconstructive outcomes and strategies. Whilst empirical research alone cannot reconceptualise, rationalise or reposition the justifications for international sentencing decisions, what it can do is to explore the different contexts for achieving particular penal outcomes.

Reconceptualising Rights

The reconceptualisation of rights for international criminal justice means grounding rights in the reality of outcomes. By this I mean that rights must not remain mere rhetorical devices whose values are enshrined in the preambles of treaties, and whose norms remain symbolic. In order for rights to engage with collective forms of justice the possibility must exist for their processual integration.

Evaluating victim participation against particular rights paradigms invites an examination of procedural traditions which support the assertion of victims' rights in sentencing, rather than adopting conventional models which seeks to protect the defendant in the pre-trial and trial phases of the criminal process. Since the latter generally suggest minimal guarantees of access to justice and fair trial for victims, knowledge must be provided which can inform the future direction of the construction and harmonisation of sentencing principles at the international level. This suggests more balanced notions of justice which endeavour to connect with the developing place of victims within restorative justice and feature conceptualisations of victim access and interests beyond measures of individual harm and just deserts.

The conceptualisation of access to justice and victims' rights within this context can be distinguished in the following way:

- *Access* is concerned with the existence of procedural and processual rules (legal, bureaucratic and administrative norms) which may be regarded as compatible with the achievement of principled goals (normative imperatives). The latter are considered as minimum requirements for a criminal trial process to conform with a certain value system (the nature, prevalence and ideological function of such value systems is taken as conjectural).
- *Rights* are envisaged as the corollary to access; namely, as procedural rules (legal norms) designed to ensure that the aspirations (values) embodied in the norms of access are *actually* upheld.

However, whilst acknowledging the cultural relativity of such concepts, I would promote the idea of access to justice in sentencing as an instrumental notion. This is consistent with the view that the processes of judicial legal reasoning and discretionary decision-making within the trial are seen as the fundamental determinants of sentence outcome. By this is implied a conceptualisation that is purposeful, one which provides a context where the ideological and philosophical rationales that inform policy and structure are negotiated in ways that reflect meaningful connections between the institutions of punishment and citizens. In this sense, the dynamics of the judge/victim paradigm are the key to understanding the determination of rights in practice.

Belief that law should be viewed as instrumental and transformative is evidenced by an equation of access to justice with a distinct conceptualisation of victim participation for sentencing which suggests that victims should participate fully and have a significant input into those discretionary decision-making processes that determine sentence occurring throughout the criminal trial. This position implicitly recognises that the sentencing decision should be conceptualised as an amalgam of process decisions rather than simply representing the processual climax of those decisions.

Furthermore, an appreciation of discretionary decision-making within the trial process as instrumental and transformative is crucially important for connecting with notions of restorative justice that resonate with the concerns of victims and communities. This is because it encourages insights into those factors which promote the relative differentiation between notions of 'truth' and justice for victims and 'significant others' within their respective communities. I have suggested that in conventional trial paradigms the moral legitimacy of process (including punishment) is equated with the nature and function of the process rather than what it *actually* signifies. In order for legitimacy to be considered in such terms requires the establishment of some conceptual linkage between the moral justifications for the process and how these are transformed in processual terms to connect with notions of moral legitimacy for victims and communities. In the context of sentencing, this position forces us to examine the rationalisations for process, what they represent as moral values, and how they are embodied in legal norms and transformed into relevant normative imperatives.

It is suggested that the extent to which this notion of access to justice for victims is achieved as a matter of practical reality involves an examination of three key areas:

1. The degree of victim integration in processual decision-making.
2. The degree to which sentencing outcomes engage with victims and communities.
3. The extent to which procedural norms providing for victim participation are supported by enforceable rights for victims.

It is therefore necessary for future research to focus on the extent to which access to justice for victims in sentencing is *actually*[8] achieved through the comparative contextual analysis of those discretionary decisions which impact on trial process and outcome, and the nature and operation of norms purporting to protect victims' rights. By approaching the analysis on this basis it will be possible to assess the relationship between the degree of normative support for victim participation and the rights protection available to victims in criminal trials in so far as it concerns sentencing.

Concluding Remarks

Each new conflict prompts renewed debate regarding the appropriate mechanisms for the trial and punishment of war criminals and those who have breached the norms of international humanitarian law. Such developments provide constant challenges for those charged with dispensing international criminal justice and the so-called international community of nation states on whose behalf they act to consider the extent to which individuals, victims, and communities consider as legitimate that which is perpetrated in their name, and the extent to which the outcomes of international criminal trials actually advance the causes of peace and reconciliation. This book has addressed these vitally important questions and suggested how the theoretical and methodological insights provided by comparative contextual analysis can provide a significant tool for understanding whether the justifications for international punishment are clear; whether they are regarded as legitimate in the eyes of those directly affected by them; what controls should exist over the development of sentencing principles in international criminal trials; and, how victims of international crimes and the communities in which these crimes are perpetrated might be able to participate in the international sentencing process.

Ultimately, the arguments put forward are at odds with those which conclude that normative flexibility in international criminal proceedings, particularly for the ICC, is undesirable and potentially dangerous, and that the solution lies in the more rigorous drafting and enforcement of procedural rules (Zappala, 2003, p.258). The polemic of this book is that the penality of international criminal justice will not be perceived as fair and just merely through a strengthening of respect for procedural norms. On the contrary, the crucial signifier of legitimacy can only be achieved by ensuring that the structures and norms of international criminal process are

[8] The emphasis is made to stress the need for understanding the significance of the law in action. Moreover, the focus on contexts of discretionary decision making confirms an interest in examining how value is added to fact, and what this signifies for trial participants.

reinforced by a rationality which promotes a normative framework flexible enough to accommodate outcomes and strategies sufficiently meaningful for all those who demand justice.

Acknowledging the relativity of justice does not render it meaningless. Justice is all about closure, whether achieved through operationalising retributive or restorative ideologies, or a combination of these or other rationales. The ability of trial process to assimilate and give effect to different perceptions of what is, and what will constitute, justice in post-conflict societies is what matters. International criminal trials should not simply legitimise partisan versions of truth because their decision-making processes implement particular ideologies and norms. Decision-making processes should be capable of objectifying the subjective realities of trial participants' experiences in ways which are meaningful, impartial and consistent. Processual justice which remains symbolic, rhetorical and biased cannot be morally justified. For international criminal process to command universal respect its legitimacy must be derived from the fact that it has moral integrity in the eyes of all significant parties.

I have argued that normative flexibility positioned within parameters for rational decision-making which are geared to constructive and relevant outcomes will gradually promote the development of a sentencing jurisprudence in international criminal trials which is responsive and creative, and whose instrumental capacity can be exploited constructively by sentencers in the exercise of their discretionary decision-making powers to satisfy the relative demands of victims and different communities of justice in post-conflict societies. Only in this way will international criminal justice ever come to be perceived by significant others as just and fair.

Bibliography

Akhavan P (2001) 'National Perspectives and Reservations' Paper presented to the International Conference, *From a Culture of Immunity to a Culture of Accountability: International Criminal Tribunals, the International Criminal Court, and Human Rights Protection* University of Utrecht, The Netherlands, 26–28 November

Albrecht H-J (2001) 'Post-Adjudication Dispositions in Comparative Perspective' in M Tonry and R Frase (eds) *Sentencing and Sanctions in Western Countries* Oxford: Oxford University Press, 293–330

Allen J (1999) 'Balancing Justice and Social Unity: Political theory and the idea of a Truth and Reconciliation Commission' *University of Toronto Law Journal* 49: 315–353

Alvarez J E (1998) 'Rush to Closure: Lessons of the Tadic Judgment' *Michigan Law Review* 96: 2031–2122

Alvarez J E (1999) 'Crimes of States/Crimes of Hate: Lessons from Rwanda' *Yale Journal of International Law* 24: 365–483

Amann D M (2000) 'Harmonic Convergence? Constitutional Criminal Procedure in an International Context' *Indiana Law Journal* 75: 809–873

Amann D A (2002) 'Group Mentality, Expressivism and Genocide' *International Criminal Law Review* 2: 93–143

Amnesty International (1999) *The International Criminal Court: Ensuring an Effective Role for Victims* AI Index: IOR 40/10/99

Ashworth A (1983) *Sentencing and Penal Policy* London: Weidenfeld & Nicolson

Ashworth A (1989a) 'Criminal Justice and Deserved Sentences' *Criminal Law Review* 340–355

Ashworth A (1989b) 'Techniques for Reducing Subjective Disparity in Sentencing' in Council of Europe, *Disparities in Sentencing: Causes and Solutions*, Collected Studies in Criminological Research, Vol. XXVI, Strasbourg: Council of Europe, 101–131

Ashworth A (1993) 'Victim Impact Statements and Sentencing' *Criminal Law Review* 40: 498–509

Ashworth A (1994) *The Criminal Process: An Evaluative Study* Oxford: Oxford University Press, 1st ed

Ashworth A (1996) 'Crime, Community and Creeping Consequentialism' *Criminal Law Review* 43: 220–230

Ashworth A (1998) *The Criminal Process: An Evaluative Study* Oxford: Oxford University Press, 2nd ed

Ashworth A (1999) *Principles of Criminal Law* Oxford: Oxford University Press, 3rd ed

Ashworth A (2000a) *Sentencing and Criminal Justice* London: Butterworths

Ashworth A (2000b) 'Victims' Rights, Defendants' Rights and Criminal Procedure' in A Crawford and J Goodey (eds) *Integrating a Victim Perspective within Criminal Justice* Aldershot: Ashgate, 185–204

Ashworth A (2002a) *Human Rights, Serious Crimes and Criminal Procedure* London: Sweet and Maxwell

Ashworth A (2002b) 'Responsibilities, Rights and Criminal Justice' *British Journal of Criminology* 42: 578–595

Bagaric M (2001) *Punishment and Sentencing: A Rational Approach* London: Cavendish

Bagaric M and Amarasekara K (2000) 'The Errors of Retributivism' *Melbourne University Law Review* 24: 124–189 available online at http://www.austlii.edu.au/au/journals/MULR/2000/5.html

Bagaric M and Amarasekara K (2001) 'Feeling Sorry? – Tell Someone who Cares: The Irrelevance of Remorse in Sentencing' *Howard Journal of Criminal Justice* 40: 364–376

Ball H (2004) 'US Opposition to the ICC: A Political Perspective on International Criminal Justice' Paper presented to Third International Conference *International Criminal Justice: A Transatlantic Dialogue* at the European Parliament and the Royal Flemish Academy for Sciences and Arts, Brussels, 7–8 May

Banakar R (2000) 'Reflections on the Methodological Issues of the Sociology of Law' *Journal of Law and Society* 27: 273–295

Banakar R (2003) *Merging Law and Sociology: Beyond the Dichotomies of Socio-Legal Research* Berlin: Galda and Wilch Verlag

Bassiouni M C (1996) 'Searching for Peace and Achieving Justice: The Need for Accountability' *Law and Contemporary Problems* 59: 9–28 available online at http://www.law.duke.edu.journals/lcp/articles/lcp59dfall1996p9.htm

Bassiouni M C (1998) *The Statute of the International Criminal Court: A Documentary History* Ardsley: Transnational Publishers

Bassiouni M C and Manakas P (1996) *The Law of the International Criminal Tribunal of the Former Yugoslavia* Irvington-on-Hudson, NY: Transnational Publishers

Bauman Z (2000) 'Social Uses of Law and Order' in D Garland and R Sparks (eds) *Criminology and Social Theory* Oxford: Oxford University Press, 23–45

Bayles M (1990) *Procedural Justice: Allocating to Individuals* Dordrecht: Kluwer

Beccaria C (1764) *Of Crimes and Punishments and other writings [Dei Delitti e delle Pene]* edited by R Bellamy and translated by R Davies with V Cox and R Bellamy, Cambridge: Cambridge University Press (1995)

Becker H (1973) *Outsiders* New York: Free Press, 2nd ed

Behrens H-J (1998) 'Investigation, Trial and Appeal in the International Criminal Court Statute (Parts V, VI, VIII)' *European Journal of Crime, Criminal Law and Criminal Justice* 6/4: 429–441

Bell J (2001) *French Legal Cultures* London: Butterworths

Bennett W L and Feldman M S (1981) *Reconstructing Reality in the Courtroom: Justice and Judgment in American Culture* London: Tavistock Publications

Beresford S (2002) 'Unshackling the Paper Tiger: The Sentencing Practices of the ad hoc International Criminal Tribunals for the Former Yugoslavia and Rwanda' *International Criminal Law Review* 1/1: 33–90

Bohlander M (2000) 'Prosecutor v Dusko Tadic: Waiting to Exhale' *Criminal Law Forum* 11: 217–248

Bohlander M (2001) 'The Direct Application of International Criminal Law in Kosovo' *Kosovo Legal Studies* 1: 7–13

Bohlander M (2002) 'The Joint Advisory Council (JAC) Draft Criminal Code of Kosovo of 13 August 200: Some Comments on War Crimes, Crimes against Humanity and Security Council Resolution 1244' *Kosovo Legal Studies* 3: 39–44

Bohlander M (2003) 'Last Exit Bosnia: Transferring War Crimes Prosecution from the International Tribunal to Domestic Courts' *Criminal Law Forum* 14: 59–99

Bohlander M and Findlay M (2002) 'The Use of Domestic Sources as a Basis for International Criminal Law Principles' *Global Community Yearbook of International Law and Jurisprudence* 1: 3–26

Bottoms A E (1998) 'Five Puzzles in von Hirsch's Theory of Punishment' in A Ashworth and M Wasik (eds) *Fundamentals of Sentencing Theory* Oxford: Clarendon Press, 53–100

Bottoms A E (2003) 'Some Sociological Reflections on Restorative Justice' in A von Hirsch *et al.* (eds) *Restorative Justice & Criminal Justice: Competing or Reconcilable Paradigms?* Oxford: Hart Publishing

Bottoms A and Brownsword R (1982) 'The Dangerousness Debate after the Floud Report *British Journal of Criminology* 22: 229–254

Bourdieu P (1977) *Outline of a Theory of Practice* Cambridge: Cambridge University Press

Braithwaite J (1994) 'Thinking Harder About Democratising Social Control' in J Alder and J Wundersitz (eds) *Family Conferencing and Juvenile Justice: The Way Forward or Misplaced Optimism* Canberra: Australian Institute of Criminology

Braithwaite J (1999) 'Restorative Justice: Assessing Optimistic and Pessimistic Accounts' *Crime and Justice: A Review of Research* 25: 1–110

Braithwaite J (2002) *Restorative Justice and Responsive Regulation* Oxford: Oxford University Press

Braithwaite J and Pettit P (1990) *Not Just Deserts: A Republican Theory of Criminal Justice* Oxford: Clarendon Press

Bush R and Fogler J (1994) *The Promise of Mediation: Responding to Conflict through Empowerment and Recognition* San Francisco: Jossey-Bass Publishers

Caplan M (2001) 'International criminal court sounds a wake up call' *The Times* April 10

Carcano A (2002) 'Sentencing and the Gravity of the Offence in International Criminal Law' *International and Comparative Law Quarterly* 51: 583–609

Casanovas P (1999) 'Pragmatic Legal Contexts' Paper presented at the International Pragmatics Conference on *Pragmatics and Negotiation*, Tel Aviv University/Hebrew University of Jerusalem, 13–16 June

Cassese A (1999) 'The Statute of the International Criminal Court: Some Preliminary Reflections' *European Journal of International Law* 10: 144–171

Cavadino M and Dignan J (1996) *The Penal System: An Introduction* London: Sage Publications

Cavadino M and Dignan J (1997) 'Reparation, Retribution and Rights' *International Review of Victimology* 4: 233–253

Cavadino M and Dignan J (2002) *The Penal System: An Introduction* London: Sage, 3rd ed

Chiavario M (2002) 'Private Parties: The Rights of the Defendant and the Victim' in M Delmas-Marty and J R Spencer (eds) *European Criminal Procedures* Cambridge: Cambridge University Press, 541–593

Chinkin C (1997) 'Due Process and Witness Anonymity' *American Journal of International Law* 91/1: 75–79

Christie N (1977) 'Conflicts as Property' *British Journal of Criminology* 17: 1–15

Christie N (2000) 'Dangerous States' in M Brown and J Pratt (eds) *Dangerous Offenders: Punishment and Social Order* London: Routledge, 181–193

Christodoulidis E A (2000) 'Truth and Reconciliation as Risks' *Social & Legal Studies* 9: 179–204

Cicourel A (1968) *The Social Organisation of Juvenile Justice* New York: John Wiley

Cockayne J (2001) 'Procedural and Processual Synthesis in the International Tribunals. Part 1: The Context of Synthesis' (unpublished paper)

Cockayne J (2002) 'Conference Report for the International Criminal Trial Project' on the conference *Internationalised Criminal Courts and Tribunals: Practice and Prospects* University of Amsterdam, The Netherlands, 25–26 January

Cohen S (1993) 'Human Rights and Crimes of the State: The Culture of Denial' *Australian and New Zealand Journal of Criminology* 26/2: 97–115

Cohen S (1995) 'State Crimes of Previous Regimes: Knowledge, Accountability and the Policing of the Past' *Law and Social Inquiry* 20/1, 7–50

Condorelli L (2002) 'Is there a Need for Internationalised Courts and Tribunals?' Paper presented at the conference *Internationalised Criminal Courts and Tribunals: Practice and Prospects* University of Amsterdam, The Netherlands, 25–26 January

Cotterrell R B M (1992) *The Sociology of Law: An Introduction* London: Butterworths, 2nd ed

Cotterrell R B M (1995) *Law's Community: Legal Theory in Sociological Perspective* Oxford: Clarendon Press

Cotterrell R B M (1997) 'A Legal Concept of Community' *Canadian Journal of Law and Society* 12/2: 75–91

Cotterrell R B M (1998a) 'Why Must Legal Ideas Be Interpreted Sociologically?' *Journal of Law and Society* 25: 171–192

Cotterrell R B M (1998b) 'Law and Community: A New Relationship in Legal Theory at the End of the Millenium?' *Current Legal Problems* 51: 367–391

Cotterrell R B M (1999) *Emile Durkheim: Law in a Moral Domain* Edinburgh: Edinburgh University Press

Cotterrell R B M (2002a) 'Global Law in a Moral Domain' *Socio-Legal Newsletter* 37: 6

Cotterrell R B M (2002b) 'Seeking Similarity, Appreciating Difference: Comparative Law and Communities' in A Harding and E Orucu (eds) *Comparative Law in the 21*st *Century* The Hague: Kluwer, 35–54

Cotterrell R B M (2002c) 'Subverting Orthodoxy, Making Law Central: A View of Socio-Legal Studies' *Journal of Law and Society* 29/4: 632–644

Cottingham J (1979) 'Varieties of Retributivism' *Philosophical Quarterly* 29: 238–246

Council of Europe (1989) *Disparities in Sentencing: Causes and Solutions* Collected Studies in Criminological Research Vol. XXVI, Strasbourg: Council of Europe (1/15)

Council of Europe (1993) *Consistency in Sentencing*, Recommendation No. R (92) 17 Strasbourg: Council of Europe Press

Crawford A (2000) 'Contrasts in Victim–Offender Mediation and Appeals to Community in France and England' in D Nelken (ed) *Contrasting Criminal Justice* Aldershot: Ashgate, 205–229

Crocker L (1995) 'The Upper Limit of Just Punishment' *Emory Law Journal* 41: 1059–1098

de Bertodano S (2002) 'Judicial Independence in the International Criminal Court' *Leiden Journal of International Law* 15: 409–430

Dennis I (1997) 'Human Rights and Evidence in Adversarial Criminal Procedure: The Advancement of International Standards in J Nijboer and J M Reijntjes (eds) *Proceedings of the First World Conference on New Trends in Criminal Investigation and Evidence* Open University of The Netherlands, The Hague

Dennis I (2001) 'The International Criminal Court Act 2001' *Criminal Law Review* 48: 767–768

de Sousa Santos B (1995) *Towards a New Common Sense: Law, Science and Politics in the Paradigmatic Transition* New York and London: Routledge

Dezelay Y and Garth B (1996) *Dealing in Virtue: International Commercial Arbitration and the Construction of Transnational Legal Order* Chicago: University of Chicago Press

Dignan J and Cavadino M (1996) 'Towards a Framework for Conceptualising and Evaluating Models of Criminal Justice from a Victim's Perspective' *International Review of Victimology* 4: 153–182

Dolinko D (1991) 'Some Thoughts about Retributivism' *Ethics* 101/3: 537–559

Dolinko D (1997) 'Retributivism, Consequentialism and the Intrinsic Goodness of Punishment' *Law and Philosophy* 16/5: 507–528

Douzinas C (1996) 'Justice and Human Rights in Postmodernity' in C Gearty and A Tomkins (eds) *Understanding Human Rights* London: Mansell, 115–137

Drumbl M (2000) 'Punishment, Postgenocide: From Guilt to Shame to *Civis* in Rwanda' *New York University Law Review* 75: 1221–1326

Drumbl M (2002) 'Sclerosis: Retributive Justice and the Rwandan Genocide' *Punishment and Society* 2/3: 287–307

Drumbl M (2002) 'Lessons for International Criminal Justice from Rwanda' Washington & Lee Public Law and Legal Theory Research Paper Series, Research Paper No. 02-13, December, available from http://ssm.con/abstract_id=355300

Drumbl M (2003) 'Towards a Criminology of International Crime' *Washington and Lee University Public Law and Legal Theory Research Paper Series, Working Paper No. 03-07*, May

du Bois F (2001) 'Nothing But the Truth: The SA Alternative to Dilemmas of Corrective Justice in Transitions to Democracy' in E A Christodoulidis and S Veitch (eds) *Lethe's Law* Oxford: Hart Publishing, 91–114

Duff R A (1986) *Trials and Punishments* Cambridge: Cambridge University Press

Duff R A (1996) 'Punishment, Citizenship and Responsibility' in H Tam (ed) *Punishment, Excuses and Moral Development* Aldershot: Avebury, 17–34

Duff R A (1998) 'Desert and Penance' in A von Hirsch and A Ashworth (eds) *Principled Sentencing: Readings on Theory and Policy* Oxford: Hart Publishing, 2nd ed, 161–179

Duff R A (2001) *Punishment, Communication and Community* Oxford: Oxford University Press

Duff R A (2003) 'Penance, Punishment and the Limits of Community' *Punishment and Society* 5/3: 295–312

Duff R A and Garland D (1994) 'Introduction: Thinking about Punishment' in R A Duff and D Garland (eds) *A Reader on Punishment* Oxford: Oxford University Press, 1–43

Durkheim E (1982) *The Rules of Sociological Method and Selected Texts on Sociology and its Method* London: Macmillan, Translated by W D Halls

Durkheim E (1984) 'Two Laws of Penal Evolution' in S Lukes and A Scull (eds) *Durkheim and the Law* Oxford: Basil Blackwell, 101–132

Edwards I (2001) 'Victim Participation in Sentencing: The Problem of Incoherence' *Howard Journal of Criminal Justice* 40: 39–54

Emerson R M (1969) *Judging Delinquents* Chicago: Aldine

Emmerson B and Ashworth A (2001) *Human Rights and Criminal Justice* London: Sweet and Maxwell

Evered T C (1994) 'An International Criminal Court: Recent Proposals and American Concerns' *Pace International Law Review* 6: 121–156

Ewald W (1998) 'The Jurisprudential Approach to Comparative Law: A Field Guide to "Rats"' *American Journal of Comparative Law* 46: 701–707

Feeley M M and Simon J (1992) 'The New Penology: Notes on the Emerging Strategy of Corrections and its Implications' *Criminology* 30/4: 449–474

Feinberg J (1970) *Doing and Deserving* Princeton: Princeton University Press

Feinberg J (1984) *Harm to Others* Oxford: Oxford University Press

Fenwick H (1997) 'Procedural Rights of Victims of Crime: Public or Private Ordering of the Criminal Justice Process' *Modern Law Review* 60: 317–333

Findlay M (1999) *The Globalisation of Crime* Cambridge: Cambridge University Press

Findlay M (2001) 'Synthesis in Trial Procedures? The Experience of International Criminal Tribunals' *International and Comparative Law Quarterly* 50: 26–53

Findlay M (2002) 'Internationalised Criminal Trial and Access to Justice' *International Criminal Law Review* 2: 237–259

Findlay M and Henham R (2001) 'Methodology and the Comparative Contextual Analysis of Trial Process: A Preliminary Study' available online at http://www.nls.ntu.ac.uk/CLR/ICTP/index.htm

Findlay M and Henham R (2005) *Transforming International Criminal Justice: Retributive and Restorative Justice in the Trial Process* Cullompton: Willan Publishing

Finnis J (1980) *Natural Law and Natural Rights* Oxford: Oxford University Press

Fitzpatrick P (1992) *The Mythology of Modern Law* London: Routledge

Fitzpatrick P (2001) *Modernism and the Grounds of Law* Cambridge: Cambridge University Press

Floud J and Young W (1981) *Dangerousness and Criminal Justice* London: Heinemann

Forsythe D (1994) 'Politics and the International Tribunal for the Former Yugoslavia' *Criminal Law Forum* 5: 401–422

Frase R (1998) 'Comparative Criminal Justice Policy' in *Comparative Criminal Justice Systems: From Diversity to Rapprochment.* Proceedings of the International Conference for the 25th Anniversary of the International Institute of Higher Studies in Criminal Sciences, Siracusa, Italy, 16–20 December 1997, Nouvelles Etudes Penales, No. 17. International Association of Penal Law, Toulouse: Editions Eres, 109–121

Frulli M (2001) 'Are Crimes against Humanity More Serious than War Crimes?' *European Journal of International Law* 12/2: 329–350

Gardner J (1998) 'Crime: In Proportion and in Perspective' in A Ashworth and M Wasik (eds) *Fundamentals of Sentencing Theory* Oxford: Clarendon Press, 31–52

Garland D (1990) *Punishment and Modern Society* Oxford: Clarendon Press

Garland D (1996) 'The Limits of the Sovereign State: Strategies of Crime Control in Contemporary Society' *British Journal of Criminology* 36: 445–471

Garland D (2001) *The Culture of Control* Oxford: Oxford University Press

Gavron J (2002) 'Amnesties in the Light of Developments in International Law and the Establishment of the International Criminal Court' *International and Comparative Law Quarterly* 51: 91–117

Giddens A (1977) *Studies in Social and Political Theory* London: Hutchinson

Giddens A (1979) *Central Problems in Social Theory* London: Macmillan

Giddens A (1984) *The Constitution of Society: Outlines of a Theory of Structuration* Cambridge: Polity Press

Gluckman M (1955) in Bohannan P (ed) 'The Judicial Process among the Barotse' *Law and Warfare: Studies in the Anthropology of Conflict* New York: The Natural History Press, 1967, 59–91

Goffman E (1969) *The Presentation of Self in Everyday Life* London: Allen Lane

Green E (1961) *Judicial Attitudes in Sentencing* London: Macmillan

Grosselfinger N (1998) 'Sentencing in the International Court' Paper presented at the *American Society of Criminology Annual Meeting*, Washington DC, 12 November

Hall C (1998) 'The Fifth Session of the UN Preparatory Committee on the Establishment of an International Criminal Court' *American Journal of International Law* 92: 331–339

Hampton J (1988) 'The Retributive Idea' in J Murphy and J Hampton *Forgiveness and Mercy* Cambridge: Cambridge University Press, 111–162

Harding A and Orucu E (eds) (2002) *Comparative Law in the 21st Century* The Hague: Kluwer

Hart H L A (1968) *Punishment and Responsibility: Essays in the Philosophy of Law* Oxford: Oxford University Press

Hayner P (2001) 'Truth Commissions and National Courts' Paper presented to the International Conference *From a Culture of Immunity to a Culture of Accountability: International Criminal Tribunals, the International Criminal*

Court, and Human Rights Protection, University of Utrecht, The Netherlands, 26–28 November
Henham R (1994) 'Attorney General's References and Sentencing Policy' *Criminal Law Review* 499–512
Henham R (1997) 'Protective Sentences: Ethics, Rights and Sentencing Policy' *International Journal of the Sociology of Law* 27: 45–63
Henham R (1998) 'Human Rights, Due Process and Sentencing' *British Journal of Criminology* 38: 592–610
Henham R (1999a) 'Bargain Justice or Justice Denied? Sentence Discounts and the Criminal Process' *Modern Law Review* 62: 515–538
Henham R (1999b) 'Theory, Rights and Sentencing Policy' *International Journal of the Sociology of Law* 27: 167–183
Henham R (2000a) 'Problems of Theorizing Sentencing Research' *International Journal of the Sociology of Law* 28/1: 15–32
Henham R (2000b) 'Sentencing Theory, Proportionality and Pragmatism' *International Journal of the Sociology of Law* 28/3: 239–263
Henham R (2001) 'Theory and Contextual Analysis in Sentencing' *International Journal of the Sociology of Law* 29: 253–276
Henham R (2002) 'Developing Theory and Methodology for Understanding International Penality' (unpublished working paper)
Henham R (2003a) 'Some Issues for Sentencing in the International Criminal Court' *International and Comparative Law Quarterly* 52: 81–114
Henham R (2003b) 'The Philosophical Foundations of International Sentencing' *Journal of International Criminal Justice* 1/1: 64–85
Henham R (2004) 'Conceptualising Access to Justice and Victims' Rights in International Sentencing' *Social & Legal Studies* 13/1: 21–55
Henham R and Findlay M (2001) 'Theory and Methodology in the Comparative Contextual Analysis of Trial Process' (unpublished working paper)
Henham R and Findlay M (2002) 'Criminal Justice Modelling and the Comparative Contextual Analysis of Trial Process' *International Journal of Comparative Criminology* 2/2: 162–186
Henham R and Mannozzi G (2003) 'Victim Participation and Sentencing in England and Italy: A Legal and Policy Analysis' *European Journal of Crime, Criminal Law and Criminal Justice* 11/3: 278–317
Hodgson J (2000) 'Comparing Legal Cultures: The Comparativist as Participant Observer' in D Nelken (ed) *Contrasting Criminal Justice: Getting from Here to There* Aldershot: Ashgate, 139–156
Hogarth J (1971) *Sentencing as a Human Process* Toronto: University of Toronto Press
Hood R G (1972) *Sentencing the Motoring Offender* London: Heinemann
Hood R (1992) *Race and Sentencing* Oxford: Oxford University Press
Honore T (2002) 'The Necessary Connection Between Law and Morality' *Oxford Journal of Legal Studies* 22: 489–495
Howland T and Calathes W (1998) 'The UN's International Criminal Tribunal, Is it Justice or Jingoism for Rwanda? A Call for Transformation' *Virginia Journal of International Law* 39: 135–167
Hudson B (1996) *Understanding Justice: An Introduction to Ideas, Perspectives and Controversies in Modern Penal Theory* Buckingham: Open University Press, 1st ed

Hudson B (2003) *Understanding Justice: An Introduction to Ideas, Perspectives and Controversies in Modern Penal Theory* Buckingham: Open University Press, 2nd ed

Hunt A (1993) *Explorations in Law and Society: Towards a Constitutive Theory of Law* London: Routledge

Hutton N (1995) 'Sentencing, Rationality and Computer Technology' *Journal of Law and Society* 22: 549–570

Johnstone G (2001) *Restorative Justice: Ideas, Values, Debates* Cullompton: Willan Publishing

Jorda C and de Hemptinne J (2002) 'The Status and Role of the Victim' in A Cassese, P Gaeta and J Jones (eds) *The Rome Statute of the International Criminal Court: A Commentary* Oxford University Press: Oxford, 1387–1419

Jung H (1997) 'Plea-Bargaining and its Repercussions on the Theory of Criminal Procedure' *European Journal of Crime, Criminal Law and Criminal Justice* 5: 112–122

Kamenka E (1979) 'What is Justice?' in E Kamenka E and A E-S Tay (eds) *Justice* London: Edward Arnold

Katzenstein S (2003) 'Hybrid Tribunals: Searching for Justice in East Timor' *Harvard Human Rights Journal* 16: 245–278

King M (1978) 'A Status Passage Analysis of the Defendant's Progress through the Magistrates' Court' *Law and Human Behaviour* 2: 167–221

King M (1993) 'The Truth about Autopoiesis' *Journal of Law and Society* 20/2: 218–236

Kittichaisaree K (2001) *International Criminal Law* Oxford: Oxford University Press

Kress C (1998) 'Penalties, Enforcement and Cooperation in the International Criminal Court Statute (Parts VII, IX, X) *European Journal of Crime, Criminal Law and Criminal Justice* 6/4: 442–460

Lacey N (1987) 'Discretion and Due Process at the Post-Conviction Stage' in I H Dennis (ed) *Criminal Law and Justice* London: Sweet and Maxwell, 221–235

Langbein J H (2003) *The Origins of Adversary Criminal Trial* Oxford: Oxford University Press

Layder, D (1994) *Understanding Social Theory* London: Sage

Legrand P and Munday R (eds) (2003) *Comparative Legal Studies: Traditions and Transitions* Cambridge: Cambridge University Press

Leigh L H (1977) 'Liberty and Efficiency in the Criminal Process – The Significance of Models' *International and Comparative Law Quarterly* 26: 516–530

Lemert E M (1972) *Human Deviance, Social Problems and Social Control* Englewood Cliffs, NJ: Prentice Hall, 2nd ed

Lewis C S (1971) 'The Humanitarian Theory of Punishment' in L Radzinowicz and M Wolfgang (eds) *Crime and Justice Vol 2: The Criminal in the Arms of the Law*

Linton S (2001a) 'Cambodia, East Timor and Sierra Leone: Experiments in International Criminal Justice' *Criminal Law Forum* 12: 185–246

Linton S (2001b) 'Rising from the Ashes: The Creation of a Viable Criminal Justice System in East Timor' *Melbourne University Law Review* 25: 122–180

Loughlin M (2001) 'Rights, Democracy and Law' in T Campbell, K D Ewing and A

Tomkins (eds) *Sceptical Essays on Human Rights* Oxford: Oxford University Press, 41–60

Luhmann N (1985) *A Sociological Theory of Law* London: Routledge

McBarnet D (1981) *Conviction: Law, the State and the Construction of Justice* London: Macmillan

MacCormick N and Garland D (1998) 'Sovereign States and Vengeful Victims: The Problem of the Right to Punish' in A Ashworth and M Wasik (eds) *Fundamentals of Sentencing Theory* Oxford: Clarendon Press, 11–29

McCoy C (1994) 'What We Say and What They Do: Prosecutors' and Judges' Sentencing Decisions at Guilty Plea versus Trial', Paper presented at the *American Society of Criminology Annual Meeting*, New Orleans, November

McCoy C and Henham R (2004) 'Guilty Plea Discounts in American and English Courts: An Empirical Description and Ethical Critique of the Trial Penalty' (unpublished paper)

McGoldrick D (1999) 'The Permanent International Criminal Court: An End to the Culture of Impunity' *Criminal Law Review* 48, 644–655

Mackie J L (1982) 'Morality and the Retributive Emotions' *Criminal Justice Ethics* 1: 3-9

Mannozzi G (2002) 'Are Guided Sentencing and Plea Bargaining Incompatible? Perspectives of Reform in the Italian Sentencing System' in C Tata and N Hutton (eds) *Sentencing and Society: International Perspectives* Aldershot: Ashgate, 110–132

Mannozzi G (2003) 'Positioning Mediation in the Criminal Justice System' in L Walgrave (ed) *Repositioning Restorative Justice: Restorative Justice, Criminal Justice and Social Justice* Cullompton: Willan Publishing, 284–295

Mashaw J (1987) 'Dignitory Process: A Political Psychology of Liberal Democratic Citizenship' *University of Florida Law Review* 39: 433–478

Mathiesen T (1990) *Prison on Trial* London: Sage Publications

Matza D (1964) *Delinquency and Drift* New York: John Wiley

Matza D (1969) *Becoming Deviant* New Jersey: Prentice Hall

Meron T (2004) 'Procedural Evolution in the ICTY' *Journal of International Criminal Justice* 2/2: 520–525

Minow M (1998) *Between Vengeance and Forgiveness: Facing History after Genocide and Mass Violence* Boston: Beacon Press

Moghalu K (2001) 'The Role of International Criminal/Humanitarian Law in Conflict Settlement and Reconciliation' Paper presented to the International Conference *From a Culture of Immunity to a Culture of Accountability: International Criminal Tribunals, the International Criminal Court, and Human Rights Protection*, University of Utrecht, The Netherlands, 26–28 November

Moore M (1987)'The Moral Worth of Retribution' in F Schoerman (ed) *Responsibility, Character and the Emotions* Cambridge: Cambridge University Press, 179–219

Moore M (1993) 'Justifying Retributivism' *Israel Law Review* 15–49

Morris A (2002) 'Critiquing the Critics: A Brief Response to Critics of Restorative Justice' *British Journal of Criminology* 42/3: 596–615

Morris V and Scharf M (1995) *An Insider's Guide to the International Criminal*

Tribunal for the Former Yugoslavia Irvington-on-Hudson, NY: Transnational Publishers Inc

Morris N and Tonry M (1990) *Between Prison and Probation: Intermediate Punishments in a Rational Sentencing System* New York, Oxford: Oxford University Press

Murphy J (1979) *Retribution, Justice and Therapy: Essays in the Philosophy of Law* Dordecht: Reidel

Nagel T (1972) 'War and Massacre' *Philosophy and Public Affairs* 1: 123–144

Narayan U (1993) 'Appropriate Responses and Preventative Benefits: Justifying Censure and Hard Treatment in Legal Punishment' *Oxford Journal of Legal Studies* 13: 166–182

Nelken D (ed) (1997) *Comparing Legal Cultures* Aldershot: Dartmouth

Nelken D (1998) 'Blinding Insights?: The Limits of a Reflexive Sociology of Law' *Journal of Law and Society* 25: 407–426

Nelken D (2000) 'Telling Difference: Of Crime and Criminal Justice in Italy' in D Nelken (ed) *Contrasting Criminal Justice* Aldershot: Ashgate, 233–264

Nelken D (2002) 'Legal Transplants and Beyond: Of Disciplines and Metaphors' in A Harding and E Orucu (eds) *Comparative Law in the 21st Century* The Hague: Kluwer, 19–34

Nelken D and Feest J (eds) (2001) *Adapting Legal Cultures* Oxford: Hart Publishing

Nemitz J C and Wirth S (1999) 'Some Observations on the Law of Sentencing of the ICC' online at http://www.ishr.org/ice/detail/nemitz.htm

Nobles R and Schiff D (1995) 'Miscarriages of Justice: A Systems Approach' *Modern Law Review* 58/3: 299–320

Nollkaemper A (2002) 'Procedures for Establishment' Paper presented at the conference *Internationalised Criminal Courts and Tribunals: Practice and Prospects*, University of Amsterdam, The Netherlands, 25–26 January

Norrie A (1996a) 'The Limits of Justice: Finding Fault in the Criminal Law' *Modern Law Review* 59: 540–556

Norrie A (1996b) 'From Law to Popular Justice: Beyond Antinomialism' *Social & Legal Studies* 5: 383–404

Norrie A (2000) *Punishment, Responsibility and Justice* Oxford: Oxford University Press

Norrie A (2001) *Crime, Reason and History* London: Butterworths, 2nd ed

Nozick R (1981) *Philosophical Explanations* Oxford: Clarendon Press

Osiel M J (1995) 'Legal Remembrance of Administrative Massacre' *University of Pennsylvania Law Review* 144: 463–704

Osiel M (1997) *Mass Atrocity, Collective Memory, and the Law* New Brunswick, NJ: Transaction

Othman M (2002) 'East Timor' Paper presented at the conference *Internationalised Criminal Courts and Tribunals: Practice and Prospects*, University of Amsterdam, The Netherlands, 25–26 January

Owens M W (1995) 'California's Three Strikes Law: Desperate Times Require Desperate Measures – But Will it Work?' *Pacific Law Journal* 26: 881–919

Packer H (1968) *The Limits of the Criminal Sanction* Stanford: Stanford University Press

Pakes F J (2001) 'Styles of Trial Procedure at the International Criminal Tribunal for the Former Yugoslavia' Paper presented at the European Society of Criminology, First Annual Meeting, University of Lausanne, Switzerland, September

Pakes F (2004) *Comparative Criminal Justice* Cullompton: Willan Publishing

Pangalangan R (2002) 'Cambodia' Paper presented at the conference *Internationalised Criminal Courts and Tribunals: Practice and Prospects*, University of Amsterdam, The Netherlands, 25–26 January

Parker H, Sumner M and Jarvis G (1989) *Unmasking the Magistrates* Milton Keynes: Open University Press

Parmentier S (2003) 'Global Justice in the Aftermath of Mass Violence: The Role of the International Criminal Court in Dealing with Political Crimes' *International Annals of Criminology* 41-1/2: 203–224

Pickard D B (1997) 'Proposed Sentencing Guidelines for the International Criminal Court' *Loyola of Los Angeles International and Comparative Law Journal* 20: 123–157

Pizzi W T and Marafioti L (1992) 'The New Italian Code of Criminal Procedure: The Difficulties of Building an Adversarial Trial System on a Civil Law Foundation' *Yale Journal of International Law* 17: 1–40

Polat N (1999) 'International Law, the Inherent Instability of the International System, and International Violence' *Oxford Journal of Legal Studies* 19/1: 51–70

Pratt J (1995) 'Dangerousness, Risk and Technologies of Power' *Australian and New Zealand Journal of Criminology* 28: 3–31

Pratt J (1998) 'Towards the "Decivilizing" of Punishment' (1998) *Social & Legal Studies* 7/4: 487–515

Pratt J (2000) 'Emotive and Ostentatious Punishment: Its Decline and Resurgence in Modern Society' *Punishment & Society* 2/4: 417–439

Radzinowicz L (1966) *Ideology and Crime* London: Heinemann

Ratner S (2003) 'Belgium's War Crimes Statute: A Postmortem' *American Journal of International Law* 97: 888–897

Retzinger S and Scheff T (1996) 'Strategy for Community Conferences: Emotions and Social Bonds' in B Galaway and J Hudson (eds) *Restorative Justice: International Perspectives* Monsey, NY: Criminal Justice Press, 315–366

Rex S (1998) 'A New Form of Rehabilitation?' in A von Hirsch and A Ashworth (eds) *Principled Sentencing: Readings on Theory and Policy* Oxford: Hart Publishing, 2nd ed

Roberts P (2002) 'On Method: The Ascent of Comparative Criminal Justice' *Oxford Journal of Legal Studies* 22: 539–561

Roberts P (2003) 'Restoration and Retribution in International Criminal Justice: An Exploratory Analysis' in A von Hirsch *et al.* (eds) *Restorative Justice and Criminal Justice: Competing or Reconcilable Paradigms?* Oxford: Hart, 115-134

Rogers L J and Erez E (1999) 'The Contextuality of Objectivity in Sentencing among Legal Professionals in South Australia' *International Journal of the Sociology of Law* 27: 267–286

Roht-Arriaza N (1995) *Impunity and Human Rights in International Law and Practice* New York: Oxford University Press

Roht-Arriaza N (1999) 'Institutions of International Justice' *Journal of International Affairs* 52/2: 473–491

Romano C (2002) 'Procedures for Establishment' Paper presented at the conference *Internationalised Criminal Courts and Tribunals: Practice and Prospects*, University of Amsterdam, The Netherlands, 25–26 January

Rubin A P (2001) 'The International Criminal Court: Possibilities for Prosecutorial Abuse' *Law & Contemporary Problems* 64: 153–166 available online at http://www.law.duke.edu/journals/lcp/articles/lcp64dWinter2001p153.htm

Rudner, R (1966) *Philosophy of Social Science* Englewood Cliffs NJ: Prentice Hall

Ryan, A (1970) *The Philosophy of Social Sciences* London: Macmillan

Sanders A, Hoyle C, Morgan R and Cape E (2001) 'Victim Impact Statements: Don't Work, Can't Work' *Criminal Law Review* 447–458

Saphire R (1978) 'Specifying Due Process Values: Towards A More Responsive Approach to Procedural Protection' *University of Pennsylvania Law Review* 127: 111–195

Salter M (1996) 'The Impossibility of Human Rights within a Postmodern Account of Law and Justice' *Journal of Civil Liberties* 1: 29–66

Schabas W (1997) 'Sentencing and the International Tribunals: For a Human Rights Approach' *Duke Journal of International and Comparative Law* 7: 461–518 online version at http://www.law.duke.edu/journals/djcil/articles/djcil7p461.htm

Schabas W (2001a) *An Introduction to the International Criminal Court* Cambridge: Cambridge University Press, 1st ed

Schabas W A (2001b) 'Protective Measures for Victims and Witnesses Versus the Rights of the Defendants' Paper presented at the International Conference *From a Culture of Immunity to a Culture of Accountability: International Criminal Tribunals, The International Criminal Court and Human Rights Protection*, University of Utrecht, The Netherlands, 26–28 November

Schabas W (2002) 'Towards a Universal Criminal Justice System?' Paper presented at the conference *Internationalised Criminal Courts and Tribunals: Practice and Prospects*, University of Amsterdam, The Netherlands, 25–26 January

Schabas W (2004) *An Introduction to the International Criminal Court* Cambridge: Cambridge University Press, 2nd ed

Searle J R (1995) *The Construction of Social Reality* London: Allen Lane

Seiber U (2003) *The Punishment of Serious Crimes: A Comparative Analysis of Sentencing Law and Practice* Vol. 1 Expert Report; Vol. 2 Country Reports, Max Planck Institute for Foreign and International Criminal Law: Freiburg im Breisgau, Germany

Shearing C (2001) 'Punishment and the Changing Face of the Governance' *Punishment and Society* 3/2: 203–220

Skolnick J H (1966) *Justice Without Trial* New York: John Wiley

Sparks R (1996) 'Penal "Austerity": The Doctrine of Less Eligibilty Reborn?' in R Matthews and P Francis (eds) *Prisons 2000* London: Macmillan, 74–93

Spencer J R (2002) 'Introduction' in M Delmas-Marty and J R Spencer (eds) *European Criminal Procedures* Cambridge: Cambridge University Press, 1–75

Sprack J (2004) *A Practical Approach to Criminal Procedure* 10th ed. Oxford: Oxford University Press

Sriram C L (2004) 'Globalising Justice: From Universal Jurisdiction to Mixed Tribunals' *Netherlands Quarterly of Human Rights* 22/1: 7–32

Steiner H (1999) 'Do Human Rights Require a Particular Form of Democracy?' in E Cotran and A O Sherif (eds) *Democracy, the Rule of Law and Islam*

Strohmeyer H (2001) 'Collapse and Reconstruction of a Judicial System: The United States Mission in Kosovo and East Timor' *American Journal of International Law* 95: 46–62

Sudnow D (1965) 'Normal Crimes: Sociological Features of the Penal Code in a Public Defender Office' *Social Problems* 12: 255–276

Sykes G and Matza D (1957) 'Techniques of Neutralisation: A Theory of Delinquency' *American Sociological Review* 22: 664–673

Tamanaha B Z (1997) *Realistic Socio-Legal Theory* Oxford: Clarendon Press

Tata C (1997) 'Conceptions and Representations of the Sentencing Decision Process' *Journal of Law and Society* 24/3: 395–420

Tata C (2002) 'So What does "and Society" Mean?' in C Tata and N Hutton (eds) *Sentencing and Society: International Perspectives* Aldershot: Ashgate, 1–39

Thomas (1970) *Principles of Sentencing* London: Heinemann, 1st ed

Thomas D A (1979) *Principles of Sentencing* London: Heinemann, 2nd ed

Thomas D A (1982 as updated) *Current Sentencing Practice* London: Sweet and Maxwell

Tochilovsky V (1998) 'Trial in International Criminal Jurisdictions: Battle or Scrutiny?' *European Journal of Crime, Criminal Law and Criminology* 6/1: 55–59

Tonry M (1992) 'Selective Incapacitation: The Debate over its Ethics' in A von Hirsch and A Ashworth (eds) *Principled Sentencing* Edinburgh: Edinburgh University Press, 1st ed, 165–180

Tulkens F (2002) 'Negotiated Justice' in M Delmas-Marty and J R Spencer (eds) *European Criminal Procedures* Cambridge: Cambridge University Press, 641–687

Twining W (1999) 'Narrative and Generalisations in Argumentation about Questions of Fact' *South Texas Law Review* 40/2: 351–365

United Nations (2000) 'Basic Principles on the Use of Restorative Justice Programmes in Criminal Matters' online at www.restorativejustice.org/.ents/UNDecBasicPrinciplesofRJ.htm

van der Vyver J D (2004a) 'National Experiences in International Criminal Justice: Truth Commissions' Paper presented to Third International Conference *International Criminal Justice: A Transatlantic Dialogue* at the European Parliament and the Royal Flemish Academy for Sciences and Arts, Brussels, 7–8 May

van der Vyver J D (2004b) 'National Experiences with International Criminal Justice: Universal Jurisdiction' Unpublished Conference paper

van Roermund B C J (2001) 'Rubbing Off and Rubbing On: The Grammar of Reconciliation' in E A Christodoulidis and S Veitch (eds) *Lethe's Law* Oxford: Hart Publishing, 175–190

van Zyl Smit D (1999) 'Life Imprisonment as an Ultimate Penalty in International Law: A Human Rights Perspective' *Criminal Law Forum* 9: 5–54

van Zyl Smit D (2002) 'Punishment and Human Rights in International Criminal Justice' Inaugural lecture as Professor of Comparative and Penal Law, University of Nottingham, 30 January

Vaughan B (2000) 'Handle with Care: On the Use of Structuration Theory within Criminology' *British Journal of Criminology* 41: 186–200

Vogler R (2000) 'Three-Dimensional Justice: Towards a Comparative Theory of Criminal Process' Paper presented at the *British Society of Criminology Conference*, Leicester University, July

von Hirsch A (1976) *Doing Justice* New York: Hill and Wang

von Hirsch A (1986) 'Deservedness and Dangerousness in Sentencing Policy' *Criminal Law Review* 33: 79–91

von Hirsch A (1993) *Censure and Sanctions* Oxford: Clarendon Press

von Hirsch A (1999) 'Punishment, Penance and the State' in M Matravers (ed) *Punishment and Political Theory* Oxford: Hart Publishing, 69–82

von Hirsch A and Ashworth A (eds) (1998) *Principled Sentencing: Readings on Theory and Policy* Oxford: Hart Publishing

von Oppeln C (2002) 'Victim's Protection in International Law: The Normative Basis and a Look into the Practice' *European Journal of Crime, Criminal Law and Criminal Justice* 10/2-3: 233–252

Walker N (1969) *Sentencing in a Rational Society* Harmondsworth: Penguin

Walker N (1991) *Why Punish? Theories of Punishment Reassessed* Oxford: Oxford University Press

Wexler L S (1996) 'The Proposed International Criminal Court: an Appraisal' *Cornell International Law Journal* 29: 665–725

Wilson R A (2001) *The Politics of Truth and Reconciliation in South Africa* Cambridge: Cambridge University Press

Wood D (1998) 'Dangerous Offenders and the Morality of Protective Sentencing' *Criminal Law Review* 424–433

Zappala S (2003) *Human Rights in International Criminal Proceedings* Oxford: Oxford University Press

Zedner L (1994) 'Reparation and Retribution: Are They Reconcilable?' *Modern Law Review* 57: 226–250

Zedner L (1995) 'In Pursuit of the Vernacular: Comparing Law and Order Discourse in Britain and Germany' *Social & Legal Studies* 4: 517–534

Index

The index covers all parts of the text, including notes, n, and figures, f. *Case names* are given in italics.